8 95

New Strategies for
Public Affairs Reporting

Investigation, Interpretation,
and Research

GEORGE S. HAGE

EVERETTE E. DENNIS

ARNOLD H. ISMACH

University of Minnesota

STEPHEN HARTGEN

The Ohio State University

PRENTICE-HALL, INC., Englewood Cliffs, New Jersey

Library of Congress Cataloging in Publication Data
Main entry under title:

New strategies for public affairs reporting.

Includes bibliographies and index.
1. Reporters and reporting. I. HAGE, GEORGE
SIGURD.
PN4781.N33   070.4'49'35   75-35635
ISBN 0-13-615831-5

Dedicated to the memory of CHILTON R. BUSH and RALPH
O. NAFZIGER, pioneer journalism educators and exemplars
in the teaching of public affairs reporting who insisted on
the practical application of research findings

© *1976 by PRENTICE-HALL, INC.*
Englewood Cliffs, New Jersey

Printed in the United States of America

10 9 8 7 6 5 4 3 2 1

PRENTICE-HALL INTERNATIONAL, INC., London
PRENTICE-HALL OF AUSTRALIA PTY. LIMITED, Sydney
PRENTICE-HALL OF CANADA, LTD., Toronto
PRENTICE-HALL OF INDIA PRIVATE LIMITED, New Delhi
PRENTICE-HALL OF JAPAN, INC., Tokyo
PRENTICE-HALL OF SOUTHEAST ASIA PTE. LTD., Singapore

Acknowledgments

The authors are grateful for permission to quote or paraphrase excerpts from the following sources:

JONATHAN D. CASPER, *American Criminal Justice: The Defendant's Perspective* (Englewood Cliffs, N.J.: Prentice-Hall, Inc., 1972). By permission of Prentice-Hall, Inc.

EDWIN DIAMOND, "Fairness and Balance in the Evening News," *Columbia Journalism Review* 11 (Jan.-Feb., 1973). By permission of the *Columbia Journalism Review* and the author.

DORIS A. GRABER, "Press Coverage Patterns of Campaign News: the 1968 Presidential Race," *Journalism Quarterly* 48 (Autumn, 1971). By permission of *Journalism Quarterly*.

STEPHEN HARTGEN, *A Guide to Public Records in Minnesota* (Minneapolis: Minneapolis Star and Tribune Company, 1975). By permission of the Minneapolis Star and Tribune Company.

PHILIP MEYER, *Precision Journalism: A Reporter's Introduction to Social Science Methods*, Copyright © 1973 by Indiana University Press. Reprinted by permission of the publisher.

JAMES O. MONROE, JR., "Press Coverage of the Courts," *Quill* 61 (March, 1973). By permission of the *Quill*, published by The Society of Professional Journalists, Sigma Delta Chi.

"The Newsman's Guide to Legalese." By permission of the Pennsylvania Bar Association.

WILLIAM J. VANDEN HEUVEL, "The Press and the Prisons," *Columbia Journalism Review* 11 (May-June, 1972). By permission of the *Columbia Journalism Review* and the author.

CHRIS WELLES, "The Bleak Wasteland of Financial Journalism," *Columbia Journalism Review* 12 (July-Aug., 1973). By permission of the *Columbia Journalism Review* and the author.

Contents

part two

PUBLIC AFFAIRS SETTINGS

APPENDIXES

Preface

A society replete with new pressures, constraints, and demands requires a thoughtful and well-organized approach to interpreting and understanding its problems. This is, of course, the historic mission of public affairs reporting. While social change has come to the public arena, so has it come to the newsroom. The accelerating thrust of social change renders old modes of understanding obsolete. Happily, many journalists are responding to it with new strategies for public affairs reporting. At times this response has meant specialization, at times it has meant revising the old beat structure in the direction of news coverage more oriented to topics, issues, and trends.

Reporters' attitudes and roles are changing, too. And changing with them is the nature of news. As old standards of news judgment crumble, a new standard for news that is relevant, pertinent, and salient to its audience emerges. Thus, news in the public arena becomes consumer-oriented and reporters ask: "What utility does this story—and the way it is written—have for people in the community?" Such an approach is a far cry from mechanistic coverage of public meetings and other activities that often stood alone without linkage to meaning or substance.

While directed toward the future, this book at the same time recognizes the practicalities of the contemporary newsroom, examining what is, as well as what could be. The book does not offer a clinical synthesis of the country's journalistic practices with regard to public affairs reporting, but rather a strategy for fuller investigation, interpretation, and research. Thus, it attempts to bridge conventional practice and journalistic potential. In the first part we offer several chapters that focus on new strategies for public affairs reporting. This focus directs attention to what is common to public affairs reporting, regardless of the setting. In the process we comment on investigative journalism, interpretative methods, and such modes of research as precision journalism, which pushes the reporter toward social science. At the same time, we are concerned about the traditional reportorial process and how it might be improved.

The second part of the book examines the special problems and opportunities of particular news settings. Here the legal process, executive agencies, politics, law-making and other areas of specialization are presented in terms of their uniqueness. We suggest strategies for innovation and offer examples of competent coverage drawn from widely diverse news presentation in large cities and small. This is done to demonstrate the applicability of the new strategies that are already being practiced in many newsrooms.

In an age of women's liberation, we are mindful of the sensitivities of those who urge a feminist critique of the media. We have used the term "journalist" instead of newsman and in many instances have used the plural form to avoid "he." But, with apologies, for readability we frequently do use the generic "he." We do this in the hope that a more acceptable form may emerge before we write our second edition.

We have written this book for advanced students of reporting. In many schools, the course that we address ourselves to is called "Public Affairs Reporting." But whatever the name, it is usually the second journalistic writing course for the student. Thus, we have written the text with a minimum of review material and have concentrated on the substantive issues and problems that the Public Affairs Reporting student will face in the classroom, in community assignments, and eventually on the job. By emphasizing *strategies* and *settings* and de-emphasizing a review of remedial reporting practices, we have tried to avoid becoming a superficial civics book. Though we do touch on the unique problems of news settings (and in some instances that requires special training), we have attempted to show how a reporter can become a sophisticated investigator-researcher in his evaluations of public affairs. To do this, it is understood that a full grounding in state and local government, economics, and law, as well as in other subjects, is needed. We suggest ways in which the student, and eventually the reporter, can become proficient in covering such specialized areas as courts, but we stop short of synthesizing a civics course. This, we feel, is the function of a liberal education that can only be reinforced in public affairs reporting.

It is our hope that the book will enhance the values of social responsibility taught elsewhere in the journalism and mass communication curriculum and lead students toward a thoughtful and analytical approach to public affairs reporting, one that will help them adapt to and cope with change.

We are grateful to many editors, reporters, and broadcast journalists from whom we have drawn examples. Similarly, we are grateful to several generations of students in public affairs reporting classes whose questions and critical comments have helped shape our perceptions. Our special thanks to three Minnesota colleagues: Robert L. Jones, director of the School of Journalism and Mass Communication; Professor Emeritus Mitchell V. Charnley for continued encouragement and support; and Professor Donald M. Gillmor for a critical reading of Chapter 6. Others whose technical expertise was especially helpful: Stewart R. Perry, Minneapolis attorney; and Patrick J. Starr, associate professor of mechanical engineering at Minnesota. We are also grateful to the following journalism educators for reviewing the manuscript: Benjamin H. Baldwin, Northwestern University; Jim Davis, California State University at Long Beach; David Grey, San Jose State University; John Griffith, University of Florida; Albert L. Hester, University of Georgia; Don R. Pember, University of Washington; Ed Weston, University of Florida. The manuscript was expertly typed by Karen Danninger.

part one

Public Affairs Strategies

chapter one

The World of the
Public Affairs Reporter

*Our society needs an accurate, truthful account of the
day's news. . . .*

COMMISSION ON FREEDOM OF THE PRESS

A democratic society depends on an educated and informed electorate. This fundamental truth of democratic theory is the rationale for the American system of freedom of expression, which is guaranteed by the First Amendment. Time and again, the Supreme Court of the United States has commanded that there shall be no interference with the news media in their pursuit of a full and robust discussion of public issues and events.

A realistic assessment of the press in a democratic society, however, suggests that most of the public does not make an effort to keep pace with public affairs. Indeed, most people read little below the headlines or see little beyond the television newscast. Studies show that the public looks to the media for escapist fare, for entertainment, rather than for news and information as it is currently presented. Nonetheless, the need for information persists. If that need is to be met—and the democratic ideal brought closer to reality—information must be presented in a manner that is of interest and makes sense to people in their daily lives.

Public affairs reporting is carried out in a variety of news organizations by many types of reporters. Four types are examined here.

In a medium-sized Southern city, a tough-minded young man walks briskly into the city hall hearing room. At 26, Tom Greene has spent five years as a reporter for the city's 10,000-plus circulation daily newspaper, most of them as city hall correspondent. Greene observes the zoning commission as it considers public opposition or support for a proposed change in one of the city's residential zones. It is the first time a public

3

hearing has been held on the issue—just two procedural steps away from final approval or denial by the city council.

As the doors of the criminal courts building in a large, northeastern city open, 46-year-old Susan Kahn, whose salt-and-pepper hair is the only hint of her age, walks toward a cavernous room labeled "Court Chamber No. 6" where a bank vice president and civic leader, charged with a $450,000 embezzlement, will go on trial. The jury has been chosen, and today's session will hear opening statements by the attorneys. Kahn is an expert reporter who earned this assignment after years of metro daily desk and reporting experience.

Shaking dust from yellowing file folders, Harold Copeland searches laboriously through land records as he traces the ownership of several parcels of land that have recently risen in value because of major county road improvements. The 35-year-old Copeland scans page after page of deeds and other land and property descriptions. As editor and part owner of a 4,500 circulation midwestern weekly, Copeland is in pursuit of a story that will determine the "real" owners of fertile farmland scheduled for development by an out-of-state firm.

In the regional office of the state health department, 21-year-old Chester Bond enters a door marked "Chief, Preventive Programs." He has arrived for an interview with a public-health planner who is developing a new program for exceptional children. Only three months out of journalism school, Bond is preparing a series for a western tri-weekly that circulates mostly among suburban families.

Each of these four reporters has gone to a public office or proceeding because he or she believes that a worthwhile news story is likely to result. Even though there are potentially hundreds of other places in the community where these reporters might be pursuing the news, their decisions to cover these stories are not accidental.

On the morning that Tom Greene decided to spend two hours with the zoning commission there were three other meetings of interest at city hall. Susan Kahn's assignment was only one legal proceeding out of eight in her city that day. Harold Copeland might have spent his time with several hundred different kinds of public records. Chester Bond selected one social problem out of hundreds, one agency out of dozens.

Varying degrees of personal initiative helped to account for these selections. City editors assigned Tom Greene and Susan Kahn to their particular stories—although both were regulars covering city hall and courts. Harold Copeland picked his story idea on the basis of a healthy suspicion of corruption. Chester Bond presented an idea to a news editor who nodded approval.

Every public affairs story, from idea, through development, to finished copy, is the result of several levels of decision-making. Former *Wall Street Journal* reporter Ronald Buel says that journalism has five layers of decision-making.

1. Data assignment: who decides what is worth covering and why?
2. Data collection: who decides when enough information has been gathered?
3. Data evaluation: who decides what is important enough to be put into a story?
4. Data writing: who decides what words to use?
5. Data editing: who decides which story gets a big headline and goes on the front page, which stories to cut, which stories to change? [1]

Biographies of Four News Stories

Suppose you as a student had the opportunity to ask the managing editors of the previously mentioned newspapers why each of the four situations is deemed *newsworthy*. Tom Greene's editor would tell you that zoning meetings are always covered by his paper because they are public business. If a zoning variance is approved at today's hearing—and subsequently approved by the city council—it will have an impact on the city. It will change a neighborhood by mixing commercial purposes with residential. This alteration, the editor asserts, may have a positive or negative effect depending on how you look at it and what you think public policy should be. He tells you that the zoning hearing is likely to draw a large group of citizens, mainly residents of the neighborhood where the zoning change would be implemented. "People are interested in this zoning issue," he might say, "and because it has an impact on the lives of people, we should and will cover it." And furthermore, he might add, the zoning hearing is the most important thing happening in city hall today—surely it ranks above a citizens' committee planning a May Day parade, a meeting of the city council safety committee, and a group of businessmen discussing a preliminary plan for a paint up-fix up campaign.

No doubt Susan Kahn's editor would think you naïve if you were to ask why the paper had decided to cover the trial of an accused embezzler, who happened to be a prominent citizen. Few details of the embezzlement have been disclosed, the editor explains, but now, presumably, all of them will be made known, and thousands of depositors have an indirect interest.

Harold Copeland is his own editor. His search of records is important to his paper because it may disclose a conflict of interest. Did the county commissioners line their own pockets by ordering extensive road work in an area in which some of them had commercial interests? As a first step, Copeland says, it was necessary to search county land records. The land in the area was owned by several local and out-of-state corporations—but who owned the corporations? That question, thought Copeland, might lead him to an important revelation. In this instance, a thorough investigation, based on an educated suspicion, was the impetus for the story. And the public policy and public interest implications of the story are evident.

As a college student, Chester Bond took courses in abnormal psychology. His personal interest in exceptional or retarded children led him to suggest the story he was seeking in the interview with the health department official. As his editor put it, "This is a good story for our readers. It affects thousands of them directly or indirectly. And since retardation is so often a family problem and our paper is directed to the suburban family, the newsworthiness of this story is clear."

On the Nature of News

On the surface, the editors' explanations are logical enough. They say they chose the four story assignments because they (a) were important, (b) affected people in the community, (c) would arouse public curiosity, and (d) would serve what they believe to be "the public interest." But clearly, neither reporter nor editor in any of the four cases was thinking of theoretical definitions of news. They were instead thinking of how their papers could present an "image of reality" of their community. For news is "in the largest sense that material which is most likely to be looked to and accepted as the image of reality." [2] There are, of course, many images of reality; thus the editor and reporter determined which image would constitute the news of the day. In a perceptive essay, sociologists Raymond and Alice Bauer observed that "the concept of 'news' which dominates our reporting media dictates that an event is news only if it is discontinuous with preceding events and if it is relatively recent in occurrence." [3] While some stories, of course, linger on for second and third day treatment, in general, issues, events, and happenings in the community that do not meet these criteria are usually not deemed to be newsworthy.

It is possible to find many lofty, theory-laden explanations of what *is* and *is not* news, but there is really only one operational definition of news: it is the editorial content of what appears in the newspaper or on the radio or television newscast. Items selected for inclusion in the media are news; those rejected or otherwise excluded are not. As Buel's five layers of decision-making indicate, news is also human interaction and conflict. The result of the compromise between and among the various individuals involved in the news story from conceptualization to the final rewritten words on paper is *news*. Political scientist Leon V. Sigal says that "the ability to get information into the news and to prevent rivals from doing so is at once a tactic and a stake in that fight [for news]." [4] Sigal continues:

> Four bargaining games run concurrently: those among newsmen inside their organizations, among reporters on the beat, between the reporter and his news sources, and among those sources, mostly officials in various government positions. Outcomes in one game can affect outcomes of the others. From the standpoint of bureaucratic politics, then, news is an outcome of the bargaining interplay of newsmen and sources. [5]

Thus, news is a highly complex concept, not easily categorized or abstracted. And yet, the content of most newspapers and newscasts has remarkable similarity. This similarity is due to the conventions of news-gathering and the use of the standard journalistic form by news gatherers. With these thoughts about the nature of news clearly in mind, we return to the four public affairs stories.

What the Reporters Did—and Why

The zoning hearing that Tom Greene attended was like a thousand others in as many cities across the country. The meeting was called to order by a lean, angular man who served both as chairman of the zoning commission (a committee of the city council in this case) and as a member of the city council. He explained that a request for a change in the R-1 zoning regulations for residential areas in the northeastern section of the city was being considered by the commission. In measured language, he explained that the commission would hear both from proponents and opponents of the measure.

A well-dressed man, a consumer-relations director for a major oil company, strode to the front of the room. He explained that his firm wanted to build a large central pumping facility (a service station designed to serve a large community area) on the edge of the northeast neighborhood. Anticipating objections to the plan, the man said the building would be "architecturally consistent" with the neighborhood. It would have no gaudy signs, but a pleasant neo-Colonial facade. He offered copies of engineering studies that dismissed the idea of extra noise in the neighborhood and promised that the pumping station would close every night by ten. His presentation took twenty minutes. It was highly professional and accompanied by visual aids and a handsome model of the proposed station.

The chairman said the commission would then hear citizen response to the proposal—to both the firm's specific proposal and the general idea of varying the zone. Six citizens testified. One represented the neighborhood improvement association, another the parent-teacher association. Others spoke for themselves, and one man testified for the chamber of commerce.

The testimony was mixed. The neighborhood improvement spokesman said the station would deface and degrade the neighborhood. It might, he said, lower property values and cause danger in the event of an explosion. Others objected to the potential noise and the additional traffic flow into the quiet neighborhood. Only the chamber of commerce representative saw any virtue in the plan, but even he was careful to qualify his statements, "allowing as how the citizens did have a point." For two hours there was heated debate as the oil company spokesman was called back for cross-examination. First, the four commissioners quizzed him; then members of the audience of about 150 persons. Eventually, a commissioner moved to recommend approval. The motion failed three to one.

Tom Greene left the meeting thinking about the result, the discussion, and how he would write his story. By the time he reached his desk in the newspaper office he had a lead in mind. And eyeing the sheaf of notes he had taken, along with reports distributed by the various spokesmen, he began to write his story. It began:

> The City Zoning Commission today rejected a plan that would have allowed construction of a gasoline pumping facility in the city's Northeast corner.
>
> By a vote of 3-1, the Commission rejected a request by the Moon Oil Company. The firm had asked for a change in the present zoning from residential to a mixed commercial-residential designation.
>
> In a spirited meeting that attracted 150 persons, Moon representative Robert Stevens argued that the proposed facility "will enhance the neighborhood, both in terms of convenience of gasoline and architecturally." Stevens presented a model of the proposed station and various reports.
>
> Michael Malloy, president of the Northeast Improvement Association, disagreed sharply, saying that the station would "deface the neighborhood and cause great inconvenience, especially noise."
>
> Malloy and several others who testified also maintained that there was potential danger to the community should the gasoline tanks explode.

Citing engineering studies, Stevens discounted this claim. "An explosion is virtually impossible," he said.

In this vein, the story continued for nearly twenty column inches, adding more quotations, more details, and eventually explaining the background of the zoning issue, how it occurred, and other concerns.

After leaving the meeting, Greene had nearly two hours to complete his story. And he had the assurance of the city editor that a twenty-inch story was desired. A facile writer, Greene was able to go over his notes and consider which quotes to use, which to discard. Because his story would fill a news hole on page one, he chose a conventional news style. He made only one phone call to check a factual detail, but otherwise relied completely on his notes and memory.

Susan Kahn knew that court would convene at 9:30, allowing time to file a breaking story for the first edition at 11:15. She hadn't expected, however, the kind of information she got as the prosecution outlined its case. It would show, the prosecutor said in his opening statement, that the accused, as manager of branches, had taken an average of $50,000 a year for nine years by making out loans to fictitious persons and covering them with "repayments" from new fake loans. Revealed for the first time in the prosecutor's statement was the information that senior bank officials had tried to cover up the loss in the hope that the accused would be able to repay the sums he had taken. Only when it became apparent that he couldn't, did they notify authorities. The accused, said the prosecutor, had used the money to live up to the image of the prosperous banker—large home, summer place, cars, and boats—on a salary of $18,000. While the prosecutor was still talking, Kahn had gone to a phone in the clerk's office and dictated the following lead:

> Top officers of the Blank National Bank tried to cover up an alleged $450,000 embezzlement by one of their vice presidents in an effort to avoid adverse publicity, District Attorney John Jones said today as the vice president went on trial in County Court.

In his search of land records, Harold Copeland learned that three of the six tracts of land affected by the road improvements were owned by the Resthaven Land Corporation, a local firm. The others were owned by two local men and an out-of-state firm, Cable Development Company, of Houston, Texas. A labored check of public records indicated that both Resthaven and Cable were owned by a holding company in the capital city. A telephone call to an attorney in the secretary of state's office brought him the information he wanted. Among incorporators in Post Road Holding Company were two members of the county board of commissioners, and a private citizen who owned one of the six tracts. Copeland checked and rechecked the records, interviewed a knowledgeable and friendly local banker, then confronted the three men involved. One of them called him a "damned snoop" and all refused to confirm the report. But neither did they deny it. So, Copeland wrote:

> Two members of the County Board of Commissioners and a local real estate broker may have benefited financially from road improvements the board approved recently.
>
> The three, supervisors Richard Bemis and Sidney Cohen, and realtor James Hoffmeister, are incorporators of the Post Road Holding Company which controls 500 acres of land in the Post Road area, according to state corporation records and county land records.
>
> The County Commission, with both commissioners voting "yes," approved extensive road construction in the Post Road area last spring, and as a result the assessed valuation of the land increased about 30 percent, according to the county assessor's office.

The story continued with heavy documentation. Copeland cited authority for his explanations, but carefully refrained from specific charges. He reported the unwillingness of the three men to discuss the land ownership with him. While Copeland saw a number of other potential conflicts of interest in the case as he searched public records, he could not get corroboration and thus left them out of the story.

Chester Bond spoke to the public-health planner who briefed him on the problems of mentally retarded children in the suburban area where his paper circulated. He got facts and figures about the state's program and how the planners proposed to extend and accelerate services. From the planner's office he visited two psychiatrists who treated retarded children, the president of a parents' association, two day-care centers for the retarded, a state hospital, and a convention of the state psychological association. The interviews were coupled with considerable reading about the problem and a call to the National Institute of Mental Health in Washington, which provided national statistics and a statement about the nature and scope of the problem. After three weeks of interviews and research for background information, done while covering other, routine stories, Bond was ready to write. He sent his editor this memo:

> I'm planning a five-part series, each story running 20–25 inches. They would be (1) "The Plight of the Retarded—A Family Dilemma," which would outline the nature of the problem and have several good anecdotal examples; (2) "What's Being Done," which would focus on present treatment practices and programs; (3) "Who Are the Retarded?" their lives and potential; (4) "From Back

Wards to the Community," a story looking at the changes in care and treatment of the retarded with an emphasis on community centers and home-visiting programs; (5) "What of the Future?" a look at the state plans and reaction of citizen groups.

The memo continued, detailing the series, indicating what sources had been consulted and why. Bond began his first story:

Jack Brown is a 37-year-old family man with three healthy children, a working wife, and a promising future. Unusual? No, except for one thing—thirty years ago, Jack Brown was diagnosed as "mentally retarded."

The story continued (Jack Brown was a pseudonym) humanizing the problem, explaining the potential of retarded persons. Bond wrote expansively. He was not worrying much about space limitations because his belief that he was writing about a major public-health problem was buttressed by the knowledge that the publisher's wife was a board member of the state Association for Retarded Children—and the chances of full use of the story were excellent.

A Look at the Stories

Returning to Buel's five layers of decision-making, it is evident why each of the stories was assigned—at least in terms of the editors' surface rationale. Obviously, a small daily should give considerable attention to a zoning meeting that will have an impact on a number of local citizens. When 150 of those citizens appear at city hall on a weekday morning—in a small city—that itself is news. It shows the intensity of concern. But such rationale was not really in play when the city editor agreed with Greene that the story should be covered. Zoning meetings are standard fare for public affairs reporters and barring another, more important assignment, Greene always covers the zoning commission, especially when it is about to make a decision.

To some extent Susan Kahn's presence at the courtroom was also routine. Following up a continuing story on her criminal justice beat is standard practice. That she would be present in the courtroom was guaranteed by the coverage already given the case. However, even the most vital cases sometimes get diminished treatment if a major, national catastrophe, such as a presidential assassination, occurs. The degree to which news values inhere in any story depends on what else is happening —in the community, state, and nation.

In deciding how much information to gather for their stories, the four reporters were all guided by time and space constraints. In two hours, Greene could hardly write a short history of zoning. He decided to concentrate only on the meeting and what happened there. Of course, as the regular city hall reporter, he went to the meeting with a considerable fund of knowledge about the subject. What was a routine assignment for him might not have been routine for a new reporter.

Similarly, Susan Kahn had already covered the pretrial aspects of the embezzlement story, so she had no trouble composing a conventional lead under pressure of an early deadline. Harold Copeland concentrated only on those records relevant to his suspicion that there might be potential conflict of interest on the County Board of Commissioners. And he used only those items that could be confirmed elsewhere.

Chester Bond had the luxury of doing a multisource story in which he was able to spend several weeks tracking down information, conducting interviews, and thinking about what he was going to write.

And in all of these instances space was pretty much guaranteed, barring last-minute developments. Not one of the reporters had to fight with the city editor to get the story into the paper.

All of the reporters had to sort out the trivial from the significant. This process was especially true of the zoning meeting coverage, the transcript of which would have covered several newspaper pages. At the other extreme, the retardation story was the product of considerable planning. Bond spent little time with irrelevant sources, although he collected a large stack of written material that required sorting and sifting.

In writing the story, Greene hurriedly prepared his copy with little thought and time for rewriting. The story was routine and it was handled with dispatch. Similarly, the trial story was quick and to the point. Copeland was much more careful in his use of language. The potential for a libel suit, even though his subjects were public officials, was great and he didn't want to take any chances. The economic constraints of a possible suit were very real to him as an owner of the paper. And so he took special care in checking and rechecking the information. Bond, in the retardation study, had more research time, which permitted the use of anecdotes, case histories, description, and dialogue. Finally, each of the stories was published with only a few editing changes.

The four stories presented here are typical assignments for public affairs reporters. We may never know precisely why the reporters did what they did, but at least there are some clues to their behavior. Like these stories, every news story has many complex variations. And depending on newsroom interactions, space, time, and other constraints, the results may vary considerably. The lot of the public affairs reporter is dynamic, one that requires an inquiring mind, specialized knowledge, and an ability to adapt and adjust as news changes and situations alter.

The four hypothetical case studies are an introduction to the goal of this book: to provide a thoughtful framework for consideration of the public affairs reporter—his problems and priorities. The book follows the reporter and his search for news, and it moves toward a new definition of news, one adaptable to change and geared to the future. It analyzes approaches to the coverage of public problems, including traditional strategies (for example, beats), direct and indirect observation, the search of public records, interviewing, and the writing process. Variations in the approach to coverage and writing style are also considered. Differences in reportorial practices demanded by different kinds of media settings and different time restrictions are also examined.

Attention is next directed to ways in which the public affairs reporter can enrich his work by using social science methods such as surveys and field experiments. Similarly, the utility of an understanding of social indicators and statistical methods is stressed.

After considering the strategic problems in public affairs reporting, we turn to public affairs news settings, placing special emphasis on coverage of the legal process, government agencies and services, politics and elections, the legislative process, specialized coverage of such areas as the environment, education, and consumerism. Finally, we discuss the future of public affairs reporting as it appears from the contemporary vantage point.

Our emphasis is more on strategy than setting because it is clear that many of the techniques and thinking processes useful to the public affairs reporter in one setting apply to other news settings as well. Where there are differences and a need for specialized skills particular to a field, we attempt to cover them.

Thus, this book is developed not as a rigid road map for the public affairs reporter, but as a stimulus to thinking and analysis. By underscoring communication strategies, it is our hope that the material that follows will help reporters of public affairs to keep pace with the future demands of the communications industry regardless of the form it takes.

NOTES

1. Ronald A. Buel, *Dead End: The Automobile in Mass Transportation* (Baltimore: Penguin Books, 1973), p. 220.

2. Raymond A. Bauer and Alice H. Bauer, "America, 'Mass Society' and Mass Media," *Journal of Social Issues* 16 (No. 3), 1960, 50–51.

3. Ibid., p. 52.

4. Leon V. Sigal, *Reporters and Officials: The Organization and Politics of News-making* (Lexington, Mass.: D. C. Heath, 1973), p. 5.

5. Ibid.

chapter two

Toward a New Definition of News

What is history but a fable agreed upon?

NAPOLEON BONAPARTE

The parson, the geologist, and the cowboy were all standing together and gazing for the first time at the Grand Canyon.

"One of the wonders of God," said the parson.

"One of the wonders of science," said the geologist.

"What a helluva place to raise a cow," said the cowboy.

So much for objectivity.

With that bit of pointed whimsy, Detroit newspaper executive Derick Daniels dismissed a bit of hard-core journalistic dogma: that objective reporting is the one path to truth and reality.[1] The long-running debate about objective versus interpretative reporting is largely over. Interpretation has earned a secure place as an accepted member of the journalistic family. There are, of course, those who retain an uncomplicated faith in the sublime dynamics of objective reporting to fulfill society's information needs adequately. The columns of newspapers are still largely populated with the classic, one-dimensional objective story in which the reporter serves as uncritical transmission belt, giving equal weight to all positions presented at an event. Still, few editors today deny the need for stories that go beyond the immediate event, adding meaning to complex news situations.

One reason for the survival and dominance of the objective form is the history of its hard-won acceptance. Herbert Brucker, former editor of the *Hartford* (Conn.) *Courant,* summed up the virtues of objectivity with this observation:

No one can argue away the fact that American journalism has now struggled for a century and a third to replace partisan propaganda with reporting that gets within hailing distance of the truth. And that kind of reporting is too valuable, not only to journalism, but to self-government itself, to be discarded now in an emotional reaction fueled by the current political distemper.[2]

But objectivity, long the Eleventh Commandment for journalism's faithful, is now often regarded with the same irreverence as other mortal rules. "Outside" press critics and inside professionals alike are subscribing in increasing numbers to a new orthodoxy which argues that interpretation is needed in the reporting of *all* public affairs. The complexity of contemporary life, the diversity of modern society, the rapid changes brought by new technology and shifting cultural values—all demand explanation if the public is to be adequately informed. Yesterday's one-dimensional journalism yielded not neutrality but superficiality. The news media, both print and broadcast, deluged their audiences with what Eric Sevareid once termed "the daily needle shower of unrelated facts." They reported the events—especially the sensational and the graphic—but ignored the antecedents of those events. They covered the visible artifacts of society's turmoil, but not the conditions responsible for that turmoil.

Communications researcher James W. Carey goes a step beyond faulting objective reporting for what it hasn't accomplished. He believes it has also compromised the independence of the journalist and allowed news sources to use the press for their own purposes. Carey writes:

> First, as an adjunct of objective reporting there developed norms and procedures governing the manner in which reporters could utilize sources. The net effect of the press conference, the background interview, the rules governing anonymous disclosure and attribution of sources, and particularly the growing use of the public information officer within government, is to routinize the reporter's function and to grant to the source exceptional control over news dissemination. As a result, not only can government and other sources deliberately place messages, without alteration, before the public, but through the "leak" and other forms of anonymous disclosure, they can utilize the press as an alternative channel for diplomatic and other private communication. The "canned" press conference in which questions are planted and to which "safe" reporters are admitted by pass further strips away the independent, critical function of the journalist.
>
> Second, the psychology of the reporting process also chips away at the reporter's independence. Because the reporter mediates between audiences and sources, he is pulled in two directions; serving the interests of the source and the interests of the audience, interests

which are rarely identical. Often, if not usually, the reporter develops contempt for both parties he serves: the audience because it is so often apathetic and uninterested, the source because it is so often dishonest. Resolution of the strain in the reporting process normally supports the interests of the source rather than that of the audience.[3]

Awareness of journalism's failings, and support for interpretative reporting, did not arrive full-blown with the 1970s. The seeds of the metamorphosis were sown a hundred years before. The strident personal journalism of the nineteenth-century American press, which sought to persuade rather than enlighten, gradually gave way to an objectivity spawned by two forces. One was a profound change in the ownership pattern of newspapers, with the editor-publisher giving way to corporate publishers more interested in profit than politics. The other was the growth of the wire services and syndicates, which served the same news material to clients of varying biases. The press associations served to standardize style at the expense of individualized reporting. The result was an objectivity so narrow that it removed all context from news stories. It was the dominant reporting form by World War I.[4]

Challenges to blind objectivity began to appear in the 1930s, in book form,[5] but the first substantial public criticism of this approach was expressed in 1947 by the privately-funded Commission on Freedom of the Press. It called on newspapers to give the public "a truthful, comprehensive and intelligent account of the day's events *in a context which gives them meaning.*" [6]

The commission, however, was composed of laymen distinguished in fields other than journalism. Its chairman was educator Robert M. Hutchins. Editors and reporters are not renowned for sitting at the feet of those who have "never met a deadline," and the press Establishment reacted predictably to the commission's recommendations: it ridiculed them and then ignored them. It wasn't long, however, before prominent voices within the profession began espousing the cause of news interpretation. One was Erwin D. Canham, editor of the *Christian Science Monitor,* who challenged convention by contending that "the balancing fact should be attached directly to the misleading assertion." Another was philosopher-critic Harry S. Ashmore, who, while editor of the *Little Rock* (Ark.) *Gazette,* summed up the growing sentiment for interpretative reporting this way:

It remains journalism's unfulfilled responsibility to somehow provide perspective and continuity . . . to add the "why" to the "what". . . . I think we have got to get over the notion that objectivity is achieved by giving a sinner equal space with a saint—

and above all of paying the greatest attention to those who shout the loudest. We've got to learn that a set of indisputable facts does not necessarily add up to the whole truth.[7]

A turning point came in the early 1950s, when Senator Joseph R. McCarthy of Wisconsin capitalized on the media's slavish devotion to objectivity and became a national figure in the process.[8] His unsubstantiated charges of treason, subversion, and communism in federal government were reported as "straight" news by the media. Thus his accusations of one day stood alone on the front pages, while the denial followed later, if at all, on the inside pages. The flaw in the process was eventually recognized by most journalists. The prevailing culture of journalism, which held objectivity as its central tenet, was jarred into a new era. It is an irony of sorts that a principal legacy of McCarthyism has been a beneficial effect on a press system that the senator used and abused.

The move from one-dimensional objectivity was by no means universal or consistent. Ground rules for the use of interpretative reporting are selective, and the public figure today can still manipulate the objective tradition to his advantage. Washington Correspondent Peter Lisagor observed this potential in the 1972 re-election campaign of Richard Nixon. "The rules of objectivity are such," he said, "that a man can make political capital out of them in the way he presents a particular issue." [9] Lisagor was referring to Nixon's practice of including a sensational, if suspect, charge in his speeches. The objective tradition persuaded reporters to use the accusation as the lead of their stories. Time for rebuttal or denial was not available because Nixon not only knew what made a good headline and lead, but also the deadlines for Eastern papers and networks.

Timothy Crouse, in his intimate portrait of presidential campaign reporters, *The Boys on the Bus,* concluded that a strict anti-interpretation rule was imposed on most journalists. While the reporter covering the town council might add context to his story, the campaign reporters were confined to conduit status. Said Crouse: "If the candidate spouted fullsome bullshit all day, the formula made it hard for the reporter to say so directly—he would have to pretend that "informed sources" had said so. . . . A reporter was not allowed to make even the simplest judgments; nor was he expected to verify the candidate's claims." [10]

Yet the evolution from rigid objective reporting has come far in the decades since McCarthy. Journalism has moved into two modes of reporting. One is straight news, the conventional journalism that despairs of reporting anything but occurrences. The other is interpretative, which attempts to explain change and relate events to each other. Strangely, they coexist in many newspapers, and this dual approach is perhaps the prevailing method for reporting public affairs in the 1970s. The principal effort is still devoted to the coverage of events. A small percentage of these stories lead to subsequent interpretative stories, variously labeled in professional jargon as backgrounders, situationers, interpretatives, news analyses, think pieces, or, derisively, "thumb-suckers."

The assumption in this schizoid approach to reporting public affairs is that fact-gathering and interpretation are separable reporting functions. Many would argue, however, that they are indivisible for the same reasons that objectivity is unattainable: The very selection (and rejection) of facts, their order of presentation, and other matters of reportorial judgment are, in effect, elements of interpretation. For these and other reasons, the cutting edge in public affairs reporting today is moving toward adequate interpretation in each story produced. The thrust in more progressive newsrooms is toward the full-dimensional story, one in which the reader gets both an accurate account of an event or situation *and* enough additional information to assure understanding. The reporter, to use a medical metaphor, is being allowed to both take the X-ray and read the film.[11]

What Is "News?"

If there is consensus in the newsrooms regarding the inadequacy of classical objectivity and the need for interpretation, are we then on the threshold of a journalistic utopia where the news media will adequately fulfill their obligations to society? Few serious observers of the press take so sanguine a view. The reasons are several. Today, editors talk more of fairness than of objectivity, and subscribe to the need for interpretative reporting. Yet the implementation of these convictions is often spotty or half-hearted. Habits die hard, rituals persist. Changing the genes of the journalistic process may be as difficult as restructuring the DNA molecule; those who rely on a hopeful Darwinism in which change will come in due time are perhaps more patient than realistic.

The conventions of journalism, the very structure of news organizations with their reliance on generations-old systems of news gathering (the rigid "beat" system with its arbitrary geographical divisions, the training of reporters as generalists, the sometimes exclusive value placed on timeliness and proximity) are factors that are now seen to thwart effective reporting. Most important, perhaps, is the realization that the objectivity versus interpretation debate was just a preliminary bout in a related but much more basic battle: the redefinition of news.

Interpretative reporting and the definition of news are related to each other as an arm is to a wrist, a switch to a lamp, a turntable to a record. Confront one and you confront the other. Success in fulfilling journalism's appointed role depends as much or more on the subject matter selected for attention as on the method of presentation. The problem then becomes a question of emphasis: is the more basic concern substance, or process?

In Chapter 1 the editors of the four hypothetical newspapers justified the story assignments they made by citing their importance to readers or to the community at large. Many editors would invoke similar notions in attempting to define news. But it was also suggested in Chapter 1 that there was really only one workable, all-embracing definition of news: that which appears in the newspaper or on the newscast. Acknowledging this reality averts a good deal of semantic quibbling and goes directly to the underlying question: What *should be* in the newspaper or on the newscast? The "what" in the question doesn't limit the answer to choices among discrete subjects. News has never been selected on the basis of categorical classification alone. One speech is covered, another ignored; one meeting gets front page treatment, a similar meeting goes unnoticed—a tree falling in the forest. It has always been thus in the news business. Factors other than topic influence the choice of events and situations that are made into news.

What, then, are these factors? As noted in Chapter 1, the Bauers considered two factors as determinants of news: a distinct event, and recency.[12]

The Commission on Freedom of the Press concluded thirty years ago that the journalist's definition of news, in an operational sense, is something that happened within the last few hours and which will attract the interest of customers. The criteria of "interest," the commission observed, are recency, proximity, combat, human interest, and novelty. Notable for their absence in the list are considerations of significance or pertinence. Critics of the press since that time haven't improved on the commission's observations. The criteria usually lead journalists to report on single events (recency) in their cities of publication (proximity) which contain elements of drama or conflict (combat) or of pathos (human interest) or oddity (novelty). These criteria could lead one to conclude that the ideal story might be about a local beauty queen who mugged the mayor in front of a brothel last night so that she could get enough money to pay for a heart operation for her critically ill younger brother.

Such exaggeration may be unfair, but the inescapable observation is that most news is event-centered. It is typically about a recent happening, and is generally uninterpreted, with minimal context, unrelated to other situations and events. This contrasts with what has been termed process-centered news—interpretative presentations of conditions and situations in society that are related in broad context and over time.[13] This latter category is not an academic invention, an ideological improbability nurtured in the ivy tower. It is an approach increasingly occupying the public affairs reporter, fostered by progressive news organizations, large and small.

Process-centered news treatments are appearing on op-ed pages, in Sunday feature sections, on front pages, and as "special reports" on radio and television. Sometimes they are written by nonjournalists with expertise in the subject. Frequently, editors assign staff reporters to this kind of story. Newspapers such as the *Wall Street Journal* and the *Christian Science Monitor* have been pioneers in this trend, giving full-dimensional treatment each day to subjects such as an evaluation of the performance of federal regulatory agencies, and the implications for farmers and consumers of the 1974 midwestern drought. Other newspapers, such as the *Los Angeles Times, Chicago Tribune, New York Times,* and Long Island's *Newsday,* have assigned reporters for extended periods to pursue beneath-the-surface explanations of news events. *Newsday* sent a team of reporters to France to probe the origin of heroin smuggled into the United States. The *Los Angeles Times* reserves column one on page one each day for depth treatment of such subjects as the reasons for the sudden spurt of interest in the mid-1970s in police work as a career, after years of decline.

The practice is not limited to major metropolitan newspapers, either. The 90,000-circulation *Riverside* (Calif.) *Press-Enterprise,* for one, devotes a section-opening page each day to subjects ranging from the growth of fundamentalist religious groups to the backyard impact of inflation-recession. Five reporters are assigned full-time to this task. Other medium-sized dailies are also attempting the process-centered approach, within the limits of staff availability.

These examples are still exceptions to the norm. The norm is still covering the mayor's speech, the school board vote, the street demonstration, the unusual crime. The norm in journalism does not yet include discovering the mayor's thoughts and plans when he is publicly silent, or probing the cross-currents of educational thought that never surface before the school board, or exploring the viewpoints and conditions of disadvantaged groups before there are demonstrations, or examining the culture of crime rather than its spectacular artifacts. The reporter and his editor might ask:

Does racism exist only when there is a riot?
Is there a problem in education only when parents protest at a public hearing?

Are there public concerns about zoning, garbage disposal, or park facilities only when they appear on the city council agenda?

The answers are obvious, but the notion that a topic is not newsworthy until something "happens" has been pervasive. By restricting the definition of news to events, significant phenomena fall outside the reporter's vision, and less significant events, often contrived, get attention. By this criterion, the public doesn't learn of important forces in society until they erupt suddenly and often traumatically, in events. The recent past is filled with such examples. It required sit-ins, marches, and riots to bring out the state of mind and living conditions of blacks in the 1960s. It required a comic-opera burglary at Watergate to expose the moral poverty of a national administration in the 1970s.

Why is the press so often a prisoner of this dysfunctional definition of news? Press critics and professionals offer a variety of explanations, some harsh, some empathetic. Critic Max Ways blames the situation on the media's decision to focus on governmental decisions, as well as the "event trap."

> Journalism still clings to the legislative act and the presidential decision because they are relatively easy to get into focus. By contrast, such gradual and multicentered changes as the lessening of parental authority or the increase of consumer credit or public acceptance of a new technology are more difficult to pinpoint. They are not events. They did not happen "yesterday" or "today" or even "last week." They do not fit the journalist's cherished notions of a "story." Yet their consequences and implications are far more potent than an isolated legislative act or presidential decision which gets the attention of reporters and space or time in the media.[14]

Journalism educator Donald McDonald also regards the event mentality as the most pernicious cause of editorial anemia. But he suggests that other journalistic conventions—the penchant for oversimplification, the preference for the bizarre, the addiction to speed—combine to hamper process-centered reporting. On the question of reducing public issues to a two-sided scenario, McDonald points out that simplification "often destroys the opportunity for understanding, for if anything is characteristic of public affairs, it is complexity."[15] Regarding the rush to get today's news into print or on the air immediately, he observes that it "is axiomatic that the more serious and consequential the public affairs, the untidier they will be and the more unmanageable they will be by any of the metronomic standards set by the print and electronic media."[16]

Sociologist Gaye Tuchman, in her detailed field studies of the professional behavior of journalists, adds yet another explanation for the normative definitions of news. What McDonald termed conventions, she described as "strategic rituals" that are followed more from habit than reason.[17] The rituals are used defensively to validate the newsman's performance. Objectivity is one such defense. Tuchman also views the organizational and operational structure of the news media as a chief determinant of what is considered news.[18] "The way something happens" thus often defines news. If an event occurs on a recognized beat, it has legitimacy and therefore will appear in print. A similar event occurring elsewhere may be rejected or pass unnoticed—an accident of geography.

Clearly, the question of news definition isn't easily answered. Reporters and editors struggle with it daily, as they do with the difficult choice between straight and interpretative treatment. The four story situations in Chapter 1 illustrate these alternatives. Two were spot news treatments, two interpretative. Depending on circumstance, each might have been treated in either mode. Moreover, interpretative stories could have been developed *before* the events in some cases.

Tom Greene's coverage of the zoning meeting was in straight news style. He told what happened at the meeting. It could have been reported in broader context, however. What are the implications of a major service station at that location? Is it an indicator of change in development patterns, of transit problems? What significance does it hold for those who didn't attend the meeting but who may be affected by the decision?

Chester Bond's series about the mentally retarded could have been treated as a brief announcement of a new state program, and left at that. Similarly, if there were no such program—no "event"—Bond could have developed an interpretative story on the possible need for one.

Harold Copeland's investigation of corruption is the type of story that may itself produce an event, in this case a criminal charge, or a recall action by voters. The digging by Copeland could have been done by an official such as the county attorney, with the result that spot news stories would follow. It was the combination of press and official investigations that distinguished the long Watergate burglary probe and its aftermath, with segments of the press doing much more than covering court appearances.

Susan Kahn led her story with the disclosures of the cover-up by bank officials, a predictable "spot" news treatment. In future stories, she would be likely to write about other developments in the embezzlement trial. But the disclosures may suggest stories of much greater import than the trial itself. How often do business executives attempt to paper over crime in their own establishments to protect their images with the public? What is the extent of white-collar crime in relation to more sensational and publicized misbehavior? These and similar questions are worth exploring, whether or not there is an embezzlement case in progress.

Decisions of the types demanded by these story situations go a long way toward determining whether a newspaper is predictable and dull or stimulating and relevant for the reader.

The Broadcast Dilemma

If the structure and heritage of the news system often turn the print reporter toward shallow treatment, the broadcast reporter is almost forced into that mold. The strictures of time and the assumptions of audience interest make radio and television news programs a bulletin board of recent events. News items are rarely allotted more than a minute or two, with the length of those on television frequently dictated by the availability of film. Broadcast reporters, in an effort to capsulize and simplify, tend to use few sources for a given story. Time constraints, complicated for television by the processing, editing, and transmission of film, are even more severe for the broadcast than for the print reporter.

The generally acknowledged communication effectiveness of television, therefore, isn't exploited on regular news programs to give the viewer a full account of the forces in society. Despite these limitations, the broadcast journalist has often produced interpretative essays of exceptional quality. His opportunity to do so depends on the availability of staff, money, and air time for documentaries and other special news programs. This opportunity varies with the station and the network, although the advent of new technology and inexpensive videotape may soon ease this stricture at many stations.

Network devotion to the documentary has been episodic. The trend, however, is away from regularly scheduled documentaries in prime time (7:30 to 11 P.M.), and toward late-night magazine-format shows that offer briefer interpretations of several subjects.[19] The amount of network prime time devoted to public affairs on a regularly scheduled basis averaged 2 per cent at the start of the 1970s.[20] Prime time is obviously the preserve of fantasy, not reality. Still, network journalists are producing programs of merit with increasing regularity. A sample of memorable documentaries of the 1970s would include "The Selling of the Pentagon," a critical examination of the Defense Department's propaganda operations, by CBS; "The Blue Collar Trap," an Emmy winner by NBC, which probed job dissatisfaction in an age of affluence; and "Close-Up," a series of special investigative reports on issues such as the energy crisis and world famine, in prime time on ABC.

Noncommercial public television, chiefly educational stations, devotes more time to public affairs programming than either the networks or local commercial stations. Limited funds, however, restrict these efforts at most stations. The Corporation for Public Broadcasting (CPB), chartered and financed by Congress, distributes some funds to local stations and to the Public Broadcasting Service (PBS). Through PBS and similar special production services funded by CPB and private foundations, high quality documentaries are shared by hundreds of public stations. But PBS, subject to political pressures and budget control by Congress, has wavered in its support of the public affairs documentary. Several regularly scheduled programs, including the award-winning "Great American Dream Machine," were abandoned in the early 1970s.

Local commercial stations provide the largest potential outlet for interpretative reporting. The amount of such programming varies widely, but as the networks and the PBS have reduced their efforts, local stations seem to be expanding theirs. Stations such as KNXT and KNBC in Los Angeles, KING in Seattle, WCCO in Minneapolis, and WABC in New York are noted for their extensive public affairs programming. Others across the nation react promptly to examine in depth a highly salient local issue when it surfaces, such as busing for school integration. Some local investigative documentaries are change-producing vehicles; an outstanding example is "Willowbrook, the Last Great Disgrace," by WABC-TV in New York. This exposé of conditions at a state hospital for the retarded won a host of prizes for the station and reporter Geraldo Rivera, as well as corrective action by the state. Such efforts aren't restricted to the largest stations; Salt Lake City's KUTV won kudos for "Warrior without a Weapon," a documentary on the plight of the Gosiute Indians.

Despite these efforts, documentaries don't constitute a major fraction of programming time or budget. The news special is typically relegated to daytime or late-night hours, when viewing is light. The vast majority of interpretative news available to the public is still found in newspapers and magazines, not on the airwaves.

The Audience Connection

Any doubts about the lack of effectiveness of conventional public affairs reporting are erased by studies which show that public knowledge of current events is extremely limited.[21] For example, most citizens can't remember the names of their congressmen, let alone the substance of the legislation with which they deal. Social observers and journalists alike are prone to cluck their tongues in dismay and place the blame for this ignorance on the citizen. He is variously regarded as lazy or alienated or lacking the intellectual ability to become informed about important public matters. For this deficiency, the public affairs reporter typically accepts no responsibility and sees no cure.

There is, however, an alternative and equally plausible explanation for the low level of public affairs knowledge. It holds that people don't score well on tests of current events because such tests are drawn from information appearing in the press. If people conclude that such information—events, names, places—doesn't hold much personal relevance, why should they attend to it? This explanation places the onus for an "ignorant" public squarely on the news media, which have absolute discretion to define news and the form in which it is presented. If the fault lies with the press and not the public, then the press *can* do something about it. Sterile, ritualistic, redundant, irrelevant treatment of public affairs can give way to coverage in which the reader can recognize self-interest. Relevance can be achieved through choice of subject matter and manner of presentation. The reader-centered interpretative article, the humanistic newswriting style, the emphasis on consumer orientation are examples of what some segments of the press are doing to meet this challenge.

It is here that communication research can be particularly helpful to the journalist. Unfortunately, reporters of the trenchcoat-and-felt-hat breed tend to sneer at scientific research, particularly when applied to their own craft. Those who do attempt to use research findings are often misled by the circular nature of conventional readership studies. In these studies, readers are shown copies of newspapers or lists of news items and asked to state their content preferences. Naturally, the range of these preferences is limited to precisely what the newspapers already contain. The result is that editors assume that people want more of what they've been getting, and readers assume that a newspaper is supposed to look like the product that editors have been giving them.

Audience analyst John P. Robinson of Cleveland State University's research center suggests that a more rational approach would start with an inventory of people's perceptions about their own information practices.[22] This inquiry would disclose what people want to know more about, what they think they know and do not know, and what might be a desirable mixture of the two. Actually, a substantial amount of knowledge about how people use news media and other information sources is already accumulated, waiting for practical interpretation by journalists.[23]

This observation isn't intended to imply that journalists should simply pander to public tastes in the selection of subject matter. Rather, the point is that an understanding of audience behavior may help reporters to design their stories so they will be read as well as printed. Much of the conventional wisdom of the newsroom runs counter to what is already known about when, how, and why people seek information. One such bit of folklore is the once dominant belief in the existence of a mass audience for the media. There is none, in the sense of a diverse aggregation of people "out there," isolated from one another but all connected to the media.[24] Many audiences are out there, some big and some small, and they will vary from topic to topic. The audience for a story on a new zoning plan may differ significantly in size and composition from the audience for a story in the next column on a proposed art center. More troublesome, each of the stories may have several sub audiences, each with different levels of understanding and information needs. Recognizing these differences and attempting to provide suitable information for the subaudiences is the reporter's challenge.

Another myth that needs shaking is that the chief function of the media is to transmit information. Harold Lasswell, a political scientist who has done pioneering research in mass communication, says the media's function consists of (a) surveillance of the environment, (b) correlation (interpretation) of the parts of society, and (c) transmission of the social heritage from generation to generation.[25] The evidence of recent studies, however, points to the media's various types of entertainment functions as those most used by most people.[26] Public affairs reporters must be realistic about the purposes as well as the composition of their audiences. One interpretation that could be drawn from the accumulated research is that most people are pragmatic and rational about their reading and viewing practices. If public affairs subject matter is presented to them in a fashion that clearly shows its personal relevance and value, they will pay attention to it.

Implications for Reporters

Objectivity versus interpretation.
Event-centered reporting versus process-centered news.
The dynamics of audiences.

Where does this leave the public affairs reporter of today—and tomorrow? How can he cope with the stresses of a profession in flux, and the demands of a society beset by overnight change? Public affairs reporters today are better trained and more highly skilled, collectively, than ever. Yet there is widespread agreement among editors and educators that even more is needed in the way of talent and training. There's more to good journalism than the ability to write a summary lead.

Attributes desired in the ideal public affairs reporter would vary considerably with the source consulted, but a composite list of advice to the reporter-in-training would probably contain many of these suggestions:

Great writing is often a variation of the conventional. The reporter should master the techniques of event-centered straight reporting, with its attendant devotion to accuracy, brevity, and clarity. This is still the criterion in the news business, despite the growth of interpretation. Reporters will have to cover speeches, meetings, and disasters for a long time to come, and they'll be judged on their abilities to follow the standard model, with speed.

Reporters can't expect to function as independent entities, free to shape their own roles. They work, in varying degrees, under supervision and subject to pressure from colleagues and news sources. They should learn something about the care and feeding of editors and recognize that editors will often have superior news judgment. This awareness will help them to cope successfully (if not with equanimity) with the contrasts in journalistic philosophy that are bound to confront them. An appreciation of an editor's values and standards enables the reporter to work through them to serve his own interests, and helps to avoid fruitless confrontations. The sociology of the newsroom shapes both opportunities and limitations. Equally important but perhaps more intractable are the conflicts that arise between a reporter and his sources. The source sees the reporter as a needed ally or a valuable conduit. The reporter sees the source as a vital lifeline. These perceptions and their implications collide with the reporter's own role perception as an objective observer, as well as the role expectations of his editors and the public. How he walks this delicate line is the measure of his professionalism.[27]

Interpretative reporting requires basic intellectual skills and an understanding of the social forces, power systems, and group behavior patterns that have shaped our world. The reporter should also develop specialized knowledge in an area that is likely to be valued by news organizations. The choices may range from public administration to home economics. The long-term trend in the newsroom is toward increasing specialization.

News professionals are discovering that a little theory makes the practice of journalism, like sex, more interesting, more understandable, and less dangerous. More and more, they are looking to communication research and theory for a better understanding of how people use information. Increasingly, this knowledge is helping to shape news decisions.[28]

Journalism today, both print and broadcast, is largely a business of communicating with an urban audience. More than 80 per cent of the United States population is in urban centers. The public affairs reporter, therefore, should become familiar with the dynamics of urban living and the particular traits of his own community and region. Communication researcher Jack Lyle suggests these areas of knowledge as useful to all reporters: [29]

Demographics. The characteristics of people differ markedly from city to city, even neighborhood to neighborhood. Reporters will want to know the attributes and distinctions of their audiences—major occupational groupings, income and education levels, recreation and leisure practices, religious preferences, value systems. Much of this information is available from census data.

Community Organization. Patterns of formal organization in his community are the reporter's road maps. He should learn the structure of organizations, both public and private, and their interrelationships.

Communication Systems. Each city and region develops its own communications complex, serving special information needs beyond the reach of mass circulation newspapers and television. These subsystems range from school newsletters to the underground press. They can tell the reporter much about his audiences and their information practices.

These suggestions have a common thread. They imply that the reporter should guard against insularity, both in his newsroom and in dealing with the relative handful of news sources to which many newspapers restrict themselves. It is the danger of this type of parochialism that Philadelphia newspaper editor William B. Dickinson may have had in mind when he told a gathering of editors:

> We have become accustomed to covering certain beats: police and fire, the city hall, the courts, the Chamber of Commerce, and so on. We are not yet accustomed to covering the new beats, the very people who are transforming our world—the scientists, the physicians, the economists, the engineers, the architects, the educators, the management elite, the planners, the thinkers.[30]

Clearly, to meet Dickinson's challenge public affairs reporters face demands that were unheard of in a simpler journalistic age. To succeed, they will need talent and training, and journalism will need to agree on a new definition of news.

NOTES

1. Derick Daniels, "The World of Multi-Media," *The Quill* 58 (July, 1970), 8.

2. Herbert Brucker, "What's Wrong with Objectivity?" *Saturday Review* 52 (Oct. 11, 1969), 77.

3. James W. Carey, "The Communications Revolution and the Professional Communicator," *Sociological Review,* monograph 13 (Keele, Staffordshire, U.K.: University of Keele, 1969), 33–34. For convenience, English spellings have been changed to the American form.

4. See Edwin Emery, *The Press and America,* 3rd ed. (Englewood Cliffs, N.J.: Prentice-Hall, 1972), pp. 465ff.; Curtis D. MacDougall, *Interpretative Reporting,* 6th ed. (New York: Macmillan, 1972), pp. 12–16; and William L. Rivers and Wilbur Schramm, *Responsibility in Mass Communication* (New York: Harper & Row, 1969), pp. 150–51.

5. For one such critique, see Herbert Brucker, *The Changing American Newspaper* (New York: Columbia University Press, 1937).

6. Commission on Freedom of the Press, *A Free and Responsible Press* (Chicago: University of Chicago Press, 1947), 20.

7. Harry Ashmore, "The Untold Story Behind Little Rock," *Harper's* ·232 (June, 1958), 19.

8. A description of Senator McCarthy's demagoguery can be found in Samuel Eliot Morison, *The Oxford History of the American People* (New York: Oxford University Press, 1965), pp. 1074ff.

9. Quoted in Timothy Crouse, *The Boys on the Bus* (New York: Random House, 1973), p. 256.

10. Ibid., pp. 323–24.

11. The X-ray analogy is taken from Alan Pritchard, "The Newspaper Responsibility," *The Quill* 54 (August, 1966), 26.

12. Raymond A. Bauer and Alice H. Bauer," "America, 'Mass Society' and Mass Media," *Journal of Social Issues* 16 (July, 1960), pp. 50–51.

13. The concept of process-centered news is developed in Todd Hunt, "Beyond the Journalistic Event: The Changing Concept of News," *Mass Comm Review* 1 (April, 1974), pp. 23–30.

14. Max Ways, "What's Wrong With the News? It Isn't New Enough," *Fortune* 36 (October, 1969), 110.

15. Donald McDonald, "Is Objectivity Possible?" *Center Magazine* 4 (September-October, 1971), 29–42.

16. Ibid.

17. Gaye Tuchman, "Objectivity as Strategic Ritual: An Examination of Newsmen's Notions of Objectivity," *American Journal of Sociology* 77 (January, 1972), 660–79.

18. Gaye Tuchman, "Making News by Doing Work: Routinizing the Unexpected," *American Journal of Sociology* 79 (July, 1973), 110–31.

19. Marvin Barrett, ed., *Survey of Broadcast Journalism 1971–1972* (New York: Thomas Y. Crowell Co., 1973), pp. 9–38.

20. Marvin Barrett, ed., *Survey of Broadcast Journalism 1970–1971* (New York: Grosset & Dunlap, 1971), p. 13.

21. Wilbur Schramm and Serena Wade, *Knowledge and the Public Mind* (Stanford: Institute for Communication Research, Stanford University Press, 1967), pp. 27ff.

22. John P. Robinson, "Mass Communication and Information Diffusion," in *Current Perspectives in Mass Communication Research*, ed. F. Gerald Kline and Phillip J. Tichenor (Beverly Hills: Sage Publications, 1972), pp. 71–93.

23. Some current perspectives on audiences may be found in Raymond A. Bauer, "The Audience," in *Handbook of Communication*, ed. Ithiel de Sola Pool et al. (Chicago: Rand McNally, 1973), pp. 141–52.

24. Eliot Friedson, "Communications Research and the Concept of the Mass," *American Sociological Review* 18 (June, 1953), 313–17.

25. Harold D. Lasswell, "The Structure and Function of Communication in Society," in *The Communication of Ideas*, ed. Lyman Bryson (New York· Institute for Religious and Social Studies, 1948), pp. 37–52.

26. Examined in Jack M. McLeod and Garrett J. O'Keefe, Jr., "The Socialization Perspective and Communication Behavior," in *Current Perspectives in Mass Communication Research*, ed. F. Gerald Kline and Phillip J. Tichenor (Beverly Hills: Sage Publications, 1972), p. 134.

27. For a discussion of reporter role conflicts, see Leon V. Sigal, *Reporters and Officials: The Organization and Politics of Newsmaking* (Lexington, Mass.: D.C. Heath, 1973); and Walter Geiber, "Two Communicators of the News: A study of the Roles of Sources and Reporters," *Social Forces* 39 (1960–1961), pp. 76–83.

28. Arnold H. Ismach, "Journalism Research: Its Use and Non-use by Newspapers" (M.A. thesis, University of California at Los Angeles, 1970). For sources of journalism research, see suggested readings below.

29. Jack Lyle, "Study of Urban Life," in *Education for Newspaper Journalists in the Seventies and Beyond* (Reston, Va.: American Newspaper Publishers Association, 1973), pp. 213–26.

30. William B. Dickinson, executive editor (ret.), the *Philadelphia Evening Bulletin* and *Sunday Bulletin* (President's Message to the annual convention of the Associated Press Managing Editors Association, San Diego, Calif., November 15, 1966).

SUGGESTED READINGS

AMERICAN NEWSPAPER PUBLISHERS ASSOCIATION FOUNDATION, *News Research for Better Newspapers*, vols. 1–6. Reston, Va.: ANPA Foundation, 1966–1973. These compilations of communication research relevant to newspapers provide useful summaries of studies from a wide variety of sources. Other sources of information about communication research include: DAVISON, W. PHILLIPS, and FREDERICK T.C. YU, eds., *Mass Communication Research: Major Issues and Future Directions.* New York: Praeger, 1974; EDELSTEIN, ALEX S., *The*

Uses of Communication in Decision-Making. New York: Praeger, 1974; SCHRAMM, WILBUR, *Men, Messages, and Media.* New York: Harper & Row, 1973.

BAGDIKIAN, BEN H., *The Information Machines.* New York: Harper & Row, 1971. Examination of potential effects of technological change on news media and society. Useful discussion of media roles (chap. 1) and audiences (chap. 3).

chapter three

New Perspectives for

Public Affairs Reporting

*I really have so much fun [as a reporter], I ought to be
arrested.*

I. F. STONE

In the early 1960s it seemed that journalism no longer had allure, was
no longer fascinating. Parodying a then-popular toothpaste commercial,
a speaker on the lecture circuit in those days used as his topic, "You
Wonder Where the Glamour Went." High school kids "no longer want
to be foreign correspondents," he advised, "and they think our field has
lost its excitement." Happily for journalism, the lamented condition was
short-lived. By 1974, as actor Robert Redford bought the screen rights
to Bob Woodward and Carl Bernstein's best-selling book, *All the
President's Men,* student interest in journalism seemed high indeed.

What happened in those intervening years both strengthened American journalism and made its job more difficult. The public affairs reporter finds this a mixed blessing. Media criticism from within and
outside the press accelerated in those years. Celebrated crimes and trials
resulted in vigorous free press-fair trial discussions; the adversary relationship between government and press grew during the Vietnam War
and peaked during the Watergate period when reporters seemed locked
in combat with the government. Revelations and exposés ferreted out
government · corruption and misdeeds. CBS produced its controversial
documentary, "The Selling of the Pentagon"; Jack Anderson's revelations about White House decision-making in the India-Pakistani War
sent shock waves through the executive branch and earned him a Pulitzer
Prize; the *New York Times* and *Washington Post* fought off extraordinary
governmental intervention and court action in their efforts to publish
the Pentagon Papers. At about the same time there arose a vigorous
discussion of reporters' sources and whether they should remain con-

fidential. The vice president of the United States and later the president, both of whom left office in disgrace, took a combative stance against the press. The public observed all these revelations and confrontations, registering varying degrees of support and interest. The credibility of the media with the public, which was never great, declined over the years with a slight upswing during the Watergate period.[1]

Concurrent with the public discussion of press and press coverage was an equally vibrant debate within the media. And for the first time working journalists were speaking openly about their newspapers and broadcast stations, challenging the old adage: "You take the King's shilling, you fight the King's war," which assumed that reporters should keep criticism of their employers to themselves. Professional and scholarly media critics attacked the concept of objectivity, long a byword of American journalistic practice. They raised questions about the journalistic form, selection of news content, hiring practices, and ethics in general. They started journalism reviews and put their views on paper for everyone—including their bosses—to read. New journalistic methods —some borrowed from literature, some from science—were suggested.[2] The ferment stimulated by internal and external critics of the media had consequences for public affairs reporters. It provided them with new perspectives.

Case Studies Revisited

Chapter 1 introduced four reporters and their stories. Tom Greene covered a zoning hearing; Susan Kahn, an embezzlement trial; Harold Copeland, conflict of interest in local government; and Chester Bond, programs for retarded children. These stories were selected because they typify the work of the public affairs reporter who operates as an observer of public decision-making, as an investigator of stories not readily apparent on the surface, and as a synthesizer of information that has utility for the public.

On the basis of some of the media criticism, mentioned earlier, it would be easy to find fault with the work of Greene, Kahn, Copeland, and Bond. Some of their work might be characterized as "routine," or "lacking in imagination." Similarly, the writing quality might vary from "interesting and competent" to "downright dull and poorly written." "Why didn't they investigate more, find more sources?" one might ask. "The stories seem so parochial. Couldn't they have provided a more national context?" another could inquire. Does Greene seem like a conveyor belt for information from city hall? Is Copeland a troublemaker in stirring up the local community over the land conflicts of the county commissioners? Have they thought about the effect their stories might have on other people? These and hundreds of other questions might be raised about the four stories and the reporters who produced them.

Although there are some general standards for reporting, substantive understanding, and writing (discussed in some detail in Chapter 4), there are also constraints and situational contingencies that must be taken into account in evaluating a reporter's performance. These factors often have considerable control over the final outcome of a reporter's efforts. Here in broad outlines we will sketch in some of these contingencies and constraints, recognizing, of course, that all of these factors are endlessly complex. First is the *paper* itself. Its size, nature, morale, staffing patterns, and economic resources can influence the kind of work the reporter does and is able to do. Second, there is the amount of *time* the reporter has to work on the story. Finally, there are the *tools* he chooses to work with—or, to put it another way, the method he is allowed to use by his editors. These factors guide, although they do not completely control, the final product: the finished story.

The Paper Itself

Frequency of publication, circulation size, and locale have a good deal to do with the reporter's work. American newspapers are incredibly diverse, ranging from metropolitan dailies with 1 million-plus circulation to rural weeklies with a few hundred. Considerable variation exists even within the standard categories, but one usually thinks of newspapers as falling into the following groupings: the large metropolitan dailies, the medium and small dailies, the suburban papers, and the community weeklies. Some metropolitan dailies—the *New York Times, Washington Post, Los Angeles Times, Toronto Globe and Mail*—have a national character with a staff and resultant content that covers the nation. Other metropolitan dailies have strong regional influence. Regionals that are *the* state paper and have an impact in nearby states include such papers as the *Louisville Courier-Journal, Milwaukee Journal, Kansas City Star* and *Des Moines Register*. Other papers in the metro category are more closely bound to their cities with little attempt to provide outstate coverage. The *Minneapolis Star* and *Wichita Beacon* exemplify this subcategory.

The circulation figures and staffing patterns of the medium and small dailies relate to the population of the city they serve. These range from papers like the *Toledo Blade* to the *Burlington* (Iowa) *Hawkeye*. Similarly, the surburban press, sometimes daily, sometimes semi- or tri-weekly, is yet another type of newspaper situation. In many instances they tend to supplement other newspapers, assuming that their readers also read the major metropolitan dailies of the nearby city. Thus, their stories amplify and localize national, state, and regional trends and may focus more carefully on the local scene, covering schools, health, and other suburban issues (e.g., the quality of life) with some vigor.

The backbone of the grass-roots press is the community weekly. It more often than not has a small staff and is preoccupied with local subjects. Its style is usually less formal, and the paper and its staff are indeed "closer" to the community. "It can't help but affect your writing when you meet your sources on the street the next day," one community editor has said.

As for the paper itself, its ownership can also be an influential factor. It can make a difference whether the paper is an independent, locally owned publication with the owner-publisher having an office in the building or whether it is a paper owned by an absentee entrepreneur who directs it from a distance. It may also be part of a newspaper group—a chain. The chains themselves vary from small ones of two or more papers to those with national holdings of fifty or more. Some papers are part of media conglomerates with diverse newspaper, magazine, and broadcasting interests. Without attempting a treatise on the sociology of media ownership, circulation size, or frequency of publication, how do these factors affect the reporter of public affairs in his work? Here are some of the constraining—and liberating—influences broken down into craft attitudes and staffing patterns:

Craft Attitudes   Craft attitudes of public affairs reporters, the result of internal and external pressures, influence the way in which the journalist does his work. Within the newsroom, these attitudes about the newspaper organization and how it produces news can be caused by the reporters' interaction with editors, by subtle pressures from the publisher, and by other socializing influences. The internal dynamics of the newsroom (as we have indicated earlier) have a large role in determining what is news. In a classic sociological study of the newsroom, Warren Breed found that its social, economic, and psychological pressures push the reporter toward conformity.[3] This trend toward conformity has also been observed in the television newsroom.[4] Craft attitudes toward writing style, definitions of news, and what sources to contact are also influenced by external community pressures. The public affairs reporter should maintain an awareness of the factors that influence his performance by reviewing the ever proliferating literature that communications researchers are generating.[5]

Staffing Patterns   The size of the staff and its composition have a large influence in determining what the final news product will be. Larger publications tend to have a greater degree of specialization. They may have, for example, an urban affairs writer or an environmental reporter. Specialized reporters may have received specific training, such as science writing, or they may be self-taught; in any event, they spend more time keeping up with their field and cultivating their sources. Specialization is often determined by the nature of the local community. Stannie Anderson of the *Topeka Capital-Journal* is an authority on medical-mental health coverage. A large part of her beat is Topeka's sizable "psychiatric community," which includes that city's famed Menninger Foundation and several state institutions and private facilities. Steven Green of the *Seattle Post-Intelligencer* covers environment, a subject of considerable interest in the Pacific Northwest.

A key factor in staffing patterns is obviously how much is spent on the editorial product. This depends somewhat on the profits of the paper, but more on the attitudes of the publisher and other management personnel. Some papers, the *Chicago Tribune* among them, go in for group journalism—team reporting. Efforts by four *Tribune* reporters in 1973, for example, led to a fully documented exposé of police brutality. Here the attitude of management, which allotted ample space and working time, was a crucial element in the success of the series.

Newspapers are relying more and more on specialists to report on technical subjects. When complex news situations involve fields of knowledge, newspapers with staff resources that permit it will assign several specialists to work jointly. An example of this team approach was the response of the *Los Angeles Times* to the energy crisis. After months of piecemeal and conflicting news reports, the *Times* sought to sift fact from myth. It assigned six reporters to the job, including specialists in the environment, finance, energy, and the federal government. The result: eight articles on aspects of the energy crisis ranging from oil industry profits to the government's role in creating the shortage.

Team journalism is more often the rule at major metropolitan newspapers, although cooperative efforts do occur on smaller papers as well. What is important is the resources allocated. Whether the paper provides ample travel money, telephone expenses, and other items is vital. One newspaper with a reputation for investing in its editorial product is the *Eugene* (Oreg.) *Register-Guard*. A series on nuclear power, for example, took months of research by the reporter, Gene Bryerton, consumed considerable space in the paper and resulted in a book published by Friends of the Earth. Similarly, the small, struggling *San Francisco Bay Guardian* did a comprehensive study of San Francisco politics by involving journalism students and other volunteers. The result was:

> *The Guardian* unleashed a pack of 40 investigative reporters last summer on the most powerful—and least understood public and private institutions in San Francisco. . . . A small paper like the

Guardian couldn't possibly publish all the information gathered by 40 volunteer reporters working an entire summer. Most of the material goes into our files and helps form the basis of our continuing editorial surveillance of San Francisco and Bay Area power centers. A good part of it is being worked up into a "Citizen's Guide to San Francisco Politics" due next year. One advantage of operating a small, independent paper in a city dominated by monopoly journalism is that an abundant supply of good stories is out there waiting to be mined—if you can get at them.[6]

A previous *Bay Guardian* summer project resulted in a book on urban growth, architecture, and building codes entitled, *The Ultimate High Rise*. In some states rather massive election coverage has been the result of team efforts with paid help and volunteers.

The Time Factor

Closely related to the staffing pattern as a factor in the reporter's performance is the amount of time allowed the reporter to work on the story. The time allotment determines in large part the scope and detail of the writing, the amount of checking and rechecking of facts, and often the depth of the reporter's understanding of the subject matter. For example, Joel Greenberg, science writer for the *Miami Herald,* demonstrated how the time investment can pay off in a series on a Florida mental hospital. The paper allowed him to spend a week in the hospital, working as an aide so that he could observe the hospital from inside. Time to observe, think about his story and do background research resulted in a graphic presentation that began:

> "Watch this," Charlotte, the psychiatric aide, smiled slyly and winked at me. "Byron? Byron, how you feel today?" A slight man with a veiny nose and shock of gray hair, Byron did not break stride as he walked briskly down the 100-foot corridor in his barefeet.
> "Awful dammit. O I feel awful," his shaky voice faded like a railroad train in the distance. We all burst into loud laughter. "Damn," we said, "if he don't always feel 'awful, dammit, just awful.'"[7]

Greenberg's story, after providing some humanistic lead-ins, discussed modes of treatment, staff personnel, and types of psychiatric problems in a detailed, sensitive story. Its empathetic view of patients and those who care for them reflected considerable thought and was a refreshing departure from the commonplace exposé stories that so often sensationalize prison, mental hospital, and other institutional conditions.

Massive time investment does not always result in a payoff for the reporter. In a story in the New York journalism review, (*More*), Brit Hume tells how Denny Walsh, a reporter for the *New York Times,* spent several months investigating a story regarding San Francisco Mayor Joseph Alioto's testimony some years earlier about alleged Mafia connections. Hume described Walsh's experience as follows:

> During his three-month investigation, Walsh returned several times to Washington, where he is based, to visit his family and, on one occasion to obtain what he considered a crucial piece of documentation. He also made trips to Los Angeles and San Diego. Most of his time, however, was spent in San Francisco poring over the voluminous record of the libel case [Alioto v. Look Magazine] and seeking documentation for instances where his sources had raised questions about the mayor's testimony. He accumulated a massive amount of material. . . .[8]

The *Times,* for reasons questioned sharply by Hume, refused to run the story, due in part to potential litigation.

Time constrains the reporter in many ways. It determines how many sources can be interviewed, how much background research can be done, how much planning can go into the story, and how much attention can be given to improving the prose and revising it. For many reporters, a fast-breaking story at deadline may have to be done in a matter of minutes. Other stories, like those of long, extended trials, may be planned precisely with ample time for special sidebar features and interviews with peripheral sources that would not get into a one-day-only deadline story.

Sometimes background knowledge about the person to be interviewed and a minimum of research can result in a brightly written story with considerable information value. For example, Ruth Heckathorn of the *Decatur* (Ill.) *Daily Review* wrote this about naturalist Euell Gibbons:

> The man that members of the Federated Women's Clubs of Delaware voted they'd most like to be lost in the woods with came to Decatur yesterday afternoon.
> "It's not all that much of a compliment," insists writer and wild food gatherer Euell Gibbons. "Obviously, they were more interested in the food rather than the man." Many more people are intrigued by the Texas-born Quaker who strode into the public spotlight after reworking a fanciful novel about a school teacher into a back-to-nature book.[9]

The Gibbons story could have been prepared partly in advance by reading his books and checking standard biographical sources.

Within time constraints on stories, one must consider how facile a writer the reporter is and how much background knowledge he has. Either of these factors can affect even a fairly constrained deadline situation. For example, Roy Reed of the *New York Times* wrote an imaginative story after the 1974 trial of a Louisiana Ku Klux Klan leader. Having covered the trial and absorbed days of testimony, the reporter was able to select an interesting post-trial angle to construct a story headlined, "How Beckwith Was Cleared in Bomb Case." Reed set the scene for his story:

> Byron De La Beckwith's ideal Christian republic would have no Jews, Orientals or Negroes and would place very little trust in Roman Catholics.
>
> Imagine his consternation then, when he found himself in this polyglot city, 300 miles from his home in the Mississippi Delta, being arraigned by two Federal magistrates—the first a Negro and the second an Oriental—defended by a court-appointed lawyer who was a Roman Catholic, and tried before a jury that included a black man as a regular juror and another as an alternate, on the charge of possessing a time bomb that, according to contentions by the police outside the courtroom, was being carried into the city to blow up the home of a Jew.
>
> If ever a man was delivered into the hands of his enemies, Mr. Beckwith said to his friends, that man was he.[10]

What followed was a story that discussed Beckwith's defense, the jurors' response, and the government's case. Of course, such a story would have taken a reporter without Reed's background from covering the trial days to research.

Application to the Case Studies

How would time, staffing patterns, and the newspaper situation itself have altered the four stories in Chapter 1? In the instance of the zoning story, additional time probably wouldn't have made much difference. A larger newspaper might not have given the story as much play; a smaller one might have given it more. Additional staff might have allowed for more background prior to the meeting and a possible follow-up story several days later.

Similarly, the embezzlement trial story wouldn't have been greatly affected. The reporter was working for a paper with specialists and she was the specialist in charge of court reporting. A general assignment reporter might not have had enough expertise in covering events of this kind and might have required more time to write it.

The story that involved the search of county land records could have been done faster and more extensively if there had been more staff. Indeed, in this instance, a small weekly was doing an extraordinary job of investigative reporting. Larger papers might do this kind of reporting more often, while many small dailies would simply not want to invest the resources unless the chances for a real payoff in terms of a story were assured.

The exceptional children story was motivated in part by the writer's personal interest in the story, and the publisher's wife's interest. A generalized topic of this kind might be covered by a small daily, but probably wouldn't be by a rural weekly. It is more often the kind of story that is particularly attractive to the metro daily and the suburban newspaper. The reporter had ample time for his work, although he might have been assisted by another reporter. Perhaps the result would have been better.

The Reporter's Tools

The impact of media criticism, mentioned earlier, has been felt in the nation's newsrooms, where various methods of reporting and writing have been challenged. Three methods to emerge from the discussion—although they are used in varying degrees and in some instances not at all—are investigative reporting, precision journalism, and reportage (sometimes called "the New Journalism"). None of these approaches to writing is new per se, but each has been given an added impetus in the last few years.

Investigative Journalism   This method is simply an intensification of journalism's traditional way of assembling information. It involves a more concerted effort to gather exhaustive information and make comparisons with checks for consistency. It probably stems from Lincoln Steffens' legendary muckraking exposés (*The Shame of the Cities*) at the turn of the century. Investigative reporting may have a reformist bent, seeking to reveal corruption in government, business, or labor, for example. The complete investigative reporters by contemporary standards are probably Bob Woodward and Carl Bernstein of the *Washington Post*. Their doggedly determined investigation of the Watergate break-in and its aftermath is regarded by some critics as partially responsible for toppling a government. Their work was thorough and involved checking and rechecking sources as well as creatively seeking new information from old and new sources. Woodward's celebrated meetings with an unnamed source called "Deep Throat" were carried out in a clandestine atmosphere. As writer Aaron Latham put it:

> Woodward would arrive at a dark garage and park outside. He would go inside the echoing building, where he would walk down ramp after ramp, deeper and deeper into a subterranean world which seemed like a metaphor for the twisting, convoluted, shadowy plots he was uncovering. Two stories beneath ground level, Woodward says, a man would appear out of the shadows. The reporter and his wary informant would huddle between empty cars and talk about political espionage. The stories which the reporter would later write would in a literal sense be Notes from the Underground.[11]

Investigative reporting is not often as exciting and glamorous as that of Woodward and Bernstein. More often it involves laborious checking of public records, finding documentation for the story. Also a part of the Watergate coverage was the work of the *Providence Journal-Bulletin*'s reporter Jack White who broke details of Richard Nixon's minimal tax payments in 1970 and 1971. Usually investigative reporting in the public sector centers on misuse of funds, mismanagement, or outright corruption. Some newspapers take their investigative reporting so seriously that they even hire accountants, lawyers, and private investigators to assist with the gathering of sensitive information. One example is the *Birmingham* (Ala.) *Advertiser,* which has won national recognition for its exposés of corruption. Investigative reporting involves a considerable investment in time and human resources for the papers that engage in it. Often stories require concerted efforts over several months. Investigative stories are often rather adversarial in nature, stating a suspicion, then following it with documentation. They are also moralistic in tone, sometimes taking a "holier than thou" stance. One of the nation's chief journalistic moralizers, for example, is columnist Jack Anderson, who describes himself as an investigative reporter. Anderson's work frequently involves the news leak or short item for a column, but in the last decade his efforts at stories with more continuity have included an exposé of conflict of interest in the activities of the late Senator Thomas Dodd of Connecticut, which is detailed in a book by a former Dodd aide.[12] Other Anderson stories have been less than successful. A 1972 allegation that Democratic vice presidential nominee Thomas Eagleton had been arrested frequently for drunken driving proved untrue.[13]

Precision Journalism   The term "precision journalism" is most often associated with the work of Philip Meyer, a national affairs correspondent for the Knight newspaper group. Meyer pioneered the use of social science methods in the newsroom in follow-up studies of the Detroit riots of the late 1960s. His work was hailed by the National Commission on Civil Disorders as exemplary journalism which gave encouragement to his later efforts, including a study of Miami's black community and a series on Berkeley's rebels several years after the campus unrest in 1964. Meyer believes that journalism should use social science methods—especially the survey, field experiment, and content analysis—in gathering the news. This view goes well beyond the pioneering efforts of such newspaper opinion polls as the *Minneapolis Tribune*'s Minnesota Poll, a regional version of the Gallup operation. Meyer, a former science writer who was trained in social science methods and computer applications while a Nieman Fellow at Harvard, put his thoughts into a book entitled *Precision Journalism*.[14]

Precision journalism, which is a break with journalism's usual impressionistic standard, differs from the standard polls and articles about survey data in a number of ways. Meyer says reporters should learn to use the social science tools themselves, rather than rely on others. Further, the tools should be used for news-gathering purposes, not for sociological sidebars. Others who advocate the use of precision journalism methods also suggest that editors and reporters should be better trained to make use of survey and other empirical data already available to them. Meyer, for example, has said that the census should be one of the major stories of the day because it is the most complete and precise index on the American people. Precision journalism also involves a blending of survey data with personal interviews and humanistic examples. But the person interviewed is always cast in the context of the survey data. In 1973, the *Philadelphia Inquirer* launched a seven-month study of court records that resulted in a series on the breakdown in criminal justice—"the jailing of the innocent, freeing of the guilty." As the *Inquirer* explained it, "the study, a sophisticated computer analysis of the way violent crimes are handled in the courts, was based on the cases of 1,034 persons indicted during 1971 for murder, rape, aggravated robbery, and aggravated assault and battery." [15] And the first story in the series began:

> Soft judges . . . a tough district attorney . . . crowded courtrooms . . . light sentences. These are the catch phrases used today to describe what is happening in many big city criminal justice systems. But how soft are the judges? Is the district attorney really tough? Are courtrooms crowded by necessity? How light are the sentences? For seven months, a *Philadelphia Inquirer* investigative reporting team sought the answers to these questions and scores of others during an intensive probe into the administration of justice in this —the nation's fourth largest city. . . . The findings [ranged] from the existence of broad patterns of discrimination on the part of

judges to extreme sentencing disparity and the jailing of innocent persons. . . .[16]

The point is that precision journalists with computer assistance can go well beyond myth and rumor, finding instead hard data to back up their assumptions. And what they do with the social science tools and the computer is either impossible without them or so time-consuming that it would never be attempted.

Precision journalism is not confined exclusively to big cities. The *Dubuque Telegraph-Herald,* for example, is using its business machines to aid with reportorial tasks. Reporter John McCormick studied public records to determine why and where traffic accidents happen in that city. (Precision journalism is discussed in more detail in Chapter 5.)

Reportage, or the New Journalism   No doubt the most controversial of the new methods open to reporters is what is called reportage or the New Journalism. There is considerable disagreement about what it is—how it is defined—but out of the criticism come some clear notions. Reportage is an ancient form of writing that goes back at least 250 years to Defoe's *Journal of the Plague Year.* It is simply the application of such methods of fiction as dialogue, interior monologue, and extended description to the practice of journalism. It usually involves a bombardment of detail for the reader and extensive description. The work of Tom Wolfe, Gay Talese, and Truman Capote is probably the New Journalism in its pure form. Variations on the theme are found in the writing of Hunter S. Thompson and Gail Sheehy, among others.

Those who defend the New Journalism contend that its practitioners do not fictionalize, but simply use fiction methods. Talese, for example, says that he asks persons he is interviewing, "What did you think when that happened?" Thus he gets the source's thoughts as well as his words.

Much of the New Journalism is appropriate to the magazine form, rather than the newspaper and it is most often found in such publications as *New York, Esquire,* and *New Times.* Its virtue is that it breaks out of the traditional journalistic form and provides the writer with new freedom. New Journalists are often participatory journalists. They more than observe from the sidelines—they are frequently involved in the action. Sometimes unconventional interviews result. As Sheehy wrote in *Hustling,* a book describing prostitution in New York City (expanded from articles in *New York* magazine):

> We arrived at David's [a pimp] penthouse in full dress but without a scrap of paper or a pencil between us. Every fifteen minutes I had to excuse myself and dash for the bathroom to make notes with an eyebrow pencil on the back of a checkbook. (Without access to other

people's bathrooms, writers would be nowhere.) To stay out of the reader's way, in the story I took the disguise of "the actress." [17]

Sheehy's celebrated story, "Redpants and Sugarman," for *New York*, aroused the ire of the *Wall Street Journal*, which learned that the prostitute she wrote about was a composite character. Actually, Sheehy had originally cautioned readers about this in her story, but her qualification was omitted by a magazine editor.

Critics of the New Journalism say it is subjective and dwells too much on details and trivia—clothing, furniture, facial expressions. Dwight Macdonald has called the new form "parajournalism" or a bastard form, one that is neither journalism nor literature.

The critics aside, one must admit that many of the features of reportage do enhance journalism and the once lifeless form of the inverted-pyramid style. There is also evidence that, increasingly, newspaper writers are adopting some of the magazine conventions. Description of people, once commonplace but later nearly taboo in newspapers, is returning, as this story about Lee Radziwill indicates:

> "For the first time, I really feel true to myself," she said, in her throaty, well-modulated voice, as she put one of her navy shod feet on the coffee table in front of her. "I think there's nothing that makes you happier than to be really involved in something. I can't imagine a totally idle life." [18]

The description, along with Radziwill's words, makes a more complete picture and sets the tone without editorializing.

At the very least, the devices that the New Journalists find so captivating should be considered by public affairs reporters. The use of dialogue, extended description, interior monologue, and the hectoring narrator can prove useful. Dialogue can set the tone of a story, humanize the source. Interior monologue, which involves reporting the source's thoughts, is especially important in relating the activities of persons who are not particularly adept at verbal communication. The hectoring narrator, a more controversial practice, usually amounts to having the writer heap invective on some nonexistent person to set a scene or create a mood. While not always practical for day-to-day journalism, or fast-breaking news, the new journalism forms can be useful in background pieces and have the advantage of showing the reader the ultility of information in a vivid, exciting way.

A cautionary note: many, if not most, of the new journalists mastered the standard journalistic form, and their variation is done deliberately and for a purpose. A writer like Tom Wolfe liberated his style after a long apprenticeship on newspapers and magazines. Effective use of New

Journalism techniques takes an exceptionally bright and creative journalist and they are not advised for everyone. A second caution is that many copy desks simply will not accept material written in this style, although increasingly it is being included, especially in feature stories and in long background pieces.

Could the New Journalism have been useful to any of the reporters in our original case studies? The zoning story might have been enhanced with more description and dialogue. The embezzlement trial story probably would not have benefited from reportage techniques. The public records story might have been brighter and more interesting with New Journalism techniques as long as they did not get in the way of the hard information being offered. The exceptional children series, however, definitely would have been improved with stylistic innovation. Imaginative ways of helping readers understand the plight of the retarded child would have enhanced its presentation.

Would the approaches of precision journalism also have been intriguing for our four reporters? Perhaps already existing data could have pointed up something to Tom Greene about the community where the zoning was to take place. The character of a neighborhood cannot always be "eyeballed." Hard data, from the census for example, might have been helpful, if not in the initial news story, certainly in background work. Susan Kahn, working on the embezzlement trial, might be interested to know of the *Philadelphia Inquirer* work because it points up aspects of the legal system that a perceptive reporter should know and could use in coverage. Similarly, Harold Copeland's job might have been made easier with all those dusty records if he had had the aide of a computer— even a very simple one. If he weren't knowledgeable in this area, he could have called on a social scientist at a nearby college. Chester Bond's series might also have been enlarged and perhaps greatly influenced by hard data, such as precision journalism yields. He wrote about exceptional children by talking with authoritative sources, but their comments were impressionistic and they might have been brought into question after a thorough analysis of data.

Thorough investigative methods were used by Harold Copeland and to a lesser degree by Chester Bond. They might have been applied subsequently to Tom Greene's work on zoning, as well as to the subject of white-collar crime suggested by Susan Kahn's coverage of the embezzlement trial.

Summary and Conclusion

The means and methods of seeking new perspectives for public affairs reporting mentioned in this chapter are only a few of the avenues open to reporters. What is most important is that reporters be aware of their opportunities and limitations in covering the public arena. Some techniques simply aren't feasible because of time, money, or other resources. Some methods of writing will work in some stories and under some circumstances while others will fail, but at the very least reporters and students of public affairs reporting should keep pace with the future by maintaining an awareness of modes and methods in reporting and their potential application to their own work.

NOTES

1. For a useful discussion of external pressures on the media during these dozen years, see James Aronson, *Deadline for the Media* (Indianapolis: Bobbs-Merrill, 1972), and Ben H. Bagdikian, *The Effete Conspiracy, and Other Crimes of the Press* (New York: Harper & Row, 1972) and *Press Freedoms under Pressure* (New York: Twentieth Century Fund, 1972).

2. See Lee Brown, *The Reluctant Reformation,* (New York: David McKay, 1974); Aronson, *Deadline for the Media,* especially chapters on journalism reviews; and Everette E. Dennis and William L. Rivers, *Other Voices: The New Journalism in America* (San Francisco: Canfield Press, 1974).

3. Warren Breed, "Social Control in the Newsroom," *Social Forces* 33 (May, 1955), 326–35.

4. Daniel Garvey, "Social Control in the Television Newsroom" (Ph.D. diss. Stanford University, 1972).

5. See Leon V. Sigal, *Reporters and Officials, The Organization and Politics of Newsmaking* (Lexington, Mass.: D. C. Heath, 1973); Alex Edelstein, *Perspectives in Mass Communication* (Copenhagen: Einer Hancks Forlag, 1966); Phillip J. Tichenor, et al., "Community Issues, Conflict and Public Affairs Knowledge," in *New Models for Mass Communication Research* ed. Peter Clarke (Beverly Hills: Sage Publications, 1974); Jeremy Tunstall, *Journalists at Work* (London: Constable, 1971); and John Johnstone, et al., "Professional Values of American Newsmen," *Public Opinion Quarterly* 36 (Winter, 1972–1973), 522–40. A forthcoming book by Johnstone, *Newsmen and News Work: A Sociological Portrait of the American Journalist* (Urbana: University of Illinois Press, 1975) should also prove useful.

6. "Findings of the Guardian's Second Annual Investigative Project," *San Francisco Bay Guardian* (Nov. 1, 1972), p. 13.

7. Joel Greenberg, "One Week in a Mental Ward," *Miami Herald* (Nov. 25, 1973), p. 1-F.

8. Brit Hume, "The Mayor, the Times and the Lawyers," *(More)* 2 (August, 1974), p. 1.

9. Ruth Heckathorn, "The Sport of Food Foraging," *Decatur Daily Review* (Oct. 23, 1973), p. 1, sect. 2.

10. Roy Reed, "How Beckwith Was Cleared in Bomb Case," *New York Times* (Jan. 21, 1974), p. 10.

11. Aaron Latham, "How 'The Washington Post' Gave Nixon Hell," *New York* (May 14, 1973), p. 49, See also, Bob Woodward and Carl Bernstein, *All the President's Men* (New York: Simon & Schuster, 1974).

12. James Boyd, *Above the Law* (New York: New American Library, 1968); see also Charles Peters and Taylor Branch, *Blowing the Whistle: Dissent in the Public Interest* (New York, Praeger Publishers, 1972).

13. See Jack Anderson with George Clifford, *The Anderson Papers* (New York: Random House, 1973).

14. Philip Meyer, *Precision Journalism: A Reporter's Introduction to Social Science Methods* (Bloomington: Indiana University Press, 1973).

15. "Crime and Justice," republished series from the *Philadelphia Inquirer*, p. 2.

16. Ibid.

17. Gail Sheehy, *Hustling: Prostitution in Our Wide-Open Society* (New York: Dell, 1973).

18. Judy Klemesrud, "For Lee Radziwill, Budding Careers and New Life in New York," *New York Times* (Sept. 1, 1974), p. 42.

SUGGESTED READINGS

ARGYRIS, CHRIS, *Behind the Front Page, Organizational Self-Renewal in a Metropolitan Newspaper*. San Francisco: Jossey Bass, 1974. A thinly disguised portrait of the internal operations of the *New York Times* by an insightful management specialist.

ARONSON, JAMES, *Deadline for the Media*. Indianapolis: Bobbs-Merrill, 1972. A leading press critic's searing analysis of problems affecting reporters and a useful overview of what is new in journalism.

CHARNLEY, MITCHELL V., *Reporting* (3rd ed.). New York: Holt, Rinehart & Winston, 1975. A briskly written new edition of the most widely adopted reporting textbook, one that likely has a considerable influence on the socialization of reporters.

DENNIS, EVERETTE E., and WILLIAM L. RIVERS, *Other Voices: The New Journalism in America*. San Francisco: Canfield Press, 1974. Several chapters chronicle changes in American journalism and the form that journalists use.

HOUGH III, GEORGE A., *News Writing*. Boston: Houghton Mifflin Co., 1975. A readable, straightforward textbook that focuses strictly on the writing aspects of reporting.

POLLAK, RICHARD, ed., *Stop the Presses, I Want to Get Off*. New York: Random House, 1975. A collection of media criticism from the pages of *(More)*, the New York journalism review, which provides a basis for a discussion of journalistic ethics.

chapter four

Strategies for
Covering Public Affairs

Reporters have four main techniques in gathering information: direct observation of an event; search of secondary and primary documents such as morgue clippings, police blotters and reference works; the receipt of unsolicited information via tips from government or press agent handouts, and direct interviewing of people who are involved in, concerned with or informed about a news event.

EUGENE J. WEBB AND JERRY R. SALANCIK
The Interview; or, The Only Wheel in Town

Public affairs reporters travel a long and rugged road as they move from an original story idea or assignment to the final written product. While there is no explicit road map to help them along the way, for public affairs reporting requires creative strategies, there are many guideposts that should be checked.

Some of these guideposts are raised in this chapter. They will help reporters explore three of the techniques for gathering information identified above by Webb and Salancik: (1) direct and indirect observation of the news situation; (2) the interviewing process; and (3) the search through public records. They will also help in the use of a fourth newsgathering technique: participation in the event. Finally, we offer some observations about writing—the process by which public affairs reporters deliver to their readers the results of using the techniques, of following the guideposts.

The public affairs reporter at times uses any or all of the techniques. Most often, his information is obtained by direct observation, watching an event as it occurs—a speech, a city council meeting. In this kind of coverage, the reporter rarely intervenes, and his story is often limited to what he passively observes.

At other times, getting the information requires the reporter to move outside the boundaries of the event. This may involve something as simple as leafing through clippings from the morgue, or as complex as contacting a number of secondary sources for confirmation, reaction, or explanation. And there are times when getting the information involves participation by the reporter. He creates an event by asking questions. The press conference, the man-on-the-street poll, the investigative story are common examples of reporters themselves "making" news.

The framework in which most public affairs reporters work, however, puts constraints on many of these techniques. That framework is the traditional information-gathering structure employed by almost all news organizations—the "beat" system. The system makes a reporter responsible for a particular area of news, usually an echelon of government. That's his beat, at once his horizon and his anchor.

The news media, perhaps the last bastion of the generalist in an age of increasing specialization, have employed the beat system for decades. This may be partly a gesture to the virtues of specialization, and partly a statement about the importance of certain aspects of society that are given beat status. Today, we find an accelerating trend toward the establishment of new beats and reporting specialties.

Once the police station, city hall, the courts, the statehouse and the federal building made up the universe of beats. The list is now three or four times that length in many newsrooms. It will vary, of course, with the size of the news organization. Some specialties come and go with the whims of news fashion. The civil-rights beats of the 1960s, for example, are largely abandoned, but big on today's scene are environmental specialists.

Broadcast news operations typically have fewer beats and specialties. At medium or large dailies, however, many of these beats are likely to be found: politics, business, education, agriculture, labor, science, urban affairs, religion, medicine, consumer news. Some newspapers, because of unique developments in their circulation areas, will employ unusual specialists. The Oak Ridge (Tenn.) *Oak Ridger,* for example, has an atomic energy writer, a specialty few metropolitan newspapers find necessary. And some newspapers, attempting to overcome barriers inherent in a balkanized beat system, have moved toward consolidation of related beats. The criminal justice specialty, combining police, courts, and correction systems, is an example.

The bulk of what we have defined as public affairs news is produced on the governmental beats found in the smallest and largest news organizations—police and courts, and city, county, state, and federal governments. Their universality testifies to the journalistic norms of news value: drama, involving individuals, emanating from the police and courts, which enforce the laws, and significance emanating from government agencies, which levy taxes and write and administer laws. In addition to their focus on government, these beats have another common characteristic. Each is usually contained within a single building, enabling the reporters to do most of their news gathering at one location. These characteristics endow the beat system with some of its strengths— and weaknesses.

Before examining these, let's look at how beats are covered, and how they often shape the reporter's strategies. The odds are high that, as a reporter, you'll be assigned to a beat early in your career. Let's say it's city hall. Again, our description of the beat may vary considerably with the size of the organization, but in all likelihood you'll spend most of your working day on your beat.

Your day may start with a visit to city hall. You'll greet the receptionist in the lobby and then perhaps check in with the city manager. As often as not, he'll be busy, so you'll speak to an aide instead, or a secretary. Part of your job—a big part—is developing and maintaining friendly relations with city employees. You'll spend seemingly unproductive time with them, engaging in small talk, sharing their problems and interests. You'll want to learn their eccentricities, their habits, their personalities, which will help you determine how you deal with them, and they with you. They're important to you, and their friendly cooperation is your lifeblood—access to information.

On some days, you'll have a specific story you're following, or one that requires more information to complete. It may be in the planning department, or the license bureau, or any of a dozen other city departments. You'll visit them with specific sources and specific questions in mind. Or you may just visit, passing the time of day with department heads, assistants, public information specialists, clerks, and secretaries. If you work in a large city, there will probably be a press room in city hall, and you'll drop in there to chat with reporters from other media. It's there where you'll probably write your stories, telephoning or teletyping them back to your city desk.

Perhaps the most frequent demand on your time will be attendance at meetings. In a large city, these go on morning, afternoon, and evening, five days a week. You pick and choose among them, rationing your time to the most significant (very often "significant events" can be translated as those your city editor wants covered, or those that competing media are covering). You may find yourself covering many meetings by telephone, a hazardous practice forced on you by your work load. A wide acquaintance with city officials may enable you to use them as surrogate reporters. It's a common practice, although the dangers of allowing error and bias to creep into your stories demands confirmation from others when relying on secondhand observation.

The most important city hall meeting is usually the council meeting, weekly or biweekly in smaller cities, daily in the metropolis. In truth, council meetings are often routine in large cities, because the debate and decisions occurred earlier in committee meetings. Nevertheless, your newspaper may want you to sit through every minute of every council meeting; or you may just pop in and out, attending only when those items about which you plan to write are being discussed. You decided on those items in advance by studying the agenda, which you received in the mail or picked up from a clerk.

The same procedure is repeated with the meetings of any of a number of council committees, city commissions, and agencies. The result: After your early round of hellos, you spend the day at one or more meetings. You leave only to write your stories.

The routine is somewhat different for the broadcast reporter who covers government news. He's probably assigned to several levels of government, not just city hall. He'll be more selective in the events he decides to cover—the quantity of broadcast news is a fraction of that found in a daily newspaper. His choices will usually be made on the basis of the overriding broadcast news values: conflict, drama, and, in the case of television, visual possibilities.[1]

The newspaper reporter should be alert to what broadcast reporters are covering, and not solely because of competition. He knows that, increasingly, people are learning about spot news events first from radio or television. The newspaper function on the same story then becomes one of providing the background and interpretation that limited broadcast coverage doesn't provide. Media watchers and critics complain that newspapers often neglect this function. It will become even more important as electronic communication systems, such as cable television, expand.[2]

How do you get the news in the hypothetical city hall beat exercise just described? Partly through direct observation, and partly through interviewing sources. You'd find yourself operating in much the same way at the courthouse, the federal building, the legislature, and at the police and sheriff's offices. Some conditions will vary. There are few meetings at the police station, for example, and direct observation falls off markedly. You'll rely more on personal contacts and relationships. Still, the strategies of beat reporting, and the principles guiding them vary little from building to building, agency to agency.

What are the strengths of the system? They are few, but significant.

Sources. The development of sources may be the chief advantage. Daily contact can lead to friendship, trust and cooperation from news sources. Personal contact is as important with the mayor's aide as with the mayor himself, for the reporter needs tips, fast help in getting information, and quick access to top officials.

Continuity. The reporter who follows the same story day after day, who deals with the same people month after month, develops insight and expertise that help produce accurate, complete stories. He's less likely to miss an angle, or find an important door closed to him. Continuity, in other words, is a major benefit.

Surveillance. The regularity of beat coverage also helps the reporter to perform one of the principal functions of journalism, surveillance of the environment.[3] It's an efficient way to monitor activity in those areas of the social environment that regularly yield news.

The "outside" reporter who breaks into a beat for a specific news event finds himself handicapped on these counts. He often doesn't know who to contact for information. Those he does contact may not know him —or trust him. Rather than cheerful help, he may be confronted with guarded answers or obstructionism from bureaucrats who have learned to fear the damage potential of the printed word.

But the outside reporter also brings assets to the task, which can best be seen by examining some of the pitfalls of beat reporting. These pitfalls include:

Cronyism. The beat reporter values his sources, sometimes to the extreme. He eventually tends to protect them from damaging stories, adopting the rationale that he'll need their goodwill another day on another story.

Bias. There's a tendency—the social scientists call it socialization— to acquire the beliefs and values of people with whom you work. This undercuts what many editors consider the first principle of reporting: objectivity. The beat reporter who talks to policemen all day, who goes on coffee breaks with them, who may meet them after work for a friendly drink, not only develops good sources. He also begins to think like a cop. If you doubt it, ask a defense lawyer; he'll never accept a police reporter on a criminal jury.

Myopia. The beat reporter tends to lose perspective about the relative importance of the subjects he covers. What may seem trivial to his editor appears significant to the reporter. His beat is his world, and he sometimes fails to see the world as viewed by those anonymous observers and readers out there in medialand.

Ego. He may come to view his beat as his personal property. He may resent other reporters stepping in to cover stories on *his* turf. By the same token, he's reluctant to move into someone else's beat to follow a story that naturally leads there. He loses sight of the fact that beats are inventions, arbitrary boundaries that news situations may not follow.

Narrowness. This pitfall is an extension of the one involving the ego. It leads to stories that are parochial because beat boundaries become psychological walls, blocking the reporter from adequately developing story situations. Consider the court reporter who attends a sanity hearing. He listens to testimony about dismal conditions at a mental hospital. The more important story might come from an investigation of conditions at the hospital. But the mental and physical blinders of the beat system may well convince the reporter to limit his efforts to the statements made in court. Of course, editors can and do assign follow-up stories, or bring in other reporters. Truncated coverage produced by the beat approach abounds, however, and these remedies are restricted by the limits of time, manpower, and vision.

Dilution. There is a tendency for the beat reporter to try to cover everything in the building. The outsider may be more objective, and parcel out energy where it counts most. The beat reporter sees and hears *too* much, and tends to equalize rather than separate information. By dividing his time among the trivial and the important, he has less time available to work on the more significant stories. A principal effect of this self-imposed time constraint is shallowness. There's no time to check with secondary sources, or to do the background research necessary for a complex story. The cure is a willingness by reporters and editors to invest time in the surveillance function, without expecting a payoff for each hour on the job. In practice, however, there's a tendency to expect production from any major effort. Thus, if a television film crew spends a couple of hours at a political rally, some of that film is likely to be aired even if the event itself turns out to be a dud.

The competent reporter, naturally enough, is aware of these pitfalls, and attempts to avoid them. Editors, while devoted to the efficiency of the beat system, also attempt to overcome its limitations. One way is periodic rotation of beats among different reporters, to minimize the perils of cronyism, bias, and myopia. Another is the use of other reporters or teams of reporters in news situations too broad for proper handling by the beat reporter. A more difficult trap to avoid in covering public affairs, however, is one not unique to the beat approach: a tendency to rely almost wholly on direct observation for some stories.

Direct and Indirect Observation

As a strategy for gathering information, direct observation is sometimes invested with an almost mystical authority. Newspaper lore puts great stock in the eyewitness account, citing both accuracy and vividness as products. When the eyewitness and reporter are one, this belief holds, conditions approach the ideal. Who, What, Where, When, Why, and How will be served, and the prose will throb with color and fidelity.

In some ways, on some occasions, the pure, direct observation model will satisfy these expectations. The delivery of a speech—if all we need to know are the words of the speaker. The report of a ball game—if the reporter also knows the scores of past games and the number of those still to be played. The description of a natural disaster—if the reporter's field of vision includes the entire scene. This is the old mirror-image school of journalism, one that the conventional wisdom heralded as the path of objectivity. Report what you see and hear, the injunction went, and truth will out.

This simplistic hope of the direct observation approach has come under increasing attack since the 1940s and '50s.[4] Restricting the reporter to direct observation (or, as is often the case, the reports of other direct observers) produces its own distortions. Consider these limitations:

Reporters are restricted to writing about events. If nothing *happens*, there is nothing to report. We can all see, however, that often situations are more important than isolated events. Sometimes the fact that *nothing* has happened is newsworthy. Consider the police reporter who spends his days writing about crimes and fatal traffic accidents. If a month goes by without a traffic death, or a year without a murder, news value is the outcome of a nonevent. Which is more worthy of a reporter's—and reader's—time: an account of a fire, or an investigative story that deals with fire hazards in retail stores and enforcement policies of building and fire inspectors?

A preference for direct observation pushes journalists into writing about lesser events, when audience interest and needs would be better served by developing stories about general situations and collections of events. Scattered coverage of a dozen medical malpractice trials over a year may be a less worthy accomplishment than an investigation of the "why" of malpractice litigation, and the characteristics of doctors who are involved.

The inclination to report on events, because by definition they are news, leads reporters to amplify pseudo-events. News manipulators stage events—a press conference, a demonstration, a contest, a speech, a meeting—because they know that this type of activity attracts media attention. As a reporter, you should make a practice of casting a skeptical eye at events to assess their intrinsic worth, and the motivation underlying them.

The news values that result in an emphasis on events and direct observation often work to restrict the number of sources available to the reporter. The delegation that speaks at a city council meeting has its viewpoint reported. Affected groups and individuals not present at the meeting don't get exposure to the public. This skewed-source emphasis not only introduces bias, but it also blocks from view important dimensions of a situation. Consider the housing authority meeting at which plans for a high-rise development are discussed with builders. Not present at the meeting are representatives of a nearby airport whose operations would be affected by the buildings. Nor are small businessmen, police officials, school administrators, and others whose activities might be affected by the high-rise. In cases like this one—and they are common— the reporter must supplement his direct observation with efforts to uncover these other dimensions. They are best presented in the initial story, but they can be done in follow-up stories. Too often, these follow-ups depend on the initiative and awareness of affected individuals, a tenuous condition, or on the alertness of the reporter and editor.

Time is another victim of heavy reliance on direct observation. The reporter who devotes his working hours to events is governed by those events. He is unable to pursue other information more essential to his story. Nevertheless, public affairs reporting is about events and happenings. Journalistic norms specify it, and the audience has been conditioned to expect it. The reporter, then, must develop methods of observation to supplement direct observation and minimize its limitations. These indirect information-gathering strategies can be categorized as pre-event and post-event procedures.

The term "pre-event observation" sounds like a contradiction. How, after all, can you observe an event before it happens? What the term implies, however, is getting information needed for intelligent coverage of the event, whether it's a meeting, a speech, an interview, or a backgrounder. The procedure starts with anticipating the story situation, with deciding on its probable audience, its significance, its dimensions. This preparation leads to questions that should be asked and answered, and points you toward the required pre-event research.

Often it starts with a search of the newspaper's morgue to gain both historical perspective and a beginning set of facts. If your own morgue doesn't include information on the subject, consider other available sources, such as the *New York Times Index*. One word of caution about morgue clippings: They may contain errors of fact that can easily be perpetuated. The best practice is to read the entire file for later correction stories.

Other pre-event research might include getting background information about individuals. Many biographical directories are available. If the person is an author or specialist in some field, you may want to become familiar with his published work. You should also consider contacting other authorities in his field to get an assessment of his work and some potential questions.

Contacting expert sources in advance is useful in preparing for any complex subject. Let's say you're going to a press conference about a claimed breakthrough in solar heating for residential housing. You could find someone knowledgeable in this field at a local college or university who will be able to direct you to published material as well as suggest questions for the press conference.

Public records are another strategic weapon in the reporter's observational arsenal. Is it a story about a proposed housing development? Tax and land records can tell a lot about ownership and prices. Does the story concern a mass transit system? Census reports provide accurate information about population densities and commuter patterns. Does the subject have to do with a legal matter? Many court records are open for inspection. Checking records, before and after the event, is laborious but profitable. A separate section of this chapter offers detailed advice on how to go about it.

By going through these preliminaries, you'll arrive at the event prepared to do something more than passively take notes. You'll have made a preliminary evaluation of the situation, organized the story in your mind, and devised some informed questions to ask. You'll also have facts against which you can measure what you see and hear.

But the observation job doesn't stop with the end of the event. If the news situation is complex, and involves several categories of people (directly or potentially), you'll want to represent all of them in your story whether or not they appeared at the event. An unfortunate maxim of the news business is the injunction to get "both sides" of the story. It traps us into thinking that there are only two sides to an issue, when often there are three, four, or more. If the event offered only two, you must seek out the others afterward. On the high-rise apartment story, for example, representatives of groups not present—the police, the zoning board, the school board, the airlines, the control tower—should be contacted to produce a rounded story.

Sometimes independent sources, who can verify or contradict suspicious claims made at an event, should be called upon. For the solar heating press conference, an independent source may be the same expert you contacted before leaving the office. A word of caution is in order about this type of source, however. People, reporters included, tend to place great faith in specialists, particularly scientists. You must remember that experts can and do disagree. One engineer may hold a belief about solar heating that another rejects out of hand. If you contact just one, you may not discover the conflict, or the truth. Worse, neither will your readers. One way to overcome this danger is to ask your source if there are differing opinions on the subject; most professionals are sufficiently honest to tell you if there are. Another approach is to contact several experts on the same subject. Here, numbers alone are likely to protect the story against bias or distortion. This multiple-source approach also lends credibility to the story.

The technique of direct observation in getting information for a public affairs story, then, may have a number of variations, and these may have varying degrees of complexity. Some of the variations, as we have noted, draw on interviewing, a technique that requires its own set of guideposts.

The Interview Process

Interviewing in public affairs reporting is not a simple art, nor is it simply explained. There are as many interview styles as there are individual personalities of interviewers—and they conjure up vivid images:

With a firm, forceful manner, Clark R. Mollenhoff of the *Des Moines Register* directs a blunt, lawyeresque question to a senator's aide as he investigates influence peddling.

Nodding quietly and listening keenly, Lois Wille of the *Chicago Daily News* chats with a youthful gang leader on Chicago's South side.

Lacing his language with superlatives, Johnny Carson of NBC's "Tonight Show" turns to an aging trouper and asks a question designed to get a laugh.

Empathy is evident in his eyes and his voice as radio interviewer Studs Terkel queries a factory worker about his inflation-riddled income.

Becoming an actual participant in the event, an unclothed Gay Talese manages a massage parlor, "interviewing" customers in preparation for a book on sex in America.

These are but a few examples of the diversity one finds in the journalistic interview. To be sure, the journalist is not the only professional who uses the interview as a tool of his trade. Doctors, lawyers, social workers, social science researchers, and many others are also interviewers.

Because so many people are interested in interviewing, the literature on the subject is expanding rapidly. This growing interest suggests that interviewing is something to which the journalist should devote considerable thought and study. Interviewing is not something one learns and then pursues mindlessly. Instead, it is a purposeful process that requires continual reassessment and readjustment.

All interviews involve verbal interaction between two or more persons, but they are usually initiated for a specific purpose and they usually focus on a specific matter. In this way an interview differs from a casual conversation between friends. The interviewer's objective is always to keep his subject on the point, dealing with relevant information. The interview requires an element of *control*. Just how the interviewer gains that control is sometimes a dilemma. Journalistic interviewers normally try to maintain control regardless of their mode of interviewing: (1) the face-to-face personal interview, or (2) the telephone interview. In some rare circumstances—the Pope used to be interviewed this way—written interrogatories are submitted for answers. Press conferences have some of the elements of the interview, but are usually too unstructured and uncontrolled in content to be termed an "interview" in the sense that we are considering it here. Obviously the reporter has greatest control in the private interview.

When a reporter decides that the interview is the appropriate method for gathering information for a particular story, time and distance usually dictate the method of interviewing. Telephone interviewing offers a major advantage if the reporter has only a short time to gather information—or if the person to be interviewed is not personally available. Major disadvantages of the telephone interview stem from the lack of interpersonal contact and the interviewer's inability to exercise persuasion by his presence in coaxing out more information than the source would be likely to give over the phone—especially to a stranger. For persons who already have rapport, the telephone interview can be a quite acceptable device.

While knowing and understanding the interview process is helpful to the reporter preparing for an interview, so is an examination of the interview's components. In the next few pages those steps—interview preparation, the interview setting, questioning techniques, recording and evaluating interview information, as well as writing the interview story— are examined.

Interview Preparation   Good interviewing requires planning— planning who should be interviewed and obtaining background information about the person and the subject area. Here the thoughtful reporter should consider a number of questions: Who should be interviewed? Is this person a knowledgeable and appropriate source? What is the extent of his competence? When is he clearly outside his field of expertise? Some sources are willing to speak out on any and all subjects— and every reporter knows such persons, whether they be public officials or self-proclaimed commentators on the state of the world. Often a reporter tends to rely on the most available source, who may not be the best source. Sometimes an agreeable and cooperative source may not necessarily be the right source either.

Securing background information about the interview topic is also important. Many an interview has gone sour because the reporter squandered precious time asking questions that could be answered by a quick search through the morgue or by consulting a standard reference like *Who's Who in America*. The knowledgeable reporter-interviewer who is well-briefed is better able to achieve depth and real substance in an interview. Minneapolis television interviewer Henry Wolfe, who is the host of a local talk show, is usually so well-read and well-backgrounded that he makes a strong, positive impression on his guests. "It shows them that you care enough about them and their subject to have done some work in advance," Wolfe says. Questions that reflect poor preparation can have a disastrous effect on an interview. If, for example, you are interviewing an author and haven't read his latest book, you can offend him. Or uncertainty about the source's background can arouse doubts in the mind of the source about the interviewer's competence—which can lead quickly to distrust.

Interview Setting   Before making arrangements for the interview, some thought should be given to the place where it will be conducted. What setting will give the reporter the best understanding of the person? In a work milieu—an office, a factory, or a laboratory? Or at home where the interviewee is seen with family members in a relaxed atmosphere? Usually, the location is dependent on the type of information desired. In an interview that requires frank questioning—perhaps of a somewhat unwilling source—a psychologically neutral environment should be found. An empty room, an intimate restaurant, or an airport lobby may offer a certain neutrality.

For the person who is likely to be interrupted by frequent telephone calls, an interview in a car may be appropriate. Grady Clay of the *Louisville Courier-Journal* is a devotee of the automobile interview. Of course, the auto interview has obvious problems for the recording of information—particularly if the car is moving. Friendly, feature interviews are sometimes conducted in the source's home, or in a neighborhood bar with a convivial atmosphere. Naturally, not all interviews can be conducted under ideal conditions and many are so impromptu that the setting cannot be planned at all. They occur on the spur of the moment in a courthouse corridor or on a street corner.

Television news interviewers like Mike Wallace of CBS News have a singular psychological advantage because the source is usually surrounded by cameramen, cameras, and other apparatus. Under such conditions, some interviewees must feel a sense of entrapment as the inquisitory, slightly hostile Wallace zeros in with one question after another. Wallace is clearly in control, and his style has yielded formidable results as sources blurt out information, often embarrassing to themselves.

Murray Fisher of *Playboy*, who is responsible for the highly successful "Playboy Interview," says that the "hostile interview gives you a feeling of dancing across a bed of coals. Our most successful interviews are those that make the source feel completely relaxed and comfortable—and sort of coax them into a level of trust that opens them up." [5] Thus, the *Playboy* interviews are conducted in settings that enhance this objective.

Questioning Techniques   Questioning techniques differ considerably with the personal style of the interviewer. Even so, most journalists agree that advance planning is useful. A list of questions might be prepared, for example, although they should not be followed so rigidly that they keep the interviewee from expressing himself. Yet question planning is helpful in maintaining control over the interview, steering it on the intended course. Tone and substance of questions are adjusted to the interviewer's purpose. They can range from direct, frontal attack questions—like those of Mike Wallace—to a meandering reinforcement technique used by the conservative columnist and television interviewer William Buckley. Buckley is a master of the technique developed by psychologist Carl Rogers wherein sentence endings are repeated as a device to keep the interviewer talking. "Well, it's not very much like that," the interviewee says. "Not very much like that?" repeats the interviewer. This technique encourages the source to elaborate and expand without having the interviewer phrase another question.

Experienced interviewers advise against questions that can be answered with a simple yes or no. As Robert Maurer of NBC's Monitor News put it, "If you say to your guest (interviewee), 'When the accident happened were you walking along the lake?' the person can reply in one word—'Yes.' But if you say, 'When the accident happened, what were you doing?' the subject will have to give you a more detailed answer." [6]

Another Monitor interviewer once demonstrated the exhibitionist question. It is the kind of question that shows off the interviewer's superior knowledge without leaving anything for the interviewee to say. For example:

> Q. Buddy Rogers, you and your wife, Mary Pickford, live in one of
>   Hollywood's great showplaces, "Pickfair." It has been described
>   as a great, big, white country English manor house right in the
>   middle of Beverly Hills, with a great winding driveway, with a
>   big, sprawling lawn, with three floors filled with great antiques
>   and a unique collection of Chinese pieces, and you've enter-
>   tained celebrities from all over the world as well as the Holly-
>   wood greats. Isn't that so, Buddy?

As the interviewer commented later, a better way to have asked the question would have been to say, "Buddy Rogers, you and your wife,

Mary Pickford, live in Hollywood's great showplace, 'Pickfair.' Would you describe it for us." [7]

Stanford communications researchers Eleanor and Nathan Maccoby suggest six guidelines for question clarity in interviewing:

1. Avoid words with a double meaning.
2. Avoid long questions.
3. Specify exactly the time, place and context which you want the respondent to assume.
4. Either make explicit all the alternatives which the respondent should have in mind when he answers, or make none of them explicit.
5. When the interview concerns a subject with which the respondent may not be very familiar, or one in which he may not have the necessary technical vocabulary, it is sometimes desirable to preface questions with an explanatory statement or an illustration which will set the stage for the question the interviewer wants to ask.
6. It is often helpful to ask questions in terms of the respondent's own immediate (and recent experience), rather than in terms of generalities.[8]

Of course, in addition to the actual wording of questions, the manner of the interviewer in asking them is important. Good eye contact is usually desirable, as is psychological reinforcement for the person being interviewed. It is important for the interviewee to know that the interviewer appreciates the information being imparted. Occasionally nodding or making verbal reinforcements—"Uh-huh," "Right," "Yes"—can be helpful. Some persons become particularly conscious of the method being used to record the interview information and slow down their usual speech pattern as the interviewer takes notes. Others get nervous when a recorder is used.

Researchers have found that people speak at a more rapid rate when they are particularly anxious. And sometimes anxious people leave sentences unfinished. According to Eugene J. Webb and Jerry R. Salancik, "breaking into an ongoing sentence with a new thought, repeating words or phrases, stuttering, using, 'I don't know' not as a reply but as an interjection, and shifts of the loudness of voice were all related to the amount of anxiety present in the situation." [9]

At times the interviewer is confronted with an uncooperative source, one who simply refuses to talk or who answers questions evasively. In such a situation the first task of the interviewer is to determine *why* the source is uncooperative. Some understanding of this uncooperative behavior will determine the interviewing strategies needed. Sources can be uncooperative because they have something to hide or fear that too much discussion of the subject will cast them in an unfavorable light. Or they are not used to being interviewed and therefore are shy and uncomfortable. Still others can be blasé—tired of being interviewed, of being asked the same questions. This apathy is notably true of celebrities, like entertainers.

There are a number of different ways in which to conduct an interview with the uncooperative source. When the source is uncomfortable, special care needs to be taken to establish rapport. One such method is *identifying* with the interviewee. You might explain that you understand and empathize with the individual's plight. Studs Terkel, who has produced three extraordinary books of interviews with the "little people," [10] says he "reveals his own vulnerability" to the source. Thus Terkel, a middle-aged, upper-middle-class white man, is able to establish lively discussions with people in very different social circumstances. The Terkel technique is particularly useful with those who are reluctant to talk. He is able to convince people who normally do not get interviewed that their views are worth hearing.

For the source who has something to hide or is otherwise unwilling to speak to the press, the interviewer must be well prepared. He may want to confront the source with someone's charges, or with evidence that suggests a particular explanation of an event. This approach may jolt the uncooperative source into cooperating. Sometimes the uncooperative source can be won over if the reporter frankly and fully explains the nature of the story he is doing, or offers a specific rationale why the person's help is needed. At other times a tough interview style, using accusatory questions (based always on evidence the reporter has gathered), may be appropriate. Some reporters use various bluffing techniques suggesting to the source that they know more than they do. While this device may work on occasion, it is fraught with ethical problems and ought to be employed rarely—and with great care.

In mid-1974 a reporter for the *Baltimore Sun,* Gordon Chaplin, was preparing a story about the efforts of former Vice President Spiro Agnew to sell his house, which had benefited from many government-financed improvements. The reporter posed as an attorney for a prospective buyer, contacted the real-estate agent and arranged for a visit to the Agnew house. After inspecting the house, Chaplin (at his city editor's suggestion) called the real-estate agent and confessed his ploy, then asked for photos of the house. The agent suggested he contact Agnew directly. When Agnew spoke with Chaplin he called him a "son of a bitch" and "lower than scum" for misrepresenting himself." [11] Eventually, to the reporter's dismay, the paper rejected the article because it was "not sufficiently 'revealing' to justify the use of misrepresentation and 'invasion of privacy.'" [12] The article subsequently appeared in (*More*), the New York journalism review. Again, ethical questions must be raised when the interviewer uses misrepresentation to obtain a story.

Lewis A. Dexter, an authority on elite and specialized interviewing, has suggested that the difficult-to-interview celebrity or public figure is often willing to help the interviewer shape the questions, thus eliminating irrelevant, routine inquiries. Dexter says that the interviewer who enlists the source's aid in exploring questions often gets a better story. Dick Cavett of ABC-TV often asks unusual questions of his guests, eliciting the response, "Nobody ever asked me that before." A fresh question, probing a new subject, or looking at an old one in a different way, can be challenging and intriguing to the blasé person who is tired of trite questions.

Recording Interview Information   Facing the reporter is the problem of recording interview information accurately and in detail without inhibiting the interviewee. Tom Wolfe and Truman Capote, who have both been called New Journalists, represent two extremes of the information recording spectrum. Wolfe takes meticulous Gregg shorthand, while Capote has developed an aural memory system in which he attempts to memorize all of the elements of the interview conversation. Most reporters use neither method. It is common for the note-taking reporter to develop a personal "briefhand" system so that the essence of the conversation and other interview information can be ascertained. Other reporters use tape recorders and are thus able to spend more time observing physical phenomena—the appearance of the subject, the furniture in the room, and so forth. An obvious disadvantage to tape recorders is the difficulty in transcribing recorded material. In a study of newsmen's interview techniques, journalism professor Jim R. Morris found that about 75 per cent of the metropolitan news reporters he interviewed were negative about using tape recorders. In the same study, Morris offered some helpful hints about note-taking:

1. Be as inconspicuous as possible. A flashy notebook can be inhibiting to the interviewee. If you sense that he objects to notetaking, don't do it. "The important thing is to get a person to say something."
2. If you don't take formal shorthand develop your own style. A form of speed writing used by most reporters consists of omitting vowels and endings by abbreviating whenever possible.
3. Notes should be taken simply to jog the memory later. Writing down key words and phrases probably will suffice for this. Get to a typewriter as soon as possible to fill in the gaps.
4. Don't shortcut where names, dates and places are concerned. Take a few minutes at the conclusion of the interview to check your notes for accuracy. It saves a lot of time and embarrassment later on.
5. Treat each interview situation differently. Notetaking might be inhibiting to one person, but you might impress the next with your thoroughness and concern for accuracy.[13]

Much of the emphasis on recording information centers on the words that pass from the mouth of the person being interviewed. Other behavior in an interview can be observed, however. The growing intellectual infatuation with "body language" and other nonverbal physical cues in an interview situation is worthy of consideration, but great caution should be taken in noting physical behavior in order to avoid sweeping interpretations. Does a man scratch his head because he is excessively nervous, thoughtful—or simply because his head itches?

A number of nonverbal cues surfaced in television critic Jack Gould's classic account of underworld figure Frank Costello as he appeared before a congressional committee:

> As he (Costello) sparred with Rudolph Halley, the committee's counsel, the movement of his fingers told their own emotional story. When the questions got rough, Costello crumpled a handkerchief in his fingers. Or he grasped a half-filled glass of water. Or he beat a silent tattoo on the table top. Or he rolled a little ball of paper between his thumb and index finger. Or he stroked the side piece of his glasses lying on the table. His was video's first ballet of the hands.[14]

Evaluating Interview Information   Just how valid is the information collected in an interview? Reporters usually take most of what they get at face value unless there is a clear indication that something is wrong with the information. But reporters would do well to remember that human beings are prone to selective recall and that memory often erodes at an alarming rate. By the same token, psychological studies indicate that people have selective perception, that is, they "note only parts of an event, and the notings are conditional on what we expect and what we are." [15]

Much research remains to be done before interviewers can be very certain about the recall of their sources. Webb and Salancik, in their study of interviewing, suggest two lines of checking: "The first centers on *consistency*—the internal analysis of a source's statements over time or within a single interview on the same topic. The second is *corroboration*, or the verification of a source's statement by comparing it with external evidence—the statements of others or some definitive record." [16] Could the event have happened the way the policeman said it did? Was it possible for the murder suspect to have been in the victim's home at 8:30 P.M. and across town twenty minutes later? Does the story as it was told to you make sense? Is it consistent? Thoroughgoing news coverage also requires corroboration of details and circumstances. Ben Bradlee, executive editor of the *Washington Post,* points out that his paper demanded corroboration of each detail from at least two sources in its celebrated coverage of the Watergate scandals. A single accusation was not enough—there had to be hard evidence acquired through checking and rechecking the material.

Writing the Interview Story   Most interview stories are written to blend quotes into a traditional news-story narrative. A blend of quotes and paraphrase plus some description of the interviewee are typical of the form.

In recent years, however, many newspapers and magazines have become enamored of the "Playboy Interview" approach—a simple question-and-answer technique. Often an interview is tape-recorded, then with modest editing it is reprinted verbatim. A lengthy editor's note, usually preceding the Q-A interview, sets the scene and indicates something about the background of interviewee and interviewer. This interview method is frequently ineffective because few people are articulate enough in speech for their words to be transferred to a written form. The "Playboy Interview" is not such a product, but rather a result of heavy editing, rewriting, and rechecking with the interviewee.

The importance of the journalistic interview as a means of gathering information cannot be underestimated. And the interview, because of its strong linkage with other fields and disciplines, is likely to be the source of continued study and interest. For this reason much more will be learned about the interview in the next few years. Public affairs reporters should be ready to make the interview an aspect of journalism requiring continuing reassessment and change. But in the final analysis, the interview is a highly personal tool to be adjusted to both the personality and the personal style of interviewer and interviewee.

Because it is so personal, and therefore subject to human frailties, as noted above, the public affairs reporter seeks to buttress it, when appropriate, with less subjective evidence. Such solid information comes from a variety of public records that are available sources of news and information.

Using Public Records

Several years ago, a weekly newspaper in Omaha became interested in the financial affairs of Boys Town, Nebraska, and the promotion techniques used by the famous home for boys to solicit money from the American public. The paper knew that under revised tax laws the tax records of tax-exempt organizations like Boys Town were available to the public from the Internal Revenue Service.

So the *Sun Newspapers* queried the IRS and obtained Boys Town's tax return, showing the home had assets of more than $190 million. Using the tax records as a starting point, the paper launched an investigation that exposed the home's financial affairs. Published in March, 1972, the articles won the paper a Pulitzer Prize.

The *Sun's* investigation shows the importance of knowing about public records and how to use them, and while most public records probably won't bring a Pulitzer Prize, every public affairs reporter ought to be familiar with the important public documents in the area he covers. The court reporter, for example, should be familiar with court filings, suits, liens, judgments, and injunctions. The business reporter should know about incorporation papers. The city hall reporter should know how to find out who holds a liquor license for a local tavern. Indeed, the ability to use public records is a quality honed particularly by the investigative journalist. He begins by finding out what records are likely to be open to inspection.

Open Records Legislation   Many states have open records laws that require officials to maintain records of their official duties, and that usually allow anyone to examine such records under reasonable conditions. Indeed, records of some government agencies must be certified as "true and correct" if a citizen so demands. Land records, deeds, wills, and other court records often fall into this category.

The investigative reporter usually has a thorough understanding of open records laws, of what materials are available under them, and of what is specifically excluded. Though open records laws may appear, upon first reading, to be blank checks to examine documents, most such laws have specific exclusions. For example, juvenile criminal records, private tax returns, and medical records are normally considered confidential, both by statute and court rulings.

Open records laws and court rulings on the issue usually distinguish between "public records," which are the official documents an official must keep and make available, and "working papers," such as letters, notes, memoranda and internal reports, which an official may be required to keep, but which are often considered confidential. In a way, then, the official record is only the tip of the iceberg below which lie supporting documents. Police arrest reports and offense reports, for example, are often available to the public affairs reporter, but "supplementary reports," in which police detectives provide many details of cases, are not public. A school board may have to give the reporter the text of a contract between the board and the teachers union, but may not have to reveal the negotiating "position papers" on which the contract is based.

The good public affairs reporter, then, should first be familiar with his state's open records law and its interpretation in court rulings. Then, if denied access to a particular record, the reporter can ask for a specific reason from the official who refuses to release a document. Under firm but pleasant questioning, the public affairs reporter will often get to see records that are considered open, but he must first know what his legal grounds are.

Presented below are some of the common records normally helpful in covering public affairs. It is by no means a comprehensive list, and we have omitted specific details that may vary from state to state and county to county. Nonetheless, the records here are usually organized in a clear fashion, and you should find them quickly and efficiently in your community.

Chapter 6 deals with questions of libel and privilege, but it is important to note here that a public document is neither necessarily true nor privileged—that is, immune from liability for libel because of its contribution to public discourse. Sworn testimony in court may be privileged, for example, but an affidavit by a police officer alleging that an individual has a criminal history may not be privileged if it has not been presented in court. Although a document may state a fact, the reporter should not assume that the statement is true. Obviously, documents should be used in concert with careful interviewing, the checking of other sources, and common sense.

Land Records   Let's say you want to determine who owns a particular piece of land. The place to go is the county register of deeds office in the county in which the land is located. But before you do, you'll need to know how land is mapped and surveyed. Almost all land in America is surveyed, and divided into identifiable parcels. Rural land is arranged usually according to *township, range,* and *section.* A township is a piece of land six miles square, or very close. It may have a proper name or be identified only by coordinate numbers; for example, Township 28 North, Range 18 West. T. 28 N., R. 18 W., is the normal way in which this township would be designated by coordinates. In this case, the piece of land has a name, Kinnickinnic Township. It is located in western Wisconsin, about forty miles east of Minneapolis, Minnesota, but it is typical of townships all across America.

Each township has 36 sections, each one square mile, or very close, on a side. If you have ever flown over the Midwest, perhaps you have noticed how the land appears to be "squared off." This is because roads were often built along the section dividing lines. Each section is numbered, so that, for example, section 11 of T. 28 N., R. 18 W., refers to a one-mile-square parcel of land in Kinnickinnic Township. Within the section, the land may be halved or quartered or both. For instance, one small piece of land in this section is described on a deed as being located in "the NE¼ of the NW¼ of section 11. . . ." That means that if the section is divided into quarters, and each quarter is divided into quarters, the land would be in the northeast quarter of the northwest quarter. (See Plate 1.)

PLATE 1: Kinnickinnic Township, Wisconsin

In urban areas, land often is identified by *addition, block,* and *lot* in legal descriptions. Additions are tracts of land added to real estate developments, and normally have given names. The block and lot numbers will identify only one piece of land in any particular addition.

Now let's trace the owner of a piece of land. In Minneapolis, Minnesota, on East Calhoun Boulevard, there is a large green house overlooking Lake Calhoun. Its number is 3347. Taking this address to the register of deeds office, you can ask to see the overlay map that correlates street address with legal description. You find that the legal description of the property is "Lot 13, Block 3, McCrory's Rearrangement of parts of Block 48 and 49, Calhoun Park Addition." Taking the legal description to the *tract index,* you can find every filed legal transaction on that piece of land going back several decades. You find that a *warranty deed* was filed on the property in 1969, and the entry provides a document number. You ask for the document by number, and the clerk produces a copy of a deed between Gladys S. MacLean, a widow, and Robert C. Hentges and Judith L. Hentges, husband and wife. (See Plate 2.)

You can also locate the deed if you know the name of either the seller (called the *grantor)* or the name of the buyer (called the *grantee).* Deed offices file land transactions by both grantor and grantee, and you can thus determine all the land in a particular county held by an individual under one name. There may be, of course, other names under which a person may own a piece of land. The deed tells you that Mrs. MacLean conveyed the property to the Hentges, and it appears to say that the selling price was for "One dollar and other good and valuable consideration." Do not be misled at this point into thinking that the Hentges bought the property for one dollar. They did not. In Minnesota, as in other states, the one dollar is merely a conveyance symbol.

So how much did the property sell for? Look for the *deed stamps* on the deed. The stamps on this deed total $71.50. Other states have different rates, but in Minnesota, deed stamp taxes are figured at a rate of $2.20 per $1,000 in transfer value. Knowing that formula, you can quickly figure that the property was sold for $32,500, although that amount is not stated on the deed.

Because the last entry in the tract index for this property is the warranty deed, you can state that the Hentges are the "owners of record" of the property. But you cannot be certain that they still hold the title. In Minnesota, as in other states, property may be purchased on a *contract for deed,* a document that buyer and seller agree to privately and that will convey the property to the buyer once the full purchase price is paid, often years later. Until that time, when a deed would be filed, the contract for deed need not be recorded, or filed.

3802196

This Indenture, *Made this* 29th *day of* October *,* 19⁶⁰ *,*

between Gladys M. MacLean, a widow and not remarried,

of the County of Hennepin *and State of* Minnesota *, part* y
of the first part, and Robert C. Hentges and Judith L. Hentges,
husband and wife, *, of the County of*
Hennepin *and State of* Minnesota *, parties of the second part,*

Witnesseth, *That the said part* Y *of the first part, in consideration of the sum of* One Dollar
($1.00) and other good and valuable consideration ————————————————————*DOLLARS,*
to her *in hand paid by the said parties of the second part, the receipt whereof is hereby acknowledged, do* es *hereby Grant, Bargain, Sell, and Convey unto the said parties of the second part as joint tenants and not as tenants in common, their assigns, the survivor of said parties, and the heirs and assigns of the survivor, Forever, all the tract___ or parcel___ of land lying and being in the County of* Hennepin *and State of Minnesota, described as follows, to-wit:*

Lot Thirteen (13), Block Three (3), McCrory's Rearrangement of parts of
Blocks Forty-eight (48) and Forty-nine (49), Calhoun Park, including any
portion of any street, alley, other city property, transportation right of
way, or other right of way, adjacent thereto, vacated or to be vacated,
together with all rights, privileges, easements and appurtenances thereto
attached or belonging, according to the recorded plat thereof on file and This
of record in the office of the Register of Deeds in and for said Hennepin
County. Together with the parcels described on the rider attached hereto
and made a part hereof.

~~State Deed Tax due hereon:~~ $ 71.50

STATE OF
Minnesota 10-31-69 DEPT. OF TAXATION
HENNEPIN COUNTY
DEED STAMP
TAX 71.50

To Have and to Hold the Same, *Together with all the hereditaments and appurtenances thereunto belonging or in anywise appertaining, to the said parties of the second part, their assigns, the survivor of said parties, and the heirs and assigns of the survivor, Forever, the said parties of the second part taking as joint tenants and not as tenants in common.*
And the said Gladys M. MacLean, a widow and not remarried

part Y *of the first part, for* herself, her *heirs, executors and administrators do* es
covenant with the said parties of the second part, their assigns, the survivor of said parties, and the heirs and assigns of the survivor, that she is *well seized in fee of the lands and premises aforesaid and ha* s *good right to sell and convey the same in manner and form aforesaid, and that the same are free from all incumbrances,* except easements, reservations and restrictions of record, if any.

And the above bargained and granted lands and premises, in the quiet and peaceable possession of the said parties of the second part, their assigns, the survivor of said parties, and the heirs and assigns of the survivor, against all persons lawfully claiming or to claim the whole or any part thereof, subject to incumbrances, if any, hereinbefore mentioned, the said part y *of the first part will Warrant and Defend.*

In Testimony Whereof, *The said part* y = *of the first part has hereunto set* her
hand the day and year first above written.

In Presence of

Gladys M. MacLean, by her mark

PLATE 2: Warranty Deed

71

Zoning. In many urban areas, and in some rural ones as well, land is zoned, meaning that once its use has been specified by zone—industrial, commercial, residential, and so forth—the land may be used for that purpose only—unless an exception is granted. For example, a commercial building may not be built on land zoned residential. It is common, however, for zoning changes to be made, usually upon request of the owner. If the applicant seeks a change in the zone classification, the petition is called a *zoning amendment.* If the request is for an exception to a zone requirement, the request is called a *variance.* In either case, zoning matters are heard by a municipal zoning board or planning commission, and then referred to the city council for final action.

Building Inspection   How do you find out whether a particular building is below acceptable living standards? By going to the building inspection office in the municipality in which the property is located. Many states now have uniform building codes that specify electrical, heating, plumbing, and general construction requirements. Many municipalities also have similar codes. The inspection office of the municipality maintains records of when a particular building has been repaired, what improvements have been made, and whether the owner has failed to comply with violation tags issued by inspectors. The records of the municipal inspection offices are generally organized according to street address, and these records are often a good source to determine who owns a building. While all inspection records may not be public, they will give you leads if you are checking on slum property in your community.

Taxes   Tax records are normally considered nonpublic. Nevertheless, certain types are often available for inspection. One is the property tax assessment record, normally kept by the city or county assessor's office. This record can provide a reliable indication of ownership because it is unlikely that someone without an interest in a piece of property will be paying the taxes on it. The assessment record is often organized by *plat* and *parcel* numbers, which correspond to legal descriptions and street addresses. The record will give the *estimated market value* of the property, that is, the dollar amount it might bring if sold. Normally, the estimated market value of land is a bit less than its true value, probably because assessors do not always get around frequently enough to reflect increased value. The record will also give the *assessed valuation,* the figure on which taxes are computed. The formula for computing tax rates varies from state to state and county to county, and you will have to find out the formula used in your community. The assessment record will also break down the tax paid on the land, buildings, and, sometimes, the physical assets on the property such as machinery. The record should indicate whether the taxpayer lives on the property, in which case the tax is computed at a *homestead* rate. It may also indicate whether the tax-payer is entitled to any special credit because of blindness or other disability.

Individual tax returns are confidential, but if the state or federal government files a *lien* against the taxpayer, his tax record may become part of the public record in a court filing. In asking a court for a tax lien, the government alleges that taxes are owed but have not been paid. A lien, if granted, places a "hold" on a person's property, such as real estate. It allows the government to sell the property to recover the taxes owed. Normally, tax liens are filed with either the clerk of court in the county in which the individual lives, or with the register of deeds or recorder's office.

We have already mentioned the Pulitzer Prize-winning story developed by the Sun Newspapers based on tax-exempt organization tax returns. Other tax-exempt foundations and corporations file similar returns, and as the case illustrates, these documents may, indeed, lead to important news stories.

Campaigns and Disclosure   There seems to be a trend in American politics toward greater disclosure by public officials of their financial assets and of the contributors to their campaigns. The trend is due partly to the election scandals revealed in the Watergate investigations, and it has filtered down to the state and municipal level. Many states, in recent years, have enacted campaign reform laws that require political candidates to reveal who contributes to their election campaigns. Some also require public officials to disclose their interests in financial ventures. Even when disclosure is not required, the politician who refuses to reveal either contributors or assets is risking defeat.

There are numerous records dealing with disclosure, and they may be found in a variety of state and county offices. Statewide election candidates normally file such information with the state secretary of state. County officials generally file with the county auditor, and municipal officials with the municipal clerk. Federal candidates, such as U. S. congressmen and senators, also file such statements, usually with their state's secretary of state's office.

Let's say you examine the disclosure of a state senator and find that he owns stock in several mining companies. Your next job would be to examine carefully his voting record, as well as the bills he has introduced in the legislature, to see whether there has been an apparent conflict of interest. In the case of an administrative official, you would have to examine his administrative decrees to determine whether his private holdings appeared to influence his decisions, or whether he gave special treatment to the requests of campaign contributors. Again, a word of caution is necessary here. Once you have determined a politician's financial assets or campaign contributors, you have nothing more than a circumstantial case. To round out the story, you would have to conduct interviews and compare the answers with what is shown in public documents. As with other public records, the use of campaign records requires discretion. Nothing destroys the credibility of a public affairs reporter faster than making unsubstantiated charges that are later refuted.

Corporations   One of the most difficult tasks for the investigative reporter is investigating a corporation and determining its holdings, officers and assets. The task is made more difficult by laws in many states that allow companies to operate pretty much in secret, particularly if the company's stock is held privately and not traded on the open market.

Corporations are generally required to file—with the state secretary of state, and often with the county register of deeds where they do business—articles of incorporation that set forth the purposes of the company. If you are checking on a company, the *incorporation papers* should be your first stop. In many cases, these will tell you who the owners and directors are or were at the time of incorporation. A word of warning here, too. In some states, the law allows attorneys to incorporate companies for private clients, and then turn over the control to those clients. So if you see an attorney's name as an incorporator, be cautious. The attorney may be an owner, but more likely, he is acting for a private client.

If the company is publicly owned, meaning that its stock is traded on a stock exchange, you will be able to learn more about it. A good source is the office of securities, normally in an agency like your state's department of commerce. Companies that sell stock must be registered, and often the securities office will have summaries of the company, including stock circulars and prospectuses. These give a substantial amount of information, often including the background of the individual incorporators and how much stock they hold.

An often overlooked source of information is the stock brokerage firm. Many investigative reporters own a small amount of stock through a major firm, and thereby can have access to the brokerage house's research. All you have to do is call your broker, and the brokerage firm will often send you information on a company.

There are a number of other sources for tracing a company. One is *Moody's Industrial Manual,* which lists American companies, and provides company histories, activities, officers, directors, and balance sheets. Others are the directories of major industries. A good indication of who controls or has an interest in a company is gained by checking court records on a company to see if it has ever been a defendant or plaintiff in a civil suit. If so, the file may reveal who appeared in court to represent the firm. A similar source is the zoning variance application. Often, a company seeking a zoning variance will file an application with the municipal council, which will indicate who is behind the company.

One good rule of thumb is to ask yourself if the company is regulated by the state or the federal government. Many businesses, such as banks, financial loan companies, power companies, trucking firms, and warehouses are regulated by the state, and the files of various state agencies may contain eye-opening information on them. For example, five individuals applied for a bank charter for a new bank in Minnesota in 1973, and the application gave each individual's net worth and a picture of his financial interests. One of the applicants was J. Kimball Whitney, a former state official. The file on this case contains a summary of Whitney's financial assets at the time of the bank application, including his stock holdings in other companies. (See Plate 3.)

The applicants' background and business interests and their involvement in community affairs are as follows:

(a) *J. Kimball Whitney:* age 45, is married and currently resides with his wife at 559 Harrington Road, Wayzata, Minnesota. He graduated from Phillips Academy, Andover, Massachusetts and attended Williams College, Williamstown, Massachusetts, graduating with BA degree in economics in 1950. He was in the U.S. Army, Qtr. Master Corps. from 1950–1952. From 1954–1964 he was a private school bus operator and president and chairman of the board of Minnesota Transit Lines, Inc. in Excelsior, Minnesota. From 1957–1967 and from January, 1971 to the present time he has been president of the Whitney Land Company of Minneapolis, Minnesota. From 1967–1971 he was commissioner of the Minnesota Department of Economic Development for the State of Minnesota in St. Paul, Minnesota. From 1971 to the present he has been the director of commercial development for Cedar-Riverside Associates, Inc., Minneapolis, Minnesota. He owns 1/9 of the stock in the Whitney Land Company; less than 1% of the stock in Cedar-Riverside Associates, Inc., Minneapolis, Minnesota; and less than 1% of the stock in Jonathan Development Corp., Chaska, Minnesota. He is the director of the North American Corp., Columbus, Ohio owning less than 1% of the stock. He is the trustee for three separate trusts. He is a member of the Wayzata Community Church; Vice President of the Woodhill Country Club; member of the board of governors of the Minneapolis Club; member of the National Executive Board of the Boy Scouts of America; treasurer of the Children's Home Society of Minnesota; director of the Northwest Growth Fund, Inc.; for 1½ years he was director of the North Shore State Bank, Wayzata, Minnesota.

PLATE 3: Bank Charter

Individuals   One of the most common questions asked by news reporters is "Who's he?" Many sources are available to the public affairs reporter who wants information about a person, his family, assets, politics and financial debts. Here are a few of those sources and we again remind you of the cautions suggested earlier about the verification of information from public records:

Bankruptcy.   When an individual files for bankruptcy, the public affairs reporter can get a complete financial picture of him at the time of the filing, including assets and debts. Bankruptcy files are kept by the clerk of the United States district court in the district in which the individual resides. Corporations may also file for bankruptcy, and usually do so in the district where their principal office is located.

Births, Deaths, Marriages, and Divorces.   All these records are kept in the clerk of court's office for the county in which the action occurred or—as in the case of a marriage—was applied for. In addition, birth and death records are usually maintained by the state division of vital statistics, which is most often a division of the state health department. Birth and death records will provide a record of true names, birth dates, and parentage, although many states specifically consider records of illegitimate births and adoptions to be confidential. Marriage records will indicate the date of the marriage, as well as the names of both parties, including the maiden name of the woman. Divorce records often contain a careful tabulation of assets held by both parties which are divided at the time of the divorce. Thus, the public affairs reporter may learn whether a person kept a home in a divorce settlement or whether there was a cash settlement or alimony, and if so, in what amount.

Wills and Judicial Commitments.   Again, a will often can provide you with an inside look at an individual's assets. If you are interested in a person's financial situation, and he is in his forties or fifties and one or both of his parents are dead, be sure to check for a will for one or both of his parents. Because of life expectancy patterns, it is common to find individuals named as beneficiaries of wills who are at the peak of their political or business careers.

The portion of the will shown in Plate 4 is that of the mother of a former state senator from Minnesota. Upon her death, she left her heirs several parcels of land mineral rights, including a portion of an iron mine. Notice in the example how the land is located by legal description.

Both wills and judicial commitments are filed in the probate court of the county in which the individual died, or lived. Judicial commitments are filed when a person is committed to a mental institution, and a record of the commitment may contain medical information that normally would be considered confidential.

Additional real estate—St. Louis County, Minnesota

Description	Section	Township	Range
Und. 1/20th of SW¼ (Pioneer Mine) except a portion of the surface thereof as conveyed by Document No. 89165 and filed for record on December 6, 1967.	27	63	12
Und. 1/30th of Lot 2 except 2 acres for road	28	63	12
Und. 1/10th of Lot 5	32	63	12
Und. 7/160ths of SE¼ of NE¼, except 2 acres for road	32	63	12
Und. 7/160ths of SW¼ of NW¼, except 2 acres for road	33	63	12
Und. 1/120th of NE¼ of SW¼	25	63	13
Und. 1/120th of SW¼ of SW¼	25	63	13
Und. 1/120th of SE¼ of SW¼	25	63	13
Und. 1/120th of NW¼ of SE¼	25	63	13

Minerals only—St. Louis County

Und. 1/30th of Lot 2	27	63	12
Und. 1/10th of Lot 4	28	63	12
Und. 1/10th of NE¼ of SE¼	33	63	12
Und. 1/10th of SE¼ of NE¼	33	63	12
Und. 1/10th of NW¼ of SE¼	33	63	12
Und. 1/10th of SW¼ of SE¼	33	63	12

PLATE 4: Portion of a Will, Showing Mineral Rights

Voter Registration. Records filed with the municipal clerk where an individual lives may disclose his full name, address, and telephone number, even if unlisted. Voter registration records will also tell you if a person is a citizen and in what elections he has voted.

Military Discharges. The armed forces recommend that servicemen file their discharge papers with the county register of deeds office in the county in which they are planning to live, or lived before entering the service. These records provide a person's military history and reason for discharge. Under the category of reason for discharge, you will often find an "SPN" (Separation Program Number). By checking the number given against military regulations, available in many libraries, you can determine the reason for the discharge. It may be for a number of reasons, including psychiatric. Again, a word of caution is important here. It would be irresponsible indeed to write that an individual had a history of mental illness on the basis of a military discharge record alone.

Criminal Records. If there is one area where the warnings about unverified information apply, it is to the use of criminal records. It is libelous to falsely accuse someone of a crime, and summary arrest records, such as the type kept by the Federal Bureau of Investigation, are notoriously incomplete. Often, these records contain an initial entry at the time of arrest or inquiry, but do not indicate disposition. A person may be questioned by police and released, but that latter fact may not be recorded.

The best source for criminal records is the court of the district—state or federal, depending on the nature of the crime—in which the action occurred or the charge was filed. There you will find a complete file, showing the specific charge and the disposition of the case. Misdemeanors and other petty offenses are normally recorded by the municipal court, or court of limited jurisdiction. Felonies and gross misdemeanors are recorded by the district or superior court of the state system, and federal violations are recorded by the United States district court.

State departments of motor vehicles keep lists of driving violations, and some of these, contrary to general belief, are often available. The same is true of motor vehicle registrations. Trailer, boat, and recreational vehicle registrations also may be kept by the state department of natural resources.

Licenses. Municipalities and states often require the licensing of certain businesses and professions, ranging from taverns and automobile-towing companies to doctors and attorneys. Normally, the fact that an individual holds a license to engage in a particular business or profession is a public record. The reporter, then, can find, by checking with a state board of medical examiners, whether a particular physician is licensed to practice in that state. He can also determine, by checking with the municipal clerk's office, who holds the license of a particular tavern.

Determining whether or not there have been complaints against a professional person may be much harder. Normally, the disciplinary action taken will be public, but the allegations on which that action is taken may not be. You may learn that a particular attorney has been disbarred, but you may not be allowed to examine the hearing transcript. The same is true for a doctor whose license is suspended or revoked. The best way to proceed here is on a case-by-case basis. If you are interested in the reputation of a particular attorney, check court files to see if anyone has sued him for his practices. Check also with the state bar association, although this source may not reveal much. Check also with the state supreme court, which takes final action in such cases.

If the business or profession operates under a state-granted charter or license, check with the office which regulates the business or profession.

Some states, for example, now regulate debt pro-rate firms, which, for a fee, will help a debtor pay his obligations. The state regulatory agency files may well provide important information on the firm's business practices.

Other public agencies are to be checked as well. For instance, many states now are establishing offices of consumer affairs, to protect consumers against shoddy business practices. In some states, these agencies are connected with the state attorney general's office.

Audits. The financial affairs of state, county, municipal, and other public agencies are audited, normally, by a state unit called the public examiner's office, the state auditor, or the state department of administration. Regardless of what the division is called, it may be a particularly valuable source if you suspect financial discrepancies in the books of a public agency.

Census Data   The records described so far are typically used to obtain information about individuals or organizations. But there is another category of record that provides information about entire populations or subgroups. This kind of information can be extremely valuable to the public affairs reporter, enabling him to introduce context, background, and a large dose of precision into news stories. It also enables the reporter to test the claims of news sources against hard facts.

One such source is the U. S. census, conducted every ten years and partially supplemented in the interim. It provides enormous amounts of data about social and economic characteristics of states, counties, municipalities, and neighborhoods.

There are other similar sources, including *The Statistical Abstract of the United States,* published by the Census Bureau, and available in many libraries. State, county, and local governments also publish demographic information, as do a number of federal agencies. Private foundations and institutions make information available in specialized fields, as do corporate, trade, union, and industrial organizations. For example, the Insurance Institute publishes an annual guide with data on categories such as accident frequency, claims, and actuarial information.

Let's take an example, in case you've got the idea that public affairs reporters have no need to search for and use this kind of information. Let's say you're covering a legislative hearing on the issue of mass transit for your city. The debate centers on alternative routes for the proposed transit system, but none of those testifying offer information about the present number of commuters in each suburban community, their destinations, means of transportation or occupations, all of which are relevant to the choice of route. You have two alternatives: to forget about these factors, and to deprive the reader of important information, or to get the information yourself. This information, as well as many other facts, can be found in Census Bureau publications, particularly in the volumes of *Population Census Reports,* which are organized by state. Some of the information is cross-classified for the nation's approximately 200 metropolitan districts, called Standard Metropolitan Statistical Areas. Additional information can be found in the *Housing Census Reports,* which include data on housing patterns, ownership of homes, and rents paid.

Directories   There are hundreds, perhaps thousands, of professional directories available in America. Many of these are municipal directories, such as the Polk directories for many communities. Others are published by state agencies, professional and business associations, and municipal governments. Most contain names, addresses, titles, brief biographical sketches, professional awards, education and family information.

Directories are important to the reporter of public affairs in at least two ways. First, they can be used to provide leads. For example, the public affairs reporter wants to know something about the background of a major political figure, say a state senator. The legislative manual will provide a brief biographical sketch. Directories can also be used to cross-check information from public records. Let's say he finds a John Smith who is married to a Mary Smith. He needs to be sure he is looking at the right John Smith, so the reporter checks a directory that contains Smith's name. It tells him that Smith's wife's name is Joan. A bell ought to go off in his head at this point. Perhaps there has been a second marriage, or perhaps not. In either case, the reporter should be aware now that there may be another John Smith who might be confused with the first one.

Many directories gather information on a voluntary basis. Such information, therefore, is not likely to be incriminating, at least on the surface. A contractor you suspect of making payoffs to a city official is not going to list himself in a contractor's directory as a briber. On the other hand, you may well determine more details about his business, its location, and other facts.

The point to remember here is that using public records is a slow, cumulative process. Rarely are reporters going to find a single document to pull a particular investigation together by itself. Usually, they'll need a number of sources, including public documents, interviews, directories, and perhaps statistical data. But by using these sources together, reporters can often focus the story or the inquiry.

At the end of this chapter, we list a number of important directories which may be helpful. The list is not exhaustive, and you should check your own library to see what's available locally.

The Writing Process

Once the reporter has orchestrated his direct observations with a sharply honed interviewing style and, where appropriate, a thorough search of public records, he is ready for the writing process. Even for the most facile writer, preparing the final product can be an agonizing process. After determining that the data are complete, that all bases have been covered—or at least as many as time and circumstances allow—hard decisions must be made about emphasis and style, what to retain from the mass of notes and other material the writer has assembled. With the writing process, the reporter must shift gears, thinking in a more direct sense than he has before of editor and audience. Here is the result of one reporter's journey from a story assignment to finished product.

The assignment was routine: coverage of a Sunday afternoon meeting of laymen representing the conservative faction in a doctrinal dispute that threatened the unity of the second-largest synod of the Lutheran Church.

The reporter was 27-year-old Peg Meier, a wispy but tough-minded journalism school graduate with five years' experience on general assignment, the first two on a small daily, the last three on the *Minneapolis Tribune.*

She made the customary preparation: checked the fat morgue file on the Missouri Synod, Lutheran Church; phoned the local office of the synod to confirm the meeting's time and place; checked with the photographer assigned to accompany her; interviewed by phone a minister identified with the moderate faction.

Her report of the meeting opened this way:

Mayer, Minn.—When Edwin C. Weber was studying for the Lutheran ministry in 1935, his professors warned that no church body in history had survived more than 100 years without a major dispute over beliefs.

"They told us to be on guard so when the time came we would stand up for the doctrine we believed in," he said. "Now is the time."

The Rev. Dr. Weber, now first vice president of the 127-year-old Lutheran Church's Missouri Synod, one of the most conservative synods of the church, continued: "Trouble has been brewing for the last 25 years. Now it's out there in the open and the laymen are getting concerned."

More than 1,200 laymen were concerned enough Sunday to turn out for an afternoon meeting about the synod's problems—problems that threaten to split their congregations. The meeting was sponsored by the conservative element of the synod.[17]

"I had trouble with that story," Meier said afterward. "I must have fiddled with the lead for a full half hour. The desk wanted me to try for a local angle because the meeting had been out of town, but there was no way."

A more traditional lead might have read: "The first vice president of the Lutheran Church's Missouri Synod yesterday told more than 1,200 laymen that "now is the time" to stand for the doctrine they believe in. The Rev. Dr. Edwin C. Weber addressed a meeting sponsored by the synod's conservative wing to air the doctrinal dispute that threatens the synod's unity."

The element that makes the first lead an inspired departure from tradition is its unexpressed reference to the root of the controversy: suspension of the president of the synod's seminary for favoring a "liberal" interpretation of the Bible—the background that most readers could be expected to know.

Offbeat or traditional, public affairs reporters can follow their bent in reporting public affairs on more and more newspapers today. But their bent must never violate the standards of effective communication, and the most important of these are accuracy, clarity, economy, vigor, and specificity.

You have already survived the rigors of a basic reporting or journalistic writing course. You are, as a consequence, alert to the necessity for verification of such essentials as dates, addresses, titles, place names, ages and correct spelling of proper names. These are only the start of the discipline. In reporting public affairs, you move into a world where the complexities of procedure lay snares for the reporter who is too shy or too sloppy to ask the questions that minimize the chance of inaccuracy. Does the appeals court's decision to remand mean a decision in favor of the appellant? Does the planning commission's recommendation of a variance mean a change of zoning? Does a filing in bankruptcy justify use of the term bankrupt? Failure to understand procedure, readiness to assume that appearances are reliable, reluctance to seek the verifying, or clarifying, answer—all of these are marks of the undisciplined reporter. The road to inaccuracy is paved with misunderstandings and faulty assumptions.

Nonetheless, we assume that basic training has instilled in you a passion for lucid expression. Like precise diction: That you don't use "continually" when you mean "continuously," "comprise" when you mean "compose," "uninterested" when you mean "disinterested," "imply" when you mean "infer." And like well-ordered sentence structure: That related words should not be separated; that modifiers belong as close as possible to the word they modify; that coordinate ideas demand parallel construction. Reporting public affairs demands that these writing rules, among others, be adhered to. As suggested above, the world of public affairs can be a jungle of jargon for the unguided reader. Legalese lurks behind every bench. If, for the sake of precision, you must use such terms as writ of certiorari, codicil, quitclaim deed, subornation of perjury, bench warrant, peremptory challenge, or deposition, you should translate, or, at the least, provide the context that permits understanding.

How, you may ask, can writing on such subjects be both clear and economical? It's not easy; good writing seldom is. But clarity and economy march in lockstep by avoiding such redundancies as "the reason is because," "he personally," "period of time," as well as by pruning all words and phrases that do not contribute to meaning: "the fact that," "needless to say," "he made a speech," "they held a meeting," "the delegate made a motion," "the judge handed down a decision," "the senator put the bill in the hopper."

Many of these verbal excesses are the clichés of public affairs reporting, and as such, they rob writing of vigor. (Less windy but almost as tedious are last year's "viable," this year's "thrust" and "machismo," and that barbarism of an entire decade, the free-floating "hopefully.") Let a few of these creep into writing that is tranquilized by passive verbs and nonstop sentences and you have encouraged the lassitude with which too many readers yawn through news of government.

Involvement, not indifference, is the attitude the public affairs reporter should seek to encourage in his readers. We wonder how much alienation, how much of the pervasive you-can't-fight-city-hall defeatism can be attributed to inadequate reporting and dull writing about public affairs.

How much can you involve your reader? You don't need to be an advocate; the desired involvement is the reader's, not the reporter's. This is where specificity comes in. Concreteness. Humanizing. The *Wall Street Journal* has been showing the way for years with its trend stories. Consider this one describing a trend among colleges to award scholarships on merit rather than need. The lead loses no time in particularizing a generalization: "To many American families, the problem Alan Weiss faced last year sounds only too familiar." Alan's problem, the reader learns, is that his parents' income boosts them out of the needy class but not into the affluent class that can afford college without strain. No matter. Alan, like an increasing number of his contemporaries, got a scholarship on merit, the *Journal* notes.[18]

Or consider the *Journal*'s exposition of an increasingly numerous character in the business world: the corporate, or in-house, economist.

The article provides a lot of general information about this new breed: estimates of their number range from 3,500 to 5,000; they are "largely a phenomenon of the last 20 years"; "their jobs are becoming harder"; their problems include "the persistence of inflation," shortages of energy and materials, "the growing involvement of many companies in international markets." The article quotes a number of such economists, along with a professor of economics. But the story's interest, and the reader's involvement through empathy, are heightened by its focus on a specific example, Stanley V. Malcuit, chief economist at Alcoa. "On his desk one recent day: a request from a sales executive for information for a speech . . . about the 1974 outlook; a request from the public relations department to review the script for a state-of-the-company movie Alcoa is making for hourly workers; a request from the Federal Trade Commission for information that will help it sharpen its definition of industries." And to help in labor negotiations, Stan (he is Stan by this time) had to "figure out how much the consumer price index might rise over the life of the contract." The reader learns more about Stan through comment by other corporate economists to whom he is "something of a crusader." He sounds like a crusader when he tells the reporter: "First of all, I love Alcoa. That's a horrible thing to say, but I almost literally love this company." And the *Journal*'s readers can doubtless empathize with Stan as he rides a bus to work, "figuring the time is well-spent in reading" (he's a speed-reader) and returns to his "substantial nine-room house in a fancy Pittsburgh suburb" where a handyman does the yard work because Stan doesn't care much for that sort of puttering.[19]

Obviously, the device is not universally applicable in public affairs reporting. But the principle of specificity, of concreteness, is applicable, and when applied, it lessens the distance between the reader and city hall.

So how do you put it all together? Journalism professor David L. Grey has defined these steps in *The Writing Process:* pre-writing (conceptualization, observing, checking sources, interviewing); writing; rewriting and editing; reaction and reassessment.[20]

Most reporters don't wait to start writing the story until they get to typewriter or telephone. They are already formulating the lead and organizing the body as they leave the interview or scene of the event. What is the essence of the event or the situation? What are its most significant elements, the essential components of the lead? The persons? If so, how are they to be identified? The action? If so, how is it to be defined concisely yet graphically? The place? The time? Or is cause or manner of greater significance? Which of these is going to be of greatest interest to readers? Which can be subordinated? Does the nature of the material demand exposition? narration? description? dialogue?

The reporter, if he's lucky, may be aided in the process by the necessity of a summary, oral report to city desk before beginning to type or dictate. Space limitations set by the desk may determine how tight or how detailed the account is to be. In any case, it must have coherence and unity, whatever the limits of space or pressure of deadline. And that means careful selection and logical organization of significant detail. Marilyn Bender, for example, in an extended piece for the *New York Times* on General Motors' failure to surmount the energy crisis with smaller models, noted deep in her story: "The men who do succeed at GM accept compromise by committee. They govern from the southeastern wing of the 14th floor of corporate headquarters, a grey edifice furnished in faint-hearted modern monotony." [21]

The reporter's problem of organization may be complicated if she has covered a city council meeting or a news conference, at either of which the agenda might encompass a number of unrelated topics of almost equal news value. A good practice to follow in writing such a story, she knows, is to devise a summary lead that breaks into item-by-item capsule statements of the various topics, each of which is amplified in turn in the body of the story.

If there is time when she has finished writing and copy editing, she will scan her notes to insure that no needed detail has been overlooked. If there is time, she will read the piece again: Are there holes? Is it clear? Is it balanced? Is it fair?

She may not be sure until she sees the piece in print. Or until her telephone rings or the letters to the editor start coming in. From Missouri Synod Lutherans—conservatives and moderates.

NOTES

1. See, for example, Don R. Pember, *Mass Media in America* (Chicago: Science Research Associates, 1974), chap. 7, and especially pp. 211–14. Many critics have argued that the desire for film dominates broadcast news decisions.

2. For a recent exploration of the complementary roles of television and print news, see Ben H. Bagdikian, "Newspapers: Learning (Too Slowly) To Adapt to TV," *Columbia Journalism Review* 12 (Nov.-Dec., 1973), 44–51.

3. The belief that mass media should perform a surveillance, or scanning, function has been put forth by many communication theorists. The first and fullest exposition of this concept is by Harold D. Lasswell, "The Structure and Function of Communication in Society," in *The Communication of Ideas,* ed. Lyman Bryson (New York: Institute for Religious and Social Studies, 1948).

4. Useful discussions about reporting objectivity can be found in Donald McDonald's "Is Objectivity Possible?" *Center Magazine* (September-October, 1971), pp. 29–42, and in the introduction to Philip Meyer's *Precision Journalism: A Reporter's Introduction to Social Science Methods* (Bloomington: Indiana University Press, 1973).

5. Murray Fisher, comments at Symposium on the Journalistic Interview (Department of Journalism, Kansas State University, Manhattan, Kansas, April, 1972).

6. Robert Maurer, taped comments on interviewing practices prepared by Monitor staff for symposium in note 5.

7. Ibid.

8. Eleanor and Nathan Maccoby, "The Interview: A Tool of Social Science," in *Handbook of Social Psychology,* Vol. 1, ed. Gardner Lindzey (Cambridge: Addison-Wesley, 1954), p. 546.

9. Eugene J. Webb and Jerry R. Salancik, "The Interview; or, The Only Wheel in Town," *Journalism Monographs* 2 (November, 1966), 15.

10. Terkel's books provide excellent case studies of different kinds of interviews. They include: *Division Street America* (New York: Avon, 1967); *Hard Times: An Oral History of the Depression* (New York: Pantheon, 1970); and *Working: People Talk about What they Do All Day and How They Feel about What They Do* (New York: Pantheon, 1974).

11. Claudia Cohen, "Enterprise Reporting or 'Invasion of Privacy?' " (*More*) 4 (March, 1974), 9. See also Gordon Chaplin, "Eclipse in Baltimore," same issue of *(More),* 8–9.

12. Cohen, "Enterprise Reporting," p. 9.

13. Jim R. Morris, "Newsmen's Interview Techniques and Attitudes Toward Interviewing," *Journalism Quarterly* 50 (Autumn, 1973), 540.

14. "Costello: TV's First Headless Star—Only His Hands Entertain Audience," *New York Times* (March 4, 1951), p. 1.

15. Webb and Salancik, "The Interview," p. 4.

16. Ibid., p. 6.

17. Peg Meier, "Laymen Come to Grips with Theology," *Minneapolis Tribune* (March 25, 1974), p. 1.

18. Roger Ricklefs, "More Colleges Grant Scholarships Based on Merit, Not Need," *Wall Street Journal* (March 25, 1974), p. 1.

19. John V. Conti, "Corporate Economists Give In-House Advice on Future's Course," *Wall Street Journal* (March 26, 1974), p. 1.

20. David L. Grey, *The Writing Process* (Belmont, Calif.: Wadsworth Publishing, 1972).

21. Marilyn Bender, "Energy Pinch Has Stunted GM Profits, Sales," *New York Times Service* in *Minneapolis Tribune* (March 28, 1974), p. 8A.

SUGGESTED READINGS

DEXTER, LEWIS A., *Elite and Specialized Interviewing.* Evanston: Northwestern University Press, 1970. An excellent treatment of the "elite" interview with special implications for political scientists and oral historians that can be adapted by journalists especially with regard to letting the subject help structure the interview.

GILLELAND, LaRUE W., "Simple Formula Proves Helpful to Interviewers," *Journalism Educator* 26 (Summer, 1971), 19–20. A journalism educator's method for improving interviewing skill.

HARTGEN, STEPHEN, *A Guide to Public Records in Minnesota*. Minneapolis: Minneapolis Star and Tribune Co., 1975.

SHERWOOD, HUGH C., *The Journalistic Interview* (2d ed.). New York: Harper & Row, 1973. A reporter's analysis of the journalistic interview. Rich with anecdotal material, but ignores social science literature on the subject.

WEBB, EUGENE J., and JERRY R. SALANCIK, "The Interview; or, The Only Wheel in Town," *Journalism Monographs* 2 (November, 1966), 1–49.

A Checklist of Useful Directories for the Public Affairs Reporter

The following list includes directories that are generally national in scope. There are many local and regional directories, and the public affairs reporter should become familiar with those in his area.

Architecture. The American Architects, Directory lists professional architects and architectural firms in the United States. It is a valuable "first source" on the qualifications and career histories for the reporter checking on buildings and construction projects.

Businesses and Corporations. Moody's Industrial Manual is a guide to industrial corporations and enterprises across the nation. It has a geographic index, and provides a brief history of companies, their activities, subsidiaries, officers and directors, and consolidated balance sheets. The *World Bank Directory* lists bank officers and bank holdings. Many states have directories of manufacturing, such as the *Minnesota Directory of Manufacturing*. These are often published by the state, and include the size and type of business firms by region or community or both. Chambers of commerce also publish similar directories for their regions. See also the *Standard & Poor's* business directory, which gives more information on business firms and officers.

Consultants. Technical advice in many fields is provided by consultants and consulting organizations. The *Consultants and Consulting Organizations* directory offers a guide to these individuals and associations.

Education. State educational directories list teachers and administrators in various school districts. There are similar guides for colleges and universities.

Engineers and Scientists. Several directories of engineers and scientists have been published. See *Engineers of Distinction,* the *International Engineering Directory, Engineering Consultants, The American Society of Mechanical Engineers Membership Directory, The Institute of Electrical and Electronics Engineers Membership Directory,* and *The Directory of Engineers in Private Practice.*

Government. There are many government directories at the state, local, and federal level. The public affairs reporter should certainly be familiar with his state's *Legislative Manual.* States, counties, and municipalities also publish directories of personnel and guidebooks to their governmental structure. Similar guides are published for federal public officials and employees, and some are organized topically, such as the *Directory of Governmental Occupational Safety and Health Personnel.*

Lawyers and Law Firms. The Martindale & Hubbell legal directory lists practicing attorneys in the United States, and law firms. It also includes lists of the firms' "representative clients," so the reporter can get an idea of which law firm represents which corporations and businesses.

Medicine. Many medical directories exist, such as those of the *American Association of Endodontists,* the *American Academy of General Practice,* the *Aerospace Medical Association* and the *American Psychoanalytical Association.* See also the directories of the *American College of Surgeons* and the *American College of Physicians,* and the *American Medical Directory.*

Newspapers. Editor and Publisher Yearbook lists the editorial staffs and management personnel of daily newspapers, along with the names of weekly newspapers and press associations. It also presents statistical information about a newspaper's circulation and advertising rates, as does the *Ayer Directory of Publications.*

Who's Whos. There are many who's whos, divided both by region and profession. Some of the more useful ones, which provide biographical sketches on individuals, are the *Who's Who in: College and University Administrators; Engineering; Insurance; Electronics; the Securities Industry; Public Relations; Advertising; Railroading; Computers and Data Processing; American Art;* and *American Theater.* Be sure to see the regional who's who for your area, such as *Who's Who in the Midwest.*

chapter five

New Techniques

for Monitoring Public Problems

One of the great tragedies of life is the murder of a beautiful theory by a brutal gang of facts.

LA ROCHEFOUCAULD

The two researchers had many important questions, but few answers.

Are certain kinds of criminals more likely than others to be imprisoned?

What circumstances are related to different sentences for the same type of crime?

Is there discrimination in the courts against blacks? Against young people? Against women?

Do judges of different races and political affiliations treat the same types of crimes differently?

To get at the answers, the researchers pored over trial transcripts. They interviewed judges, prosecutors, defense lawyers, victims, and defendants. They examined more than 1,000 case records, abstracting 100,-000 pieces of information from them. The data ranged from the age, race, and sex of the defendant and victim to the type of location of the crime—more than 100 variables in all, filling almost 10,000 cards. When the research was completed, and 4,000 pages of computer printouts were analyzed, they had the answers. Their conclusion: The assumption that justice is equal for all in the Philadelphia criminal courts is a myth.[1]

The researchers in the seven-month-long investigation weren't criminologists or sociologists, conducting an academic study of the legal system. They were Donald L. Barlett and James B. Steele, reporters for the *Philadelphia Inquirer*. Their research led to a series of articles that challenged widely held beliefs about the criminal justice system: that judges are "soft," that district attorneys are "tough," that courts have a "logjam" of cases, that justice is dispensed with an even hand. Instead, they found patterns of apparent bias on the part of judges. They found district attorneys "talking tough" but recommending light sentences for many criminals. They found extreme disparity in sentencing for similar crimes. They found innocent persons in jail. They found that Philadelphia's judges handle fewer cases than judges in other major cities.

Answers to their questions weren't available from regular news sources. A reporter going to court officials or defense lawyers for information of this kind would probably come away, at best, with self-serving, impressionistic accounts devoid of supporting evidence. The only way Barlett and Steele could approach their goal was to conduct their own study, in this case a scientific analysis of public records. For the research design and computer programming, they were joined by Philip Meyer of the *Inquirer's* parent company, Knight Newspapers. Meyer is the chief evangelist and principal practitioner of the type of reporting represented by the *Inquirer* study: precision journalism (Chapter 3).[2] This newest of the New Journalisms is, in essence, the use in interpretative reporting of social science research methods—the survey, the experiment, content analysis.

Scientific research doesn't mean dry, statistics-laden stories. Precision journalism requires the use of case studies, examples, and focused quotation to make the statistics come alive. In their initial article describing the uneven quality of justice in Philadelphia, Barlett and Steele began this way:

> Angus Williams, a 57-year-old laborer, was arrested in November 1971 and charged with the street robbery of a retired North Philadelphia machinist. For five months he sat in jail awaiting trial, unable to post the $3,000 bail.
>
> In the end, he was acquitted of the charges. As it now turns out, Angus Williams—who never went to school, who cannot read or write, who had never been arrested before—was indeed innocent. Another man committed the robbery.[3]

The story goes on to detail other cases in which judges acted with apparent inconsistency. Only after "humanizing" the material with these illustrations do Barlett and Steele present the statitsical findings from their study.

When traditional reporting methods can't produce the information desired, as in the Philadelphia illustration, precision journalism techniques can mean the difference between a comprehensive story and no story at all. In other situations, empirical research may be employed by journalists to confirm or enhance the accuracy of assertions, and the implications of limited data. If city officials say, for example, that a new antilitter program has reduced the amount of debris on downtown streets, a simple experiment might be designed to test the assertion. Similarly, if a business group contends that shoppers avoid the downtown district because of inadequate parking, a survey could verify the claim.

These, of course, are cases that would require sufficient staff time and funds to pursue. Even those few news organizations that already have ventured into research don't do it on a daily or weekly basis. Short of formal research projects, however, precision journalism techniques are being used to add power to the less elegant methods of information gathering used by reporters in their daily work. All that is required is an awareness of the principles upon which scientific research is conducted. The reporter who systematically checks several sources on one subject rather than relying on a single source has, in effect, committed an act of precision journalism. As an example, the statehouse reporter for a metropolitan daily wants to learn the likelihood of passage of a bill. He has several options. He could question every member of the legislature. He could conduct a formal sample survey, questioning perhaps a fourth of the members, selected randomly. He could search out a handful of legislators, perhaps several from each faction or party, and ask for their estimates of the vote. Or he could seek the answer from just one friendly legislator who is willing to speak, relying on that person's predictive acumen. The four approaches range from the most rigorous (the first) to the most casual of reporting techniques (the last), and testify to a journalistic truth—that reporting, like politics, is the art of the possible. But any move toward precision should be welcomed by journalists, and their critics.

The research situations described thus far might be classified as "active" uses of precision journalism. Although several news organizations have moved vigorously into research undertakings, most have not. The costs in time and money are inhibiting factors, as is the fear that journalists can't be trained to perform adequately as researchers.[4] The principles of quantitative research, however, need not be limited to "active" projects. They can be applied to almost every facet of public affairs reporting on a daily basis. This latter application represents what might be termed the secondary use of precision journalism. The only requirement is knowledge of research methods and statistics. Many may consider these secondary uses more important than the primary uses, simply because of the wide utility of the former and the infrequency of the latter.[5] It's a rare day when the average newspaper doesn't publish several stories that include research-based information. Every time a news source gives reporters the results of an empirical study, the situation calls for familiarity with the techniques used in that study. Indeed, a source presentation without benefit of a research element is often a signal to the reporter to question the information.

Reporters on most beats confront these situations regularly, from the political writer presenting the results of an election poll, to the medical writer passing along the findings of an experiment; from the governmental reporter confronted with conflicting conclusions in two feasibility studies, to the police reporter trying to find significance in quarterly crime reports. All signify danger to the unwary. Research conducted by investigators with a point of view to defend may be suspect because of bias; research coming from independent sources may be flawed by methodological or statistical improprieties. The reporter (and his editor) must have at least a minimum knowledge of research methods and analysis in order to recognize these faults. Only then can he interpret the information accurately, or be alert to the need for checking with a competent authority. Otherwise, the error is passed along uncritically to a public even less able than the journalist to evaluate research findings. The files of newspapers are filled with examples of this failing.

The case for precision journalism as part of the professional's standard repertoire, then, is based on three benefits:

1. Original research to obtain information not available through other sources.
2. More accurate procedures for conventional news-gathering.
3. Interpretation and evaluation of the increasing amount of quantitative research that is flowing across newsroom desks.

Traditional modes of news reporting—direct observation of events, such as covering a trial, or indirect observation of events, such as a press conference—serve well in the appropriate situation. Often, however, they can't meet the demands of a given situation. That new models are needed for contemporary journalism is apparent from the criticism of straight reporting as discussed in previous chapters. In the introduction to his seminal work, *Precision Journalism,* Meyer suggests a rationale for the scientific method as a successor to other reporting models. Objectivity of the old-fashioned variety, Meyer writes, presents few problems to the reporter. He merely records, so the myth goes, what he observes. He needs no thoughts of his own about the subject. But the shift to interpretation in news-writing requires the reporter to have a reference point, an anchor, on which to base his analysis. Objectivity not only doesn't require a reference point—it prohibits one.

Anchor points for interpretation can be supplied by the reporter's personal convictions, by ideology shared with a group, or by prejudices shaped by consensus. Meyer suggests abandoning these anchor points because they jeopardize the journalist's goal of truth. "Instead of starting from a base of personal conviction, ideology or conventional wisdom," he writes, "we can start with intensive and systematic fact-finding efforts." [6] This approach, he contends, is not a return to the old model of abject objectivity, but is intended "to reduce the size of the leap from fact to interpretation, and to find a more solid basis of fact from which to leap." [7] The effect of such systematic fact-finding can be objective interpretation rather than simplistic objectivity.

Meyer and the *Detroit Free Press* put this conviction into practice with a sample survey of racial attitudes following the 1967 Detroit ghetto riot. It was a landmark in the journalistic use of social science research methods—and required only three weeks from conception to newsprint. It demonstrated that newspapers can do what social scientists can't: develop a capacity for "fire engine research" to examine significant news events "even as they happen." [8]

Some precision journalism efforts by newspapers predate the Detroit survey, of course. For many years, untrained reporters using invalid methods have conducted surveys of a sort for a number of newspapers. An example of this genre is the "person-on-the-street" poll, in which the reporter stops the first twenty, or thirty, or fifty persons he meets on the street and asks their opinions on some issue. The results are published as a reflection of what people in the city believe. Few well-edited newspapers are guilty of this travesty today, although survey research of questionable accuracy is still conducted and published. Most quality research efforts by newspapers have been devoted to opinion polls. The *Minneapolis Tribune's* respected Minnesota Poll, perhaps the oldest, has been operating since the 1950s. The *Tribune* has also developed a sophisticated election prediction model, based on a sampling of about 100 precincts. With it, statewide election results have been predicted long before official returns are tabulated. Similar election models have been employed by the television networks since the mid-1960s.

A more common journalistic use of survey research is the commissioned poll, conducted by a commercial research organization. The practice is hardly new; *Fortune* magazine during the 1930s published a notable series of essays on national issues, accompanied by the results of opinion polls. The weekly newsmagazines frequently commission survey research on special topics. Newspapers such as the *Detroit News,* the *Los Angeles Times,* and the *New York Times* sponsor and publish local surveys regularly. The trend to "in house" research conducted by the news organization itself, however, is relatively recent.

A confluence of factors may account for today's greater sophistication in the journalistic uses of research. The growing acceptance of precision journalism may be an extension of wider press understanding of the social sciences since World War II. It may also originate in what newspaper critic Ben Bagdikian described as "the disappearing anti-intellectualism" of the press.[9] Editors are more willing to accept specialized training for their staffs, and make use of it in their newspapers. Some impetus for change has undoubtedly come from demands by critics that the media develop better ways to translate complex issues accurately and understandably. And news professionals themselves have testified to the desirability (and inevitability) of precision journalism. In 1973 J. Edward Murray, then president of the American Society of Newspaper Editors, called for a major shift in reporting emphasis toward the use of social indicators, statistical models, and opinion polls.[10] A year later, an association of precision journalists was founded by working newsmen who attended a summer institute in research methods.

While these developments may herald the oncoming age of precision journalism, prospects for the availability of journalists equal to the task are not so sanguine. Reporters once were expected only to read and write well. Now they are also being asked to count. The untrained reporter can meet the opportunity—and challenge—of precision journalism in two ways. The first is to rely on social scientists for advice. Most cities have colleges rich in authorities who can guide and backstop the journalist. Obviously, there are limits to the extent of this type of help, so it is clear that journalists must themselves come to terms with the business of research and analysis. This means formal training—enough to speak the language of science, to recognize danger areas, and to conduct studies appropriate to the skills acquired. It is not essential for the journalist to match the rigor or sophistication of the professional researcher. As Meyer notes:

> Not all the rules can be observed all the time, but it is important to know them so that you are aware of what you are doing when you break them. There will always be occasions when quick and dirty research is the only kind a newspaper is capable of. If designed with its limitations in mind, such research can still take you closer to the truth than pure intuition or thumb sucking.[11]

For the college student, training is easily obtained. Courses in statistics, research methods, data analysis, and computer operation are offered by several departments at most universities. Some journalism departments also have courses in these subjects, shaped to fit press interests. For the working professional, extension courses are often available, and summer workshops in precision journalism are likely to become more numerous.

This chapter is intended to offer an elementary introduction to some of the concepts and techniques of precision journalism. The sections that follow on statistics and research methods can be considered as curtain raisers; the student who plans to develop his own research capability, or properly report on the research of others, must go on from here to more thorough study.

Statistics and Elephants

To eat an elephant standing in your path, according to an old African proverb, you must first cut it into small pieces.

Reporters and their publics frequently are confronted with elephants in the form of complex phenomena. What are the reasons for low reading scores among sixth graders? Is there a solution to the conflict between economic development and environmental protection? How can we predict the effects of welfare programs on the components of society? To get at these questions, we usually try to reduce the information to digestible portions.

There are many ways to look at, or analyze, information in the sense of arriving at conclusions. We can rely on experience, common sense, or intuition; we can decide by consensus or voting; we can rely on authority; we can apply logical reasoning; and we can use statistics, if the information is quantifiable. People commonly use the word "statistics" to refer to specific facts or figures. Scientists, however, apply the term "data" to accumulations of information, and reserve "statistics" for reference to methods of summarizing, analyzing and interpreting data.

The use of statistics as an analytical tool dates back to humankind's earliest time, but the field has flowered in this century because of great advances in data-gathering methods, measurement techniques, and electronic computing. Particularly in the social sciences, certain attributes once considered as qualitative (e.g., intelligence, apathy) are being cast in numerical terms.[12]

Social scientists distinguish between two branches of statistics, *descriptive* and *inferential*.* Descriptive statistics involves measurement or counting of observable objects or their attributes. The compilation of batting averages, weather records, the listing of occupations according to income, are examples of descriptive statistics. This statistical approach simplifies masses of data by classifying, comparing, and ordering them. Inferential statistics deals with phenomena that are less easily observed,

---

* The terms and concepts described in this chapter can be studied in more detail in any of a number of excellent books. Several are listed in the suggested readings at the end of the chapter.

and attempts to explain or predict outcomes on the basis of partial information. Underlying these attempts are the laws of probability, which determine the accuracy (validity) of the predictions. Examples of inferential statistics are those determined by predicting student grades on the basis of previous grades of other students, or those determined by isolating the probable causes of juvenile delinquency through an examination of relevant hereditary and environmental factors. Some fundamental scientific concepts and statistical terms will be examined next.

Scientific Method   The reporter's minimum goal is to describe events. Sometimes he also attempts to explain and predict events, which brings him into league with the scientist. The scientific method imposes order to the effort of describing, explaining, and predicting events. Typically, the process begins with an informal observation of facts, which leads to beliefs—guesses, if you will—about relationships among these facts.

The reporter who finds inconsistencies in the state's handling of two liquor license applications is at this first stage. If his suspicions carry him beyond that stage, he may begin a systematic examination of the disposition of all license applications for the past year. Such an examination would be the second stage of scientific inquiry—formal observation to confirm an initial guess about the functional relationship among facts. If the relationship is confirmed, a "law" may be established; in this fictional case, the general law may be that liquor licenses are awarded on the basis of political campaign contributions. If our persevering reporter discovers in later investigations that political contributions indeed seem to benefit the giver in a variety of situations, he may arrive at the third stage in the scientific process: developing a theory. A statement that functionally relates at least two sets of laws is a theory.

Journalists, as do other people, invoke theories frequently, except that they don't call them theories. When an editor exhorts a reporter to limit his sentences to fifteen words, he is following a theory that holds that short sentences are more understandable. When a reporter uses the most dramatic element of an event for his lead, he too is applying a theory. Journalists' theories are often passed off as *reasons* for doing things the way they do; they are rarely explicit or testable. Scientists demand that theories be explicit, and subject to verification by test. To accomplish this task, scientists follow one of two rigorous courses: field studies or experiments. Field studies are attempts to observe functional relationships among events as they occur in nature—the equivalent of the reporter examining a year's liquor license applications. Experiments use the controlled setting of the laboratory in an effort to avoid the accidents of nature that often contaminate field studies. In the liquor license example, a reporter-experimenter could arrange to submit license applications by persons who did and who did not contribute to the governor's campaign, with all other factors about the applicants being equal. The pattern of license awards would then tend to confirm or disconfirm the theory of political favoritism.

In both field and experimental studies, scientists try to describe their observations in numerical terms. This procedure allows different studies to be compared, and permits statistical tests to measure accuracy.

Measurement   Underlying all quantitative analysis is measurement, but all measurement is not the same. In a pre-election poll, registered voters may be classified as Republicans, Democrats, or independents. The count of each category is known as *nominal* measurement, the lowest order of scientific measurement. If there are more Democrats than Republicans, and more Republicans than independents, arranging the categories in that order is known as *ordinal* measurement, the next level on the precision scale. If the same voters are classified according to how many times they have voted in the past ten years, the result would be *interval* measurement. Each vote is an absolute and equal quantity, qualities required of interval scales. The most refined measure, *ratio*, might be represented by the ages of voters. Ratio measurement requires a scale with a true zero point, a quality possessed by age. The significance of the type of measurement lies in the statistical tests that can be performed on them. Only weak tests are possible for nominal scales, but stronger tests are possible for ordinal, interval and ratio scales.

Averages   Most people understand and use averages, but the layman usually considers only the arithmetic mean—the sum of all values in a group divided by the total number in the group. There are, however, several other "averages" that indicate mid-points in a group of values, each with its own special advantage. The scientist finds it useful to distinguish among these types because some give a better picture of reality in certain situations. The most commonly used measures of centrality are the arithmetic mean, the median, and the mode. The *median* is the point at which a set of values can be cut in half, with an equal number of cases above and below that point. It is preferred to the mean when a distribution has extreme scores on either end, or is not symmetrical. An example would be family income in a heterogeneous population. The *mode* is simply the point at which the greatest number of values occur. It is used primarily as an indicator of the most common score, or "the typical case." An example would be an examination of grades. If more students receive C's than any other grade, then C is the modal grade. Sometimes averages don't provide enough information about a set of measurements; they may distort reality, as when two sets of values have the same average but major internal variations. In such cases, measures of *dispersion* provide more useful indicators. These measures show the configuration of individual values within a group. For example, two groups of employees may have the same average salaries, but one group may have several very high salaries and many low salaries, while the other group's salaries all hover near the average. The true differences in the groups' incomes can't be seen by looking at their means, but can be observed in dispersion statistics, which measure internal variability. The most useful measure of dispersion is the *standard deviation,* which summarizes the differences of all individual values in a set from the mean value of that set. It is a sort of average of individual deviations from the mean. The standard deviation has widespread use in statistical analysis, because it is used to compute correlations between two or more sets of values, and to determine the amount of error likely in these computations.

Probability   The ability to make confident predictions from a set of observations is founded on the laws of probability. Everyone is familiar with probability in the form of odds. Most often we estimate probability objectively, by observing a large number of events. Sometimes probability estimates are subjective, such as the degree of confidence a person has about catching a fish. Another person may assign different odds to the same proposition. Probabilities, which are usually expressed as proportions, can be determined for any event by empirical methods. Once determined, they can be applied to future events that are identical to the original in all significant respects.

Sampling   The procedure that makes possible field research, such as opinion polls, is sampling. Samples are based on probability determinations of the number of units of a population required to faithfully reflect some characteristic of all units in the population. They allow predictions to be made about whole populations after studying just a relatively few members of that population. With proper sampling methods, a group as small as 1,000 can reflect, within a known range of accuracy, the characteristics of a population of 100,000,000. That principle bothers many people, including some journalists, who object that such generalization is impossible. What makes accurate generalization possible is the *probability sample,* in which each unit of the population has an equal or known chance of being selected. Accuracy then depends on the size of the sample, but large samples (above 2,000) don't substantially improve accuracy. There are several types of probability samples, but the most basic is the *simple random sample.* Random does not mean accidental; the researcher must assure that all segments in a population have an equal or known chance of selection. Nonprobability samples, in which a researcher selects population segments with a special purpose in mind, are often employed, but have limited value in prediction because the degree of error can be estimated only with true probability samples.

Confidence and Significance   Scientific findings are viewed with the hope that they represent reality. This hope is measured in terms of *confidence levels* and *statistical significance*. A confidence interval refers to the degree that the mean of a sample used is likely to represent the mean of the entire population. The .95 level is commonly used in the social sciences as an arbitrary, acceptable confidence limit. It means that in 95 cases out of 100, the sample mean will be the same as that of the population in question. Statistical significance measures the probability that differences in sample means are genuine and did not occur by chance. A variety of significance tests, based on normal probabilities, is available for different types of data. Generally, social scientists rely on significance levels of .05 or smaller. This would mean there are only 5 chances in 100 that the differences in the data came out that way by chance rather than because of the factors being examined.

Some disagreement exists among scientists, however, over the (logical) significance of (statistical) significance.[13] In studies with large samples, the very size of the group studied will in itself produce statistical significance, despite relatively minor variations. Many choose to ignore statistical tests in favor of what is sometimes called the "interocular eyeball test": if the data really mean something, it should be apparent by looking at the raw figures.

Types of Analysis   Generally, data are collected and analyzed to see if they are generalizable to a larger population, or to discover causal relationships. Generalizations are accomplished more often than causal conclusions. Cause-and-effect relationships are usually considered beyond the proof available from surveys.[14] The controls possible in experiments (eliminating extraneous factors) make that research approach more desirable than surveys for testing causal hypotheses. Head counts, in the form of means and proportions, and correlations are the types of interpretation usually applied to survey data.

For the public affairs reporter, it is important to remember that the correlation of two factors means only that they are observed to change at the same time by a fixed amount. Whether one causes the other to change is an inference made at great risk. For example, it was widely reported in the early 1970s that the incidence of blood clots in women taking birth-control pills was higher than in those not taking them. The two factors were correlated significantly. Yet the contention that birth-control pills caused clotting can't be sustained by the correlation because the data were gathered from women in hospitals, some for treatment of clotting problems, some for other reasons. It could well have been that women with a tendency to clotting problems were incidentally also users of birth-control pills.

To claim a causal relationship, three types of evidence are necessary: that the variables change in the way predicted before measurement; that the causal variable precedes the other in time of occurrence; and that other factors do not determine the change.[15] The last requirement is the one that usually negates the causal connection. It is often impossible to rule out "third variable" explanations, where some unknown or un-measured factor may be the true cause of the change. Correlations may also be spurious, with the association between two variables coincidental, and not the result of even a third-variable condition. A rise in the sale of artichokes accompanied by a drop in movie attendance would be an example of a spurious correlation.

There are a variety of measures of correlation, designed for different types of measures—nominal, ordinal, interval, ratio. Most show the rela-tionship in a range from -1 to $+1$, with the extremes indicating perfect correlation, and numbers closer to zero a weak association. Interpreting the intensity of a correlation must be done with good sense; sometimes even a weak association is meaningful, and a high correlation may not be nearly as high as should be expected for two factors.

Correlations, and comparisons of data summarized in the form of means and proportions, are the two modes of analysis reporters confront most often. The same underlying cautions for correlations apply to the interpretation of means and proportions. These are usually presented in tabular form, with the differences between categories or samples the focus of interest. It is easy to make causal assumptions in examining such data because of a natural tendency to look for relationships. Tests of signifi-cance and third-variable questions should routinely be applied to such analysis, however. In other words, reporters should be confident that the data did not take its form by chance, and that other equally plausible ex-planations for the results have been considered.

Field Survey Methods

Sample surveys are the Fords and Chevies of the research business. The journalist is likely to see more of them than any other type of scientific study in the course of his work, and if he does the research him-self, he will probably use a field survey. The qualifier "field" means that the research is conducted not in the laboratory, but somewhere in the real world where the subjects of interest reside. The term "sample" means that only a part of the study's universe, or population, is being examined.

The field and the population can range from all voters in the United States, to homeowners in a defined neighborhood in a city, to all members of the county medical society.

Field surveys can be conducted in several ways. One is by direct observation, viewing the behavior of a specific group of people in a systematic manner. To find out how many government cars are parked in restaurant lots after 5 P.M each day, the reporter might resort to a direct observation study. More typical of survey research is the self-administered questionnaire, in which subjects in a sample respond to a fixed set of written questions. The questionnaire can be mailed to respondents, or delivered and retrieved by the researcher. A third method, the most expensive and often considered the most accurate, is the interview. This can be done in person or by telephone. Each method has its advantages and disadvantages.

If surveys differ in method, they also differ in purpose. Some seek only descriptive material about the respondents, such as demographic characteristics or purchasing habits. Food price comparisions are a common use of descriptive surveys by newspapers in this age of consumer consciousness. Other surveys attempt to measure attitudes or predict behavior. These are the types of surveys most frequently found in the news media—the Gallup, Roper, and Harris polls are examples—and the types most likely to be undertaken by journalists.

Public-opinion polls and election polls are merely special cases of field surveys. They are the ones to which the public is exposed most frequently, and the ones that have generated both skepticism and criticism of survey research in general. Election polls in particular have been faulted, for allegedly influencing voter decisions on the one hand, and for failing to accurately measure opinion on the other. The first complaint, that polls create "bandwagon" effects favoring the leading candidate, or create sympathy votes for underdogs, has been largely dismissed. Witness after witness testifying before a congressional hearing on polling practices in 1972 discounted the existence of either effect.[16] As to the validity of the attitude and opinion measured, most researchers in the field share the public's qualms to some degree. Leo Bogart, one of the leading figures in survey research for a generation, distinguishes between good research and bad (and laments that the media rarely make this distinction). But even the best opinion surveys, he says, fall short of the goal of capturing reality. "There is a vast difference," Bogart writes, "between the reality of public opinion and the polls that measure shadows cast, as in Plato's myth, upon the wall of the cave." [17] One of the reasons for this lack of agreement between opinions held and opinions measured is the intrusiveness of the survey question itself, which often limits the range of responses open to the interviewees, or conditions their answers. As Bogart describes it, "The paradox of the scientific method is that we change phenomena by measuring them." [18] Michael Rappeport, an executive of a commercial research organization, points to another weakness of survey methodology: "Before assuming that a poll reflects public opinion, we should find out just what proportion of the adult public has any opinion to reflect . . . substantial minorities or even majorities of people questioned do not have even the barest minimum of factual material on which to base an opinion." [19] Rappeport contends that "don't know" or "no opinion" response categories don't correct for this problem because people prefer to give a specific answer. "It is human nature," he contends, "not to want to admit ignorance." [20]

Despite these fundamental problems and others equally troublesome, sample survey research shows no signs of withering. The challenge to commercial, academic, and journalistic researchers is to follow proper procedures rigorously and to seek better methods. Whatever the purpose and form of the survey, there are a number of steps common to all.

Defining Objectives   Decisions about what the survey is attempting to discover must come before anything else. A clear picture of the information desired will help determine the proper survey method, the appropriate population group, and a useful line of questioning.

Sample Design   Proper sampling is crucial to survey accuracy. As discussed in the previous section, probability samples are required if generalizations to a larger population are to be made. The pure random sample, in which every member of the population is in the original pool from which names are drawn, is rarely used in field surveys because of the high cost of locating persons scattered throughout the population. Other probability methods, such as the systematic, stratified, cluster, and sequential samples, enable the researcher to confine the study to convenient geographic areas. Some use census tract maps; others, directories of some kind. All, however, possess the quality of unbiased selection. Non-probability samples, on the other hand, introduce bias because the researcher's judgment determines the selection of the respondents. Sometimes such a "purposive" sample is appropriate, as when a decision is made about items to be included in a cost of living index. One type of nonprobability sample, however, the convenience, or "accidental," sample, is rarely justified. This type of sample is employed in the discredited newspaper "person-on-the-street" polls.

Sample Size   The layman is often surprised by the small numbers involved in sample surveys, and becomes skeptical of the results. National polls generally use samples of from 1,200 to 1,600 respondents. Some local surveys, such as the statewide Minnesota Poll, use 600 to 800.

Depending on the degree of accuracy desired, the type of data sought, and the size of the population to be surveyed, samples as small as 200 can still be useful. Formulas and tables to help choose sample size are available. If it is randomly drawn, a sample of about 1,200 will provide an error margin of ±3 per cent or less for surveys in cities, states, and the nation. Larger samples reduce the error potential only fractionally, and are therefore uneconomic.

© King Features Syndicate 1973.

Forcing survey respondents into a box by limiting their response choices may distort results—just as Hagar's height is distorted in this comic strip.

Questionnaire Construction   A large body of literature exists solely on the topic of questionnaires. The error potential in the wording of questions is obvious. Questions should not "lead" the respondent to a particular answer. They should be easy to understand and unambiguous. They should produce answers that speak to the question. It's not a simple task. There are two schools of thought on the subject of question style. Some researchers prefer the closed question, in which respondents must choose from a fixed number of specific responses ("Do you approve

————— or disapprove ————— of a special tax for mass transit?" Others believe that the closed question leads to distortion, and advocate instead the use of open-ended questions in which respondents provide answers in their own words. ("How do you think funds should be obtained for mass transit systems?") The disagreement is likely to go on for some time.

Pretesting   After the questionnaire is completed, prudence demands that it be tested on a small group to discover flaws, such as ambiguous wording. Pretest subjects should be similar to those who will participate in the larger survey, but not the same respondents, of course.

Data Collection   If interviewers are used, they should be thoroughly trained in procedures and techniques. Excellent instructions can be found in a monograph published by the University of Michigan's Institute for Social Research, the *Interviewer's Manual*. Two major cautions for interviewers will help protect the integrity of the survey: the sampling plan should be followed faithfully, and respondents should not be coached on their answers.

Data Processing   The final steps in a survey include coding the responses so they can be transferred to computer cards, tabulating by computer, and analyzing the results. Most cities have commercial firms that will prepare computer cards from code sheets supplied by the customer. Computer time is also widely available on a rental basis. The researcher need not be a computer programmer, either. Many data analysis programs, written in non-mathematical language, are available, as are consultants at computer facilities. It is a good idea, however, to study the computer program that will be used *before* designing the questionnaire, so that responses can be coded to conform to the program. The analysis of data may consist simply of counting responses in different categories. If this is the case, and if there are few variables and a small sample, the counter-sorter machine may substitute for the computer.

Reporting Results   Although studies differ according to subject matter and findings, certain information should be included in published accounts of all surveys. This information gives the reader a basis for judging the validity of the findings. The National Council on Public Polls suggests seven disclosures that are necessary: sponsorship of the survey, if not evident; dates of data collection, if relevant to interpretation of the poll; method of interviewing (mail, personal interview, phone interview); wording of questions; size of sample; population sampled. and the data base used for the findings if it is less than the total sample. (The last item refers to situations in which only a portion of the sample responds to a question.) The American Association for Public Opinion Research advocates similar reporting guidelines, with one addition: an indication of the allowance that should be made for sampling error (the "confidence interval").

The foregoing is a skeletonized checklist of procedures followed in most surveys, small or large. It can serve as a starting point for the journalist who plans to undertake a survey, although much more is involved than the steps outlined here. A number of books offer detailed instructions on how to conduct a survey, including Meyer's *Precision Journalism,* Charles Backstrom and Gerald Hursh's *Survey Research,* and others listed at the end of the chapter.

That rigorous surveys are feasible projects for news organizations is evident from the increasing number appearing in print and on television. Consider this sampling of published work:

Staff writer John McCormick of the *Dubuque* (Iowa) *Telegraph Herald* produced this story on the results of a survey completed as part of a precision journalism workshop in 1974:

> SAGINAW, Mich.—The first pre-election survey since President Nixon's resignation indicates that Watergate continues to haunt Republican candidates, even though voters list inflation as their main concern.
>
> The survey, which involved 411 randomly selected citizens in Michigan's traditionally Republican Eighth Congressional District, found that voters currently perceive no difference between Republican and Democratic positions on economic and other non-Watergate issues.[21]

Although politics occupies a central position in newspaper research efforts, other subjects are often surveyed. Philip Meyer and reporter Michael Maidenberg conducted this questionnaire survey of 230 former college students. It appeared in the Knight chain of newspapers:

> The young men and women who began the student rebellion five years ago in Berkeley, Calif., are older and wiser now. Age has made them a little more settled and less visible, but it has not made them feel less radical.
>
> This finding, based on a six-month search for the rank-and-file Berkeley rebels of five years ago, contradicts a hope cherished by much of the older generation. The young movement is not a passing fling by over-active children. Its effects linger when their childhood is gone.[22]

The sample survey in the form of a statistical prediction model was employed in this 1974 study by reporter Bernie Shellum of the *Minneapolis Tribune:*

> Teachers will play a disproportionately powerful role in the shaping of a Democratic-Farmer-Labor platform and in the party's upcoming endorsement of candidates for the Minnesota House of Representatives. . . .
>
> In caucuses held in thousands of neighborhoods Tuesday night, the teachers, who represent less than 2 per cent of the state's voting age residents, were elected to fill 15 per cent of the DFL's precinct delegate spots. . . .
>
> Projections from the Minneapolis Tribune's 100-precinct model indicate that members of Common Cause, the so-called citizens' lobby for political reform, won 10 per cent of the DFL seats.[23]

These examples demonstrate the role played by precision journalism in obtaining information not available from conventional sources. The list could be expanded with dozens of stories both more and less elaborate than those described above. There is no dearth of available subject matter suitable for inquiry. Every time a reporter covers a story that leaves questions unanswered, he has a potential subject for research. Consider these:

Student Values. What are the values of high-school students today? An attitude survey might produce findings that run counter to expectations.

The "Lemon." There is always coffee-table conversation about automobile "lemons"—cars that are in the repair shop more often than out. What proportion of new cars are lemons? What do people do about them? A sample survey could provide the answers.

Food Prices. Food-market chains advertise prices that apply to all of their stores, but what about prices of nonadvertised items? Do these vary from store to store? Is there a relationship between price variation and the economic level of the neighborhood served by the stores? A careful survey could test this hypothesis.

Anyone can make up a list of researchable questions that would interest the public. Some, like those above, might be suitable for field surveys. But others may require experiments, and still others the analysis of available records and documents. These methods will be examined next.

The Field Experiment

Field surveys, it was noted earlier, are limited in their power to identify causes. So many factors operate at once in the real world that isolating one or two to examine alone is virtually impossible. Because of the many unmeasured factors in any survey environment, the researcher can rarely be sure that one or more of them isn't causing the phenomenon he's studying, rather than those he has chosen to measure.

A researcher may believe, for example, that voting is a function of the educational level. If a representative sample of voters is examined, it is likely that a relationship between regularity of voting and amount of schooling will be found. Still, the claim that more education leads to faithful voting habits can't be made with confidence; a number of other factors are possibly greater influences on voting (e.g., income level, cultural values, occupation, social pressure, distance from the home to polling place). Even if we manage to measure some of these other variables, there is always the possibility of still other variables that haven't been considered. The most likely explanation is that several factors account for voting habits, and the researcher's task is to identify all of them, measure them accurately, and attempt to determine through statistical analysis the relative magnitude of influence for each.

In the search for causes, experiments get around some of these problems. An experiment is a controlled situation in which the relationship between two or more variables can be examined by deliberately changing one and observing whether this change is accompanied by a change in the other.[24] In the jargon of science, the variable that is deliberately changed is known as the "treatment" or the "independent" variable. The one that is examined for effect is known as the "criterion" or the "dependent" variable. The researcher selects his subjects, or experimental groups, through unbiased random procedures. Typically, two groups are used in experiments: one receives the treatment, or suspected causal factor; the other, the control group, does not. Inasmuch as subjects for both groups were chosen randomly from a common population, it is assumed that they are equivalent on all extraneous factors. Many experimental designs are more complex than the one described, but it nonetheless illustrates the advantage of experiments over surveys because it can minimize third-variable explanations.

The procedure is so clean and logical that experiments are the preferred method in much of science, from biology to psychology. Most often they are conducted in laboratory settings, where conditions can be controlled. Unfortunately, they are more difficult to execute in dealing with social relations. Experiments can be conducted in the field by finding a treatment or independent variable that can be applied selectively to large population groups, but it is a difficult and expensive procedure. People are not easily accessible and manipulable in large numbers for extended periods. For a hypothesis such as the voting-education relationship, it would be impossible to "apply" education to one group, much less withhold it from another.

Even so, the field experiment is an option open to the social researcher and the precision journalist, and it is sometimes used. An example of its use in a communication context is the testing of different advertisements for a product in different marketing regions to see which has the greatest effect. The news media have rarely employed the field experiment as a reporting tool, but one approach has been widespread in recent years: the consumer protection study in which a product (e.g., an automobile or a television set) is purposely damaged before it is brought to repair shops. News stories then report which shops correctly identified the fault, which padded the bills with unneeded repairs, and the range of prices charged. The studies are sometimes done without proper controls, but they are experiments in a basic sense.

A clever use of the field experiment was demonstrated by the *Miami Herald* in 1973 and 1974. Dade County officials ruled that Spanish would be the county's second official language, requiring all government agencies to deal with the Spanish-speaking population in its native tongue. About a month after the ordinance was passed, the *Herald* selected 80 municipal agencies throughout the county, and had a Spanish-speaking reporter call each one and ask for assistance. In only about 8 per cent of the cases did the reporter get help in Spanish. The stories that followed the experiment made quite an impact. But a year later when the *Herald* repeated the experiment it found that the number of public agencies that could respond to a plea for help in Spanish had actually declined. (So much for the power of the press.)

Few news organizations use the experimental method, yet academic research provides many examples that could be adapted by journalists. One such example is offered by Meyer in *Precision Journalism:*

> Stanley Milgram of the City University of New York has reported how his students devised an experiment to test the relative helpfulness and trustingness of city dwellers as compared to residents of small towns. Two boys and two girls rang doorbells, told whoever answered that they had lost a friend's address, and asked to use the phone. They did this 100 times in middle-income housing developments in Manhattan and 60 times in small towns in Rockland County, N.Y. Girls had more luck than boys in getting in, regardless of location, but the city-town distinction was even greater. All four did at least twice as well in gaining entry to the small-town homes as they did in the city.[25]

Another example: A student in a precision journalism class at the University of Minnesota designed an experiment to test for apparent sex bias among employment agency job counselors. She arranged for men and women students to apply for jobs with a randomly selected group of agencies. Each applicant gave the same background description of himself or herself, and asked about identical job opportunities. The finding: more women than men were routed toward clerical jobs.

Imagination is the only limit to the range of field experiments possible for journalists, given time and resources. The method requires meticulous attention to detail and careful controls, as well as some knowledge of analysis procedures suitable for experiments. It is worth the journalist's attention both for the opportunity it presents to answer questions that defy other approaches, and for understanding the work of professional experimental researchers.

Mining Available Data

Surveys and experiments can be powerful reporting tools in trained hands, but they also have drawbacks. They usually are costly and time-consuming; few can recover information from the past; and they tend to produce biased data (i.e., people and their responses are changed by the very act of measuring them). These weaknesses are overcome by another research approach: analysis of public records, documents, and data archives.[26]

The use of records to gather information—from sifting through the daily police log to painstaking examination of property deeds—is a common reporting technique. Some of these uses were examined in Chapter 4. Searches of this type, however, are typically focused on a single person, transaction, or subject. Social science objectives in analyzing records have a broader target: aggregate information about larger populations or general topics. As with surveys and experiments, the purpose is to examine the relationship of one category of data to another. Though records can provide purely descriptive information, their greater use is to confirm or disprove beliefs, and to uncover trends. The Philadelphia criminal justice study described in this chapter is an example of the extensive use of court records to test hypotheses.

Court records have, in fact, become a prime source for precision journalists. The range of suitable archival material, however, is much broader. There are police files; voting registers; city, county, and state clerks' records of births, deaths, and much human activity between those extremes; and statistics compiled by governmental agencies at all levels. There are also records of private groups, such as trade associations, that are sometimes available to the reporter. Another source is the data archives gathered by several universities, which often are available to the public. The Survey Research Center at the University of Michigan is one such source, offering data from its lengthy series of national election studies, among other materials. Another depository is the Roper Public Opinion Research Center at Williams College, which collects data from more than forty commercial and academic survey organizations in the United States and abroad. Usually, this data is available on computer tape, making analysis less expensive and more convenient.

Computers have enabled newspapers to undertake massive records examinations that were previously beyond the practical reach of journalism. The *Dubuque* (Iowa) *Telegraph Herald* analyzed almost all traffic accidents in the city for a period of one year with the help of a university computer, and came up with these findings:

> Drivers who cause injury accidents are likely to be charged with fewer violations than drivers causing only property damage.
>
> Men tend to commit different traffic violations than do women.
>
> The high number of accidents occurring on streets slickened by weather conditions may evolve from a common fallacy: it appears that many drivers don't realize that treacherous road conditions linger hours or days after rain, snow, or sleet has stopped.[27]

In a similar computer-assisted study, reporters with the *Roanoke* (Va.) *Times* examined campaign finances in a state election and discovered that the candidates for governor spent a third of a million dollars more than their principal campaign organizations had reported spending.[28] The data was available under new election spending laws, but required 130,000 pieces of information on 13,000 data cards to analyze it usefully.

The granddaddy of all record sources is, of course, the U.S. Census. It presents an almost limitless body of information for the reporter with a computer who wants to analyze independently the characteristics of any defined geographic unit, from a city street to an entire state. Although census data is voluminous, much of it is unanalyzed, awaiting the enterprising journalist.[29] It is available both on computer tape (at major libraries and research centers) and in bound volumes, found in almost any community. Some of the data (age, sex, color, or race; marital status; and relationship to head of household) is based on interviews at every household in the nation, and is broken down by city blocks. Other questions are asked only of samples of the population (e.g., income, occupation, place of work, mother tongue), and the answers are available only for larger geographic units known as census tracts.

Though the comprehensive census of population is conducted at ten-year intervals, more current data is provided by the annual Current Population Survey, based on a sample of 35,000 households. Another useful records source is the *Statistical Abstract of the United States,* published annually and containing selected census information as well as other government-generated statistics.

How can reporters make use of census information? The possibilities range from extensive analysis of, say, voting patterns and population characteristics in a city, to bits of information that add perspective and meaning to breaking news stories. An example of the latter was demonstrated by several reporters covering the 1974 school busing protests in Boston. The neighborhood focus of the protests enabled the reporters to gain from the census books the data needed to describe the relevant characteristics of the residents: income levels, amount of schooling, national origins, size of families, and so on.

Sometimes, census information can generate an idea for a story. Reporter Randy Furst of the *Minneapolis Star* found that occupational listings for Minnesota showed sixteen categories in which all employees were men, and thirty-three occupations in which women constituted 2 per cent or less of the work force. Armed with that information, he developed several stories probing for reasons.[30] At other times, census data provides most of the information for stories, with the reporter adding confirmation or reaction to the statistics from field sources. Reporter Carl Griffin Jr. of the *Minneapolis Tribune* followed that route in developing a story on commuting practices in a thirteen-county region.[31] Census books provided information about the percentage of the labor force commuting to Minneapolis and Saint Paul, and their points of origin.

Sources need not always be formal records. Some of the most useful and accurate information is produced by simple observation or comes from unintended sources. In their monograph, *Unobtrusive Measures,* Eugene Webb and his co-authors describe many ingenious ways researchers have obtained otherwise inaccessible information.[32] How, for example, can whisky consumption be measured in a town that is officially "dry"? One researcher's method was to count empty bottles in trash cans. In another case cited by Webb and his colleagues, the question was raised about the effect of a newspaper strike on retail shopping. An answer was found by examining parking meter revenues before and during the strike.

Whatever the source of the data, systematic methods must be employed in order to assure validity and accuracy. Records involving large numbers of units can be approached with the same random sampling procedures used for surveys. A first step is defining the "population" to assure consistency—for example, all the Democrats on the voter lists, or all the murders and homicides from court records. After that, a unit of analysis must be determined so that the same attribute is measured or counted for each case. If health conditions in restaurants were the subject under study, for example, the unit of analysis might be an employee serving food and the presence or absence of hairnets.

Caution must be exercised in records analysis, as with any other research method. Just because the source is a record does not assure it is accurate. Reporters should determine how the records were compiled, and whether they contain built-in biases. They should also tread carefully when making comparisons among records from different sources. Some criminal acts, for instance, are felonies in one state but misdemeanors in another. Unless this fact were known, a study comparing rates of felonies in the two states would be distorted. The danger of making careless causal inferences because of an observed association between two factors is also ever-present. Records can be a gold mine for the alert reporter, a mine field for the unwary.

Social Indicators

One of the growth fields of social science in the 1970s, if not *the* glamor field, has been the development and use of social indicators. A social indicator is a relatively easily obtained measure of a population characteristic that permits inferences about another characteristic that can't be measured. The first measure is often a simple counting statistic, such as average income; the second an abstraction, such as happiness. Some might say the higher the average (real) income, the higher the happiness in a community.

Indicators themselves aren't new. Some, like employment rates and school attendance, have been used for decades to tell us something about the state of the economy and the culture. Until recently, however, many indicators weren't sufficiently refined to provide precise predictions or valid representations of current conditions. In the past few years social scientists in several disciplines have turned to the development of new and better indicators. The activity has been so widespread and intense that the Institute for Social Research at the University of Michigan has described the investigations as "a new frontier in social science." [33]

The area of greatest interest and activity has been in the "quality of life" studies. Indicators have been developed to evaluate important aspects of community life, enabling planners, political leaders, and citizens to be guided in decisions about community needs and priorities. They also permit comparisons between communities, and measurement of progress over time.

One of the more active organizations in the social indicators field in the United States is the Urban Institute, of Washington, D.C. It began in 1969 to take available measures in many areas of concern (e.g., health and crime) and to develop models in order to interpret the indicators in relation to human welfare. One such model measures the state or condition of human well-being in terms of consumption of goods and services.[34] This model has been applied to several areas of social concern, such as housing and neighborhoods, and learning and education.

One of the Urban Institute's major works, and one that attracted massive news media attention,[35] was a study comparing eighteen large metropolitan regions on fifteen quality-of-life categories.[36] Each category was measured by one available statistic. For example, health was measured by infant deaths per 1,000 live births; citizen participation by the percentage of the voting-age population that voted in recent presidential elections. On infant mortality, as one illustration, Minneapolis-St. Paul was rated best among the eighteen cities, Chicago worst.

Some quality-of-life studies are based on discrete behavioral data, such as the Urban Institute's indicators. Others, such as those sponsored by the Institute for Social Research, tend toward psychological indicators, measured through field surveys.[37] An example would be social or political alienation, obtained through tests of sample populations. The psychological measures reflect public perception of the quality of life; the behavioral measures a more objective assessment of that quality.

Interest in social indicators appears to be high in the news media, judging by their use of reports on the studies. Journalists are going much beyond the mere reporting of formal studies in their use of indicators, however. *Time* magazine examined statistics describing trends in income distribution among blacks in 1972, and discovered a growing schism between blacks who are catching up with the white population in income, and those who are falling behind. These income statistics were interpreted by *Time* writers to indicate the creation of two societies within black America—separate and unequal.[38]

Another use of available statistics for indicating social conditions and prospects is demonstrated by this excerpt from an article in the *Washington Monthly:*

The 1970 census reveals another major demographic fact: that the potential for migration of poor people (mostly Southern blacks) to the cities has sharply declined. . . . The absolute number of blacks outside the metropolitan areas diminished only slightly in the last 10 years. With almost 60 per cent of all blacks now living in the central cities, one of America's historic migrations is coming to an end, at least relatively, and quite possibly in absolute numbers. The lessening of this influx of poor people will reduce the demand on city budgets for public services. This reduced migration, when coupled with declining birth rates for both blacks and whites in the cities, should reduce the pressure for the spread of ghettos.[39]

Of course, much use of social indicators by the news media is not so heavily interpretative. Economic indicators are presented in news columns almost daily, ranging from the familiar stock market price indicators to the cost-of-living index, the wholesale price index, and literally hundreds of other indexes compiled for specialized interests by government, business, and other institutions. The opportunity for journalists to discover and use indicators applying to their own communities—or to develop their own indicators—is new and challenging.

The key to developing indicators is the discovery of suitable available statistics, or the collection of such statistics. Often, social indicators are index numbers (such as the cost-of-living index) that must be constructed with skill and caution. Index numbers sometimes represent simple averages or, more frequently, weighted averages of a series of data. A given average is taken as a base (e.g., cost of certain goods and services in 1970), and the other averages for the same goods and services in later years are expressed as ratios or percentages in relation to the base. The result is an index number. Usually, index numbers are expressed as a percentage of some base value, which is taken as equal to 100. If the cost of a market basket of goods in the base year was $50, the base becomes 100. If the cost of the same market basket rises to $75 a year later, that would become 150 on the index scale.

Although the development of new indicators is an option open to journalists, most will probably rely on existing measures. Some of the measures used in the Urban Institute study of eighteen cities included: [40]

Social Disintegration: estimated narcotics addiction rates per 10,000 population.

Mental Health: reported suicides per 100,000 population.

Racial Equality: ratio between white and nonwhite unemployment rates.

Community Concern: per capita contributions to United Fund appeals.

Poverty: percentage of households with incomes less than $3,000 per year.

With these and other established indicators, the news media can monitor the quality of life in a community on a continuing basis. The public would be served with a psycho-social weather report, telling it about its climate of life at one point in time and providing it with an early-warning system for problems ahead. Used with caution, appropriate advice, and training, social indicators offer the news media another opportunity to bring interesting and useful information to their viewers and readers.

Statistics and Bikinis

Statistics, a perceptive wag once remarked, are like bikinis. What they reveal is interesting. What they conceal is vital.

Disraeli was more direct. There are, the British statesman said, three kinds of lies: lies, damned lies, and statistics.

Others are more charitable. Figures, they say, don't lie, but liars figure. Author Darrell Huff capitalized on that belief with what may be the all-time best seller among books dealing with numbers. His irreverent

monograph, *How to Lie with Statistics,* has gone through more than twenty printings since it first appeared in 1954.[41]

Applying this aura of pervasive if healthy incredulity about statistics to the field of precision journalism, a double challenge arises. The reporter must conduct his own research in a way that doesn't mislead his audience. He must also guard against distortion from statistical information that comes through the newsroom door from other sources. Whether the error comes from intent or from honest mistake, the problem remains: when the reporter is gulled, his public also is gulled. The increasing amount of social science and other quantitative research in the news today testifies to the potential of the problem. Two examples, one a report on "outside" research, the other a case of newspaper enterprise, will show the range of the problem:

On November 9, 1965, the greatest power failure in history darkened New York City and most of the Northeast. About 30 million people were without lights, in some areas for more than twelve hours. The impish question in everyone's tongue was, "What did you do when the lights went out?" The implication was that bereft of television and other energized diversions, people would naturally turn to bed. Together. The *New York Times* decided to test this theory nine months later. Its story, picked up by newspapers all over the world, appeared on August 10, 1966: "A startling increase in the birth rate has been reported by hospitals here in the last 36 hours, exactly nine months after the big blackout." [42]

The *Times* based its conclusion on a survey of eight hospitals in New York City. One had twice the normal daily average of births. Five reported slight increases, and two reported no change. The only problem with the conclusion was that it was wrong. The *Times* did not include enough hospitals in its sample, nor were the eight selected randomly. A few days later, after reports from 100 hospitals throughout the city were studied, a different picture emerged. The number of babies conceived on that dark November night was actually slightly lower than normal.[43] Stories correcting the initial error appeared, but myths die hard. Seven years after the baby boomlet was deflated, this item appeared in a national magazine:

LONDON—Having ordered television off the air by 10:30 P.M. to conserve energy, the British government is now concerned that earlier bedtimes will lead to a baby boom similar to that which occurred in New York nine months after the Northeastern U.S. was blacked out by a massive power failure in 1965.[44]

The *Times* mistake was caused by improper sampling for a rudimentary descriptive survey. Sometimes the journalist must confront much more complex research questions. Consider the second example.

"TV Violence Held Unharmful to Youth," read the headline in the *New York Times* of January 11, 1972. Under it, a story by television editor Jack Gould gave details of the U.S. surgeon general's report on the effects of television violence on children.[45] The series of studies on which the report was based, Gould wrote, indicates that there is no compelling evidence that viewing violence leads to aggressive behavior in children.

A week later, hundreds of other newspapers ran headlines similar to this one in the *Seattle Post-Intelligencer:* "Study Links TV Violence to Children, Says Official." [46] The story that followed quoted Surgeon General Jesse L. Steinfeld as saying that research showed for the first time a link between television and real-life violence.

Why the disparity between these two stories (and many others that appeared in the same time period)? Gould based his story on an eighteen-page summary of the research findings that he had obtained a week before the official release date. He was forced to rely on his own interpretation of the findings. When the report was officially released to the press on January 17, Steinfeld backed away from the "no connection" conclusion that appeared in the summary.

Complicating the situation for reporters was a dispute over the meaning of the findings among members of the research teams that had participated in the thirty-month, million-dollar project. Some contended that a link between television and aggression was not definitely established. Others asserted that the connection was proved. Their conflicting claims appeared in a 260-page cover report that accompanied the five volumes of data produced by the study.

The point of this discussion is not which group of scientists was correct, but rather the role of journalists in presenting and interpreting complex research. The failure of reporters in properly presenting the television-violence report is widely recognized. The public endured weeks of inconsistent stories until the press finally dropped the subject. Many of the researchers blamed the press for the confusion. Asked for their reaction to media coverage, fifteen of twenty-one project investigators responding to a questionnaire said it was, in general, "inaccurate." [47]

One of the investigators, Steven H. Chaffee of the University of Wisconsin, blamed the inaccuracies on what he described as the media's "scoop mentality," and the fact that few reporters have had training in social research methodology. Said Chaffee in a report to a professional research group two months after the report was released:

> In all, then, we should not be surprised that the first news story on the committee report was written a week before the report was issued, that the article was inaccurate and misleading, that the headline was much more so, and that—since the story appeared in the New York Times—it set the tone for subsequent reporting on the committee report.[48]

The problem for journalists was pinpointed by Newsweek magazine,[49] which concluded that it would require "an almost professional familiarity with sociological parlance" to grasp the significance of conflicting arguments in the cover report. "Such expertise," the Newsweek writer allowed, "is not readily available around most newspaper city rooms."

The solution is obvious. Journalists must develop at least a minimum level of sophistication about social research methods. The television-violence fiasco might be interesting only from a historical standpoint if similar situations didn't occur with depressing frequency. On the premise that one can learn from the mistakes of others, here is a sample of just a few types of press mishandling of research information:

Crime statistics are a staple item for news organizations. Police and sheriffs' departments, state agencies, and the Federal Bureau of Investigation regularly issue reports on crime rates. Stories developed from these reports are familiar to all:

> Serious crimes in the city went up (or down) 11 per cent in the past three months, Police Chief Bruce Stalwart reported yesterday.

or:

> The rate of burglaries in Integrityville increased last year, while the rate in Pottstown decreased, according to state crime statistics released today.

The only problem with these stories is that the data on which they are based are notoriously inaccurate. Crime reporting procedures vary markedly from city to city, and even within cities. Residents in some communities report a larger percentage of crimes to police than do residents of other communities. Some police departments manipulate statistics to inflate law enforcement achievements. Different bases for records are often used. These and other flaws in crime statistics are spelled out in a series of studies conducted in 1973 and 1974 for the Law Enforcement Assistance Administration of the U.S. Department of Justice.[50] The message for reporters is clear: Qualify stories about crime statistics, and warn readers about their evaluation. One other opportunity is always present. News organizations can conduct their own field surveys, perhaps annually, to serve as a check on police reports of crime rates.

Sampling irregularities account for a major portion of research mistakes, with the self-selected sample a chief offender. A Chicago daily in 1973, for example, asked its readers to "vote" on whether they favored giving reconstruction aid to North Vietnam. About 1,700 responded, with the vote almost 10 to 1 against aid.[51] This percentage was projected to reflect sentiment in Chicago, rather than the 1 per cent of that newspaper's readers who responded. In a similar case, a national Sunday newspaper supplement, with a circulation of 12 million, published a questionnaire in one issue. It received "more than 25,000 replies," on which it based conclusions about "typical" parental concerns about children's television programs.[52] Another common mistake that gets into print is the survey by congressmen, which usually pops up a month or two before election day. These surveys typically send questionnaires to all households in a congressional district, with response usually at the rate of 10 per cent.

Each of these examples involves large samples, certainly as large as, or larger than, those used by commercial pollsters. Yet sample size alone does not guarantee accuracy, unless it approaches 100 per cent of the population. More important, as discussed earlier in this chapter, is the quality of randomness. When a survey permits respondents to select themselves as participants, bias must be assumed. All types of people don't answer surveys; studies have found that certain types of people will usually respond, and others will never respond. Those who do participate are hardly representative of the population as a whole.

Comparing findings from two different studies is a particularly dangerous practice. The results of a Gallup poll and a Roper poll on the same subject may differ markedly, despite valid sampling procedures. One reason for the difference may be the timing of the two surveys. If they were done in different weeks, events may have intervened to change public opinion. Another reason is differences in the wording of questions. Subtle differences in language are known to produce different results. Reporters should also look for comparability in the data bases in two surveys. Consider this story distributed by a news service in 1974:

WASHINGTON, D.C.—Two new studies show that teen-agers are just as likely to run afoul of the law in rural areas as in big cities.

In rural Oregon, a study by the University of Oregon showed that 25 per cent of the 16- to 18-year-old males in one county had a record with the juvenile department, excluding minor traffic violations.

In a Philadelphia study . . . 35 per cent of the teen-age boys had a juvenile record, including traffic offenses.[53]

Two sources of invalidity are evident. The age groupings differ, with one including all teen-agers, the other covering only three years. One study included traffic offenses, the other didn't. Beyond that, there is no indication that other categories of juvenile crime were recorded similarly in the two regions, or that enforcement practices in rural Oregon and urban Philadelphia are comparable.

The three classes of potential error just described represent the tip of an iceberg. Dozens of other analytical traps await the unwary—or un-trained—reporter. In addition to inadequate samples and inappropriate comparisons, a list of the more common pitfalls would include:

Miscounting. Perhaps it isn't surprising, but the most common statistical error is a mistake in computation. Checking addition, subtraction, multiplication, and division should be a reportorial routine.

Correlation. Interpreting a correlation between two factors as evidence of a causal connection is rarely justified. Always look for spurious associations and other variables that may explain the findings.

Percentages. Many people use percentages improperly. A rise in the cost of living from 100 to 150, for example, is a 50 per cent increase, not 33 per cent. A classic misuse of percentages is in applying them to small numbers. If there are only two copy boys in a city room, and one of them is eventually hired as a reporter, it would be misleading to say that 50 per cent of copy boys become reporters.

Charts. Manipulation of the scales on charts or graphs can distort the meaning of the data. Choosing the proper scale is a judgmental matter, with no fixed rules, but critical examination is always wise in order to avoid deception. If a chart doesn't contain a zero point, for example, try to ascertain whether it would make a difference in the configuration of the data. Also, see if representing data in percentages gives a different impression than would the raw figures.

Exaggerated Accuracy. Presenting statistical projections to the second decimal point can lead to spurious accuracy. If a health agency is quoted as estimating the number of new cases of tuberculosis at 112,426 next year, compared with 108,079 this year, the precision of the figures themselves claims more accuracy than deserved. These and similar estimates are often based on samples, and rounding the numbers would avoid imparting undeserved confidence in them.

Statistics and Style

A central tenet of good reporting is reader identification, demonstrating the relevance of news situations to the individual. Unless the reader can see himself related to the story in some way, he's not likely to go beyond the headline and lead paragraphs.

Helping the reader to identify with story content is more difficult with the quantitative approaches of precision journalism. How, after all, can someone find himself in a percentage? Yet the presentation of aggregate data is often essential to an understanding of civic and social problems. Author and journalist Martin Mayer once observed succinctly that "societal as distinguished from individual reality is always statistical." In the journalistic context, his observation means that writing exclusively about individuals can't produce an accurate picture of the larger community. The challenge to reporters, then, is to make the statistically-described societal reality palatable by bringing in the individual reality as well.

This approach was illustrated in the *Philadelphia Inquirer* court study quoted at the beginning of the chapter. Some of the people who made up the percentages used later in the story were described first. They became flesh-and-blood humans, who served to illuminate classes of people lumped into statistical categories.

The Berkeley rebels study mentioned earlier deals with the attitudes and behavior of 230 former students. By tabulating their responses to standard questions, writers Meyer and Maidenberg were able to describe the group as a whole. Anticipating the need for individual reality, however, the writers interviewed thirteen of the respondents personally. From these interviews, they obtained enough quotable material to illustrate any of the statistical findings in the study. The survey found, for example, that 70 per cent of the former students considered themselves more radical five years after their participation in the Free Speech Movement. Meyer and Maidenberg evoked personal reality for that statistic with passages like this one:

> But for the few flamboyant leaders like Jerry Rubin, there were many followers like Jane Nielsen: quiet, soft-spoken, out of the public eye. She works as a letter-sorter in the Berkeley post office, trying to earn enough money to go back to school. . . .

"Since FSM I've become more radical, really," she says. "Then I had some qualms about sitting in as a means of demonstrating. Now my only problem is with violence, would I be aligning myself with it or not. I would condone it but I don't know if I would be there." [54]

Interviewers conducting surveys can obtain useful quotes for later consideration by writers. In a survey of residents following a speech by President Nixon on the Watergate affair, the *Seattle Post-Intelligencer* found that almost half of the respondents thought the president was not telling the truth. A third said they believed his version of the burglary, and the remainder were uncertain. To illustrate these groupings, newspaper interviewers obtained quotes that added dimension and emotion to the cold statistics:

"What does he take us for? Idiots?" said one Bellevue resident. "No, I don't believe him."
"I've been standing here cooking dinner, thinking about it," said a resident of southeast Seattle. "I wholeheartedly think he knew nothing about it. I'm shook up, but I still have faith in the president." [55]

Obviously, statistical and individual reality complement each other in this example. The approach is similar to a reporting method known as "humanistic newswriting," in which the focus is placed on the impact of news on the individual. Journalism professors Alex S. Edelstein and William Ames, who coined the term, define humanistic writing this way: "It is individualized and personalized, in the hope that the reader will see common threads of experience between his own life and that of another individual. . . . If the reader can identify with another person's experience, he feels less isolated as a human being. He develops a greater understanding of others and becomes more able to cope with events." [56]

An example of humanistic reporting and its straight news counterpart can be seen in these leads about a rise in real-estate and housing costs. First, the conventional treatment:

The price of a new single-family house has risen more than twice as fast as the increase in the consumer price index in recent years, according to a report by the National Industrial Conference Board.[57]

The same subject was introduced this way in the *Wall Street Journal*:

There is this married woman in the East who is in love with this airline pilot in the West. And he is in love with her. So they have made plans to marry.

But they cannot start out on a shoestring. Expenses of a divorce, a wedding, a new home were to have been paid from the pilot's stock portfolio. Until the market dropped. There are other examples:

While the pilot is postponing his marriage, a 73-year-old Cleveland man is postponing his retirement. A Boston man is having second thoughts about buying a $24,000 Mercedes. The backers of a screenplay have pulled out. And a Chicago executive has ordered his wife to serve cheaper cuts of meat.[58]

There is a danger in the case-study approach, of course, that the writer will restrict his story to examples. To be useful, the story must move from the specific to the general. Economist Herbert Stein complains that journalists sometimes resort to this technique, attempting to draw general significance from a few selected cases. "These vignettes really aren't significant unless the people represent some general category," Stein writes. "And we can only tell that from the statistics, however unreliable they may be." [59]

Stein's challenge to reporters is being met today in those news organizations that value fluency in numbers as well as fluency in language. The marriage of precision journalism and humanistic newswriting is fortuitous, stable, and productive.

NOTES

1. Philadelphia *Inquirer* (Feb. 18, 1973).
2. The descriptive phrase "precision journalism" was suggested to Meyer by Everette E. Dennis, a co-author of this book. See Meyer, *Precision Journalism: A Reporter's Introduction to Social Science Methods* (Bloomington: Indiana University Press, 1973).
3. "Equal Justice for All? . . . It's a Myth," Philadelphia *Inquirer* (Feb. 18, 1973, p. 3).
4. Training of journalists in research methods is examined by Philip Meyer, Social Science Reporting" (pp. 149f), and Jack Lyle, "Study of Urban Life" (pp. 213–26), in *Education for Newspaper Journalists in the Seventies and Beyond* (Reston, Va.: American Newspaper Publishers Foundation, 1973).
5. Opportunities and problems in newspaper reporting of social science subjects are exhaustively examined in Frederick T. C. Yu, ed., *Behavioral Sciences and the Mass Media* (New York: Russell Sage Foundation, 1968).
6. Meyer, *Precision Journalism,* p. 13.
7. Ibid.
8. Ibid., p. 15.
9. Ben Bagdikian, Chapter 3, "A Review of Session One," in *Behavioral Sciences and the Mass Media,* p. 47.

10. J. Edward Murray, speech to the Georgia Press Institute (Athens, Ga., February 23, 1973).

11. Meyer, *Precision Journalism*, p. 292.

12. A brief treatment of the history and uses of statistics can be found in Boris Parl, *Basic Statistics* (Garden City, N.Y.: Doubleday, 1967), pp. 1–4.

13. Both sides of the question are treated in Denton E. Morrison and Ramon E. Henkel, eds., *The Significance Test Controversy* (Chicago: Aldine Publishing, 1970). See also Meyer, *Precision Journalism*, p. 94.

14. Hubert M. Blalock, Jr., *Causal Inferences in Nonexperimental Research* (New York: Norton, 1964) offers a thorough examination of the causation in survey research.

15. Claire Selltiz, Marie Jahoda, Morton Deutsch, and Stuart W. Cook, *Research Methods in Social Relations* (New York: Holt, Rinehart and Winston, 1959), p. 422.

16. U.S. Congress, House Subcommittee on Library and Memorials, Committee on House Administration, *Public Opinion Polls*, hearings on H.R. 5003, 93rd Cong., 1st sess., 1972 (Washington: U.S. Government Printing Office, 1973).

17. Leo Bogart, *Silent Politics* (New York: Wiley, 1972), p. 17.

18. Ibid., p. 18.

19. Michael Rappeport, "The Distinctions the Pollsters Don't Make," *Washington Monthly* 6 (March, 1974), 13.

20. Ibid.

21. *Dubuque* (Iowa) *Telegraph-Herald* (Aug. 26, 1974).

22. *Miami Herald* (Jan. 1, 1970), p. 1.

23. *Minneapolis Tribune* (March 3, 1974), p. 1.

24. Definition adapted from Barry F. Anderson, *The Psychology Experiment* (Belmont, Calif.: Wadsworth Publishing, 1966), p. 21.

25. Meyer, *Precision Journalism*, p. 249.

26. See Eugene J. Webb et al., *Unobtrusive Measures: Nonreactive Research in the Social Sciences* (Chicago: Rand McNally, 1966) for exploration of the range of archival material.

27. *Dubuque* (Iowa) *Telegraph Herald* (Dec. 1, 1974), p. 1.

28. *Roanoke* (Va.) *Times* (Feb. 10, 1974), p. 1.

29. Meyer, *Precision Journalism*. Chapter 12 contains a detailed description of census examination procedures.

30. *Minneapolis Star* (July 22, 1974), p. 1B.

31. *Minneapolis Tribune* (Jan. 27, 1974), p. 1B.

32. Webb et al. *Unobtrusive Measures*.

33. University of Michigan, Institute for Social Research, *Newsletter* (Summer, 1974), 3.

34. Harvey A. Garn, Michael J. Flax, Michael Springer, and Jeremy B. Taylor, "Urban Institute Working Paper 1206–11," Mimeographed (Washington: Urban Institute, 1973).

35. *New York Times* (Oct. 21, 1973), p. 1.

36. Michael J. Flax, *A Study in Comparative Urban Indicators: Conditions in 18 Large Metropolitan Areas* (Washington: Urban Institute, 1972).

37. University of Michigan, *Newsletter.*

38. *Time* (Sept. 3, 1973), p. 75.

39. Michael Rappeport, "The Cities Turn a Corner," *Washington Monthly* 4 (March, 1972), 30.

40. Flax, *Study in Comparative Urban Indicators.*

41. Darrell Huff, *How to Lie with Statistics* (New York: Norton, 1954).

42. "Births Up 9 Months After Blackout," *New York Times* (Aug. 10, 1966), p. 1.

43. Another aspect of the Northeast blackout is reported in an essay by W. Phillips Davison, "The Russell Sage-Columbia Program in Journalism and the Behavioral Sciences" in *Behavioral Sciences and the Mass Media,* p. 221: "During the New York power failure last November, many of the news media reported that, in the face of the shared calamity, New Yorkers became more friendly, more neighborly. A survey conducted by the Columbia Bureau of Applied Social Research during the blackout found that such a reaction was indeed characteristic of those belonging to the higher educational and income groups. Poorer, and more ignorant people, on the other hand, tended to feel more isolated and to show more signs of apprehension. The research thus suggests that journalists assigned to cover popular reactions during similar emergencies might well be advised to seek out representatives of different social classes when making interviews. Indeed, awareness of class structure and of the different reaction patterns of different population strata is probably relevant to a great many news stories. . . ."

44. *Playboy* 21 (May, 1974), 61.

45. Surgeon General's Report, *Television and Growing Up: The Impact of Televised Violence* (Washington: U.S. Government Printing Office, 1972).

46. *Seattle Post-Intelligencer* (Jan. 18, 1972), p. A1.

47. Matilda D. Paisley, "Social Policy Research and the Realities of the System: Violence Done to TV Research" (Stanford, Calif.: Institute for Communication Research, Stanford University, March, 1972).

48. Steven H. Chaffee, "Television and Growing Up: Interpreting the Surgeon General's Report" (Paper presented to the Pacific chapter, American Association for Public Opinion Research, Asilomar, Calif., March, 1972).

49. *Newsweek* (March 6, 1972), p. 55.

50. Reports on the National Crime Panel surveys were carried in newspapers of April 15, 1974 and Nov. 28, 1974.

51. Reported in *Time* (April 9, 1973), p. 10.

52. *Parade* (March 4, 1973), p. 12.

53. Newhouse News Service article, published in the Minneapolis *Star* (Sept. 18, 1974), p. 10C.

54. *Miami Herald* (Jan. 1, 1970), p. 1.

55. Seattle *Post-Intelligencer* (May 2, 1973), p. A-1.

56. Alex S. Edelstein and William E. Ames, "Humanistic Newswriting," *The Quill* 58 (June, 1970), 28.

57. Ibid., p. 30.

58. Ibid.

59. *Newsweek* (July 29, 1974), p. 11.

SUGGESTED READINGS

Andriot, John L., *Guide to U.S. Government Statistics*. Washington: U.S. Government Printing Office, 1974. An annotated listing of more than 1,700 recurring government publications, along with more than 3,200 titles in major statistical projects.

Backstrom, Charles, and Gerald Hursh, *Survey Research*. Evanston: Northwestern University Press, 1963. An intelligent cookbook approach to the conduct of a field survey, taking the reader step by step through all required procedures.

Blalock, Hubert M., Jr., *Causal Inferences in Nonexperimental Research*. New York: Norton, 1964. Examines the difficulty of determining cause from survey findings, and suggests new approaches.

————, *Social Statistics*. New York: McGraw-Hill, 1972. A comprehensive and well-written introduction to basic statistics, for the serious student.

Campbell, Donald T., and Julian C. Stanley, *Experimental and Quasi-Experimental Designs for Research*. Chicago: Rand McNally, 1966. A small paperback, with information vital to the proper design of experiments.

Hyman, Herbert, *Survey Design and Analysis*. Glencoe, Ill.: Free Press, 1955. The standard work for years, and an excellent reference for problem-solving.

Kish, Leslie, *Survey Sampling*. New York: Wiley, 1965. Standard definitive work on sampling procedures and limitations.

1970 Census User's Guide. Washington: U.S. Government Printing Office, 1970. Necessary reference for getting the most from available census data.

Parl, Boris, *Basic Statistics*. Garden City, N.Y.: Doubleday, 1967. Reviews briefly statistical concepts and procedures ranging from the elementary to the advanced.

Phillips, John L., Jr., *Statistical Thinking: A Structural Approach*. San Francisco: W.H. Freeman, 1973. Introduces statistics without computation, concentrating on concepts. Ideal for beginners.

Sheldon, Eleanor B., and Wilbert E. Moore, eds., *Indicators of Social Change*. New York: Russell Sage Foundation, 1968. Comprehensive treatment of concepts and methods employed in social-indicator research and applications.

Webb, Eugene J., Donald T. Campbell, Richard D. Schwartz, and Lee Sechrest, *Unobtrusive Measures: Nonreactive Research in the Social Sciences*. Chicago: Rand McNally, 1966. Readable presentation of nonconventional approaches to research.

Williams, Frederick, *Reasoning with Statistics*. New York: Holt, Rinehart and Winston, 1968). Practical and lucid guide to data analysis.

chapter six

Understanding Communication Law

No system of freedom of expression can succeed in the end unless the ideas which underlie it become part of the life of the people. There must be a real understanding of the root concepts, a full acceptance of the guiding principles, and a deep resolve to make the system work.

THOMAS I. EMERSON
The System of Freedom of Expression

The inadvertent turn of a phrase or an accusatory statement may be among the issues that bring a reporter into a legal conflict. In spite of the absolute ring of the First Amendment ("Congress shall make no law. . . ."), the rights of the press frequently collide with the rights of individuals, groups, or even the government. When this happens, communication law litigation involving such issues as libel, privacy, and free press-fair trial may result.

It is almost a truism to say that public affairs reporters should maintain an interest in, and knowledge of, the law of mass communication if for no other reason than self-protection. Schools and departments of journalism usually insist that their students take at least one course in communication law, but beyond this requirement there are few efforts to keep journalistic practitioners aware of legal trends and circumstances.

Yet the public affairs reporter who does make an effort to stay current with communication law can have a real advantage over his colleagues who may slavishly rely on the timid advice of the company lawyer. This is not to suggest that reporters should second-guess their newspaper's or broadcast station's attorney, but they should know enough

126

about the law as it affects them to ask substantive questions. A vigilant reporter who follows the law with care may know more about libel law, for example, than a company lawyer who spends most of his time on financial matters, labor negotiations, and tax problems.

Sometimes thorough investigative reporting requires tough-minded articles that ease toward the ragged-edge of libel. Many of the exposés of government officials' wrongdoing were initially threatened by libel suits. Even the *New York Times* would have averted its celebrated 1971 confrontation with the Federal government over the Pentagon Papers had the editors followed the cautious legal advice of the firm representing the newspaper. Sanford Ungar in his account of that case, *The Papers & The Papers,* chronicles the resistance of the *Times's* lawyers and how they were eventually overruled.[1]

Journalists covering the complexities of the public arena commonly hear legal threats and thus must be especially careful in their work while maintaining a delicate balance between justifiable caution and appropriate revelation. This chapter attempts to suggest some parameters for that balance, to mention briefly important areas of communication law, and to chart a direction for the conscientious journalist who wants to keep pace with communication law. No attempt is made here to offer an exhaustive compendium or guide to self-protection. The law is dynamic with frequent contours and changes. Keeping up with it, even in a specialized area, requires an energetic commitment by the journalist.

The Law of Libel

State laws of libel, which frequently confront reporters, were "intended to protect the individual against unfair damage to his reputation."[2] Samuel G. Blackman, a general news editor of the Associated Press, says that "from a practical standpoint, the chief causes of libel suits are carelessness, misunderstanding of the law of libel, the extent of the defense of privilege and the extent to which developments may be reported in arrests."[3] Defining libel, communications scholars Harold L. Nelson and Dwight L. Teeter write: "Libel is defamation by written or printed words, by its embodiment in physical form, or by any other form of communication which has the potentially harmful qualities characteristic of written or printed words."[4] Libel, explains legal scholar Thomas I. Emerson, "applies to a communication that subjects a person to ridicule, hatred or contempt in his community or lowers him in the estimation of his fellows."[5] Dean William L. Prosser, a distinguished authority on tort law, suggested that of all laws defamation law is one of the most complex. There is no agreement on what precise interests must be damaged in order for libel to exist, but according to Emerson some of them are said to include:

1. Injury in one's trade, profession or other economic pursuits.
2. Injury to prestige or standing in the community, which affects one's position as decision-maker or participant in the community.
3. Injury to feelings, arising out of an affront to one's dignity, distortion of one's identity, reflection on one's honor, or lessening of the approval of one's peers.[6]

Naturally, many news stories that reflect negatively on persons might be considered libelous. Communication law scholars Donald M. Gillmor and Jerome A. Barron say it is necessary to determine whether the libel is actionable and what defenses the journalist can offer. They explain that actionable libel requires "(1) defamation, (2) identification, and (3) publication." [7] Thus, there must be an injury to reputation; the injury must be applied to an identifiable person; and the statement must be published or broadcast. (Group libel and criminal libel, which involves the government, are not treated here.) Importantly, the burden of proof in a libel suit must be understood. Gillmor and Barron explain:

In the first instance, the person bringing a libel action must persuade the court that a defamatory publication has been made concerning him. Ambiguity is for the jury. Since the law presumes that a defamation is false, the publisher then has the burden of pleading an affirmative defense such as truth, good motives, privilege or fair comment. The burden then shifts to the plaintiff to show that a defense of privilege or fair comment has been nullified by malice on the part of the publisher, or that a defense of truth has been lost for want of good motives or justifiable ends.[8]

There are four defenses against libel that the press can invoke in litigation: truth, qualified privilege, absolute privilege, and fair comment and criticism. There is "only one complete and unconditional defense to a civil action for libel," [9] says an Associated Press report on libel: "That defense is that the facts stated are provably true." Note well the word, *"provably."* Though often repeated, this assumption is not quite accurate. Other unconditional defenses to a libel suit are: (1) consent, (2) the statute of limitations and (3) political broadcasts under the Equal Time provisions of Section 315 of the Federal Communications Act. These are absolute defenses. Furthermore, truth alone is an unconditional defense in only about half of the states.

Privilege is an exemption in the law in which the social good in communicating certain information in the public interest overrides damage to individual reputation. Absolute privilege applies to individuals testifying at official court proceedings or before legislative bodies. As Nelson and Teeter put it: "Anyone who reports proceedings is given an immunity from successful suit for defamation; and for the public at large, 'anyone' ordinarily means the mass media. The protection is ordinarily more limited for the reporter of a proceeding than for the participant in the proceeding. It is thus called 'qualified' (or 'conditional') privilege, and is qualified in that it does not protect malice in reports." [11]

The fourth defense in libel actions—fair comment and criticism— has undergone considerable change in recent years. Originally, it was intended to protect persons (including the press) in assessing public officials, institutions, and other visible public activity. Fair comment and criticism applied as long as there was no malice, but unfortunately for years the courts had a variable standard of malice and no one was ever sure what it was. In 1964 the defense of fair comment and criticism was more fully defined in the landmark Supreme Court case of *New York Times* v. *Sullivan*. In that case the court ruled that a public official is prohibited from recovering damages for a defamatory falsehood relating to his official conduct unless he proves that the statement was made with "actual malice—that is with knowledge that it was false or with reckless disregard of whether it was false or not." [12] That, in effect, provided the long-needed definition of malice. The *New York Times* doctrine was eventually extended from public officials to public figures ("persons caught up in the vortex of public discussion") in a series of progeny cases. By 1971 when the *Times* malice rule had been extended to purely private persons caught up in public events, some commentators thought that "the law of libel has been all but repealed." [13] Although this assumption did not seem unreasonable at the time, the number of libel suits continuing after this period necessitated abandoning it. In 1974, the Supreme Court pulled back from its liberal standard (as developed further in *Rosenbloom* v. *Metromedia*) in the case of *Gertz* v. *Welch*. "It is clear," wrote D. Charles Whitney in *The Quill*, "that the ruling destroys musing that libel suits are a thing of the past." [14] The result of the case, as Whitney wrote, was:

A private individual, even if speaking on a public issue can now collect actual damages in a libel suit if he can prove negligence on the part of the publisher. In addition to collecting the actual damages to his reputation, the person can collect for personal suffering and mental anguish. To collect punitive damages, however, a person must prove "actual malice" on the part of the publisher. It is up to the state courts now to determine who is a private individual, as opposed to a public citizen, and define the boundaries of negligence.[15]

A 1974 memorandum prepared by Arthur B. Hanson, general counsel to the American Newspaper Publishers Association, states "that publishers no longer have the protection of the *New York Times* rule when libel is alleged by a private individual, involved in matters of public interest, who seeks to recover actual provable damages." [16]

What the *Gertz* case indicates is the dynamic nature of the law and particularly the law of libel. Resources for reporters who want to keep pace with libel law are given at the end of this chapter.

Reporters and Privacy

As with libel, reporters often find that the rights of a free press can collide with the right of individual privacy. Emerson offered this keen observation in distinguishing between privacy and libel:

> Communication that invades the inner core of the personality, assaulting the dignity of the individual by depicting matters of a wholly personal and intimate nature, may be subject to government control. Under existing legal doctrine, if such a communication contained matter that was false and defamatory, it would be governed by the law of libel. If the matter was not false, it would be subject to a privacy action.[17]

For years scholars have spoken of the "law of privacy" as differentiated from the "right of privacy." The right of privacy is implicit in the Constitution and in various social and political rights. The law of privacy, first proposed by two legal scholars in a law review article in 1890,[18] is narrower and more specific. It refers to the specific statutory provisions for the protection of privacy, for the right "to be let alone." Statutes for privacy protection in the United States are relatively recent in origin, and vary considerably from state to state. Dean William Prosser, the leading authority on torts, has written that there are four kinds of torts included under privacy. They are:

1. Intrusion on the plaintiff's physical solitude.
2. Publication of private matters violating the ordinary decencies.

3. Putting plaintiff in a false light in the public eye, as by signing his name to a letter attributing to him views he does not hold.

4. Appropriation of some element of plaintiff's personality—his name or likeness—for commercial use.[19]

Privacy scholar Don R. Pember says that courts dealing with press privacy cases must work toward a "desirable compromise":

> In almost every case the problem before the court could be reduced to this simple question: Which is more important, the protection of society by a free and unfettered press, or the individual's claim to personal solitude? When the publication has involved commercial or false material, the court usually has sided with the individual. In this case the public interest involved was not great enough. When the publication has been a truthful or factual account of even private or personal affairs, the court usually has sided with the press. Here society's interest in a free press took precedence.[20]

Usually two defenses are advanced by the press in privacy cases. They are (1) newsworthiness and (2) consent. In the first instance, courts decide that the publication of the material, even though it invaded a person's privacy, was in the public interest. In the second, the individual simply gave consent to have the information published, either by signing a release or by seeing the reporter in the first place. Of course, complex arguments can be marshalled in both areas as the adversary process of a trial unfolds.

Not until 1967 did a privacy case reach the Supreme Court of the United States. In *Time Inc.* v. *Hill* the Court extended the *New York Times* malice rule (reckless disregard or knowing falsehood) to privacy cases and ruled that in some instances the First Amendment prohibited state courts from imposing liability upon a publication for an invasion of privacy. Privacy, like libel, is an active area of the law and bears careful observation.

Free Press-Fair Trial

Another focal point for rights in conflict between the press and the public is in the area of free press-fair trial wherein the First Amendment right of a free press runs head on into the Sixth Amendment "right to a speedy and public trial, by an impartial jury. . . ." Celebrated public trials in which the press offers heavy, detailed and sometimes sensationalized coverage have led to considerable conflict between the press and the bar. The conflict came to a head in the mid-1960s when the American Bar Association appointed an advisory committee on fair trial and free press headed by Justice Paul C. Reardon of the Supreme Judicial Court of Massachusetts. The Reardon commission, working concurrently with a number of statewide bar-press efforts, recommended some standards for the release of material in criminal trials. The recommendations, however, were generally rejected by the press.

While the bar-press discussions on reporting restrictions did not have the force of law, they were generally adopted by many courts and by the U. S. Justice Department.[21] Agreements generally ran along the lines of this press-bar code adopted in the State of Minnesota:

Recommended Guidelines of
The Fair Trial-Free Press Council of Minnesota
Relating to Adult Criminal Proceedings:

The following information generally SHOULD be made public at, or immediately following the time of arrest:

1. The accused's name, age, residence, employment, marital status and similar background information.
2. The substance or text of the charge, such as is, or would be contained in a complaint, indictment or information.
3. The identity of the investigating and arresting agency and the length of the investigation.
4. The circumstances immediately surrounding an arrest, including the time and place of arrest, resistance, pursuit, possession and use of weapons, and a description of items seized at the time of arrest.

The following information generally should NOT be made public at, or immediately after, the time of arrest:

1. Statements as to the character or reputation of an accused person.
2. Existence or contents of any confession, admission or statement given by the accused, or his refusal to make a statement.
3. Performance or results of tests, or the refusal of an accused to take such a test.
4. Expected content of testimony, or credibility of prospective witnesses.
5. Possibility of a plea of guilty to the offense charged or to a lesser offense, or other disposition.
6. Other statements relating to the merits, evidence, argument, opinions or theories of the case.

Cooperation between the bar, law enforcement officers, courts, and the press is substantial, especially at the local level, students of free press-fair trial agree. In numerous cases, however, the potential for prejudicial publicity is high. In fact, one recent study linked prejudicial pretrial publicity to adverse jury verdicts.[22] The massive press coverage of the Watergate period made it difficult for the courts to find impartial jurors. The reasoning of courts in proceeding to try cases even in instances of heavy publicity, says Lesley Oelsner of the New York *Times,* is as follows:

It is impossible in an age of mass communications to find reasonably intelligent jurors who have heard nothing about famous cases; defendants in sensational cases should not be freed before at least an attempt has been made to try them; the courts can often meet the problem of prejudicial pretrial publicity by delaying the trial until the publicity abates, moving the trial to a town where publicity is less extensive, sequestering the jury, ordering lawyers and witnesses not to talk to the press, and interviewing prospective jurors carefully.[23]

Although some agreements have been worked out between the press and the judicial system, the area of free press-fair trial is by no means settled. Jack C. Landau, Supreme Court reporter for the Newhouse News Service and a trustee of the Reporters Committee for Freedom of the Press, has suggested that a long-term, bitter institutional conflict between press and courts is likely unless so-called "gag orders" by judges are controlled. Gag orders are issued without hearing or explanation when judges forbid coverage of certain proceedings. Four types of gag orders have been detailed by Landau:

First are direct prior restraints on information obtained out of court. Second are restrictions on access to information in court. These access limitations are mechanical; they limit the numbers of reporters admitted to the courtroom. Third are restrictions on attorneys, police and other officials with responsibilities in a given case. Very frequently the press argues the prosecution has had a terrific advance start on publicity—and the defense wants its point of view known. Finally, there is the problem of confidential sources —the cases where the attorney is ordered to divulge his source or go to jail. [24]

Organizations such as the American Society of Newspaper Editors, Reporters Committee on Freedom of the Press and American Newspaper

Publishers Association have kept a close watch on the free press-fair trial issue. In most states there are free press-fair trial councils and compacts.

Other Areas

The long-standing debate over "shield laws" recognizing the right of reporters to protect confidential sources has raged in recent years. The heavy use of subpoena power by the Department of Justice in the early years of the Nixon administration, which led to some celebrated court cases, has heightened the interest in shield laws. The result has been a call for a national shield law and the passage of shield laws (some absolute, some qualified) in many states. These cases usually arise in instances when courts cite the press for contempt for refusing to reveal sources. Pointing to practical and conceptual difficulties, the Supreme Court in *Branzburg* v. *Hayes,* a 1972 case, said that the newsman's privilege was defined by the court as being outside its purview. As Justice Byron White wrote in the majority opinion: "At the Federal level Congress has freedom to determine whether a statutory newsman's privilege is necessary and desirable and to fashion standards and rules as narrow or broad as deemed necessary. . . ." [25]

Of particular interest to public affairs reporters are state statutes for open meetings and open records. Although they differ considerably from state to state, the general idea is that public business should be conducted in full public view. In some instances these laws are called "sunshine" laws. A reporter should familiarize himself with the open meetings and open records legislation of his state or efforts to obtain such statutes. It is helpful in knowing whether or not a school board can declare an "executive session" and refuse to admit reporters or whether a city council can have sub-rosa ways of not discussing the public business openly in council meetings. Frequently, the absence, presence, or application of open meetings and open records laws has been the cause of conflict between public officials and the press.

Conclusion

As might be surmised from the foregoing discussion, the application of communication law to the press should be seen in the context of journalistic ethics. The legal protection and subsequent defenses come in court (sometimes called the court of last resort) when the interpersonal bargaining between the press and individuals or government ceases. Nevertheless, reporters need a good working knowledge of press law. One pathway toward that knowledge is as follows:

1. Take a course in press law or communication law in a college or university, or attend a short course or special seminar on the subject.
2. Familiarize yourself with a major treatise on the subject (for example, Nelson and Teeter's *Law of Mass Communications* or Gillmor and Barron's superb casebook, *Mass Communication Law*.
3. Familiarize yourself with the law of your particular state or locality, either through special materials developed by local publisher associations or through Arthur B. Hanson's detailed, three-volume, state-by-state compendium, *Libel and Related Torts*.
4. Keep a handy desk reference on press law—either one of the major treatises or a shortened version like Paul B. Ashley's *Say It Safely* or the Associated Press's *The Dangers of Libel*.
5. Follow current press law developments in the *Press Censorship Newsletter*, published by the Reporters Committee on Freedom of the Press; the *FoI Reports*, published by the Freedom of Information Center of the University of Missouri, or such random sources as *Editor & Publisher* and *Broadcasting*.
6. For more detailed knowledge, search law reviews (through the *Index to Legal Periodicals*) and other legal periodicals for the current status of particular cases.
7. Watch the book reviews of such publications as *Journalism Quarterly* for materials of special interest.

The importance of a knowledge of press law in competent journalistic performance cannot be overestimated. Reporters who avoid controversy, fearing litigation unnecessarily, may be doing themselves and their public a disservice.

NOTES

1. Sanford Unger, *The Papers & The Papers* (New York: Dutton, 1972).
2. Thomas I. Emerson, *The System of Freedom of Expression* (New York: Vintage Books, 1971), p. 518.
3. Associated Press, *The Dangers of Libel*, rev. ed. (New York: AP, 1969), p. 1. See also Paul B. Ashley, *Say It Safely* (Seattle: University of Washington Press, 1966).
4. Harold I. Nelson and Dwight L. Teeter, *Law of Mass Communications*, 2d ed. (Mineola, N.Y.: Foundation Press, 1973), p. 61.
5. Emerson, *System of Freedom of Expression*, p. 518.
6. Ibid.
7. Donald M. Gillmor and Jerome A. Barron, *Mass Communication Law: Cases and Comment* (Saint Paul, Minn.: West Publishing, 1974), p. 194.
8. Ibid., p. 214.
9. Associated Press, *Dangers of Libel*, p. 3.

10. *Black's Law Dictionary,* rev. 4th ed. (Saint Paul: Minn.: West Publishing, 1968), p. 1360.

11. Nelson and Teeter, *Law of Mass Communications,* p. 140.

12. *New York Times* v. *Sullivan,* 376 U.S. 245 (1964).

13. See Frederic Coonrandt, "The Law of Libel Has Been All But Repealed," *Quill* 60 (Feb., 1972), 16–19.

14. D. Charles Whitney, "Libel: New Ground Rules for an Old Ball Game," *Quill* 62 (Aug., 1974), 22.

15. Ibid., p. 23.

16. Arthur B. Hanson, "Term 'private' in Libel Ruling Stumps Attorneys," *Editor & Publisher* 107 (Aug. 31, 1974), 15.

17. Nelson and Teeter, *Law of Mass Communications,* p. 183.

18. See Samuel D. Warren and Louis D. Brandeis, "The Right of Privacy," 4 *Harvard Law Review* (Dec., 1890), 193–220.

19. Nelson and Teeter, *Law of Mass Communications,* p. 183.

20. Don R. Pember, *Privacy and the Press, The Law, the Mass Media, and the First Amendment* (Seattle: University of Washington Press, 1972), p. 249. Pember's contention is supported in two recent cases, *Cantrell* v. *Forest City Publishing Co.,* 95 S. Ct. 465 (1974); and *Cox Broadcasting Corporation* v. *Cohn,* 95 S. Ct. 1029 (1975).

21. Gillmor and Barron, *Mass Communication Law,* p. 415.

22. "Jury Verdicts Linked to News Reports," *New York Times* (Oct. 21, 1973), p. 23.

23. Lesley Oelsner, "Watergate Jury Quest: Pretrial Publicity Creates a Problem That Many Believe Is Insurmountable," *New York Times* (Oct. 11, 1974), p. 14C.

24. Jack C. Landau, "Free Press-Fair Trial," 15 *Criminal Law Reporter* (Sept. 4, 1974), 2489.

25. *Branzburg* v. *Hayes,* 408 U.S. 665, 706 (1972).

part two

Public Affairs Settings

chapter seven

Covering the Legal Process

It is one of the press's great—if not greatest—responsibility to provide the essential information regarding the administration of justice, without which no progress whatever is possible in a democratic society.

CURTIS D. MACDOUGALL
Covering the Courts

Public affairs reporting has its historic roots in the coverage of courts. One of the first collections of newspaper reportage, John Wight's *Mornings at Bow Street* (1824), provided a moving, human glimpse of English courts. It is appropriate that law, the legal process, and its consequences shall continue to absorb the attention of journalists in a democracy. "The law is, among other things, a series of commands about how people in a society ought to behave,"[1] writes political scientist Jonathan Casper. The legal process is the mechanism by which disputes are settled when informal interaction fails. Intensely human and rife with drama, the legal process is also a stage on which conflict is resolved.

Because the legal process is a highly visible index of society coping with its problems, it has been standard fare for media coverage. Even so, "the legal process is one of the most fundamental yet least understood aspects of American government,"[2] law professor Marc A. Franklin asserts. In part, this lack of understanding may be because the law and legal process are so rarely treated by reporters in the context of their total functioning, but rather as individual and unrelated cases. Not without reason, the legal scholar Morris L. Cohen has written of "the lawless science of our law, that codeless myriad of precedent, that wilderness of single instances."[3] For, as Cohen implies, the law is, in fact, cumulative and dynamic. Operating within the somewhat stable framework of the legal process, individual cases—the results of personal disputes or conflicts between the individual and the state—lead to legal principles and theories of recovery. The tendency for the reporter and for the citizen is to look narrowly at single instances—disputes in a vacuum—without considering the overall context of the legal process. One hears of a settlement in a civil suit or of conflicting testimony in a criminal case, but only as fragments of a larger picture.

The Legal Process Defined

To Marc Franklin, the legal process is the distance between the arising of a grievance between individuals (in a civil case) * or between individuals and the government (in a criminal case) and its final resolution in either the trial court or the appellate process. While there are some variations in procedure between civil and criminal cases, there is much similarity in their movements. The process, using Franklin's explanation, can be described as follows:

1. *A grievance arises.* A dispute between individuals cannot be resolved at the level of personal discussion.

2. *An attorney is retained.* The aggrieved party finds his way to an attorney who advises whether or not the issue should be pressed in a court case.

3. *The attorney identifies the relevant law.* He examines the legal consequences of the facts of the case.

4. *Researching the law.* The attorney searches the various sources of law (statutes, constitutions, court opinions) to make a systematic determination about the chances for recovery.

5. *Choosing the court system.* In the United States, there are federal courts and state courts. In both the civil and criminal areas, federal courts deal severally with federal questions arising under the Constitution or federal statutes, disputes between residents of different states and between states themselves. Most other matters are first handled in state courts.

6. *Choosing the correct court.* Once the correct court system is determined, the lawyer or, in some instances, law enforcement officers must choose the correct court within that system. The magnitude of the offense (in a criminal case) and the amount of damages or type of relief sought (in a civil case) will determine the court where the case will be tried initially. Minor cases (traffic violations, misdemeanors, small claims) are assigned to municipal or local courts, whereas more serious criminal charges, larger money claims, divorces, and real estate claims are resolved

* See Appendix A, "The Newsman's Guide to Legalese."

by district or circuit courts, which are ordinarily courts of first instance in most jurisdictions. Money amounts sought or the extent of punishment that the court may render determine the choice of the correct court. All state "blue books," or governmental directories, describe the functioning of courts and the appropriate names for the particular location. Courts, their names and responsibilities differ considerably among the various states, and the reporter must learn the idiosyncracies and nuances of his own area.*

7. *The action commences.* A legal action begins when the plaintiff's attorney does two things: "(1) starts the 'pleading' stage by putting in writing the plaintiff's 'complaint' and what he wants from the defendant; and (2) takes steps to bring this 'complaint' to the defendant's attention." [4] In a criminal case, the state issues a formal charge or presents an indictment.

8. *The complaint is served.* The defendant (or party against whom an action is brought) is served with a formal complaint, itemizing the charges or grievance against him.

9. *The defendant's turn comes.* Once notified that he is to be a party in a legal dispute, the defendant also seeks an attorney who follows many of the procedures indicated earlier.

10. *Choosing a defense.* A defense is decided upon by the attorney and his client, and the attorney drafts an "answer" to the original complaint. The complaint and the answer are called "pleadings." These are public records, open to the press (and public) for inspection. In a criminal case, the first stage of the defense is the entry of a plea. In a civil case, Franklin says, "almost always the defendant asserts that there are mistakes or inaccuracies in the plaintiff's case in one or more of four categories: (1) technical objections unrelated to the merits of the case; (2) disputes about the underlying legal rules implicit in the plaintiff's complaint; (3) claims that the plaintiff's fact allegations are not true or that he has omitted some vital facts; and (4) claims that the damages sought are too high." [5]

11. *Pretrial activities.* These are in several areas, including: (a) *judgment on the pleading.* ("The party making the motion asserts that with all the pleadings filed, no fact disputes remain so that there is no reason for a trial and the judge should decide the case now"); [6] (b) *discovery* (Through written interrogatories, oral depositions and by providing documents and other physical evidence, both sides share information about the case to narrow the dispute). Discovery is more extensive in civil cases than in criminal, but is a process that virtually prevents the kind of unrealistic courtroom confessions that take place in television dramas and also

---

* See Appendix B, "Federal and State Court Structure."

make unlikely the appearance of surprise witnesses; and (c) *conferences* (Fact disputes are narrowed and exhibits marked by pretrial agreements and discussions).

12. *Jury selection and trial beginning.* Although some parties in a case waive jury trials, jury selection is often a vital part of the case. Lawyers try to get juries that will favor their client.

13. *The trial.* The trial consists of the plaintiff's case, the defendant's case, including direct and cross examinations, and occasional rulings by the judge on objections and motions by attorneys. Eventually, the case goes to the jury and under the American system of justice, juries decide questions of *fact,* not questions of *law.* That is, the jury decides whether a car ran a red light at a particular time, not whether running the red light should be actionable. The jury eventually renders a verdict and the judge can accept it or grant a post-trial motion brought by the losing party.

14. *Post-trial motions.* These include "judgments n.o.v." which are judgments notwithstanding the verdict. The judge rules here that the jury came to an "impossible" decision (one contrary to the evidence or the law), and renders a judgment for the other party.

15. *Judgment order.* In a civil case the judge concludes that the jury was correct and directs by judgment that payment of civil damages be made. In a criminal case a sentence is pronounced.

16. *Appeals are made.* Making claims that there were errors in the trial, the losing party might ask for an appeal to a higher court. Appeals in state cases go to intermediate appeals courts (in California and New York) or to the State Supreme Court or its equivalent. There is also an appeals structure in the federal system from district courts to circuit courts of appeal to the United States Supreme Court.

17. *The appeal is decided.* A decision based on briefs presented by the opposing parties is eventually rendered by the appeals court if the case is accepted for consideration.

Each phase of the legal process as sketchily outlined here is worthy of considerable study. Unfortunately, much of the dynamic nature of the legal process is hidden from the public and is rarely treated by the news media. Such issues as how people find attorneys, the nature of legal fees, and pretrial conferences are largely ignored.

While Franklin's description of the legal process as the movement from an initial grievance to the appeal structure is useful to the reporter in considering the context of most legal disputes, the term "administration of justice" has come to have a more discreet meaning. Here the emphasis is on the various components of the legal system, rather than the process itself. For example, the system is seen as having three components: law enforcement agencies or police; adjudicatory agencies including courts and bar associations; and corrections, including jails, prisons, and facilities for forensic psychiatry. It is on these components of the system that most media coverage focuses.

Efforts to improve the quality of criminal justice in the United States during the 1970s often added a fourth component: crime prevention. It was a component aimed at reducing crime through preventive programs prior to police intervention or through rehabilitation programs at intermediate stages between courts and prisons.

Covering the Legal Process

The complexity and scope of the legal process may work against comprehensive analytical reporting. A cursory examination of most newspapers and newscasts indicates that there is more news about crime, police activities, individual trials, and prison riots than interpretative reporting of legal trends, law firms, performance of judges, or penology. Of course, this is in line with conventional news standards and news judgment.

The 1966 Reardon commission (on Fair Trial-Free Press) report found considerable cooperation between reporters and those charged with the administration of justice. But the journalist covering the legal system is often an "outsider" treated with a cold correctness. Legal sociologist Abraham S. Blumberg says that personnel throughout the legal system "are deeply suspicious of—almost hostile to any effort to unearth embarrassing material." [7] In his daily activity, a member of this system soon learns, says Blumberg, "that too often the fact that he 'talked too much' meant conviction for an accused person." Blumberg continues: "This virtually hostile attitude toward 'outsiders' is in large measure a psychological defense against the inherent deficiencies of assembly-line justice, so characteristic of our major criminal courts. Intolerably large case loads, which must be handled with limited resources and personnel, potentially subject the participants in the court community to harsh scrutiny from appellate courts and other public and private sources of condemnation." [8] Media critic Edward J. Epstein thinks reporters are at a disadvantage in covering the legal process. Pursuing truth and finding an image of reality proves difficult for the journalist. Epstein says:

> Reporters possess no such wherewithal for dealing with evidence. Unlike the judicial officer, journalists cannot compel a witness to furnish them an account of an event. Witnesses need only tell reporters what they deem is in their own self-interest, and then they can lie or fashion their story to fit a particular purpose without risking any legal penalty. [9]

In covering complex legal problems, reporters can mislead the public, Epstein maintains. In the late 1960s a series of violent incidents involving the Black Panthers led to serious misreporting. "The reporters closest to the Black Panthers could not dispute their (the Panthers') public claim that an organized campaign of genocide was being waged against them. . . ." [10] Taking a larger view buttressed by several months of research, Epstein disputed this claim in his highly praised *New Yorker* article, "The Black Panthers: A Question of Genocide." [11]

News media sources in law enforcement, courts, and corrections, as well as others interested in legal problems, promote different images of the legal process. In a study of the criminal justice system from a defendant's perspective, Jonathan Casper suggests three images of reality:

> (1) On television we see a dramatic, carefully controlled process, in which each side is represented by committed, often brilliant attorneys jealously guarding and defending the rights of their clients. Mistakes may be made, but truth and justice generally triumph: the guilty are convicted and punished, and the innocent are vindicated and set free. We see the adversary process at its finest, operating to protect the rights of defendants and to arrive at a judgment conforming to absolute truth.
>
> (2) If, on the other hand, we listen to professional prosecutors, police officers and critics of recent Supreme Court decisions, a somewhat different picture emerges. We see a victimized majority and hamstrung police and prosecutors, unable to deal effectively with those who violate the law. We see a scale balanced unevenly in favor of the criminal defendant. These critics conjure up the image of the crazed bad man—the mugger, the rapist, the junkie—free to pursue his heinous activities because of procedural protections that hamper his capture, conviction, and punishment.
>
> (3) If, finally, we examine the growing body of reformist literature dealing with the criminal justice system, we find the image of an assembly line. The system is a machine which begins with raw material consisting of those arrested. They are processed and emerge as a product; the convicted criminal, sentenced to prison or released on probation. Between arrest and disposition are a series of points on the assembly line. . . .[12]

Naturally, these points of view are fostered by different, but equally self-serving, sources for the reporter. Yet too often, coverage of law enforcement agencies, the courts, and the corrections system today has serious flaws. As journalism professor David L. Grey points out:

> The press often handles such complex fields as law by preoccupation with personalities, drama, action and other often-superficial issues.

Time magazine is the institution, of course, which has probably most glamorized news about names; but skimming or scanning most daily newspaper front pages or television newscasts shows perhaps even more preoccupation with who-just-did-what-to-whom rather than the more substantive issues of what-is-going-on-and-why.[13]

With the antagonism between police and press in the 1960s, particularly during the demonstrations and riots, has come criticism of the press's role in covering such events. A study team, reporting to the National Commission on the Causes and Prevention of Violence, found that some police complaints about press coverage were justified:

> There is some explanation for the media-directed violence. Camera crews on at least two occasions did stage violence and fake injuries. Demonstrators did sometimes step up their activities for the benefit of TV cameras. Newsmen and photographers' blinding lights did get in the way of police clearing streets, sweeping the park and dispersing demonstrators. Newsmen did, on occasion, disobey legitimate police orders to 'move' or 'clear the streets.' News reporting of events did seem to the police to be anti-Chicago and anti-police.[14]

Other observers have found that coverage of police news suffers because of attitudes and methods the police reporter brings with him. "Too soon," writes Police Lieutenant James Robertson in the *Twin Cities Journalism Review*, "the eager young reporter attempts to flex his journalistic muscle, and rather than develop rapport—at least an avenue of sound communication—he attempts to demonstrate to his superiors how adept he is in dealing with the police. Soon, there is a head-on confrontation with the police, and the reporter's effectiveness is soon diminished substantially, if not completely."[15]

Coverage of corrections institutions—prisons, lockups and workhouses—has only recently begun to deal with substantive issues. "For the most part," writes attorney William J. vanden Heuvel, "the press has accepted arbitrary and ridiculous regulations that keep it from reporting the true nature of our institutional tragedies. It has been content to report events such as prison riots."[16] He explains:

> The responsibility of the news media is to lift the veil of secrecy surrounding the nation's prisons, to give voice to both the victims of crime and of the criminal justice system, and to reveal the incredible waste that our jails and penitentiaries represent. . . .
> The simple conclusion is that the reporting of criminal justice has been grossly inadequate to the country's need. Billions of dollars are being spent on a system that does not work. Vigilant observation

of the exercise of governmental power is a basic need in a democracy. Yet large sectors of the criminal justice system—from police power through procedures of the courts into the walled recesses of the prisons—operate practically without objective scrutiny and evaluation.[17]

Some corrections officials also see the need for more complete press coverage of penal institutions and issues. In evaluating press coverage during his administration, David Fogel, former commissioner of corrections in Minnesota, writes:

> It is my belief that public information is vital to correcting corrections. The cost of an "open access to the media" philosophy can sometimes be burdensome, but I believe necessary. I would have liked more analysis than was present. Sometimes the individual parts do not make up the whole. Programs or incidents taken serially were not well connected to indicate the real issue. For example, an escape, a runaway, a lockup for a non-violent demonstration all seem, as individual acts, to show "chaos" in the prison—the press very infrequently "put it all together." [18]

Reporting Functions and the Legal Process

A heightened awareness of the importance of legal process and criminal justice stories has been evident in recent years as thoroughly researched stories about the quality of judges, police performance, specific crimes (such as rape), and court procedures have had generous treatment by various publications and broadcast outlets. The *Minneapolis Tribune,* for example, assigned three reporters in 1974 to examine the quality of juvenile justice. They wrote a seventeen-part series that included careful examination of juvenile court cases and extensive interviews with juvenile offenders, corrections officials, and judges.[19] Jack Newfield's 1972 article, "The Ten Worst Judges in New York," spoke candidly about the administration of justice in New York City.[20] The *Chicago Tribune,* in a 1973 series, examined dozens of cases of police brutality and suggested positive steps for the screening and training of police recruits.[21]

These articles, and others like them, indicate a widening role of the reporter covering police, courts, and corrections. What should be the objectives of the reporter in these areas? Several come to mind:

Helping to Control and Prevent Crime. Although reporters are not police auxiliaries, and ought not to function as a publicity arm for police departments, one of the hoped-for effects of thorough coverage of crime is to prevent it.

Helping To Provide Due Process. By considering the administration of justice story from the standpoint of the defendant in both civil and criminal cases, the press can help prevent maladministration by police, judges, and others. This approach can also give readers and viewers an empathetic view of "what it is like to be arrested, go to court, be convicted and perhaps be sent to prison." [22]

Critical Surveillance of the Legal Process. By exposing activities and practices not in the public interest, the press can help the legal system function in the best interests of all. Reporters who take this role seriously have exposed police corruption, helped unfairly convicted defendants prove their innocence, and promoted, as a side effect, legislation to improve the legal process.

Making Sense out of Single Cases. Interpretative reporting can help the public understand what the fragmented single-instances mean. Often, crimes are reported as single incidents. In many large newspapers, only major crimes are reported in any detail. By examining single cases in context, and as a group, the reporter can help make sense of the process. In 1972 the *Minneapolis Star,* for example, summarized twenty-five murders in the city in the previous six months.[23] The articles included a breakdown of the victims and suspects by age, race, and sex, as well as by location of the murders; the stories also drew comparisons between Minneapolis homicides and national patterns.

In all of these functions, the reporter should "humanize" his stories, by making them understandable to the layman. Most citizens have only an occasional brush with the legal system, usually in the form of a court appearance for a minor traffic violation, a minor civil claim against another person, or a common legal matter such as a divorce or legal title search on a piece of property. Most citizens never become defendants in a criminal felony case, nor become entangled in a complex civil suit, nor find themselves indicted by a grand jury. Most people's exposure to the trial process, for example, may come from television shows such as "Perry Mason," but such "trials" bear little resemblance to reality. The reporter, aware of his reader's lack of knowledge, should be careful to provide information that is understandable. Every story should offer the reader enough information to fully understand the case. One obvious task for the reporter, therefore, is to translate technical legal jargon into understandable English. To do that, the reporter should have a clear understanding of legal principles and terms. (Legal research is discussed later in this chapter.) This necessity does not mean that the public affairs reporter must be an attorney, although an increasing number of reporters, such as attorney-reporter Fred Graham, who covers the U.S. Supreme Court for CBS News, are trained in the law.

Covering Civil and Criminal Actions

Writing about civil and criminal cases requires different investigative, research, and writing strategies. Civil law cases generally, but not always, require more legal research on the part of the reporter. Precedents and legal interpretations are cited more often in civil cases. In legal research, the reporter gains an understanding of how the specific cases relate to trends and developments in the law. By research of cases on racial integration, for instance, the reporter can grasp important changes that led up to, and followed, the U.S. Supreme Court's landmark desegregation case, *Brown* v. *Board of Education* (1954). Since civil suits often involve several plaintiffs and defendants, the reporter should be careful to understand the legal position of each, and to weight them fairly and accurately in news stories. In interpretative reports, such as an examination of divorce law, the reporter needs to interview plaintiffs and defendants, as well as authorities on the issue who are not parties to the cases.

Accuracy is vital in reporting all types of public affairs, and it is particularly important in criminal court cases. Criminal statutes are specific, and to identify incorrectly the crime of which a person is accused is as serious an error as a false accusation of crime. Auto theft, for example, differs in some states from "unauthorized use of a motor vehicle," although both may be felonies. The reporter who assumes one is the other without checking the statute is simply being careless. It is the kind of carelessness for which a reporter and his publication may have to pay libel damages.

Criminal cases generally don't require the extensive legal research of civil cases, but the writing techniques are just as rigorous. Every effort must be made to place the trial, arrest, hearing, or other criminal proceeding in context. This effort could well involve extensive interviewing. Because prosecution officials—district attorneys, police, investigators— may be more accessible to the court reporter assigned to cover the courthouse, there is a tendency for the reporter to leave the defendant uninterviewed. At the very least, the reporter should attempt to contact the defendant's attorney, particularly if the case appears to be one worthy of extended coverage.

All of this means an approach to legal reporting that goes beyond the superficial. "The trouble is," writes one jurist, "too many newspapermen and perhaps too many lawyers and judges *act* too often, again, at least on a day-to-day basis, *as if* these things were neither important nor interesting, and scarcely worth our time." He cites specifics:

We can improve our techniques. We can cover the ball game, the trial itself, and the real evidence in court—not the before, through the eyes of a self-serving sheriff, or the after, through the eyes of the winner or loser. We can use more discretion and acuteness. We can check both sides. We can describe and report the physical facts, even help gather them; but we should not take sides in conclusions. Lawyers and judges and juries are occasionally wrong—how do newsmen get to be so cocksure? On sources, we can ask ourselves the questions: is he in a position to find out? is he smart enough to find out? did he find out the truth? does he have any reason to lie? would he lie if he did have a reason? has he told me the truth? [24]

Most criminal trials begin with a police investigation, followed by the filing of a formal complaint by a prosecutor, or indictment by a grand jury. The reporter who wants to cover such legal actions accurately must have a firm understanding of the police investigations that precede the courtroom activity.

Covering Police and Law Enforcement Agencies

The police reporter must be able to write accurately and concisely on fast-breaking news stories such as crimes, traffic accidents, fires, and natural disasters. He must be able to convey human emotions accurately and sympathetically without being maudlin, for every crime and tragedy has one or more victims. He must be able to convey police attitudes without being either "copper-hearted" or overly critical. In short, he must be an effective interviewer, and writer, with considerable energy and enthusiasm for journalism, since the police beat is a demanding one.

The relationship between police and press is often strained. As Professor Arthur Niederhoffer, a former New York City policeman, explains: "Distrust and suspicion, so deeply imbued in policemen, often alienate those agencies upon whom they depend: the press and the courts. The police need the support of the press in order to clarify their attitudes for the public. They need the cooperation of the courts because police arrests must be validated by conviction in court. Yet the police often take pains to offend journalists and judges by impugning their motives." [25] When Niederhoffer surveyed 220 police officers, he found that 72 per cent believed that newspapers in general "seem to enjoy giving an unfavorable slant to news concerning the police, and prominently play up police misdeeds rather than virtues." For patrolmen with between two and twelve years' experience, the figure was 95 per cent.[26] As a report to the National Commission on the Causes and Prevention of Violence suggests, police-press relations are particularly strained during civil disorders. The *Report of the National Commission on Civil Disorders,* which studied the causes of riots in the 1960s, found that:

> A recurrent problem in the coverage of last summer's disorders was friction and lack of cooperation between police officers and working reporters. Many experienced and capable journalists complained that policemen and their commanding officers were at best apathetic and at worst overtly hostile toward reporters attempting to cover a disturbance. Policemen, on the other hand, charged that many reporters seemed to forget that the task of the police is to restore order.[27]

The experienced police reporter recognizes the importance of maintaining trustworthy police contacts. While some police are especially critical of the news media, probably every police department has some officers who get along well with the Fourth Estate. These may be officers intent on being promoted, or on running for election as county sheriff, or they may be simply dedicated policemen who recognize that the press, as well as the police, has duties to perform. Such officers may be found at every rank, and the reporter who does not seek them out may miss many important news stories. Many officers do not want publicity themselves, but will "tip off" a trusted reporter to a particularly intersting news story. Many such stories will be "events," but such police contacts may help the public affairs reporter "get beneath" the event story and probe important issues in law enforcement, criminal justice, and corrections.

There is a line here, obviously, that the experienced reporter soon learns not to cross. A reporter on any beat can become too chummy with his news sources, and in police reporting, that may lead to special problems. The reporter who has become a close friend of a policeman may find it difficult to write about corruption in the department.

Police Department Organization

There are many types of law enforcement agencies in the United States, and the reporter assigned to cover them in his locality should familiarize himself with their structures, overlapping duties, and jurisdictions. Typically, police agencies have structured chains of command, with the department usually headed by a chief or a public safety director. Depending on the department's size, there may be one or several deputy chiefs, and beneath them in authority, various divisions, typically headed by captains and lieutenants. These divisions often include traffic, homicide, theft and burglary, juvenile, planning and research, and license inspection. If the department is in a large city, patrolmen will generally be assigned by precincts, each headed by a captain or lieutenant. Large cities may have specialized divisions as well, such as morals and vice, and narcotics. The reporter is likely to find several types of law enforcement agencies, including:

Municipal Police Departments   Most cities, towns and villages have these departments. Generally, they handle traffic control and criminal apprehensions.

Sheriffs   Sheriffs are elected officials generally, and their jurisdiction is normally countywide. Along with traffic patrol and other law enforcement functions, sheriffs and their deputies often maintain jails and lockups, provide court bailiffs, and, in some areas, collect taxes and serve legal papers such as subpoenas.

Highway Patrols and State Police   Some states have state police with crime-investigation powers. Others have patrols whose principal duties are the surveillance of state highways. In a few states, bureaus of criminal apprehension buttress local and county law enforcement agencies.

Federal Agencies   The FBI, U.S. marshals, Internal Revenue Service agents, U.S. customs officers, postal inspectors, and other federal law enforcement officers are found in many larger cities. These groups have differing judisdictions, and they vary from press-shy to publicity-seeking.

Police Information

Police departments, like other governmental agencies, have made important changes in recent years in their records-keeping systems. In some departments, the reporter may find information being logged on offense reports and arrest reports. In other departments, arrest and offense information may be in computerized form. Whatever the form, the police reporter will find that, for day-to-day news items, these two types of reports will be most helpful. Offense reports are made out for all crimes, and generally include the type of offense, the victim, and other details. They are also made out for noncriminal activities, such as accidents and lost children. Arrest reports, sometimes called "show ups" or "booking sheets" identify arrested suspects, normally by name, age, and address. They usually include a brief statement of probable cause for the arrest, and the statute or ordinance number under which the arrest was made. Departments keep other types of records, such as suspect photographs, supplemental reports on serious crimes, and reports on alleged criminal activities, such as gambling.

Normally, the police reporter will have access to offense and arrest reports, but this is by no means standard. "Moreover," writes communications researcher Michael J. Petrick, "police may refuse access to the police blotter (arrest reports) as a form of 'punishment' for a non-cooperative newsman, or for other reasons of self-interest." [28] In most states, he concludes, control of police arrest information is in the hands of local police authorities. "Occasionally, these decisions [about access] come in the form of municipal legislation and municipal court decisions. More often, however, they are administrative instruments in the form of departmental regulations, unwritten rules or 'working agreements' between the police and press." [29] Police officials tend to guard reports carefully, and the reporter who wants access may have to be careful not to offend police officials needlessly. This doesn't mean that the critical story should never be written; indeed, sometimes it is essential, and is welcomed by police officials who are interested in the furtherance of police professionalism. Nonetheless, the reporter who writes a critical story short on facts and long on unsupported allegations will find himself faced with an immediate, and extensive, stone wall. Other types of police reports are normally not available to the reporter until he has "proven" himself to the police to be "trustworthy." Many experienced police reporters maintain a few close contacts in the department who will sometimes provide such information on a "background" basis only.

Handling Police News: Some Cautions

Accuracy   Regardless of the type of police record, the reporter must exercise a high degree of caution in using police information. It is not unusual to find a wrong name, age, or address in a police report, and the reporter who accepts police information without question will soon find himself making mistakes. The best rule of thumb for the reporter is to check the facts himself.

Fairness   Occasionally, police arrest a suspect and later release him without formal charge. Some editors and educators believe the ethical course is to wait for the charge—in the form of a criminal complaint or indictment—to be issued before identifying a suspect. Some publications routinely ignore this rule of thumb. In highly newsworthy situations, most reporters and editors would not hesitate to report the arrest, say, of the mayor on an armed robbery charge, before the formal complaint is issued.

Crime Statistics   Reporters should be particularly skeptical of the "crime statistics" press release. At regular intervals, law enforcement agencies issue crime statistics, and whether crime goes up or down, the reports normally get considerable media coverage. But the reporter should be aware that the statistics are often misleading. Police departments are not above showing a "crime increase" if they are seeking a budget increase; nor are they above showing a "crime decrease" to give the public the impression they are doing their job well. Crime statistics are based on "reported crime," not on all crime. Too often, a reporter raps out a lead like, "Crime was up 10 per cent in the county in 1973 compared with 1972." Only a fraction of actual crime is reported to law enforcement agencies, and thus, it is misleading to imply that the statistics represent the full picture of criminal activity.

Police and Politics   At election time, the police reporter may find his duties similar to the public affairs reporter covering politics. While certainly not the general rule, some police and sheriff's offices insist that the chief or sheriff announce the solving of crimes. And it is not a coincidence that such releases become more common during campaigns, or when the city's police budget needs public support. In short, the astute police reporter will question whether such "news stories" are legitimate.

Writing the Police Story

How could the public affairs reporter, using techniques and strategies mapped out in the first part of this book, research, investigate, and write stories about law enforcement that get beneath the "event"? What tactics might be used? Obviously, the approach to any one story may depend, in part, on the nature of the topic itself, and the guidelines suggested here are not meant to be proscriptive. But let's take a hypothetical example:

The legal process reporter for a metropolitan newspaper writes several short stories during a several-month period about individuals killed or injured in high-speed chases with police. Perhaps, he wonders, police are not being adequately trained in driving techniques under stress conditions. Perhaps there need to be revisions in the state law that allows a police officer to pursue a fleeing suspect. On this story, the reporter might begin by building a careful statistical base. What is the rate of traffic accidents for police officers? How many officers have been injured in such accidents in the past five years? How many innocent bystanders or suspects have been hurt in crashes resulting from high-speed chases? These questions could be answered by careful examination of records from, say, the state department of motor vehicles, the highway patrol, and local law enforcement agencies. The reporter might also examine the training program for officers. How many hours of driving training are included in the police training program? Who does the training? Is that person qualified? Here the reporter might examine the training programs in other states, pulling information from police professional journals or magazines. The interviewing on such a story might be extensive, including interviews with the captain of the city police traffic division or patrol division, an academic professional with the local university's criminal justice studies department, the training personnel at the state police academy, attorneys, and legislators. Professional organizations, such as the state chiefs of police association, might also be able to provide useful information. To round out the story, interviews might be conducted with hospital and medical personnel, the victims of such chases, and, of course, some police officers who have been involved in high-speed chases. The reporter might want to use the direct observation approach here, as well, by riding along in a police vehicle on emergency runs. At the writing stage, the story might contain a main story and several sidebars, and perhaps some statistical tables, carefully explained. Because the issue is a complex one, the story might well discuss contrasting views. A similar approach might be adapted to other stories involving police training, such as gun training and arrest techniques.

If the story had involved allegations against police, such as an investigation of police brutality, then the reporter might have broadened the research base further. Careful, specific statements by alleged victims would be needed, and to be doubly safe, the reporter might seek signed affidavits from interview subjects. That is what the *Chicago Tribune* did in its eight-part series of articles on police brutality, published in 1973. The series began with a case study of a man who was beaten during a police interrogation:

> Joshie Johnson was lucky.
>
> The *Tribune* found people who were telling the truth, but still lost lengthy and expensive legal battles and were convicted of false felony charges that had been placed against them to hide a policeman's misconduct.
>
> The *Tribune* found even more people who, altho they had successfully fought bogus charges, could not get the Police Department to discipline the policemen who had brutalized them. . . .
>
> The department has consistently ignored scathing criticism of halfhearted brutality investigations from such diverse groups as bar associations, federal study groups, and respected police organizations.

The department has discarded, for apparent political reasons, the most widely praised psychological testing program in the nation for policemen, leaving it years behind departments that copied the Chicago system.

IAD [Internal Affairs Division] investigators often ignore the most fundamental rules and tools of police investigation, such as seeking out key witnesses and using the polygraph.

Discipline against guilty policemen sometimes amounts to suspensions shorter than those levied against policemen who take an unauthorized lunch break.[30]

A week after the series began, a state's attorney announced a grand jury investigation of the charges against some of the policemen named in the articles. There were calls by various civil-rights and civil-liberties groups for a cleanup in the department, including better psychological screening of police recruits. Shortly thereafter, three policemen were indicted on charges ranging from attempted murder to filing false arrest reports. "A newspaper," wrote *Tribune* publisher Stanton R. Cook in an introduction to the reprinted articles, "can be fair while being tough. . . . Fairness breeds trust. And trust, the public's belief that a newspaper makes every effort to be fair, is the life's blood of a free press. . . . Today, more than ever, a newspaper must be a spotlight on our system because only the press has the resources, energy and staff to examine such wide-ranging and complex stories as this. Whether the issue is Watergate or police brutality, today's newspaper must dig hard and dig deep. It must practice professional investigative journalism, but it must do so in a responsible manner." [31]

Covering the Courts

Earlier in this chapter, it was suggested that there is a widening role for the public affairs reporter in covering the legal process. Several objectives were suggested: helping to control and prevent crime; helping to assure due process; critical surveillance of the legal process; and making sense out of single cases. How can the reporter meet these objectives?

One way is to see courts as an integral part of the system of justice which includes police, corrections, the legal profession, and citizen groups. In covering these diverse groups, the reporter needs to have some sense of the "big picture" if he is to avoid falling into the limited day-to-day coverage of trials, arraignments, hearings, and motions that make up the daily court calendar and provide the bulk of court news for American newspapers. "So, in analyzing press coverage of the courts and the law," writes Professor Grey, "there are many reasons for doubting the 'educational value' of such actual news leads and headlines as: 'Supreme Court Convicts Martin Luther King' and 'Supreme Court Frees Tim Leary' or 'Court Denies Protest by (Chicago 7) (Manson) (Angela).' Such emphasis is usually not inaccurate or 'wrong'; it is instead simply stressing too much the actors and the action at the expense of such important legal questions as rights of dissent and of the accused." [32]

The need for writing news stories in which news is seen as a process, in which systemic issues are dealt with, is suggested by other critics of the press's coverage of public affairs. Professor Todd Hunt writes that "if the self-reflexiveness of event-centered reporting is to be avoided, news media will have to nurture a whole new breed of information gatherers. They will have to be people who are capable of going into a situation . . . and studying the event at a generic level. 'What's going on here? What are these people doing? How are they using this event? Are they all using it in the same way; if not, what differences and variations are there?' " [33] Court news, traditionally, has been oriented toward events. Arraignments, trials, pleas, motions, arguments all appear on court calendars on specific days, and the reporter who covers courts may be tempted to "scan the calendar" looking for "interesting" news stories on a day-to-day basis. Recent articles on police reporting suggest that coverage is generally focused toward "covering the crime." "Police reporters," writes one observer, "have become specialists in the art of listening to police radios and using the telephone. Communications are so rapid and thorough that *a reporter need only lift up a telephone receiver, make a few calls, and a story is virtually complete.*" [34]

But an increasing number of observers recognize that this approach to crime and court news is not adequate. "Urban courts are a disaster area," writes Professor David B. Sachsman. "They are understaffed and poorly managed. And while some court reporters have clearly documented the problems of the judicial system, most are too busy with day-to-day coverage." [35] And Illinois Circuit Judge James O. Monroe, Jr., concludes that on some topics, there is too much coverage, but on other topics, the coverage has been inadequate:

> Delay in court, the pileup of cases, the appalling bad habits of lawyers and judges, the simple remedies that are ignored—these have scarcely been touched except in petulance and periodic squawks. In every court, state and federal, and in all divisions in local courts, there are serious stories in the statistics of cases on file (the inventory), cases being filed (the input), and cases disposed of (dispositions or pace). Law reviews and bench and bar reports pro-

vide over-all studies and viewpoints. Trends in civil torts and criminal case disposition represent major philosophic developments of importance. On the dockets of all courts, we ought to know what cases are *not* called, which are reduced, which are lost or ignored or conveniently forgotten. Yet there continues to be too little coverage of all these things.[36]

Covering the courts as part of the legal process system, these writers suggest, means being able to stand back from day-to-day reporting and to look for systemic issues. Process-centered news is not necessarily current. The reporter might well examine trends in court case loads and plea bargaining, as did the *Minneapolis Tribune* in a series in 1973. In process-centered news, the writer "gives considerable attention to causes and offers suggestions as to resultant events." [37] The *Tribune's* series suggested causes for the growth of cases involving plea bargaining—in which the defendant pleads guilty to a lesser charge—and concluded:

> One of the principal reasons for plea bargaining is that there are not enough judges, assistant county attorneys or public defenders (who represent the majority of criminal defendants) to try all the cases the county has each year.
>
> Large backlogs of cases interfere with the rights of defendants to speedy trials, they cause judges to be transferred from civil cases to criminal trials and thus jam the civil calendar, and they cause problems for the prosecution because of time lag—witnesses disappear and police officers' memories diminish.[38]

Or the reporter might examine the grand jury system, as did the *Los Angeles Times* in 1974. The *Times* discussed the grand jury's strengths and weaknesses, cited current thinking of legal scholars, and provided historical perspective on how grand juries originated. The reports included interviews with members of the grand jury, together with suggestions for changes and modification of the grand jury system.[39] Or the reporter might use new social science techniques, discussed in detail by Meyer in *Precision Journalism* (see Chapter 5), to examine criminal justice in a court system, as did the *Philadelphia Inquirer* in a 1973 series. As these, and other stories indicate, a reporter assigned to cover courts need not restrict himself to day-to-day events.*

Different Courts, Different Strategies

Within the court component of the legal system, there are different courts, of varying complexity and remoteness from the local scene, and

---

* See Appendix C, "Criminal Justice and Criminal Trial Process."

these may require different reporting strategies. In local courts, the reporter may be able to become quite friendly with individual judges, attorneys, and law enforcement officials. Normally, these courts are rather informal, and the reporter sometimes needs to work closely with court officials and personnel.

District courts, or courts of original jurisdiction or of "first instance," normally have complex rules of procedure, particularly on such matters as the presentation of evidence and the taking of testimony. Few cases go to trial. In the typical civil case the parties agree to an out-of-court settlement, and in the typical criminal case the defendant pleads guilty to a lesser offense. But some cases do, of course, go to trial, and it is there, in the courtroom, that the reporter's abilities are most severely tested. The reporter must weigh hours of testimony, and perhaps piles of evidence, and from that mass select the most important items for his news story. He must judge the continuing questions of excessive publicity, yet provide readers with accurate and complete accounts of the trial proceedings. This task becomes particularly difficult during the taking of testimony. One witness may contradict another, and the purpose of calling a particular witness may not be clearly stated, but only implied. The reporter must take special care to balance his reports: a too-heavy emphasis on either the prosecution or defense performance risks distortion. At the same time the reporter must watch out for grandstanding by attorneys, behavior and remarks intended as much for the press as for the jury. Beyond the obvious need for accuracy, the reporter should try to catch the flavor of an important or interesting trial, and yet do so in a way that is neither sensational nor maudlin. And as if that weren't enough, the reporter must stand back from the trial as an "event," and ask himself questions about the administration of justice, due process, and the quality of justice as suggested by the trial. In short, he must see the trial as part of, but not the whole, legal process system.

At the district court level, the reporter is also likely to run into other components of the legal process system, such as the grand jury. Rather than simply covering the indictments and "no bills" that are routine, the reporter might well attempt to examine the components in context, providing the reader with perspective. And this objective can be accomplished in writing that is both dramatic and informative. The *Los Angeles Times* reporter Gene Blake, in a 1974 report on the grand jury system, for example, began his story this way:

> Twenty-three pairs of eyes—seemingly cold and distrusting but perhaps merely bored and apathetic—stare at a lone witness seated in a somber chamber behind a locked and closely guarded door.

He fidgets and glances nervously about. There is the man asking him the probing question—the prosecuting attorney. There is the steno-typist, carefully taking down every word for possible future use.

And there are the men and women behind the 23 pairs of eyes—all his fellow citizens—holding in their hands the fearsome power known as "indictment."

There is no lawyer to sit beside the witness, to give him advice and perhaps ask additional questions of him and other witnesses who may precede or follow. There is no judge to referee. There is no audience to pierce the veil of secrecy.

This is the grand jury.

It is a venerable institution, with roots going back to 12th century and ingrained by the American founding fathers in the Bill of Rights.

It has been called a "protective bulwark standing solidly between the ordinary citizen and an overzealous prosecutor"—which, at one point in its evolution, it was.

But hardly anyone believes the grand jury is serving that function today.[40]

Seeing the components of the legal system in context becomes particularly important when the reporter covers federal courts, for rulings here often affect state court decisions, and the functioning of state and local agencies. From obscenity and the death penalty to abortion, reapportionment, and busing to achieve racial integration, federal court rulings in recent years have had an important impact at the state and local level. Though most public affairs reporters will never cover a case before the U.S. Supreme Court, the court's decisions are often very important to the reporter at the local or state level. Local judges, in their rulings, often cite U.S. Supreme Court rulings, and the reporter who hopes to cover these issues well should be familiar with the cases that are relevant. Perhaps the reporter cannot read every federal court ruling, but he should at least read summaries and excerpts.

Legal Research

Unless he wishes to rely entirely on personal sources, many of them self-serving, in covering the legal process, the public affairs reporter must gain some knowledge of legal research methods. The legal research resources available to the reporter may vary from one community to another, ranging from a large university law library to a lawyer's private, working collection. In between there are legal libraries and collections in courthouses, city halls, community libraries, and law firms. No community is without some rudimentary collection of legal materials.

Learning something about legal research is useful to the reporter in several ways. It can provide context and background for various legal process stories ranging from individual cases to legal trends. It can also help the reporter ferret out stories that are not immediately evident in a superficial observation of the procedures followed by courts, law enforcement, or corrections. Ideally, the reporter should search legal materials on his own, but he should also consult attorneys and others schooled in the law for help in interpretation. Without some formal training, the reporter should not second-guess trained attorneys, but legal research will help him formulate better questions and should result in more understandable and knowledgeable stories.

The public affairs reporter may want to make use of some of the following materials:

Research Guides   Several research guidebooks list major sources of American law and help the reader find them. They include such works as Morris L. Cohen, *Legal Research in a Nutshell* (West, 1971), Miles O. Price and Harry Bitner, *Effective Legal Research* (Prentice-Hall, 1953), and Ervin H. Pollack's *Fundamentals of Legal Research* (Foundation Press, 1973). These are essentially guidebooks to law libraries and legal materials collections and explain how to search out information. Also essential is a copy of *A Uniform System of Citation,* published by the Harvard Law Review Association. This pamphlet identifies various abbreviations and other legal shorthand and helps in the use of court opinions, statutes, law reviews, and other materials.

Dictionaries and Encyclopedias   The search for legal definitions and brief mentions of cases in which legal principles were decided is assisted by consulting a legal dictionary. The best-known legal dictionaries are *Black's Law Dictionary, Ballentine's,* and *Bouvier's.* For more detailed treatment of legal issues, consult legal encyclopedias such as *Corpus Juris Secondum,* published by the West Publishing Co., and *American Jurisprudence 2d,* published by the Lawyer's Co-operative Publishing Co. Also useful to the reporter are various directories of practicing attorneys. The most comprehensive directory is *Martindale-Hubbell,* which provides a listing of lawyers by state and includes most cities and towns. In listing law firms, the directory gives an indication of who some of the firm's clients are.

Legal Periodicals   Keeping pace with the law and legal developments is aided considerably by a number of legal periodicals. *U.S. Law Week* covers the Supreme Court, the Federal courts and major state cases.

Law reviews, published by bar associations, university law schools, and various legal organizations, present scholarly comment on recent cases and articles about legal trends and concepts. Reading a law review article, which usually offers a nearly exhaustive search of relevant materials, can be particularly useful to the reporter and may save him considerable work in the law library, although it should be noted that law review articles are often adversarial by nature and push a particular legal view. Finding articles of interest in legal periodicals is assisted by the *Index to Legal Periodicals,* a "reader's guide" for legal materials. There are also *The Index to Periodical Articles Related to Law* (in nonlegal publications) and an *Index to Foreign Legal Periodicals and Collections of Essays.*

While the above-mentioned materials are useful secondary sources for legal research, the major sources of law are found in court opinions and statutes. Here law libraries have vast holdings that are easy to use, once you learn about citation.

Court Decisions   These include decisions of the Supreme Court of the United States, which are found in *United States Reports, The Supreme Court Reporter,* and the *Lawyer's Edition of the Supreme Court Reporter.* Federal circuit courts of appeal are covered in the *Federal Reporter* and decisions of district courts can be found in *Federal Supplement.*

State appeals court decisions are given in officially published reports (e.g. *Nevada Reporter*), but are also brought together in a regional reporter that is a part of the West Publishing Co.'s *National Reporter System.* This system divides the country into seven regions, and the decisions of appellate courts in the states in each region are collected into series of volumes. Separate series are also published for New York and California (*New York Supplement* and *California Reporter*), the two most litigious states. The West system is particularly important because a number of states have stopped publishing their own official reports and rely on the regional reporters.

In using federal or state reports, a case citation is needed. For example, 354 U.S. 449 (1957) is the citation for *Mallory* v. *United States,* a Supreme Court case. The citation is read as follows:

Volume	source (U.S. Reports)	page number
354	U.S.	449

Citations are obtained from various sources including briefs in an appeals case, in case digests, and in other materials.

Statutory and Related Materials   Statutes of the federal and state governments are another important source of law. These are usually laws passed by legislative bodies. Legal sources in addition to statutory law include constitutions, resolutions and acts of legislative bodies, treaties, interstate compacts, reorganization plans, (executive decrees and administrative regulations, court rules, and local laws and ordinances. Federal public laws in the United States are published regularly in the *U.S. Code Congressional and Administrative News,* shortly after enactment, and later in *Statutes at Large* (the official publication) as well as in the *U.S. Code* and the *Federal Code Annotated.* State laws are also codified. Similarly, some cities publish compilations of their ordinances. Uniformity in state laws, part of a growing legal trend, are found in *Uniform Laws Annotated,* or in specialized codes, such as the *Uniform Commercial Code.* Statutory citations are similar to case citations. For example, 18 U.S.C. 641 refers to:

chapter no.	source (U.S. Code)	section number
18	U.S.C.	641

This simple citation leads the searcher to the exact place in the statutes where the official law is found.

There are, of course, hundreds of other information sources and finding tools in law libraries. This discussion was designed to deal briefly with a few of them, with the understanding that serious public affairs reporters will become knowledgeable users of law libraries, whether massive ones or small collections.

The Actors: Lawyers, Judges, Juries, Clerks
As Sources, How Much Can They Say?

At the beginning of this chapter, it was pointed out that the journalist covering the legal system is viewed, generally, as an "outsider," and that personnel in the legal system are often suspicious of efforts to "unearth embarrassing material." Though civil servants and bureaucrats generally may regard the press with suspicion, there are legal constraints in the legal system that inhibit the reporter in his search for news. In most states and jurisdictions, for example, grand jurors are prohibited by law from commenting on cases before them. Legal canons of ethics warn lawyers about making statements in public that might influence the outcome of pending cases. Some judges have imposed "gag" orders on the press, prohibiting the reporting of certain cases under pain of a contempt citation.

Few journalists or lawyers, however, naïvely believe that violations of such rules and laws do not occur. The "leak" from a grand jury, or from a legal investigating agency like the Senate Watergate committee, has become routine. Such leaks may and do prejudice cases, but the "calculated leaks are a highly exaggerated tool of investigative reporting," writes Contributing Editor Bob Kuttner, in *(More).* He continues:

Most of the important revelations about the Administration—including Agnew's difficulties—came from legwork, not leakage. Where deliberate leaks occurred, as with the Ervin Committee, the result was hardly worth the typesetting. . . .

I have spoken with most of the reporters involved in these and other damaging stories, and while none, obviously, will disclose his sources, the general pattern emerges that the most fruitful sources for details of the case against the Vice-President were lawyers for other potential defendants, and possibly Agnew's own lawyers as well. To a lesser extent, some information came from prosecutors in Baltimore. Undeniably, there were also some juicy one-liners, particularly in the newsweeklies, that must have come from middle-level Justice Department sources. But this does not add up to a pattern of willful, malicious leaking.[41]

The motives behind the "leak" from a prosecutor, defense attorney, judge, or juror should be carefully considered by the reporter. Most such leaks carry a built-in bias; that is, the material "leaked" is often selective. Journalistic standards about using "leaked" material vary from paper to paper and from case to case. The reporter should consider the public interest of the material, as well as the potential to invade a person's privacy and prejudice public opinion against him. Few editors would tell a reporter to ignore "leaked" materials, but many would urge the reporter to exercise great caution in weighing the newsworthiness of the leak against the potential harm to the defendant. Walter Pincus, associate editor of the *New Republic*, suggests that newsmen ought to be less willing to take "leaked" material and more careful to consider the source's motives:

> While I believe newsmen should—must—use confidential sources, I also think the time has come for journalism as a profession to come to grips with one fact—the press is being manipulated more and more by sources whose motives for providing sensational "facts" may be newsworthy, even more newsworthy, than the information given. Newsmen, eager for scoops or wanting just to keep up with the competition, by design or through ignorance, prefer to overlook the important question of *why* the information is being given to them.[42]

So the reporter covering the legal system, then, needs to be particularly careful about sources. Discussing a case with a juror while the case is being heard, for example, could be grounds for a mistrial. But this doesn't mean that the reporter should assume all avenues are closed. Some judges will discuss cases on a not-for-attribution basis. Many lawyers will do the same, although the reporter should be aware that such comments may be self-serving. Generally, the reporter needs to establish the trust and confidence of court officials and personnel, and the best way to do that is to act in a professional manner. A quote given "not for attribution" that later shows up in the paper with the source named is likely to get the reporter very little from that source again. Similarly, a reporter who "sneaks a peak" at legal documents that are not part of the public record is likely to find attorneys and judges reluctant to discuss cases frankly in the future. Usually, legal personnel are more likely to discuss a case after it has been decided in court, and the reporter may, in the meantime, have to forego some day-to-day stories and keep his eyes on the "big" story when the case is concluded. While some important stories may be missed, the reporter may have the perspective in the future to write a more valuable story that deals with how the legal system functions. The *Los Angeles Times's* reports on the grand jury, for instance, included interviews with former grand jury members who spoke candidly about their roles and how they believed the grand jury functioned as an institution.[43] In his article on New York judges, reporter Newfield relied on off-the-record interviews with both attorneys and judges:

> No agency regularly monitors the courts—the press can go all out on one trial or another, but it is notoriously indifferent to the trial *system*—and no agency retains records of judicial dispositions. The Bar Association's files of formal complaints against sitting judges are closed to the public. For fear of reprisal, if not out of respect for the code of ethics, no lawyer I spoke to would let himself be quoted about a specific judge. And the mystique of respect that allows us to criticize poets, fighters, generals and Presidents, but not judges, silenced some of those who know the inner workings of the courts best.
>
> Nevertheless, enough people, especially several good judges anxious to redeem their own profession, did talk off the record, so that a consensus of the worst judges, reinforced by personal observation, finally did emerge.[44]

These articles illustrate that the well-timed, and sometimes off-the-record interview can be a valuable tool to the reporter who deals with press-shy court officials and personnel.

What strategies and tactics can the reporter use in covering courts as part of the legal process? Again, without being proscriptive, let's take a hypothetical example. The court system of a small city has a procedure called pretrial diversion, in which a defendant is diverted from the criminal court process and given rehabilitative job and educational training.

The purpose of the program, which is supported by a state crime commission grant, is to prevent crimes against property by giving potential thieves training so that they will be able to earn an income and not have to steal. How well, the public affairs reporter asks, does the system work? Does it really rehabilitate? Do defendants in the diversion project receive job training and educational training that really helps them?

This is a multisource story for which the reporter will need to tap different types of resource material, interview a range of authorities, and employ various techniques. To define the perimeters of the story, the reporter might begin by examining the program's grant. What does the grant say the project will do? Then, the reporter might examine how the program staff evaluates itself, keeping in mind that any such examination could be highly self-serving. Are the evaluation methods reasonable? How have other courts handled such projects? What statistical base is there for saying such-and-such a percentage of the defendants complete the job and educational training? The reporter might then turn to some of those involved with the project and interview probation officers, judges, court and corrections workers, and police. The reporter might examine police records to see whether the defendants are arrested any less often. The reporter might also ask some defendants, past and present, for their evaluation of the program. He might also talk with employers. As with the story on police training, some academic opinions from criminal justice experts would add dimension to the story. This investigation would reach across the traditional police-court-corrections beat lines by examining a problem that is centered in the court system, but which has law enforcement and correction elements, too.

Covering the Penal System

The corrections component of the legal system in America is perhaps the most difficult to cover. Unlike courts and police departments, prisons are generally closed to the public and the press, and even news dealing with a prison "event" is difficult to obtain. "The peculiar nature of covering a prison riot," writes *Chicago Daily News* reporter John Linstead, "is the ability of officials to control almost totally the flow of information. In an urban street riot, you can drive through the area, watch what the police are doing, talk to residents and rioters. In a college takeover or street demonstration, you can find leaders who may condescend to talk to you. But whom do you talk to in a prison riot?" [45] All the same, the reporter need not restrict himself to "official" accounts of what is going on inside prisons. Nor need he restrict himself to covering prison "events" such as riots, murders, escapes, and suicides, all of which are fairly common. There are other ways to handle news from corrections. At the Attica (N.Y.) prison riot, reporters soon learned to tap other sources for their stories. Says Linstead:

> We talked to so many families of hostages, camped outside the gates, that they grew sick of reporters walking up with tape machine or pencil ready. The nearby residents told us their life stories in the first few days. Local barflies soon learned to shut up when an obvious reporter type walked in. Doctors, priests, and negotiators who had been inside the prison for hours without sleep knew they'd have to answer hundreds of questions before they could get to bed. Reporters who managed to get into the prison in pools during the days before the attack grew weary of repeating to us what they had seen, heard and smelled. And a short-wave radio tuned to the police band provided a running account of police moves during the attack.[46]

"Prison riots," writes vanden Heuvel, "like cowboy movies, have a quick audience because the 'good guys' and the 'bad guys' are identifiable and they meet in violent confrontation. But as reporter Nat Hentoff has pointed out, 'Except for brief public interest during a prison rebellion, what happens inside these institutions remains unreported and, therefore, unexamined.' " [47]

Many stories need to be written about prisons, and the reporter needs to see corrections as part of the legal system. On a good number of newspapers, beats are divided into "police," and "courts," but few newspapers designate a reporter to cover corrections. Furthermore, a tendency prevails among reporters to think that once a police investigation of a crime and a trial of the defendant have been completed the story's over. The sending of a defendant to prison after a trial often means the end of the coverage of the case by the press, unless the defendant returns to the court system to file an appeal. Such appeals are covered routinely as they come up in the day-to-day court news. This approach, however, leaves important stories untouched. Vanden Heuvel suggests 30 assignments that would "revolutionize our awareness" about corrections including:

> Live TV coverage of a prison council such as in the Women's Prison of New York City, where elected prisoner delegates meet regularly with correctional personnel to discuss institutional grievances.
> A study of the correction officer, including an analysis of how he is chosen, his responsibility, training, and personal attitude toward his work.
> A feature story on prison chaplains, including prisoner reactions to organized religion and the clergy.

A visit to the court pens where prisoners await court appearances—and an analysis on any given day of the disposition of the cases on the court calendar.

A review of the prison commissary system and an accounting of the monies involved.

A profile of solitary confinement with a review of the procedures by which prisoners are sent to such quarters.

A story about the consequences to a family when the father is sentenced to prison.

An evaluation of the rehabilitation programs in any prison.

A productivity audit and itemized analysis of a correctional budget so that an average citizen can understand it.

A story about what happens to children whose mother is sentenced to prison.

An in-depth interview with an adolescent prisoner at the beginning of his sentence and when he leaves the prison.[48]

Let's follow vanden Heuvel's last suggestion to see how it might be approached by the public affairs reporter. Most likely, the reporter would want to pick out an individual who is going to prison for the first time. He could make such a selection by examining court records, including presentence investigation reports, which are normally confidential but which a reporter can often see if he is careful to explain his purpose to court officials and the sentencing judge. There is a commonly held belief that prisons, rather than reforming young offenders, merely educate them in the sophisticated ways of crime by putting them in contact with older, more experienced prisoners. In addition to interviewing the prisoner, the reporter might want to find out more about him than court records and a talk with him permit. Interviews with his family, friends, schoolmates, as well as with victims of his crime, would help here. To get perspective on the issue of prison reform, the reporter might examine statistics on recidivism rates, how they are measured and what they show and don't show. While the individual is in prison, the reporter might do frequent interviews with him, getting him to talk about the changes he perceives in himself as a result of prison. Such material could be self-serving in the extreme, but the reporter could also talk with other prisoners, prison officials, and employees and psychiatrists. When the individual is released, the reporter might do a lengthy interview, then follow it up six months later. Obviously, the reporter would have to keep a careful interview and records file on the individual so that, at the writing stage, he could show his transformation, or at least what effect prison has had on him.

By intensive research, carefully arranged questions, and a real empathy with the prisoner, the reporter might develop real insight into what it's like to go to prison for the first time. The lack of a time deadline would remove the necessity of "rushing into print" with the story. But would not the final stories, if well written, say more about prisons than the typical news story that emphasizes the escape of a certain "hardened criminal"?

Stories like this have already been done, but others of vanden Heuvel's suggestions have not. One problem is that reporters don't take advantage of access to prisons which is, in some institutions, replacing secrecy and control. "Despite our liberal inmate interview policy," says New York City Corrections Commissioner Benjamin Malcolm, "the press has not stampeded to the cellblocks to interview inmates. Most reporters have not availed themselves of the opportunity as often as we thought when we first relaxed the rules. Most interviews granted have been with a small selected group of highly vocal individuals whose cases have received front page treatment. There have been few interviews concerning the pathetic cases of inmates who may have been trapped in the judicial whirlpool." [49] The interview with an inmate or ex-convict can provide the reporter with new insights into how the criminal justice system works from a perspective that is normally different from his own. Two months after fights between black and white inmates at Minnesota's Saint Cloud State Reformatory, student reporter Greg Breining went to the prison to interview inmates. He wrote:

> But if the reformatory approximates a small society because of the occupations of its residents and the politics of its administration, then it is also a small shadow of the outside in that society's problems are accentuated by the close, intense living conditions and a population perhaps more volatile than normal. . . .
>
> Since April, tensions seem to have mellowed. Some staff members and inmates attribute this to optimism over the upcoming talks [between inmates and staff]. Others say that fewer problems arise because the inmates are separated into smaller groups in trouble spots like the ball diamond and the lunchroom. Others say that for the first time, white inmates are unified like the blacks and a balance of power exists. Other inmates, particularly blacks, say that the racial tension still exists as pervasively, and only needs a catalyst.[50]

Interviews need not be limited to inmates. "There are few things more necessary than for the public to understand the strain of the correction officer's work and the alienation he feels because of the hostility directed toward him," writes vanden Heuvel.[51]

Whatever the sources, the reporter should attempt to research and write stories that give the reader different perspectives on the problems of corrections. Fortunately, some of these attempts are already being made, for, as vanden Heuvel says, "unless the media can translate these [prisoner's] grievances into public understanding, there is little hope for prison reform. The quality of justice must be measured periodically by the press. . . . How can a prison be free of anger and grievance when an inmate convicted of selling 1/73 of an ounce of heroin receives a sentence of thirty years, while another defendant in another court guilty of the same crime is sentenced to three months?" [52] By approaching corrections issues as "events" (e.g., the riot, escape, murder, suicide), the reporter limits himself greatly. By seeing corrections issues as part of the generally unreported legal process system, the reporter can begin to make sense of single incidents. There will probably always be a need to cover the prison riot, or to investigate and write the story by which an innocent man is freed from a prison. But these stories do not, in themselves, deal with root social problems and issues.

There are many types of corrections facilities, and though the reporter needs to cover them all from broad perspectives, special investigating problems emerge with each one.

Local Lockups   The county and municipal jails and workhouses are probably the most ignored component of corrections facilities. Usually small, and carefully tucked under the wing of a county sheriff or local police department, these facilities range from adequate to poor. Some conditions border on the inhumane. Here, the reporter will need to deal with local sources in his pursuit of stories: not only lawyers and local branches of civil liberties unions and other groups interested in corrections reform, but law enforcement officials and the prisoners themselves. With enough persistence, the reporter can sometimes find a sympathetic judge, lawyer, or other official to provide information. Then comes the writing, like this moving excerpt from a story on local jails by Newfield originally published in the *Village Voice*:

> A few facts to meditate on. Almost all the inmates of the Kew Gardens jail, of the Tombs, and of the Long Island City jail have *not* been convicted of a crime. According to the Constitution, they are innocent until proven guilty, by a jury. These institutions are detention facilities, not punishment prisons. The men are detained there usually because they could not raise the $500 or $1,000 bail on the single phone call they are allowed. Most of them have been in these dungeons for six and twelve months *waiting for their trials to begin,* 25 percent on bail of $500 or less. Under any name this is preventive detention. They rot in these Cancer Wards because they are poor, and because some criminal court judges are political hacks who work only five hours a day. Most of these judges are opposed to the penal reform supported by Chief Justice Burger and Mayor Lindsay, and already adopted by the State of California, the

reform that places a sixty-day legal limit on the time between arrest and trial.[53]

State Facilities   In some states, penal institutions harbor dozens of suspicious officials who are reluctant to give the reporter any assistance in developing complex and important stories. The reporter often needs the help of other sources, such as court records, but can sometimes, through careful interviewing of officials, present processes or abuses clearly. For instance, reporter Robert Pearman, writing in *The Nation* in 1966, followed up the Arkansas state penitentiary's policy change that allowed prisoners to be whipped. He wrote:

> After O. E. Bishop, superintendent of the Arkansas state peniten-
> tiary, has sentenced a man to be whipped, he sits at his desk and
> waits until the punishment is carried out. If the door is open, he
> can hear the sounds of the strap falling in a room just down the
> hall, but Captain Bishop (in Arkansas all wardens are called 'Cap'n')
> never watches the whippings. He has no stomach for such things.
> 'I'd just rather see anything other than that,' says the superintendent,
> who took over his present job last January, after seventeen years
> as sheriff of Union County. 'I know you have to have some means
> to cope with the things that happen here. That's why I want to
> build the facilities for solitary confinement. I just think it would
> work better.' [54]

There is a continuous need for follow-up stories. In 1968, three mutilated bodies were found at the Cummins Prison Farm in Arkansas. "The state's two largest newspapers," writes *Los Angeles Times* reporter Nicholas C. Chriss, "have repeatedly lambasted the prison officials over the past years. Nevertheless, the horror stories continue to emerge." [55]

Juvenile Facilities   Juvenile justice stories are also difficult for the reporter to get because of various state laws that prohibit the release of information about juvenile offenders. Often, the reporter will have to work with sympathetic judges, lawyers, and corrections officials, as well as the juveniles themselves, to unearth these stories. The *Minneapolis Tribune's* series on juvenile justice, for example, concluded:

> The delinquent encounters a large number of competent, well-
> meaning adult workers as he wends his way through the system. But
> the sum total of the adults' efforts remains a mystery. . . . The
> question is: What does all the work accomplish? The answer is:
> Nobody knows. Oh, there are success stories. . . . But overall,
> there is no evidence that the juvenile justice system is effective—no
> evidence that it rehabilitates youthful offenders.[56]

Institutions for the Criminally Insane   These institutions exist in every state, but are little covered, at least in detail, by the press. Furthermore, few reporters probably know much about forensic psychiatry, or the tests applied legally to determine if a person is criminally insane or competent to stand trial. Traditionally, such matters are covered as they come up in court hearings, but occasionally, defense and prosecuting attorneys will parade conflicting expert witnesses who present opposite findings. Psychiatrists are more commonly seen as witnesses in court, and the phychiatrist's relationship to criminal law is one that needs more attention by the public affairs reporter covering the legal process.[57] The reporter here might consider preparing articles on the quality of care for emotionally disturbed prisoners, on the commitment process, and on the legal rights of a criminally insane person.

Community Corrections   In recent years, corrections has moved out of—at least in part—the isolated, maximum-security institution and into neighborhoods. Halfway houses, which include education and employment programs for ex-convicts, need more examination by the press, as do pretrial diversion projects, which take the nonviolent offender out of the criminal justice system and provide him with vocational training. Traditionally, the press's interest in such programs has been centered on the reaction (often disapproval) of neighborhood groups to plans to locate a drug rehabilitation center or halfway house in a neighborhood. But these programs, many of them funded by state and federal crime-prevention grants, are in need of serious evaluation by the press. The reporter, here, will have to deal with opponents, proponents, and academic scholars, all of whom have theories on whether such programs work. He will have to examine funding and granting documents, and perhaps do considerable research in professional and academic journals of sociology and criminology. As with other fields in public affairs reporting, there are dozens of stories to be done in this area at the local level.

Broader Perspectives on Criminal Justice

In recent years, state and federal government agencies have taken an increasingly broader role in various aspects of the criminal justice system. In 1968 Congress passed the Safe Streets Act, which provides federal funds to the states to improve court systems, initiate crime-prevention programs, and improve the quality of police services. These funds are administered by the Law Enforcement Assistance Administration (LEAA), a division of the U.S. Department of Justice. In every state, crime commissions review grants and disburse the funds. Traditionally, the media have covered these organizations at the state level as another state agency, and the typical story has been one that announces the awarding of major grants to various local law enforcement groups. Relatively little has been reported on the effectiveness of individual programs, and there has been little media investigation of the procedures by which funds are expended. These, as well as detailed analyses of various programs, should be more thoroughly covered by reporters in their pursuit of stories that examine the total legal process system. For example, the reporter might ask whether a small police department needs sophisticated riot-control equipment; whether a program to hire ex-convicts is working; whether computer technology to speed processing of criminal court cases improves the quality of justice; or whether a pretrial diversion program reduces crime by raising the job skills of nonviolent criminals. There are dozens of such programs in every state, and the reporter who wants to give a broader perspective to the legal process system should not ignore them.

In addition to these state and federal initiatives, local "task forces" and "commissions" have become increasingly involved in various aspects of the criminal justice system. Bar associations, associations of judges and prosecutors, and citizen groups have all begun to evaluate seriously their roles in reducing crime and making the criminal justice system more equitable. As with the LEAA programs, the media have tended to cover these developments on a one-shot basis, reporting the findings of a commission or task force, but rarely following up, perhaps months later, to see whether improvements have been initiated and wheteher they are working. For example, if a state bar association recommends changes in the state's rules of criminal procedure, the reporter might examine what the proposed changes would accomplish, then follow up the story with a look at the implementation phase. These types of stories obviously require informed investigation and interpretation, and a broad perspective on the legal process and its components.

NOTES

1. Jonathan D. Casper, *American Criminal Justice, The Defendant's Perspective* (Englewood Cliffs, N.J.: Prentice-Hall, 1972), p. 145.
2. Marc A. Franklin, *The Dynamics of American Law, Courts, the Legal Process and Freedom of Expression* (Mineola, N.Y.: Foundation Press, 1968), p. v.
3. Morris L. Cohen, *Legal Research in a Nutshell* (Saint Paul, Minn.: West Publishing, 1971), p. 228.
4. Franklin, *Dynamics of American Law,* pp. 26–27.

5. Ibid., p. 36.

6. Ibid., p. 41.

7. Abraham S. Blumberg, *Criminal Justice* (Chicago: Quadrangle Books, 1967), pp. x–xi.

8. Ibid., p. xi.

9. Edward J. Epstein, "Journalism and Truth," *Commentary* 57 (April, 1974), 37.

10. Ibid.

11. Edward J. Epstein, "The Panthers and the Police: A Pattern of Genocide," *New Yorker* (Feb. 13, 1971), p. 45.

12. Casper, *American Criminal Justice*, pp. 1–2.

13. David L. Grey, "Covering the Courts: Problems of Specialization," *Nieman Reports* 26 (March, 1972), 17.

14. Daniel Walker, *Rights In Conflict: "The Chicago Police Riot,"* (New York: Signet, 1968), p. xxv.

15. James C. Robertson, "Cooperation Needed in Police-Press Relations," *Twin Cities Journalism Review* 2 (March–April, 1974), 16.

16. William J. vanden Heuvel, "The Press and the Prisons," *Columbia Journalism Review* 11 (May-June, 1972), 35.

17. Ibid., pp. 35, 39.

18. David Fogel, "David Fogel Talks Back," *Twin Cities Journalism Review* 1 (March-April, 1973), 12.

19. Frank Premack, Doug Stone, and Peter Vanderpoel, "Juvenile Justice: A Defective System," *Minneapolis Tribune* (Aug. 4–20, 1974).

20. Jack Newfield, "The Ten Worst Judges in New York," *New York* 5 (Oct. 16, 1972), 32–36.

21. George Bliss, Emmett George, William Mullen, and Pamela Zeckman, "Police Brutality," *Chicago Tribune* (Nov. 4–11, 1973).

22. Casper, *American Criminal Justice*, p. 1.

23. Stephen Hartgen, "Murder in Minneapolis," *Minneapolis Star* (Dec. 11–13, 1972).

24. James O. Monroe, Jr., "Press Coverage of the Courts," *Quill* 61, (March, 1973), p. 24.

25. Arthur Niederhoffer, *Behind the Shield: The Police in Urban Society* (New York: Anchor Books, 1969), pp. 121–22.

26. Ibid., p. 234.

27. *Report of the National Advisory Commission on Civil Disorders* (New York: Bantam, 1968), p. 378.

28. Michael J. Petrick, "The Press, the Police Blotter and Public Policy," *Journalism Quarterly* 46 (Autumn, 1969), 475.

29. Ibid., p. 477.

30. George Bliss et al., "Police Brutality Exposed," *Chicago Tribune* (Nov. 4, 1973), p. 1.

31. Stanton R. Cook, in a foreword to a booklet of the reprinted articles on police brutality, *Chicago Tribune* (Nov., 1973).

32. Grey, "Covering the Courts," p. 17.

33. Todd Hunt, "Beyond the Journalistic Event: The Changing Concept of News," *Mass Comm Review* 1 (April, 1974), 28.

34. Mark H. Litke, "Police Beat: Still the Place There's Fast-Breaking News," *Editor & Publisher* 105 (Jan. 1, 1972), 15. Emphasis added.

35. David B. Sachsman, "Mass Media and the Urban Environment," *Mass Comm Review* 1 (July, 1974), 5.

36. Monroe, "Press Coverage," p. 23.

37. Sachsman, "Mass Media," p. 26.

38. Frank Premack and Peter Vanderpoel, "Plea Bargaining: Sure Deals behind Closed Doors," *Minneapolis Tribune* (Oct. 14, 1974), p. 9.

39. Gene Blake, "Grand Jury: 'Bulwark of Liberties' or Aid to Prosecution," *Los Angeles Times* (Nov. 3, 1974), section 2, p. 1.

40. Ibid.

41. Bob Kuttner, "The Politics of Leaksmanship," *(MORE)* 3 (Nov., 1973), 1, 15.

42. Walter Pincus, "The Usable Press," *The New Republic* (Oct. 20, 1972), pp. 17–18.

43. *Los Angeles Times* (Nov. 3, 1974).

44. Newfield, "Ten Worst Judges," p. 33.

45. John Linstead, "Attica: Where Media Went Wrong," *Chicago Journalism Review* 4 (Nov., 1971), 9.

46. Ibid.

47. Vanden Heuvel, "Press and the Prison," p. 35.

48. Ibid., pp. 39–40.

49. Quoted in Edward M. Swietnicki, "Gaps in Crime Reporting Are Noted at Symposium," *Editor & Publisher* 106 (June 9, 1973), 14.

50. Greg Breining, "St. Cloud Reformatory," *Minnesota Daily* (July 17, 1974), pp. 8–10.

51. Vanden Heuvel, "Press and the Prisons," p. 38.

52. Ibid., p. 39.

53. Jack Newfield, "The Law Is an Outlaw," in *Bread and Roses Too* (New York: E. P. Dutton, 1971), p. 342.

54. Robert Pearman, "The Whip Pays Off," *The Nation* 203 (Dec. 26, 1966), 701.

55. Nicholas C. Chriss, "New Chapter in Horror," *The Nation* 214 (Jan. 10, 1972), 50.

56. *Minneapolis Tribune* (Aug. 4, 1974), p. 9.

57. See Richard C. Allen, Elyce C. Ferster, and Jesse G. Rubin, eds., *Readings in Law and Psychiatry* (Baltimore: Johns Hopkins University Press, 1968).

SUGGESTED READINGS

BURGETT, CLAUDE, et al., "How To Cover Police Story." *Gannetteer* 30 (June, 1975), 1–8.

Cohen, Stanley, and Jock Young, eds., *The Manufacture of News*. Beverly Hills, Calif.: Sage Publications, 1973.

Friendly, Alfred, and Ronald L. Goldfarb, *Crime and Publicity: The Impact of News on the Administration of Justice*. New York: Twentieth Century Fund, 1967.

Wicker, Tom, *A Time to Die*. New York: Quadrangle-The New York Times Book Company, 1975. A personal account of the Attica prison riot that provides useful ideas on covering penal institutions.

chapter eight

Covering Government Agencies
and Services

The media generally do not value state government news very highly.

JOHN BURNS
The Sometime Governments

At all levels of government in the United States, executive departments, commissions, boards, and agencies are organized to deliver government services to people. Guided by legislative intent and checked by the courts, government agencies are administered by the executive branch of government whether at the federal, state, or local level. The executive function of government as it applies to the delivery of services is vast and complex. And these activities are administered by executives who have a number of things in common, as political scientist John C. Ries has observed:

> Whatever their titles, they share many common characteristics. They are expected to take the lead in initiating new policies. They are called upon to define public problems and to come up with solutions for them. They are required to manage the financial, procedural, and practical aspects of government. They occupy the highest offices in the vast complex of agencies through which the government operates. Because they are viewed as solely responsible for the "execution" or the carrying out of the activities of government, we call them executives.[1]

The responsibility of executive agencies may involve monitoring agricultural standards, providing civil defense protection, administering prisons and mental hospitals, dispensing welfare and public health payments, building highways and planning for future growth. Some services are direct; some indirect. Both must be reported on, interpreted and analyzed within the context of important dimensions of executive roles. As Ries puts it:

> First are the stable demands, which explains why Governor Ronald Reagan, for example, conducts many of the affairs of California much as his predecessor Edmund G. Brown did. Second are the differences which are partially accounted for by changing demands on government. Some of these changes reflect shifts in political ideology on the part of the electorate. Some of them result from advances in technology. . . . Finally, there is the personality and political ideology of the incumbent. . . .[2]

Coverage of the executive functions of government would be less difficult if it could be assumed that all agencies and departments within a single system were directly responsible to a single executive. Then, one would contact governors, mayors, and county executives. As early as 1835, the French writer Alexis de Tocqueville used words that are apt today: "The executive power of the state is represented by the governor . . . although he enjoys but a portion of its rights." [3] Municipal governments range from highly centralized "strong mayor" systems to those that are decentralized with interrelated and overlapping checks and balances. In some states, governors appoint members of their cabinets to supervise state agencies; in others, some cabinet members are elected directly by the people. In some states, a governor or mayor will have thousands of political, patronage appointments to make; in others, a tightly organized civil service will fill almost all jobs by competitive examination.

The work of the public affairs reporter is made even more complex by the interdependence of the executive agencies. No agency or department can ever be viewed as an independent entity. It must be seen in its relationship to other units in the executive bureaucracy, in its relationship to the legislature which provides its budget, in its relationship to the courts which monitor its policy. Political scientist Morton Grodzins has rightly observed that one cannot even make simplistic observations about "layers" of government. Indeed, writes Grodzins, the American system of government is more like a marble cake with federal, state, and local functions interrelated and intermingled.[4] Thus, there is the context of intergovernmental relations whereby an agency may blend federal, state, and local funds in its allocations mix.

Covering the Executive Process

While the importance of the executive process in terms of public services or monitoring nongovernmental activities for the public interest is self-evident, government agencies and departments do not attract much attention in the media. Preoccupied with coverage of the seemingly more newsworthy activities of legislatures, courts, and chief executives, the municipal, state, and federal bureaucracies often escape the scrutiny of the press. John Burns's lament that the press does "not value state government news very highly" might even be understated, though Burns himself admitted that "such news usually ranks a poor third behind national and local news." [5]

Paul Simon, former lieutenant governor of Illinois and a journalist, has urged editors "to help destroy the attitude on the part of reporters that an assignment to Springfield (or any other capital) is an assignment to purgatory." [6] Simon continued:

> Too often good reporters view the state capital as an unhappy stopping place on the way to Washington or some other assignment. A good example is Tom Littlewood of the Chicago *Sun-Times,* one of the best reporters on the state scene. After some years, he happily moved on to Washington. I don't blame him, but state government suffered a loss.[7]

To Simon and other critics of the noncoverage of government departments and agencies, partial blame can be laid to a tendency of the media not to follow through on a story. A new program for drug abuse may, for example, be announced with fanfare by a government or mayor, move through the legislature or city council with conflict and argumentation. All of this is covered with lively flair by the press. When the program moves to the implementation stage, however, to the state or municipal agency, it seems to lack news appeal. It drops out of the press's vision. Yet, whether the new program succeeds or fails may be the most important aspect of the story.

Some municipal governments get more coverage of agencies and services than do state governments—due partly to the beat system whereby a reporter covers city hall on a regular basis. But even at the municipal level the emphasis is on the day-to-day views of executives and lawmakers. Part of the problem is that many agencies and departments are covered only as they collide with the executive or legislative authorities. A health commissioner argues about a program before a city council, a county commission, or a legislative committee; a highway department director openly criticizes the governor; state employees decide to strike in defiance of the courts. These activities get coverage whereas the major part of the agency's activity, the organization and delivery of services, is ignored. One reason for this lack of systematic coverage is the exodus of reporters from a state capital once the legislature recesses. In many states there are dozens of regular legislative correspondents, but few reporters are given responsibility for covering state agencies on a regular basis. Increasingly, some of the functions of agencies are being covered by such specialists as environmental writers and medical writers. The specialist, however, covers the agency only as it relates to his particular story, making no attempt to systematically examine all of the services provided. Thus, with the infrequent coverage by legislative correspondents and the highly selected coverage by specialists, the treatment of government agencies and institutions is necessarily fragmented.

Attempting to reverse this pattern of noncoverage are groups such as the Council of State Governments. The council has organized a national task force to stimulate coverage of government services. Ralph Nader and other consumer advocates have offered vivid illustrations of the vital role state agencies and departments play in the lives of people. Schools of journalism are also now urging improvement in public affairs reporting on the state level.

Reporting Functions and Government Agencies

There are no doubt hundreds of reasons why the press should cover government agencies and services. Three that stand out in bold relief, though, are:

The Watchdog Role. As a watchdog, the press keeps an eye on the activities of government, looking for conflict of interest or other improper conduct. In this function, the press is an adversary of government, demanding that it serve the public interest through an ethical delivery of services.

The Performance-Monitor Role. In this function, the press is not necessarily adversarial, but more neutral. It looks for standards by which the work of an agency can be evaluated, judged for what it is worth on neither a positive nor negative basis.

The Service-Utilization Role. Here the press attempts to help people utilize effectively the services to which they are entitled.

Sometimes the roles overlap in the same story, of course, but the model of three roles is helpful in directing the reporter toward more thoughtful coverage of government agencies or services.

In the spotty coverage of agencies and services, the watchdog story is most common. Winners of Pulitzer Prizes for community service often engage in watchdog journalism. A notable example was George Thiem's series in the *Chicago Daily News* some years ago that proved improper fiscal management and embezzlement on the part of the Illinois state auditor. Also in this genre are the traditional exposé stories that reveal corruption in government. The exposé traces its origins to the journalism of Nelly Bly, who wrote a sensational series on life in the "madhouse" for the *New York Sun*. The exposé often involves subterfuge on the part of the reporter who poses as a prisoner or mental patient and then reveals a firsthand account of the horrors observed. The result of many exposés has been scapegoating of particular public officials (e.g., a warden) and collective legislative clucking. The exposé sometimes helps stimulate legislation, improve funding, and change conditions. However, the exposé form with its attendant sensationalism has mostly passed out of fashion. Exposés require relatively simple targets and simple, easily understood conditions. The growing recognition that social conditions are extremely complex has reduced the tendency to indulge in exposés. One notable exception has been the continuous coverage of the Willowbrook State School, an institution for the mentally retarded, on Staten Island, New York, which has been under fire for more than twenty years. Newspapers and television news shows, in a reformist bent, are still pointing to overcrowded, subhuman conditions at Willowbrook, and demanding change.

In recent years more subtle watchdogging has been apparent in the press. Quesions about agency functions are raised. Instead of searching for overt incompetence or corruption, reporters look for conditions caused not by individuals per se but by sluggish bureaucracies and inappropriate governmental structures. This story about the Chicago transit situation is an example:

> There is a model train on display at the offices of the Chicago Transit Authority. It's painted the regulation green and white. At the side of the tracks, switches flash their lights. Plastic commuters stand on the platform and wait. The train rarely gets to them. It's too slow, it stalls and nobody pays attention to it. Neglect plagues the CTA itself, with its 1,329 real subway cars, 3,300 buses, and a very real $30 million it may lose this year. It is just starting to get attention now, because its 800,000 daily riders are not plastic people, but real people who can scream and vote.[8]

Closely related to the watchdog story is the agency performance story. Inherently less sensational than the conflict stories of corruption, the agency performance story centers on the question of how well the agency is doing its job. The reporter asks about the agency's function, its interaction with other agencies, its relative power in the governmental arena. Here the reporter must learn to dissect and analyze programs and to ask the right questions. The reporter's job here is quite difficult because government officials like to talk about success, not failure. They try to accentuate programs that are highly visible and that make them look good. Programs that are less than successful are often not discussed. The information on agencies that makes news usually flows from official press releases, news conferences, and interviews with officials. The government is seldom averse to announcing new programs, but it is not nearly so zealous about following up on old ones. Status stories are released, but usually they are quite self-serving.

This article by Trudy Lieberman in the *Detroit Free Press* illustrates the subtleties of monitoring agency activity:

> The consumer press has frequently castigated government agencies for not releasing information deemed to be in the interests of consumers.
>
> But in an ironic switch, the usually zealous consumer press can be partly blamed for the elimination by the Federal Trade Commission (FTC) of press releases on flammable fabrics. For it was press indifference coupled with some well-applied pressure by the carpet industry's trade association that led the agency to announce on Nov. 9 that it was killing its release program on flammable fabrics.[9]

Inside the Agency

Reporters rarely look single-mindedly at one agency, but instead at a whole array of agencies. From them they must choose those that will be useful sources of news. The agencies that usually get the most attention are the ones that (1) are developing new programs or making major changes; (2) are building new facilities, selecting sites for new hospitals, colleges, experiment stations; (3) affect the greatest number of people; (4) fit in with topical issues of interest at the time; or (5) are deemed to be important in terms of public policy.

Agency bureaucrats usually would prefer to see stories in the press on their own terms. It is the responsibility of the reporter, however, to translate the activities of the agency into pertinent information for people. One function of agency stories only recently recognized is the service-utilization role. A typical story about a new health center might focus on a physician and quote him, using his language to explain the function of the center. It does the public little good to hear about "innovative programs," "broad panoplies of service," "crisis intervention programs," and "comprehensive modalities of treatment" without knowing what this bureaucratic jargon means specifically. The reporter must be able to translate these terms into information that makes sense to readers who are also potential users of these services. In a story aimed at helping the disadvantaged use the services to which they were entitled, Margaret Kuehlthau of the *Tucson Daily Citizen* wrote:

> Are the minority groups in Tucson, the needy and those just on the borderline of poverty, using to any great degree many agencies ready to assist them?
>
> The answer is a loud resounding, "No!"
>
> A Tucson *Daily Citizen* survey indicates that most tend to use only governmental health and welfare agencies. Spokesmen for many charitable and social agencies gave this almost unanimous response: "We could help many more poor people but they do not seem to be aware of the services which we have to offer. If they do, seemingly they do not care to use our services." [10]

In some instances it is important that citizens know the distinction among different kinds of services to save themselves long trips and long waits where services are offered. Although governmental agencies have become more concerned about providing adequate information to the public about human services, there is still no central location for such information and the press must continue to serve this vital function. As one community organizer put it, "During the heyday of the community mental health movement we were worried that we would be overwhelmed with patients demanding to use our services even though we couldn't help them with their specific problems. Good stories in the media, telling what we could and could not do, saved the day." [11]

To some reporters there is little excitement in helping people use services. They see this function as a glorified bulletin board. It need not be. The kind of reporting of services that is needed should be discerning and questioning. Here the reporter is the eyes and ears of the public, attempting to ask the questions that a consumer of services would want to know: Can I use it? Am I eligible? How good is it? How does it differ from what was available before? How do I get there? Falling into the agency bureaucrat's jargon, thus obscuring a clear view of the services, does just the opposite of helping people to better utilize public services.

Agency News Sources

The reporter covering an agency needs an understanding of bureaucracy and how bureaucrats operate. He needs to know how the agency is organized, who does what, and what's in a title. Often stories about government agencies refer to the source as an assistant commissioner or community liaison officer without any indication of what the person does, who he speaks for, and what degree of expertise he has. All too frequently the reporter deals with a governmental information officer who is sometimes "an underling whose only aim is to get the boss's name in print," [12] writes an editorialist in the *Delaware Valley News* of Frenchtown, N. J. So many government information officers these days are well-trained writer-publicists who are among the strategists trying to inspire confidence in the agency they represent. They usually provide honest, rapid information when asked, but otherwise spend their time attempting to get favorable publicity for programs and projects. Usually they are busy people with more responsibilities than they can carry out, and can both aid and mislead the reporter. One of the most misleading practices (and sometimes it is unconscious) of government information officers and government officials generally is to fail to distinguish between *planning* and *implementation*. A cautionary note: it is always important to find out the exact status of a program. Sometimes such a determination is not easy to make from an interview without asking specific questions: Is the program actually operating now, or is it just in the planning stage? When will people be able to take advantage of the service? Questions like these often lead to qualifications and a little clearer explanation—that, for example, it may be seven years before the new recreation center for teen-agers opens its doors. Usually there are announcements by various legislative bodies, the agency itself, and others long before the new facility is completed. One of the functions of the press is to provide the public with an awareness of what stages government projects and programs are in—a kind of status table. Such reporting will furnish the public with the kind of information it needs to hold the government accountable for its activity—or inactivity.

Also important for the reporter in covering government services is to recognize the distance between central office rhetoric and field office activity. Sometimes the programs perceived by supervisors in the state capital as operating are only on the drawing board in the field. Similarly, there is often a misunderstanding between the management personnel at the state or regional level and those who implement programs at the grass roots. These differences can make for interesting copy. For example, federal law enforcement initiatives should be viewed not only from the state and regional offices of the LEEA, but from the project-level firing line too. The federal government's objective may call for better preventive measures. The state, with federal assistance, may have funded a halfway house supervised by a regional state crime committee. But the day-to-day problems of this halfway house—and its battles with a middle-class community that wants no part of it—many make for a much more vital story than a dull interview with the state commissioner of corrections. It may also be more useful to the reader to get a broader view of several halfway house projects, rather than a single case.

In the 1970s federal revenue-sharing funds also complicate the local picture with less clearly defined lines of authority between local and state agencies. This growing tendency for shared funding at several governmental levels leads to interesting stories about how funds are being used and for what purpose. Making sense out of the complex web of government activity, however, is a singularly difficult assignment. Yet its importance at all levels is pointed up by Joe Pierson of the *Binghamton* (N.Y.) *Evening Sun,* a county reporter, who described his job as follows: "Perhaps a task of equal difficulty (equal to getting governments to cooperate) is transcribing in readable, if not lyrical, form the decisions, actions, details, intricacies and personalities that make the governments click or falter. In other words, the job of reporting the government's activities in depth." [13] In jocular fashion, Pierson urged reporters of government services to develop these attributes:

> The curiosity of a 4-year-old. (Government officials love to be questioned by reporters.)
> The patience of a fly fisherman. (Those same officials always seem to be busiest when the reporter wants them the most.)
> The mathematical genius of an Einstein. (To interpret those budgets and allocation formulas.)
> A law degree. (To interpret legal papers, especially reapportionment suits.)
> A diploma from a Dale Carnegie course. (To make friends and influence sources.) [14]

Reporters who look beyond their local assignments can find useful assistance on topical and agency subjects in a variety of places. The League of Municipalities and the Council of State Governments, among others, have active publications and information dissemination programs. There are also citizen groups, such as the League of Women Voters, that monitor and report on government activities. Sometimes citizen and government task forces also supply this information. At the state level useful information can be found in the state's "blue book," sometimes called a "red book" or state directory. These volumes usually have factual information about state agencies, state laws, and state constitutional requirements. Some cities also have public affairs directories which list the names of municipal agencies and their officers and explain interrelationships between intra- and inter-governmental units.

Agencies through the Executive

At the policy-making level, an agency is often perceived differently by its chief executive (mayor or governor) than it is by those inside the administrative apparatus of the department itself. This difference can be observed in the kind of information that comes from official messages to the legislature, from staff papers, and from interviews. Covering an agency that is a particular favorite of a governor, for example, can prove especially interesting to the reporter. In fact, knowing in what esteem the agency is held by the executive or his staff is usually a good indicator of its relative power. Those who followed the career of New York's master builder Robert Moses were always aware of his relationship with governors, mayors, and members of Congress. These relationships—whether warm or heated—invariably reflected the amount of support—and money—Moses was likely to get from the legislature or city hall.

Reporters also must know what involvement the executive has with a particular agency. Is there an official in his office who monitors its activities? Does the commissioner or director report directly to the governor or the mayor? Here the structural and organizational questions of who reports to whom and with what effect can be vital indicators of stories to come. Certainly it is useful to view the agency from the standpoint of the chief executive and his program. This provides valuable contextual understanding as the reporter gets a sense of where and how the agency fits into the executive's total program.

Budgets and Services

No reporter can have a full understanding of a government agency without some knowledge of public finances. Excluding the legislative body, which usually grants the funds, organization for fiscal management includes:

1. Agencies in the executive branch that must have money in order to carry out their programs.
2. Agencies organized primarily to implement the acquisition of funds and oversee their expenditure.
3. Agencies created to check on the fidelity and legality of disbursements after they have been made.[15]

The specific function and power of chief executive officers, treasurers, budget officers, comptrollers, auditors and purchasing agents must be known by the public affairs reporter. The titles—and relative position and authority—of these officials differ from one jurisdiction to another. But whatever they are called, they are important in tracing the budget process. A budget according to public administrators Russell Maddox and Robert Fuquay, is "a comprehensive plan, expressed in financial terms, by which an operating program is effective for a given period of time. It includes estimates of (a) the services, activities and projects comprising the program; (b) the resultant expenditure requirements; and (c) the resources usable for their support." [16] Tracing an agency's budget for the purpose of evaluating its effectiveness is difficult, but not impossible. Budget planning usually begins in the agency, proceeds to an intermediate budget office, and eventually is taken into consideration by the chief executive's fiscal advisers. The steps along the way, differing from state to state and city to city, are fascinating adventures in priorities and decision-making process. Eventually, the product of this negotiation becomes part of an official legislative request and often is best considered from the legislative hearing room where agency officials go to testify. Indeed, the style of these legislative presentations may be yet another clue to an agency's plight or situation. Some presentations are flamboyant and are accompanied by visual aids; others are quieter and more measured. Legislative budget hearings also offer lawmakers the opportunity to support certain officials on certain projects and to denounce others with whom they disagree. Thus, governmental budget hearings can make good news copy.

For most reporters, understanding the budget is difficult, and they have too little time in which to thoroughly analyze it and translate it into terms the public can grasp. Reporters tend to become preoccupied with how much larger—or smaller—the budget is than the previous one. Some newspapers now hire accountants and tax attorneys to assist in the complex job of making city and state budgets intelligible. Such quasi-governmental units as school boards and airport commissions are also coming in for this kind of scrutiny. In this way the annual budget story becomes comprehensible. More and more reporters are also humanizing the budget story by translating it into personal terms. For example, in the wake of the 1971 Los Angeles earthquake, the *Los Angeles Times* focused on the fiscal practices of the Small Business Administration (SBA). One story in a superb series by Robert Rawitch and George Reasons began:

> The Small Business Administration handed out $211 million to assist earthquake victims here last year, but a large share of that money went to thousands who did not deserve it. Overpayments for repairs by the SBA and misuse of the disaster funds by the homeowner probably cost the taxpayer millions of dollars, available evidence indicates.[17]

In this unusual budget follow-up story, which discussed the way in which the budget was administered along with its initial intent, the reporters interviewed more than 100 homeowners, contractors, SBA appraisers, and mortgage holders, as well as a wide range of public officials. They also made comprehensive checks of documentary sources ranging from the rolls of the county tax assessor to the public records of the SBA itself. This story, which highlighted the human consequences of governmental fiscal management after an earthquake, demonstrates the need and the interest that can be generated in budget follow-ups. The *Times* series urged reform in the emergency loan and relief programs of the federal government.

Covering Levels of Government

The *Los Angeles Times* story is also a fine example of how a news-paper can use local resources to cover a story of national significance. One way in which to use these resources is to cover federal programs from the standpoint of their impact on the local area. Most cities have a federal building that houses the regional offices of federal agencies, rang-ing from the office of the U.S. attorney, who represents the Department of Justice, to the Weather Bureau. In the regional offices, the reporter is dealing with middle-level bureaucrats who have limited contact with Washington. But finding out just how much contact they have with their federal department is important. In the early 1970s some federal offices at the regional level, partly due to revenue sharing, were given certain autonomous powers by Washington. Local federal offices can be used to present the local angle on a national story, or to get information in order to present the national background on a local story. Reporters can also get assistance on information about national programs from the staffs of senators and congressmen who usually have offices in the local federal building. Agencies are often more responsive to elected officials than to reporters; therefore, this avenue of prying loose information should be used. The Federal Freedom of Information Act, designed to make govern-ment information available to the public, can also be used as leverage to gain information from local federal offices.*

State government can be covered from the state capital, where many departments are headquartered, or in some states from the largest city, where important state functions are carried out. Of course, most state governments have some presence in almost every local community and can be covered in a manner similar to that suggested for the federal government.

Although many of the examples presented in this chapter refer to state, city and metropolitan government, they have wider application. Agencies and services exist, of course, at every level of government from

* For information about how the FOI Act can be used by the press see Ap-pendix D, "How to Use the New 1974 FOI Act."

the large federal bureaucracy to villages, townships, boroughs, counties and other political jurisdictions. There are thousands of units of government in the United States, many overlapping and interrelated. But the general assumptions about the executive process presented earlier in this chapter apply.

The tendency toward decentralization of government has also affected municipalities, which have fanned out their services to local neighborhoods in an unprecedented manner. Covering city hall may now mean getting a more thorough knowledge of local community areas. County governments, which also operate agencies and services responsible to the county board of commissioners or its administrator, have also extended their services. The growing tendency toward metropolitan government is another phenomenon that deserves the attention of the public affairs reporter. Metro governments have varying degrees of authority, but they do serve as useful sources of information about the delivery of services to an entire metropolitan area. Metro government administrators and their staffs can supply valuable insights about the interlocking and interrelated nature of various governmental agencies, thus saving the reporter much time. Similarly, many interstate compacts and other intergovernmental relationships are important in understanding how policies are conceived and how services are delivered to the public.

All these visibly interrelated workings of government may presage more broadly based coverage by the media of government and its services. The present practice of covering the city hall, the metropolitan offices, the state capitol, or the federal building should be replaced by topical coverage that looks at problems and programs of interest to people with wider vision and that draws generously from many sources for news regardless of arbitrary beat boundaries. Stories about land-use or health or mass transit should not be developed by limiting contact to one or two agencies. They should be based on many sources of information.

The public affairs reporter who prepares for coverage of public agencies and services—potentially the most important governmental story of the future as people become increasingly consumer-oriented and as government continues to play a greater and greater role in their lives—must prepare himself by studying state and local government, taxation, and urban politics. He must also keep abreast of developments in these fields. In this connection, more and more university journalism programs are being organized to assist the reporter already on the job. During 1974, for example, there was a special conference for public affairs reporters covering law enforcement. In the final analysis, the coverage of agencies and services must be seen in human terms and within the complex interplay of the executive process.

NOTES

1. John C. Ries, *Executives in the American Political System* (Belmont, Calif.: Dickenson, 1969), p. 2.

2. Ibid., p. 3.

3. Alexis de Tocqueville, *Democracy in America*, 2 vols. (New York: Vintage Books, 1954), vol. 1, p. 88.

4. Morton Grodzins, *The American System: A New View of Government in the United States* (New York: Random House, 1966).

5. Ralph Whitehead, Jr., and Howard M. Ziff, "Statehouse Coverage: Lobbyists Outlast Journalists," *Columbia Journalism Review* 12 (1974), 11.

6. Paul Simon, "Improving Statehouse Coverage," *Columbia Journalism Review* 11 (Sept.-Oct., 1973), 51.

7. Ibid.

8. Ralph Whitehead, Jr., "The CTA: Does Anybody Give a Damn?" *Chicago Journalism Review* 3 (April, 1970), 9.

9. Trudy Lieberman, "Press Indifference and Manufacturer Vigilance Kill FTC's Flammability Releases," *Media & Consumer* 1 (April, 1972), 24; reprinted from the Detroit *Free Press* (Nov. 9, 1971).

10. Margaret Kuehlthau, "Big Gap Exists in Use of Agencies," *Tucson Daily Citizen* (April 29, 1968), special supplement, p. 14.

11. Paul I. Kliger, presentation at workshop on "Understanding the Human Condition: Mental Health and the Mass Media" (American Orthopsychiatric Assn. annual meeting, March 26, 1970, San Francisco).

12. "The Press Release," *Grassroots Editor* 12 (Nov-Dec., 1971), 32; reprinted from *Delaware Valley News,* Frenchtown, N.J.

13. Joe Pierson, "The Recurring Problem of Reapportionment," *The Gannetteer* (Dec., 1965), p. 27.

14. Ibid.

15. Russell W. Maddox and Robert F. Fuquay, *State and Local Government* (Princeton, N.J.: D. Van Nostrand, 1966), p. 389.

16. Ibid., p. 393–94. For another useful treatment of fiscal administration and budgets see James W. Fesler, ed., *The Fifty States and Their Local Governments* (New York: Knopf, 1967), and Charles R. Adrian, *Governing Our Fifty States and Their Communities* (New York: McGraw-Hill, 1972).

17. Robert Rawitch and George Reasons, "Mass Fraud Found in '71 SBA Quake Loans," *Los Angeles Times* (April 10, 1972), p. 1.

SUGGESTED READINGS

Hills, William G., et al., *Conducting the People's Business: The Framework and Functions of Public Administration.* Norman: University of Oklahoma

Press, 1973. Useful commentary and readings growing out of research, consultation, training and administration of human service agencies.

REAGAN, MICHAEL D., *The New Federalism*. New York: Oxford University Press, 1972. Lucid discussion of revenue-sharing and intergovernmental administrative relationships.

State Government, journal of state affairs published by the Council of State Governments, Lexington, Kentucky, 40505. Articles by state officials, researchers and others on governmental problems and issues. Published quarterly.

WILDAVSKY, AARON, *The Politics of the Budgetary Process* (2nd ed.). Boston: Little, Brown, 1974. An analysis of the political aspects of budgetmaking. Many examples from the Federal government, but useful at all levels of executive decision-making.

chapter nine

Covering Politics and Elections

*If you were to generalize—probably outrageously—
and say you know what really is at the root of so
much of the discontent with political institutions in
this country, I think you would suppose it is the feeling that seems to be so widespread, and it goes from
the ghetto to the affluent suburb, that events are taking
place and decisions are being made in this political
process without the meaningful understanding and
participation of the people who are affected by those
decisions. This is really an indictment of the press and
the politician equally.*

DAVID S. BRODER

The shortcomings of both press and politician in fulfilling the democratic process have often been remarked by less qualified observers than
the *Washington Post*'s political columnist David Broder. And it is small
comfort to devotees of the press that the indictments of the media have
been figurative, whereas those of some politicians in recent times have
been literal. The press—despite the credit reflected on it by the *Post*'s
dogged disclosures of Watergate corruption—shares with politicians a
low regard by the public that ranges from indifference to distrust.

The public's low regard for both may perhaps best be seen in the
low voter turnout that characterizes elections in the United States—despite the inevitable urgings by media and politicians for citizens to do
their duty. The extent to which the press is responsible for voter apathy
is a subject for conjecture, but the shortcomings of the media in covering
politics have been documented again and again by responsible critics.
These shortcomings range from superficiality to outright bias, and include,

more specifically, reliance on handouts, dependence on events, a too-rigid adherence to an idealized objectivity, the herd instinct, and the misuse of polls. They also include the failure to dig: for the facts of campaign financing, for the authenticity of organizations and endorsements, and for what people—the apathetic and the not-so-apathetic—are thinking about the issues that concern them.

The criticism has come in bursts—at two- and four-year intervals, much of it being directed at coverage of congressional and presidential campaigns and elections. But politics is a continuing activity, locally as well as nationally, and apprentice reporters, whether or not their goal is a Washington assignment, need to be aware of its ramifications. The contest for power that is politics may underlie a grand jury's report criticizing administration of a state mental hospital if the jury's foreman happens to be an ardent Democrat and the board of hospital supervisers happens to be dominated by a Republican committee-woman. It should not pass unseen by reporters covering courts simply because their focus is too narrowly on the judicial process. Reporters assigned to education are myopic indeed if they fail to note that the newest appointee to the state commission on higher education was a heavy contributor to the campaign of the governor who makes the appointment. Politics, then, pervades most of the action in the public arena; it is not merely a biennial or quadrennial contest culminating at the polls. Public affairs reporters, whatever their beat, need to recognize the maneuvers and identify the players. A reporter who shows the inclination and aptitude, may move up to regular coverage of politics; it is a coveted assignment on most newspaper staffs, gained, traditionally, via city hall and statehouse experience. If the reporter's first job is on a small daily or a weekly, initiation in coverage of political events may come in an assignment to report a county convention. Or, on a larger daily, it may come in monitoring a number of precinct polling places or the county auditor's offices on election night when the entire staff is mobilized for the harvest of election returns. The county convention may seem like ritualized tedium, relieved, if at all, by committee reports and occasional balloting; and the election night, a vigil protracted by an auditor's inefficiency in reporting results in a crucial county. But as these isolated events come to be perceived in the context of the political process, the fascination of watching the exercise and pursuit of power takes hold.

The Reporter and Political Reality

Politicians, political scientists, opinion analysts, and just plain observers have long debated the extent of the influence of the mass media on elections. Those who minimized the influence of editorial page endorsements invariably have pointed to Franklin D. Roosevelt's heavy reelection majorities in the face of overwhelming newspaper opposition. Most voters are Democrats, but most newspapers back Republicans. Yet communications researcher John P. Robinson, directing a study for the University of Michigan's Institute for Social Research, concluded that the influence of newspaper endorsements is seriously underestimated; he found that newspaper support "had a significant bearing" on the votes cast for Nixon in both 1968 and 1972.[1] Other factors affecting voter behavior cited by Robinson are those most often noted in other studies: party identification, age, education, region, size of city, ethnicity, economic status.

Whatever the effect of editorial endorsements on election results, there can be little doubt of the importance of campaign coverage in the news columns and on the television screen. Political scientist Frank Sorauf, citing a Survey Research Center report "that in the 1968 campaign only 22 percent of American adults had been contacted by someone from one of the parties," concludes that "most of the voting electorate, in other words, were reached exclusively, if at all, by the mass media." [2] As two other political scientists express it: "Mass communications . . . furnish much of the material from which voters build their mental pictures of political reality." [3] Those pictures were markedly altered by television, for example, in the unique Kennedy-Nixon debates of 1960, which caused a shift in voter preference from Nixon to Kennedy.

The precedent of the "Great Debate," however, has been largely ignored ever since by politicians—particularly by the incumbents. The voter had to look closely, indeed, to catch a glimpse of political reality in the noncampaign of incumbent Nixon in 1972. At such times, the responsibility of the political reporter becomes especially large.

What is that responsibility? What are the functions that the political writer must fulfill if the voter's picture of reality is not to become hopelessly skewed, blurred, or incomplete? Those functions can be identified as follows:

Reporting and interpreting events
Defining issues
Portraying personalities
Investigating support
Identifying trends
Checking and analyzing public opinion

These functions are as applicable on the local level as they are on the state and national; the stakes may be higher in Washington, but the interest may be more intense in Goshen or Gallipolis.

Before looking at these functions, in turn, some generalizations about the reporter and the political process deserve attention. They apply to the reporter who undertakes any and all of these functions.

If ever the heat of reporters' curiosity needs to be fueled by skepticism, that time is when they are checking with political sources. It's not that the politician necessarily lies—although some do—or creates pseudo events—although many do—or withholds or only partially discloses information—although most do. It's just that the relationship between reporter and politician is essentially adversarial.[4] They need each other, but the politician's need of the reporter is as a channel to the public in his pursuit and retention of power, whereas the reporter's need of the politician is as a source of reliable information. The needs do not regularly balance out in favor of the public interest. The device of the leak, for example, discussed with reference to the legal process in Chapter 7, is used by the politician for his own ends. Those ends may be to provoke action or to undermine an opponent or to test public response to a possible course of action. The leaked information may also be useful to the reporter, though not until he has verified it with other sources. Many a reporter has been left feeling used—and abused—because his too-ready acceptance of the reliability of a source led him to publish misinformation. Furthermore, of course, some politicians are not above claiming they have been misquoted, so the reporter is well-advised to retain his notes.

The healthy skepticism of the reporter may be compromised in some instances by too close an association with a political source. The reporter may rationalize a chummy relationship with a politician in office on the grounds that it will serve him and his newspaper well by making him privy to "the real inside." But if he enjoys dining at the politician's home and is a friend of the family, how likely is he to then ask the really hard questions that may embarrass his source?

The political reporter is vulnerable enough to charges of bias without that kind of association. In an area of news where merely the publication of a public figure's name is held to be an advantage, contenders for the public's attention are quick to charge favoritism. It would appear that the political reporter whose newspaper endorses candidates is particularly susceptible to bias in favor of those the paper supports. A number of studies have shown that unfortunately a paper's editorial endorsement tends to be reflected in the news columns of the paper.[5] That reflection may lie in space allocations, which are outside the reporter's range of responsibility, but it should not show in the reporter's writing, which is well within it.

One of the most frequently voiced criticisms of political reporting is that it relies heavily on handouts. The promotional mills of political candidates and officeholders grind frequently, and always in self-interest. How much of their output gets published would seem to depend on a newspaper's policy, but also on the energy and initiative of the reporter. A study published by the American Institute for Political Communication suggests that dependence on press releases by Washington correspondents varies inversely with the amount of news competition faced by their home papers: the less competition, the more dependence.[6] There is little reason to believe that the finding would not apply as well to the use of campaign publicity at every level of government. One of the troubles with the release, of course, is that it tends to put a barrier between the candidate or officeholder and the reporter; it is the information that the originator wants the public to have, and unless the reporter probes beyond it, or rejects it out of hand, the picture of political reality suffers further diminution.

Reporting Functions
and the Political Process

Politics—"this striving to win the things one holds desirable" [7]—is limited for the political reporter to the sphere of government and public policy. Although, as we have suggested, its ramifications are not confined to campaigns and elections, "the most critical political decisions are those determining who will hold public office; for by these decisions we decide who will decide all other questions." [8] The process of such determination, then, is the essential political process. That process encompasses institutions (the parties), events (campaigns and elections), issues, personalities, and, of course, the electorate on whom the entire process is based. The accuracy of the picture of political reality provided by the media depends upon the ability of the political reporter to understand and interpret all of these components. Such, then, are his functions.

Reporting and Interpreting Events   The well-educated public affairs reporter today comes to a political assignment with a background of courses in American government and politics. He has an understanding of the two-party system: the loose confederation of sectional and state interests in both parties at the national level, the relative autonomy of state parties, the wide variations in the effectiveness of one or both parties at the local level. He knows that this two-party system is represented structurally, with wide variations among states, by functionaries and committees that tend to parallel voting districts: from precinct through ward and city (if urban) to county, to state legislative and judicial, to congressional. He knows that the party structure, for all its apparent similarity to the public's image of a political machine, is only occasionally, if ever, complete in all its parts, and that the locus of power is more often in the city or county than in the state organization. Because party organizations are regulated, in varying detail, by state statute rather than by federal law, he will be familiar with the relevant statutes of his state. He recognizes the pragmatism of party organizations at all levels by their purposes, which are recruiting, fund raising, and patronage. He also recognizes that they are considerably less concerned about issues, except as issues may help to determine the outcome of elections. If, in his state, party auxiliaries of dues-paying voluntary-membership clubs have been formed to articulate ideology, or simply to circumvent statutory regulations, he is aware of their influence. He is also conscious of the political influence of such nonparty organizations as chambers of commerce and labor unions. He appreciates the role of the parties in government, their part in organizing and promoting party interests in deliberative bodies from city councils to the national Congress. And he is aware that on the local level nonpartisan elections of commissioners (in the commission form of government) and councilmen (in the city manager form)—a practice that has grown widely in this century—do not mean an absence of politics, but rather that politics are managed by persons not responsible to party organizations.

Political science courses will also have made the educated newcomer to political reporting familiar with the key events of the political process: the primaries, the conventions, the campaigns, and the elections. The variations in practice among the states with reference to primaries alone defy generalization. Fewer than half the states have adopted the presidential primary, but all of them use direct primaries to nominate candidates for some or all local and state offices, and these primaries vary from closed to open to "blanket," which permits voting for candidates from both parties. So the political writer, just as a starter, will know which practices apply to his locale. His reader may cherish the notion that the primary serves the function for which it was intended—to democratize the nominating process by removing it from the control of party cadres—but the reporter should be able to tell him to what extent the party organization has foreclosed genuine competition, whether through prior endorsement at a convention or by the more covert dissuasion of possible candidates. The immense advantage enjoyed by incumbents and the dominance of one party in some states and electoral districts only partially account for the thinness of competition in most primaries.

Assuming that the novice political writer will not immediately be assigned to cover a national convention, he may nonetheless win spurs at county, district, or state versions of the quadrennial spectacle. Whether the purpose of the convention is to endorse candidates or elect party officials or select delegates to the next higher convention, the procedure is pretty much the same: a keynote speech, reports of committees—credentials, rules, nominating or endorsements, and platform (if any)—and debate and voting on the reports by the delegates. Conventions are usually characterized by factional struggle, much of which goes on in the committee sessions and is prefigured by the composition of the committees. Because conflict is such a traditional staple of news reporting, no reporter needs to be told to look for it. What he does need to look for are the issues, the ideologies, the personalities, and the histories that underlie the conflicts so that his report of the convention can help the reader to understand it in the context of the political process.

Conflict is obviously a staple, as well, of the series of events that constitute political campaigning. In no aspect of the political process have the media come to play a more important role. Television and radio, particularly, have brought about what is often called "the new campaigning," managed by public relations and advertising firms, whose decisions are based on public opinion polling.

It is precisely because these experts know the customs of the media journalists and exploit them to the advantage of their clients that the commonly practiced standard of objectivity is too often a disservice to the reader—and the viewer. Timothy Crouse, whose account of life with the 1972 campaign press corps, *The Boys on the Bus,* is a litany of reproaches against the inadequacy of objectivity, crisp wire service leads, and the herd instinct in reporting events, quotes Brit Hume, columnist Jack Anderson's former legman:

> "Those guys on the plane," said Hume, "claim that they're trying to be objective. They shouldn't try to be objective, they should try to be honest. And they're *not* being honest. Their so-called objectivity is just a guise for superficiality. They report what one candiate said, then they go and report what the other candidate said with equal credibility. They never get around to finding out if the guy is telling the truth. They just pass the speeches along without trying to confirm the substance of what the candidates are saying. What they pass off as objectivity is just a mindless kind of neutrality." [9]

Gene Wyckoff, himself a sought-after producer of campaign films for television, after telling how it's done in *The Image Candidates,* remarks: "Television's slavish devotion to the stopwatch may also serve to reduce the substance of political statements to incidental dialogue between dramatic characters in conflict. Newscasts typically edit a candidate's SOF [sound-on-film] remarks to the most pithy and provocative sentences and, without elaboration or evaluation of the condensed statement, juxtapose it with a contrary statement by the opposition." [10] As for more extended, face-to-face confrontations of candidates on news-feature programs, Wyck-off continues:

> Even when the candidates are given more time to answer and rebut answers of questions about campaign issues, viewers may be forced to judge style rather than substance of the arguments because candidates are often in serious disagreement as to the basic facts and such disagreements are rarely (if ever) set straight by the professional television journalists conducting the program. The failure should not be dismissed with the comment that the professional television journalists might not be prepared to inform the viewer where the truth lies. Technically it is quite feasible (and hardly more expensive) to record candidate confrontations on videotape and delay broadcast twenty-four or forty-eight hours until the facts cited by the candidates can be authenticated and appraised by inserted remarks by the program moderators.
>
> But however feasible in a technical sense, any appraisal of political candidates or their remarks by television newsmen would constitute a cardinal sin against the medium's most holy commandment: *Thou shalt not offend.*[11]

Whether motivated by fear of offending listeners or of being cut by the copy desk, the journalist who considers himself merely a conduit is serving the politician and shortchanging the electorate. A journalist who broke away from the conduit role in the 1972 campaign was NBC correspondent Catherine Mackin. The incident was so unusual that it has been recounted by a number of media critics, including Edwin Diamond:

> "Catherine Mackin has been campaigning with the President," John Chancellor noted on NBC the night of Sept. 28, "and she has some observations to make on the Nixon campaign style. . . ."
>
> With that standard introduction, the *NBC Nightly News* switched to a film report by Cassie Mackin from Los Angeles. It looked like a typical item from the wind-in-the-hair school of TV journalism: Mackin doing a "standup" outside the hotel where President Nixon had spoken the night before, too late to make the network news programs. But the script that accompanied the routine clips of Richard (and Pat) Nixon shaking hands, climbing into helicopters, and appearing at the fund-raising dinner was sharp and unequivocal.
>
> Mackin said that the Nixon campaign consists of "speeches before closed audiences—invited guests only. . . ." She reported that the press was getting only glimpses of Nixon as he campaigned. Then she added: "There is a serious question of whether President Nixon is setting up straw men by leaving the very strong impression that McGovern is making certain proposals which in fact he is not . . ."

The film cut to Richard Nixon speaking of "some who believe" in defense budget cuts that "would make the United States the second-strongest nation . . . with the second-strongest Army . . . with the second-strongest Air Force . . ." Then back to Mackin: "The President obviously meant McGovern's proposed defense budget, but his criticism never specified how the McGovern plan would weaken the country. On welfare, the President accuses McGovern of wanting to give those on welfare more than those who work—which is not true. On tax reform, the President says McGovern has called for 'confiscation of wealth'—which is not true."

It was a critical moment in NBC's coverage of the 1972 presidential campaign. Rather than merely re-amplifying a campaign attack, Cassie Mackin was offering a strong corrective—for NBC's audience of 10 million. Her gloss was too much for the men in the White House who monitor the media. NBC officials received three phone calls from Nixon Administration men protesting the Mackin item—the first call almost before the program's theme had faded.[12]

Aside from its forthrightness in interpretation, what made the Mackin newscast remarkable was its uniqueness. "Perhaps it was no coincidence that it was a woman who went for Nixon's jugular," Crouse commented in his account of the incident. "Mackin was an outsider. She had neither the opportunity nor the desire to travel with the all-male pack; therefore, she was not infected with the pack's chronic defensiveness and defeatism. Like Helen Thomas and Sarah McClendon, she could still call a spade a spade."[13]

The herd instinct in campaign coverage thus alluded to has been documented by more than one researcher. Political scientist Doris A. Graber, reporting on a content analysis of twenty newspapers she chose as a cross section of the American press, declared: "The most striking finding of the analysis of press reporting of the 1968 presidential campaign is the great uniformity in coverage. Extant press information was essentially the same throughout the country."[14] Graber concluded:

Several reasons seem to account for the similarities in press coverage. In the first place, the origins of campaign news were surprisingly uniform. Forty-one percent of all campaign news was based on information supplied by presidential candidates and another 15 percent on information released by their running mates. Thus 56 percent of all campaign news was directly linked to the campaign efforts of the presidential and vice-presidential contenders.

Uniformity also resulted from the fact that news stories were encoded by a limited group of people. While some similarity undoubtedly springs from frequent use of wire service stories, this was not as heavy as we had anticipated. It ranged from a low of

7 per cent for the New York *Times* to a high of 79 percent for the Bangor (Maine) *Daily News*. But the median was only 30 percent. Only seven of the 20 papers took as much as 40 percent of their campaign items from wire services.

Another reason for uniformity which was less influential than anticipated was use of syndicated columns. Fifteen percent of all items in the study came from columnists. But 75 percent of the columnists had columns in one paper only. Only 3 percent of the columnists had their work published in at least a third of the papers in this sample. . . .

In view of the limited unifying influence of columnists and wire service reports, one is left with the impression that common socialization, more than identity of encoders of news messages, accounted for the uniformity in campaign coverage. Newspaper personnel apparently shared a sense of what is newsworthy and how it should be presented.[15]

Part of the socialization to which Graber refers was specified by Crouse four years later as the reluctance of special correspondents, traveling with the candidates, to develop stories different from those filed by the wire services. They knew that back home in the newsroom, their copy would be compared with the wire service accounts, and justification for deviations would be demanded.

That shared "sense of what is newsworthy"—though not pack journalism—is also apparent in the reporting and interpreting of the ultimate event in the political process, the election. In national elections, the broadcasting networks' elaborate systems for reporting and computerized projection of vote totals have contributed to uniformity of broadcast presentation, if not always of results. For all their instantaneous delivery, however, they have not diminished the job of the political journalist serving the newspaper audience. He must still have his own highly organized system for gathering results from precinct polling places and county auditors' offices in his area, whether the election is local, state, or national. And the news for him, as for the broadcaster, is who won what office and by what margin.

To often, he stops right there. The editors of *Columbia Journalism Review* have faulted the media generally for their "relatively casual treatment" in interpretation of election results, and they cite examples:

On election night [1972], John Chancellor asserted confidently on NBC that much of the Nixon majority represented a shift from the 1968 Wallace vote. To say the least, this is a hypothesis worth study, but no reporter who has come to this publication's attention has actually gone to voting districts and tried to find proof.

Another example: *Time* asserted (Nov. 20) that Nixon's victory had 'splintered' the New Deal coalition of minorities, and did cite a scattering of precinct returns to support its contention. But it reached back only to 1968, whereas a large organization should not find it beyond its grasp to determine whether in fact the Democratic coalition in 1968 was still Roosevelt's, and what stage 1972 represented in its evolution or dissolution over four decades. The possibilities are great. By halting the story of the election as soon as the counting stops, news media are discarding what is perhaps their best opportunity for reporting on the whole electorate.[16]

Not all of the media, of course, do halt the story of the election when the counting stops. Even so, much of the post-election interpretation tends to be in the form of quotes from party chiefs as to how *they* interpreted the results, or in the form of the journalist's impressionistic analysis that weighs such factors as economic trends, broadening of the suffrage, and type and cost of campaigns. Or a newspaper may report the enterprise of NBC News, which "interviewed Republican voters as they left the polls, including both those who remained loyal to their candidates and those who voted Democratic. Among the loyalists, 26 percent said . . . ." And so forth. The reader's confidence is shaken when he discovers later in the story that the NBC News sample was only 211 voters, and there is no indication of how many voters leaving the polls refused to answer the reporter's first question concerning party identification.[17]

The deep-delving analysis that ranges over decades to identify and hypothesize about voting behavior is left to the social scientists, and their findings, reported in scholarly journals, are rarely noted—let alone replicated—by the journalist.

Defining Issues   If the picture of political reality tends to be distorted by conventional reporting of events, that picture risks further distortion when the writer turns to the second function of political reporting: defining issues. In this effort, the writer may be hindered, rather than helped, by party platforms and the utterances of candidates.

Given the non-ideological nature of the two major American political parties and their inclination to jostle each other for the middle of the road, it is not surprising that party platforms tend to be all things to all voters. They indulge in verbiage with little clear definition of positions on issues. As for the candidates, the strictures of the new campaigning often call for obscuring, rather than defining issues. "The very pervasiveness of television may serve to inhibit meaningful debate on campaign issues," writes strategist Wyckoff. "When a candidate is making an in-person address to a banker's luncheon or a union convention, he can presume certain special knowledge or interests on the part of his audience and not risk boring them or talking over their heads—but not so via television, where a candidate has no way of knowing who is tuned in. His fundamental purpose—to win the election—may best be served by staying 'loose' and general on the issues." [18]

Whether or not party platforms are ambiguous and the candidates "stay loose" on the issues, the political journalist has a responsibility to put those issues in focus.

"The power of the press in America," Theodore H. White has written, "is a primordial one. It sets the agenda of public discussion; and this sweeping political power is unrestrained by any law." [19] In concurrence, political scientist Bernard Cohen has suggested that the mass media may not be very successful in telling their audiences what to think, but they are "stunningly successful in telling their audiences what to think *about*." [20] In study after study, communications researchers have demonstrated the importance of the press—and coverage of politics and elections—in setting the public's agenda, in helping to sort out and crystallize the issues of a campaign. Two leading authorities on agenda-setting research, Maxwell McCombs and Donald L. Shaw, say there is a strong relationship between the issues emphasized by the news media and those that eventually have salience for the individual reader or viewer.[21] What this means is that media coverage of campaigns has a more direct impact on the voter's perception of the important issues than was previously believed by social scientists.

One aspect of a campaign that should not be ignored by the political reporter in an effort to define issues is that of political advertising. Journalism professor Thomas Bowers believes the press should pay more attention to such advertising because of the part it plays in agenda-setting. A thorough analysis of campaign advertising can tell the reporter where the candidate thinks he is weak, what issues he thinks the voters want to hear about, and what kind of image he is trying to project. In recent years, political advertising messages have often been based on the candidate's precampaign polls that indicate issues of concern to the voters. This data is analyzed by political operatives who decide how it will be used. Sometimes advertising is aimed at the general public; sometimes at specific audiences. For example, in the 1972 presidential campaign, the McGovern forces emphasized the Vietnam War in their advertising. They did this, not because the war was a "gut issue" with the voters, but because the candidate and his staff agreed that persons likely to contribute money to the campaign would be attracted by it.[22]

Whether the candidate is manipulating issues or straddling them by "staying loose," the responsibility of the political reporter is clear. The importance of the agenda-setting function of the media is such that the journalist must raise the questions and pursue the answers that define genuine issues before the electorate. If the answers from the candidates are not forthcoming, that, too, is news.

Portraying Personalities   Given the length of the ballot in most voting districts, and the limitations of newspaper space, the political writer is faced with an almost insoluble problem in fulfilling the function of adequate portrayal of candidates' personalities. And yet, under the terms of the new campaigning, the need for such portrayal is perhaps greater than ever. For the image presented on the television screen is, at best, a superficial image, one that needs the kind of fleshing out that only research, careful observation, and honest assessment in well-documented stories can provide. It is not realistic to expect this kind of portrayal of even the leading contenders in minor races, but too often the press falls short in profiling major candidates in major contests. In her analysis of the 1968 presidential campaign coverage, Graber concluded that "the press provided a very shallow portrait of the candidates based largely on general character traits. Readers learned little about the candidates' professional abilities." [23] More specifically, she reported:

> Presidential qualities were discussed in similar manner by all papers. Papers varied in the actual number of references to personal and professional qualities described as important for the presidency, but the types and proportions of qualities mentioned were surprisingly uniform throughout the entire country. Only the special audience papers and the Sunday issues of general papers showed a somewhat different pattern.
>
> With the single exception of the *National Observer,* personality attributes received the bulk of the stress. More than one third of all presidential qualities mentioned by newspapers dealt with character traits needed by the candidates. Presidential style ranked in second place, except for the *National Observer* where it ranked first and the Chicago *Defender* [a black newspaper], *Wall Street Journal,* and three out of four Sunday papers where it ranked third. Professional image—the ability to project an image of capacity in crucial policy areas—ranked third for most papers. While the man and his image were widely discussed, his professional capacities were slighted. Ability in foreign affairs, race relations, or relations with the public received scant mention. Other vital abilities were ignored entirely. Remarks concerning the political philosophy of the candidates and their plans for organizational changes also were barely touched upon. Sunday papers, in particular, emphasized personal qualities to the exclusion of nearly all other criteria for judging presidential fitness.[24]

Investigating Support   The political writer's function in checking out support for candidates traditionally takes two directions: endorsement and financial backing. In neither is the investigation usually thorough enough. Suppose the reporter surveys all the county chairmen in an effort to determine candidate preferences. Good idea. Often such questionnaires, if carefully devised, serve as accurate indicators of candidate strength. But what if a high proportion of county chairman are leaders in name only? What if many have lost touch with their constituency and represent the opinion of only a small, hard core of party loyalists? Then such a survey is no substitute for the kind of door-knocking in key areas that is counseled—and practiced—by the *Washington Post's* David Broder and Haynes Johnson.

Another kind of endorsement tactic that needs close scrutiny is the frequent claim, "endorsed by labor." What segments of labor? Which unions? Not even organized labor speaks in unison. Then there are the various "independent volunteers for . . ." and "independent citizens for . . ." and "independent voters for. . . ." A little independent checking by the reporter may disclose that volunteers-citizens-voters are one-to-a-handful of longtime partisans whose news releases are cleared, if not written, by the candidate's public-relations staff.

As for financial support, the high cost of campaigning plus the Watergate corruption have created a climate that has encouraged enactment of campaign disclosure laws in many states. These are of varying degrees of stringency, and the effectiveness of all of them depends on follow-through by the press. "Every candidate can follow a disclosure law to the letter, but the public will never know where the money came from or where it went unless newsmen relay the information," says political writer Timothy Harper. "In Iowa, where one of the toughest disclosure laws ever written went into effect last fall, too many journalists have chosen to ignore the new statute rather than assume knotty added responsibilities." [25]

Journalists who did not shirk the responsibilities of a new disclosure law in another state were a team of reporters for the *Roanoke* (Va.) *Times,* who employed a computer to study a gubernatorial race. They found that "the two candidates actually spent a third of a million dollars more than they reported," according to *Editor & Publisher.*

> The study . . . also uncovered several avenues, real and potential, for abusing the state's new election laws which require candidates to show near the end of the campaign where their money comes from and where it was spent. According to a story by [associate editor Forrest M.] Landon, "No less than 99 separate campaign committees, candidates' local headquarters, economic-interest groups and assorted organizations—some real, some imaginary or practically so— were raising money for [gubernatorial candidates] Howell and Godwin." This multiplicity of fund-raising operations, he said,

prevented the voter from getting a full and accurate picture of where the money was coming from during the election's peak. Another method of concealing donations was splitting gifts to several different organizations, although the money originated from one benefactor, the study reported.[26]

The sophisticated analysis practiced by the *Roanoke* (Va.) *Times* team is perhaps beyond the resources of most newspapers, but a careful examination of the required reports of income and expenditures by candidates and their committees is not. The report of such examination—including failures to comply—can do much to clarify the picture of financial support in the mind of the voter.

Identifying Trends   The job of the political writer is not limited to reporting and interpreting events, defining issues, portraying candidates, and investigating support. Indeed, some of his most useful work in giving the reader a picture of political reality may lie in areas less readily perceived, and for that reason, all the more interesting. Politics is a dynamic process: alignments shift, coalitions form and dissolve, new strivers for power enter the arena. The political writer is alert to signs of change and untiring in checking them out. Such enterprise resulted in a *Detroit News* story that reported that the country's schoolteachers were greatly increasing their contributions to "friendly" political candidates. John E. Peterson of the *News* Washington Bureau began his story this way:

> Washington—When a suburban Detroit teacher returned from a vacation trip this summer, her mailbox contained a letter requesting a pledge to the National Education Association's (NEA) political action fund.
>
> Eighty cents of each $1 she contributed, the letter said, would be used to support state and local candidates "friendly to education." The rest would go to the NEA's Washington headquarters for political use on the national scene.
>
> Before the start of school this fall, the NEA had collected nearly $1.1 million in political donations from the 1.6 million classroom teachers and other educational professionals who make up its membership.[27]

The story went on to report that NEA officials expected to spend 125 times more than the organization had spent on campaigns two years earlier, and that its objectives were vastly increased federal aid to education, or, in the words of the reporter, "better working conditions."

Another "trend" story, much more elaborately based, concerning increased participation in politics by teachers, has already been cited in

Chapter 5. That story grew out of an effort by the *Minneapolis Tribune* to analyze the action at party caucuses. The *Tribune* explained how it had covered them:

> From a carefully arranged list of the more than 3,900 precincts in Minnesota, a computer selected 100 by a random method. What happened in those precincts reflects accurately the state as a whole.
>
> For each precinct, one observer was recruited to attend the Republican caucus and another to attend the DFL [Democratic-Farmer-Labor]. Observers were thoroughly briefed about caucus procedures.
>
> Each observer was asked to note certain facts about the people attending, about the chairman, and about the business of the meeting. In addition, each observer also gave a questionnaire to each delegate elected.
>
> Observers phoned in some of their findings . . . and also were interviewed for their impressions about the meeting. Delegate questionnaires and information about the resolutions were mailed. The findings were coded and assembled for processing on a computer for analysis by the *Tribune*.[28]

One of the results of that analysis was the reader's awareness of an otherwise imperceptible trend: a new strength of teachers among DFL convention delegates disproportionate to their numbers among eligible voters.

Checking and Analyzing Public Opinion   The wide acceptance of public opinion polling in the political realm, for all its attendant controversy, speaks clearly to the political writer of the importance of gauging voter attitudes if his reader is to gain a clear picture of political reality. The fact is that the picture is incomplete if the political journalist concentrates on events, issues, personalities, and support, to the exclusion of voters' reaction to any and all of these. The question for him remains: How can he best fulfill this function without distorting the picture?

The answer will probably depend, at least in part, on the resources made available to him by his publisher. But whether he can command an in-house survey team or subscribe to one of the polling organizations or neither of these, his concern will be with accuracy in polling and sophistication in reporting the results. These considerations apply in double measure to his assessment of a candidate's own polls.

In any case, the political writer should be familiar with at least the rudiments of survey research methodology described in Chapter 5. In cautioning the reporter to treat leaked survey results with skepticism,

Philip Meyer has compiled a checklist, based on an advisory of the National Council on Public Polls (NCPP), that should serve as the minimum information needed to judge such results:

1. The identity of the sponsor of the survey.
2. The exact wording of the questions asked.
3. A definition of the population sampled.
4. The sample size and, where the survey design makes it relevant, the response rate.
5. Some indication of the allowance that should be made for sampling error.
6. Which results are based on part of the sample, e.g., probable voters, those who have heard of the candidate, or other subdivisions.
7. How the interviews were collected: in person in homes, by phone, by mail, on street corners, or wherever.
8. When the interviews were collected.[29]

Such information is important for the reader, as well as for the reporter, in assessing the significance of survey results. Some newspapers, as a matter of regular policy, precede every news report of a political poll with editorial comment pointing out what NCPP standards the poll does and does not meet.

It is this kind of consideration for the needs of the reader that can help to make coverage of politics a significant service by the media. The political process is too complex, and the voter's choice too important, for the reporter to be willing to settle for less than the closest approximation of reality that he is capable of making.

NOTES

1. John P. Robinson, "Perceived Media Bias and the 1968 Vote: Can the Media Affect Behavior After All?" *Journalism Quarterly* 49 (Summer, 1972), 239–46.
2. Frank J. Sorauf, *Party Politics in America,* 2nd ed. (Boston: Little, Brown, 1972), p. 84.
3. Hugh A. Bone and Austin Ranney, *Politics and Voters,* 3rd ed. (New York: McGraw-Hill, 1971), p. 35.
4. David S. Broder, "Politicians and Biased Political Information," in *Politics and the Press,* ed. Richard W. Lee (Washington: Acropolis Books, 1970), p. 63.
5. Guido Stempel, "The Prestige Press Covers the 1960 Presidential Campaign," *Journalism Quarterly* 38 (Spring, 1961), 157–63; "The Prestige Press in Two Presidential Elections," *Journalism Quarterly* 42 (Spring, 1965), 15–21;

Jae-won Lee, "Editorial Support and Campaign News: Content Analysis by Q-Method," *Journalism Quarterly* 49 (Winter, 1972), 710–16; Ben H. Bagdikian, "The Fruits of Agnewism," *Columbia Journalism Review* 11 (Jan.-Feb., 1973), 9–21.

6. Edward M. Glick et al., *The Federal Government-Daily Press Relationship* (Washington: American Institute for Political Communication, 1967).

7. Sorauf, *Party Politics in America*, p. 1.

8. Bone and Ranney, *Politics and Voters*, p. 1.

9. Timothy Crouse, *The Boys on the Bus* (New York: Random House, 1972), p. 305.

10. Gene Wyckoff, *The Image Candidates* (New York: Macmillan, 1968), p. 210.

11. Ibid., p. 211.

12. Edwin Diamond, "Fairness and Balance in the Evening News," *Columbia Journalism Review* 11 (Jan.-Feb., 1973), 22.

13. Crouse, "Boys on the Bus," p. 267.

14. Doris A. Graber, "Press Coverage Patterns of Campaign News: The 1968 Presidential Race," *Journalism Quarterly* 48 (Autumn, 1971), 502–12.

15. Ibid., pp. 511–12.

16. Editors, "The Neglected Results," *Columbia Journalism Review* 11 (Jan.-Feb., 1973), 3.

17. The *Milwaukee Journal* (Nov. 6, 1974), p. 26. The NBC sample totaled 8,000 voters.

18. Wyckoff, *Image Candidates*, p. 7.

19. Theodore H. White, *The Making of the President 1972* (New York: Bantam, 1973), p. 327.

20. Bernard C. Cohen, *The Press and Foreign Policy* (Princeton: Princeton University Press, 1963).

21. See discussion in Maxwell McCombs and Donald L. Shaw, "A Progess Report on Agenda-Setting Research" (Convention of Association for Education in Journalism, San Diego, Aug. 18–21, 1974), p. 1.

22. Thomas Bowers, "Political Advertising: Setting the Candidate's Agenda" (Paper delivered at the Media and Agenda-Setting Function Conference, Syracuse, N.Y., Oct. 25–28, 1974).

23. Graber, "Press Coverage Patterns," p. 512.

24. Ibid., pp. 506–7.

25. Timothy Harper, "Disclosures on the Campaign Trail," *Quill* 62 (March, 1974), 24.

26. *Editor & Publisher* (March 2, 1974), p. 10.

27. *Detroit News* (Oct. 28, 1974), p. 1.

28. *Minneapolis Tribune* (March 3, 1974), p. 9A.

29. Philip Meyer, *Precision Journalism* (Bloomington: Indiana University Press, 1973), pp. 185–86.

SUGGESTED READINGS

BARBER, JAMES DAVID, *The Lawmakers*. New Haven, Conn.: Yale University Press, 1965. Presents state legislators as representing four types of behavior on the basis of personality characteristics.

BOGART, LEO, *Silent Politics*. New York: Wiley, 1972. Explains and evaluates public opinion polling in the context of politics and journalism.

CROUSE, TIMOTHY, *The Boys on the Bus*. New York: Random House, 1973. A sharply critical report of the methods and mores of political writers based on direct observation in the 1972 Presidential campaign.

GREEN, MARK J., JAMES M. FALLOWS and DAVID R. ZWICK, *Who Runs Congress?* New York: Bantam/Grossman, 1972. Describes congressional organization and operation in a useful perspective for the journalist. Another view of the congressman is offered in *O Congress*, by REP. DONALD RIEGLE. New York: Popular Library 1972. In *Congress: The Electoral Connection* (New Haven, Conn.: Yale University Press, 1974), political scientist DAVID MAYHEW examines the behavior of congressmen from the standpoint of news and publicity.

HIEBERT, RAY E., et al., eds. *The Political Image Merchants: Strategies for the Seventies*. Washington, D.C.: Acropolis Books Ltd., 1975. The "new" politics discussed in a collection of conference papers, of which the most useful are those of participating campaign managers.

KELLEY, STANLEY, *Professional Public Relations and Political Power*. Baltimore: The Johns Hopkins Press, 1956. This early examination of the role of public relations in politics is still one of the best.

MEYER, PHILIP, *Precision Journalism: A Reporter's Introduction to Social Science Methods*. Bloomington: Indiana University Press, 1973. This "bible" of social science methodology has particular relevance for the political writer.

ROBINSON, JOHN P., "The Press as King-Maker: What Surveys From the Last Five Campaigns Show," *Journalism Quarterly* 51 (Winter, 1974), 587–94. A summary of studies supporting the author's thesis that newspaper endorsement influences voter's choices.

ROLL, CHARLES W., JR., and ALBERT H. CANTRIL, *Polls, Their Use and Misuse in Politics*. New York: Basic Books, 1972. A pair of professionals find ignorance about polling among media and media users. This is a readable effort to dispel it.

chapter ten

Covering the Legislative Process

You can find out more about what's going on at the state capitol by spending one night drinking with the capitol press corps than you can in months of reading the papers those reporters write for.

MOLLY IVINS
Houston *Journalism Review*

At every level of government, from the municipal council to the state legislature to the Congress, legislative bodies meet to consider laws. An idea for a law may originate with the lawmakers themselves, departmental administrators, citizens, or lobbyists, but whatever the source, there is a typical process by which an idea becomes a law. The idea is first expressed in a bill, drafted to conform to other laws and court rulings. The bill is introduced in the lawmaking body, which usually refers it to one of its committees for study. The committee may amend, revise, ignore, kill, or pass the bill; if it is of sufficient interest, the committee may hold a public hearing at which citizens and representatives of affected groups may add their views. If released from committee, the bill is considered by the entire legislative body, which may amend, defeat, refer to another committee, or approve the measure, with or without debate. If the legislative body consists of two houses, this procedure is followed in each of them, with differences resolved by a joint conference committee. Finally, if passed, the bill is considered by the appropriate executive—mayor, governor, or president—who vetoes or approves it. The lawmaking body may vote to sustain or override a veto.

Covering the legislative process, whether it is at the local, state, or federal level, requires intensive effort by public affairs reporters. Understanding the process by which a bill becomes a law is only the beginning.

Reporters must weigh the myriad proposals in terms of their significance for readers and viewers. They must consider the important ones in relationship to other laws and court decisions. They must examine the pressures that determine defeat or passage. How can the reporters assigned to cover a legislative body—be it city council, state legislature, or national Congress—provide the public with information that is both important and interesting? How can they cover "events" (i.e.: "The city council today passed an ordinance prohibiting all-night massage parlors") and at the same time, set those events in context? In short, how can they best cover the legislative process?

Functions of Coverage

An understanding of the functions of legislative coverage provides a foundation:

Providing Information   In representative government, an informed citizenry is considered essential. From Colonial times, American governmental institutions have, in theory at least, depended on the people for their authority. Clearly, the media, as principal conveyors of information about society's needs, can help the citizen to seek laws that benefit the society. Political scientist Delmar Dunn notes that the press can "lift a matter from the mire of obscurity to the light of intense attention," and in doing so, "alerts additional groups and decision makers to their stakes in the outcome" of a decision.[1]

Serving As Watchdog   From Colonial times to the present, an antagonism, sometimes latent and sometimes open, has pervaded the relationship between citizen and government. Traditionally, the press has been one of the social institutions that monitor the performance of government and government officials. "A policy-maker very often judges the success of an endeavor by the extent to which it generates press comment," according to Dunn. "If the press praises or criticizes them [officials' proposals or activities], they are affected by what they read. In fact, the press's critique of policy-makers' performances encourages them to act in ways that the press perceives as favorable."[2]

Promoting Change   The press can promote change that benefits society by exposing evil. If mental hospitals are dungeons, intensive press coverage can force corrective action by the legislature. If poverty and hunger are real, but invisible, problems, the press can instigate action by revealing the conditions. "The policy-maker," Dunn writes, "often seems desperate in his attempt to learn about his environment," and the press can help provide essential facts. Because officials "use the press to gauge public thinking," the press can influence the policy-making process.[3]

Evaluations of Coverage

For several months every two years—and in an increasing number of states, every year—state legislatures meet and pass thousands of laws. Many are routine, such as a law to change the state animal from the groundhog to the deer or to grant bonding authority to a school district to raise school-construction funds. But some are very complex, such as laws on taxation, property, public education, and the conduct of criminal trials. State laws, generally, have immediate and direct impact on the lives of citizens, perhaps more so than the ordinances of a city or village council, whose impact is within a municipality, or the laws of Congress, whose effect is often filtered through several layers of bureaucracy.[4]

Yet, despite the importance of state legislatures, press coverage, in the eyes of many observers, has been, with exceptions, inadequate. "The legislator's most commonly heard concerns," writes former state capitol reporter Thomas B. Littlewood, "are that reporters do not dig deeply enough or interpret wisely enough; do not have the time or inclination to comprehend the subtle shadings and political nuances of the legislative arena; and—by far the most serious allegation—may not really understand the legislative process." [5] Other commentators also fault the press's coverage of legislative affairs, whether the legislation is being considered at the local, state, or federal level. Discussing coverage of the Congress, reporter Michael Green writes:

> What is generally omitted from coverage of Congress, almost alone of the categories of people and events with which a newspaper regularly deals, is journalism that might portray Congressional life so as to engage the public interest. The human face of Congressmen and their aides, in all the day-to-day expressions of their small human foibles and unreported triumphs, mirrors the forces at work in the population as a whole. They color the story and, in doing so, reveal it. But the public is not allowed to know this story. Readers are told only in dry, clipped accounts the numerical fate of legislation. They are shown the final score, seldom the action itself. The smells and faces of humanity of the players is lost to them and with it the opportunity of interest. The daily weather report is more interesting to the public and seemingly has more demonstrable relationship to their lives.[6]

The process by which an idea becomes law, at the local, state, or federal level, is complex, and there are many actors and influencing ingredients in the making of any legislative decision. Too often, the reporter is caught up in the decision itself, and ignores the behind-the-scenes pressures that resulted in the legislation, as well as the more apparent effect of the legislation on the lives of his readers. "The legislative process in the states is messy—really, it defies all of the American instincts for order—and extremely subtle," says Alan Rosenthal of the Eagleton Institute of Politics at Rutgers University. "At times it may be impossible to report it clearly and consistently, since it is not always clear and consistent itself." [7] Furthermore, the path by which a bill becomes a law can lead the reporter into fragmentary reporting, in that each time a bill is debated or voted on, there is an "event" to report, and the importance of a bill may be "watered down" in a series of fragmentary news stories. "Newspaper philosophy still keys on a breaking news story," observes Joe Weisman, a political columnist for the Chicago *Sun-Times* and a veteran of statehouse coverage in Springfield, Illinois. "And the legislature least lends itself to this theory." [8]

If coverage of the legislative process is faulted by such critics, reporters and legislators involved in the process also are critical of the reporting. Carol Hilton, a student of the media, found in a 1967 study that many lawmakers "criticize the media broadly for having an appetite for sensationalism, for jazzing up coverage and rushing into print (or on the air) with half-researched stories." She also found that some reporters felt they were on a "useless errand" and that "a wide audience is achieved only by titillating copy." [9] A more recent study found that, on one hand, reporters "tend to hold a very favorable perspective toward the legislature as an institution of government. On the other hand, they tend to view legislators' qualities and roles in a negative fashion." [10]

Components of the Process

Like legislative bodies themselves, the press in its legislative coverage must engage in a dynamic process. The public may perceive the legislative process as the visible, regular, and special sessions of city councils, state legislatures, and the Congress, but it is much more than that. It is a pattern of activity and leadership. It is also a manifestation of the complex interrelationships among other branches of government and various constituencies. Some of these components are:

The Body Organizes   Through party caucuses, formal and informal meetings, legislative leadership emerges after each new election.

Sometimes the jousting for leadership positions goes on for months, even years. Witness, for example, the "revolution" of young members of Congress in 1975 when a number of leading committee chairmen were ousted and replaced by younger and more moderate members. The same pattern sometimes occurs at the state, city, and village level. The reporter observing this process needs to watch for leadership patterns, appointments to key committees, and particularly sharp conflicts that flare up. These factors may not have great meaning when they occur, but they may determine the course of legislation for the next few months. The observant reporter who knows legislative voting records from previous sessions will have early clues about the way certain legislative proposals might fare.

Party Relationships Solidify   Relationships within and between the majority and minority parties in legislative bodies make for interesting copy. In a few instances, legislative bodies are nonpartisan, but even in these cases patterns of support or nonsupport for various bills chart a picture of political philosophy in action. Thus, it may be possible to talk about a "conservative" or "liberal" caucus. Legislative splits often provide interesting copy as the conflict during a session builds. An article in the *Denver Post* by correspondent Todd Phipers describes party divisions:

> "If you guys need a doctor in here, I'll be right across the hall," State Rep. Frank Traylor, R-Wheat Ridge, chided a Democratic caucus.
> It didn't take the work of a physician, which Traylor is, but it took some political patchwork to mend the Democrats back into a House majority Monday as the party maneuvered for a delay on a bill regulating private employment agencies.[11]

As the story progressed, the writer gave a glimpse of the caucus atmosphere:

> The issue, the majority leader said, wasn't whether Democrats would support the bill when it comes to a floor vote. It was that the courtesy be given to a fellow party member to lay a bill over at her request. . . . Strategy, in other words, was the key.[12]

Molly Ivins, the editor of the *Texas Observer*, has denounced newspapers in her home state for their lifeless coverage of the legislature. Ivins says the legislature is a vital, exciting place, yet too many legislative correspondents turn out stories that leave out all the color and spontaneity. One way to avoid this is to cover the battles among party leaders and the procedural conflicts that sometimes stir spirited debate.

Agendas Are Set   Who determines what a legislature will do during a session? This is a question that reporters covering any type of lawmaking body must ask frequently, and it is a question that is answered differently depending on the locale and the political situation. In many legislatures, the chief executive (governor or mayor) has a major role in setting the agenda. He may set it through a "state of the state" message or through selected, topical messages (e.g., health, energy). As the administrator of the state departments and agencies, the governor may marshal efforts to push the program through the legislature. In analyzing these messages, reporters need to distinguish between the maintenance functions of government and new programs. Relationships between the chief executive himself or between a commissioner or department director may have a strong influence on subsequent action. These relationships are best observed by following the activities of the executive's legislative liaison staff and legislators themselves who are close to the executive. This story from the *Chicago Tribune* shows how an astute legislative reporter kept pace with an emerging legislative package:

> Governor Walker's administration is studying a series of controversial criminal justice reforms, including the elimination of prison paroles in favor of flat-time sentences with more liberal early-release provisions than now exist. Before the consideration of the 15 proposals the Walker administration had not become greatly involved in trying to change the state's criminal justice system. . . . A spokesman for the administration cautioned that "all these proposals are only on the drawing board. Don't jump to the conclusion that all of them will be introduced as bills.[13]

Understanding what issues will come before a legislature and why is a difficult task and requires a close view of both executive-legislative interaction and the relationships between certain legislators, their constituents, and lobbyists. This interplay determines the agenda. The press itself, of course, often has a role by pointing out needs or by providing publicity for persuasive spokesmen for various causes and issues.

Lobbies Function   Special interest groups, which lobby for legislation, sometimes provide the spark for illuminating legislative stories. A reporter can often provide depth for a story about a bill by finding out what motivated its introduction and what groups are supporting it. He can do so not only through interviews and observation of lobbyists at work, but also through a careful assessment of their newsletters and legislative materials. Often groups with interests ranging from gun control to public welfare will publish special bulletins during a legislative session to monitor and assess progress on actions in which they are interested.

Trends Develop   At several junctures during a legislative session, a reporter may want to assess the context and perspective of the
lawmakers' activities. Which ways are they headed? Is the executive's program making headway? What does all this legislative activity mean to the
average citizen? Legislative coverage should try to synthesize the meaning
of single-instance bills and find a pattern of activity. The dilemma posed
by trying to balance day-to-day coverage and broader interpretation is
suggested in this assessment of the *Sacramento Bee*'s legislative coverage:

> Ambiguity, in part due to management's indecision whether to
> publish a newspaper-of-record or a probing iissue-oriented news-
> paper, produces a plethora of short articles often bearing head-
> lines that begin, "Bill Advances . . ." and occasional well-written
> pieces that will turn up, almost apologetically, inside the bulky
> *Bee*.[14]

Coverage of Sessions

From the town or city hall to the state and national capitols, the
complexity of the legislative process increases, as do the problems of coverage for the reporter. At the town, city, or county level, the reporter in
search of the behind-the-scenes story may find himself drawn to public
records in search of a pattern. Or he may find himself relying on the
official meeting of the council and its official actions, which he follows
up with careful interviews.

City Councils   Most beginning reporters are likely to find themselves assigned early in their careers to covering the meetings and official
actions of a municipal council. Depending on the aggressiveness of the
reporter's publication, tradition, and access to records and key municipal
personnel, that coverage may vary from little more than a bulletin board
of official council minutes to enterprising, investigative probes of the
quality of city government. Public affairs reporters, as a first step, should
obviously become familiar with the governmental structure of the body
they are covering. Several types of structure characterize local government
in the United States, including "strong mayor," "weak mayor," commission, and city manager systems. These types, and their modifications, are
discussed in a variety of political science books, and the local municipal
library can also provide the reporter with the basics of the municipal
structure. In addition to their overall structure, municipal governments
are organized into various departments and bureaus, such as finance,
assessment, police, health, public works, licenses, and legal. These divisions have different functions and duties depending on the size and type

of municipal government, and the reporter should obviously understand their operations.

The reporter covering local legislative bodies must also understand the powers under which the local council functions. Most municipal governments operate under charters granted by the state legislature and amended from time to time by the voters. These charters grant municipal lawmaking bodies certain authority, such as the right to pass ordinances, but often that power is limited. The reporter needs to know the ways in which the local governmental body relates to the state legislature and to the federal government, particularly in matters such as mass transit and housing, in which federal funding and jurisdiction are often involved. Whatever the relationships, the reporter will often find that the major portion of his responsibility in covering the council requires surveillance of the body's committees in which most of the discussion and decision-making take place.

But not all of it. Local governmental councils, particularly in smaller communities, often are cozy gatherings of political leaders who may have close ties to the community's businesses, including its newspaper. More than one reporter covering city hall has encountered singular foot dragging when he has set out to do an aggressive investigative story.

The reporter who does look behind the scenes and ask such questions as "Who runs this city?" is likely to turn up some fascinating news stories that examine the entire decision-making process, from formal governmental structure to the personalities of officials—and nonofficials. In a series entitled "St. Paul (Minn.) Decision Makers," reporter David Nimmer found that, on a decision to build a civic center, "St. Paul suffered from a 'sugar daddy' complex—Let one of our millionaires do it for us. And there was a limit to what the wealthy men were willing to do." He found, further, that:

> members of the city council, with perhaps one exception, never took any key leadership roles:
>
> Council members were generally in the position of reacting to what the businessmen and the MIC (Metropolitan Improvement Committee) had proposed.
>
> Mayor Thomas Byrne was the only Council member who played a critical part in Civic Center decision-making, and he did that this spring when he informed businessmen that he wasn't about to see the project go down the drain because of doubts over the design of a particular building.
>
> Even when the councilmen weren't eager to support a proposal, such as the voter referendum on auditorium expansion, MIC leaders were able to persuade them with apparent ease.[15]

A similar examination of a city's power structure was carried out by *Cincinnati Enquirer* reporter Betsy Bliss. Her series, called "The Movers and the Shakers," seemed to go against a tradition of coziness between the newspaper and the city's establishment, but it "named the members of the Cincinnati power structure, described how they ran the town, and discussed their actions as viewed by city planners, educators, 'little people' and other critics. The article on the movers in politics, headlined, 'Republican Grip on city nurtured by power elite,' discussed the role of big businessmen in supporting and determining policy for the Republicans." [16]

State Legislatures   Coverage of the state legislature, like coverage of the local lawmaking body, can lead the reporter to interpretative stories on how the legislative process works. State legislatures vary in size from several dozen members to well over 100, and increasingly, legislatures have supporting bureaucracies in the form of research staffs. Because the state legislature often considers hundreds or thousands of bills during a typical session, the reporter may have difficulty making news decisions on what to cover, and in how much detail. "Many newspapers try to simplify by publishing a legislative checklist. . . ," write former reporters Ralph Whitehead, Jr. and Howard Ziff, "showing the status of different bills at different times during the session. While often helpful, this device can be seriously misleading. Merely noting the progress of bills, such checklists are not always sensitive to crucial details." [17]

A major problem in covering state legislatures is lack of accurate information. "For one thing," Whitehead and Ziff explain, "few legislators stay around long enough to develop an expertise of their own. . . . Then too, except for members of the leadership, most legislators, and most of their committees, lack staff. For the use of its 180 members, the Vermont legislature employs one research assistant, one fiscal analyst, one secretary and two draftsmen. 'It's not like Washington, where you can stroll into the offices of the Atomic Energy Commission and talk to somebody on the staff who's one of the country's top half dozen experts on nuclear power.' " [18] The Vermont situation is perhaps not typical, as legislatures have staffs of varying sizes and expertise, depending on, among other things, the complexity of issues with which the legislature deals. Littlewood explains the problem in different terms:

> In any statehouse the legislator and the journalist who is reporting his activities may be surprised to find themselves sharing a common problem: the difficulty of obtaining reliable factual information about what is really going on. For our tradition of part-time citizen-legislators has meant that the only pros in the legislature are the managerial cliques who profitably preserve their monopoly of

insight. The committee system thus is made ineffective and the legislator-in-the-ranks lacks the tools for doing his job.[19]

This problem becomes acute as the legislative session draws to a close, and legislators and reporters alike find themselves in marathon sessions in which many bills are passed without debate or discussion. Reporter Paul Hoffman describes this scene of the closing hours of the New York legislature, but his comments might well apply to other states:

> In 1967, the legislature closed shop with a twenty-one hour marathon. Hundreds of bills were passed—nearly one-fourth of the session's total—including a major revision of the law governing strikes by public employees and a controversial proposal for a state lottery. Both bills were mimeographed only minutes before the vote. Neither the lawmakers who approved them, nor the reporters who had to explain them had time to digest their contents, much less penetrate the maze of deals and compromises that lay behind them. Hundreds of other bills were killed, either on the floor of the legislature or in committee.
>
> All this meant a stream of activity on the floor of the assembly and the senate, in the leaders' offices and capitol corridors, and in the executive chamber—a stream involving more than two hundred legislators and scores of aides, lobbyists, and state officials. No newspaper had enough manpower to cover everything that happened. Few newsmen had the stamina to stay with even one development for twenty-one hours—and then write about it.[20]

The reporter faced with trying to say what a new law means has a difficult time under ideal conditions, much less under conditions like those described by Hoffman. The reporter's readers may be well-served if he follows these suggestions: don't tackle too much; get to those who know, and look for the personal relationships.

Obviously, no reporter can write definitive stories on each of the hundreds or thousands of bills that go through the typical legislature each session, or look behind the scenes at the various pressures that brought defeat or passage. While there probably is a need to provide day-to-day "overviews," the reporter should guard against overextending himself. Unlike city councils, which tend to have a more leisurely pace, legislatures can be rat races, particularly near the end of a session, and the reporter should make a conscious effort to avoid being caught up to the extent that perspective is lost.

As for those who know: lobbyists have earned reputations, sometimes deserved, as wheeler-dealers who pressure legislators behind the scenes to pass their pet bills. While that may be true in some cases, lobbyists are often valuable sources for the reporter, as well as for the legislator. The professional lobbyist may have a thorough understanding of certain kinds of legislation, and though his view is likely to be biased, balancing one such source against another can help the reporter put individual pieces of legislation in context. The same is true of research staff personnel, which many legislators now recognize as essential, if expensive. Executive departments and agencies have to administer the laws that are passed, and the reporter should see departmental staffs as potential sources of information.

There are other aspects of covering the legislature that the public affairs reporter must be mindful of, too. For example, because legislators represent different constituencies, they may see the need to "trade off" votes on some issues to gain support for their favorite projects. Furthermore, the citizen-legislator often brings biases with him to the legislature, and sometimes votes these prejudices. In a perceptive article about the Maine legislature, *Maine Times* reporter Phyllis Austin examined the relationships behind the scenes:

> A legislator introduces a bill to raise the salary of a state post. A son of the legislator holds that post. But the amount of money is small.
>
> A legislator works to switch tax money to an agency he heads. But it is a legitimate agency and the position he holds with it is unpaid. He makes no financial gain.
>
> Are either or both of these conflicts of interest? When a specific case is cited, it becomes clear just how difficult it is to define conflict of interest. But the specific cases also shed light on what makes Maine's legislature tick. . . .[21]

How do public affairs reporters proceed when they want to write this kind of story? What resources can they use? The committee hearing, the debate on the floor, the vote for and against—these are easier to take hold of. But where does the reporter turn first to get a systemic story off the ground? Let's take an example. You're covering the legislature in a western state where environmental issues are widely discussed and debated. A group of mining companies proposes to strip-mine for coal, but the group needs enabling legislation. One of its chief spokesmen in the legislature is a senator who is rumored to have some private interests in coal mining. You want to investigate what interests those might be, and examine the real pros and cons behind the strip-mining issue.

The reporter might begin here on two tracks, one a careful review of the legislator's voting record on mining issues, and two, thorough research on coal mining. Sources would include legislative voting files and the debates and minutes of committee meetings. The reporter might also turn to trade publications on coal mining and position papers by such environmental groups as the Sierra Club. The state department of taxation might provide projections on revenues generated by the coal-mining industry, and lobbyists in other industries, such as electric power, could provide data on the need for coal. The reporter might well find himself deep into newspaper stories in other states where coal mining, or other types of mining, are an issue. A statistical base on employment factors might be available from the state department of employment, or the federal Department of Labor. The reporter would then move on to middle-level interviews with mining experts, asking questions about the environmental impact, the employment projections, the effect on the state's tax base. Along the way, the reporter would develop the ability to make valuable and realistic comparisons with what is happening in other states and regions. This evaluation would free him from the necessity of depending on the opposing groups' press releases, with their assumed biases.

In the examination of the senator, the reporter might study land and deed records in areas where mining is proposed to see whether the senator has land interests there. He might also examine corporation papers to see whether the senator has an interest in a company that might benefit from mining, such as a company that supplies and distributes tires for huge earthmoving equipment. He might examine the wills of the senator's parents and of other relatives to learn if the senator owns mining company stock. A check of various business professional directories might show whether the senator is an officer or on the board of directors of a company that would benefit from mining. Last, the reporter should not overlook the senator's own statements, comparing them with his private votes or comments in committee hearings, which generally get less attention than the full-scale public meeting.

In the examination of both mining as an issue and the senator's interests, the reporter would be constantly asking comparative questions in which statements with built-in prejudices are weighed against standards and performance. The reporter might ask: Do the senator's public statements coincide with his votes recorded in committee? Do his private interests seem to be reflected in his votes? Has mining by the same mining group in other states met permit standards set by those states' pollution monitoring agencies? Have the mining companies helped or hindered efforts by other states to protect the environment, while allowing mining to continue? How have the legislatures in other states responded to pressure by mining interests? With all these questions, and perhaps dozens more, the reporter would soon begin to have a knowledge of the mining issue that would go well beyond that needed to cover individual bills as they came up in the Senate and House. Combining these investigative techniques with direct observation of, say, mining operations in other states, the reporter would be able to get behind the public event to real issues.

Congress   Much has been written that is critical of Washington correspondents and the coverage of Congress, yet recent critics still find Capitol Hill coverage inadequate. Ben H. Bagdikian writes that "the American body politic is hemorrhaging from Executive people unwatched. But the remedy, a responsive and daily accountable Congress, has also gone largely unwatched in any way significant for local voters." [22] "About 400 of these 1,400 correspondents cover Congress specifically," he explains, "but they also follow the herd, most of them working for national news organizations that concentrate on big issues and a few leaders. This is a natural and necessary concern, but it means that most members of Congress are left uncovered. This gap pretty much leaves the field to the printed press release and an even more effective instrument of political promotion: television footage represented as news when in fact, it is government-subsidized propaganda." [23]

Obviously, the reporter assigned to Congress will have to develop his own ways of covering the news "events" from Capitol Hill and of researching and writing the systemic stories. But perhaps the biggest pitfall is the press release, which is all too available and easy for the reporter to pick up. An American University team of student journalists found that:

> Eighty percent of these papers' [suburban newspapers] coverage is based on the congressmen's press releases. It apparently is common practice for releases to go straight from the Hill and into a local newspaper word for word. Unbeknownst to the reader, a congressman's legislative boasts or self-serving quotes may be lifted whole from the releases and shoveled into print with no further checking. In one two-month period, we found 84 stories (in 29 papers) that were based on press releases, and nearly half (41) of them were verbatim reprints of the release.[24]

Coverage of Public Meetings and Hearings

On any given weekday, or evening, the reporter is likely to find a number of public meetings going on in his community. There may be a specially called session of the county board of supervisors to hear citizen comments about a proposed widening of a highway. An environmental protection agency may be taking testimony from businessmen about the need for a rubber-processing plant. The next night, it might hear from opponents of the plant. The district school board might be inviting comments from parents and taxpayers about the need—or lack of it—for an addition to the high-school gymnasium. An advisory committee on the problems of aging may be taking testimony from nursing-home operators as it considers recommended changes in a state's nursing-home regulation laws. In all these cases, the reporter is faced with several problems:

Scale   The public meeting often draws only the most outspoken of opponents and proponents on public issues. The vast majority of citizens, while they may be concerned about an issue, don't bother to come. Thus, there may be important views unrepresented at a public hearing, and the reporter should ask himself what other sources could make the story complete and balanced.

Size   The beginning reporter, particularly, tends to measure the support for, or opposition to an issue by the number of people who turn out for a meeting, and the emotion-level of their participation. Thus, a crowd of 2,000 that jams into a high-school auditorium to scream about a proposed desegregation plan may be taken to represent the community as a whole. Conversely, the reporter who finds himself the only spectator as the county zoning board rules on variances may think people don't care about the proposals. The size of the audience may subtly lead the reporter to "weight" his account: the larger the crowd, the longer the story; the smaller the crowd, the briefer the account.

Interest   The reporter may assume that if he is not interested in the contents of the meeting, then surely, the public is not either. "On one occasion," writes a state representative, "a reporter asked me if a certain bill I was introducing was 'sexy' or 'exciting.' I stated I wasn't sure, but I thought it was important. The reporter agreed that it was important but since it wasn't 'sexy' or 'exciting' or controversial, no story was written." [25]

Grandstanding   Some political officials see the public hearing as a forum to impress the audience with the "rightness" of their positions. That audience often includes the press. The reporter needs to measure what an official says in a public setting against that official's record on the issue, or against what he says in private. "The only way for a reporter to look at an official is skeptically," writes journalism Professor William L. Rivers.[26] The investigative committee, Douglass Cater writes, "is geared to the production of headlines on a daily basis and even twice daily basis. It is able to create the news story which lingers week after week on the front pages to form an indelible impression on the public mind." [27]

Access   It is not unusual for public officials to meet, behind closed doors, in an "executive session" and make decisions that are than rubber-stamped at a later public meeting. Most states have laws prohibiting such closed sessions, and these apply sometimes to the meetings of municipal as well as state officials. But these laws are sometimes ignored, and the reporter should attempt to find out what decisions, if any, are being made outside the public meeting.

Impact   What happened in a public setting, such as a meeting, may not reveal the important forces that influence a legislative decision. The reporter needs to ask how important the meeting is to the outcome of an issue. Have decisions already been made? Will the public debate influence the officials? The reporter needs to follow up the meeting with questions about its importance. Often, decisions made in such settings are only part of the picture. Always, reporters must keep in mind their chief job: providing the reader with the *meaning* of an issue and how the public meeting fits into that meaning. Reporters need to evaluate the substance of the meeting in relationship to the needs of their audience. In doing so, they will often be led to the systemic story. The reporter in such situations should maintain a high level of skepticism, if not disbelief. In an article about investigative reporting, former *New York Times* reporter Robert M. Smith writes about the frustration of being lied to. "There is an old bromide imparted to young Washington reporters. Always ask yourself, they are told, 'Why is this bastard lying to me?' Being lied to becomes so much a part of the investigative reporter's life that once or twice a year he asks himself, 'Why is this guy telling me the truth?' " [28] The reporter who covers the legislative process needs to be aware that lying does occur, or, at a minimum, that often what he sees in the public forum is only part—often a small part—of the story.

How can the public affairs reporter cover a public meeting and avoid the problems inherent in the discussion? Let's take a theoretical example from the first part of this section—a meeting of the school board to consider the need for an addition to the high-school gymnasium—and look at how the reporter might cover it.

The meeting is to be held at the school district's board room, and when the reporter arrives half an hour before the meeting is to start, he finds the room already filled with parents, coaches, teachers, students, and other interested citizens. In a corner, he spots the chairman of the high school's English department, an outspoken teacher popular with her students and generally critical of spending for sports facilities at the expense of more academic programs. He also notices a couple of "meeting regulars," people who come to school board meetings frequently and who are generally critical of spending funds that require additional property taxes. And he also notes the presence of the high-school football coach, a popular figure in the community since last fall's team finished with a 10-0 record. The reporter scans the room more carefully and realizes that he does not see someone he expected: a statistics and economics professor at the local college who has served as chairman of the community's planning commission and who is generally regarded locally as an unbiased expert on public financing and cost-benefit analysis. He makes a mental note of the professor's absence, and jots the professor's name on a page of his notebook under the heading "should contact."

The meeting is lively, but orderly. The English teacher makes a case for needed textbooks and says the present gymnasium is adequate. The football coach says he could get more students involved in high-school sports if there were more practice facilities. One of the "regulars" argues that property taxes are already too high, and that the proposed addition to the gymnasium would cost too much. Board members listen intently, and one, with a reputation for "playing to the audience," assures the group that the board will do its best to make the right decision. A vote is taken, and the addition is approved unanimously. Several persons in the audience seem disgruntled, and the English teacher shrugs and leaves.

As the reporter leaves, he begins to think about what happened and what pieces are missing. To be sure, the meeting attracted a large crowd, but several important sources, including the professor, were absent. Back at the office, he gets on the telephone and begins to fill in the holes in the story. The professor tells him that the addition will cost too much in light of population trends that project a leveling off of the tax base in the community and provides him with cost-benefit statistics. He calls the English teacher, and she further describes the inadequate high-school library, and the need for books in the English program. The reporter plans his report of the meeting. One story, a relatively short one, describes the meeting; another, much longer, presents the professor's views and those of the English teacher. He supplements the package with an out-of-date reading list for an English course, provided by the English teacher, and a table of cost statistics. The group of articles runs in the next day's paper, and the reader, instead of getting only a report on the board's action and the meeting, gets reports that set that action in context.

Continuity of Coverage

The process by which a bill moves through the legislative process is complex, from introduction to various hearings in committee, to the debate and vote on the floor. Whether the proposal is a local ordinance, a bill in a state legislature, or a piece of congressional legislation, the reporter needs to develop ways of keeping track of the proposal's progress. The job is complicated by the practice of "gutting" proposed legislation.

For example, a state legislator may introduce a measure that establishes an environmental protection agency to regulate state power companies. In committee, another legislator may come along with an amendment to the proposal that strikes everything after the enacting clause and inserts entirely new language that gives the proposed agency "advisory" power only. So the first pitfall to avoid is "labeling" a piece of legislation in a way that would mislead the reader or tell the reader little about what the proposal would accomplish. As one legislator points out: "No-fault insurance, no-fault divorce, environmental rights act, equal rights amendments, fair pupil dismissal act, are just a few of these that have passed in the last two years. In every case, the bill as passed is far different from the bill as originally prepared by the author." [29] Shrewd legislators know that a certain kind of bill, sent to a hostile committee, will be permanently "postponed." A state legislative agriculture committee, for example, may have a disproportionate number of farmers, and may not be very favorable to a bill allowing synthetic milk products to be sold widely. So one part of keeping track of legislation is to watch the kind of "setting" in which a bill winds up. That will often provide the reporter with a clue to the bill's chances of getting out to the floor.

Legislatures themselves have begun to develop rather sophisticated methods of keeping track of legislation. Ordinarily, clerks of each body of the legislature function as repositories for legislation and steer bills to the right committees. This is normally under the guidance of a rules committee of the legislature. The reporter should become familiar with these and other legislative components because, obviously, it is difficult for him to trace a bill unless he understands the procedure by which bills move. Legislatures also keep journals of their proceedings, and these are helpful to the reporter too.

The Actors: Lawmakers, Aides and Lobbyists

The Congress, as Bagdikian suggests, is particularly subject to press coverage of a few "star" members at the expense of most of its members. But every legislative body has leaders. These may be either formal leaders, such as the majority and minority whips, or the chairmen of major committees, or the speaker of the house or president of the city council. Often, these individuals are party caucus leaders as well as legislative leaders, and their influence and power may vary with the size and makeup of the legislative body. Political scientist Dunn suggests that the press is used for a number of political purposes including building program support, achieving personal publicity, providing neutral information, testing public reaction with a "trial balloon," [30] and legislative leaders are probably more likely than others to employ the press for these purposes. The perceptive reporter recognizes these uses, and is cautious about self-serving statements from legislative leaders. Dunn explains that "the legislative leader, for his part, knows that his colleagues learn much of what they know about a bill from the papers, and that they measure public reaction to a proposition by reading the papers. He therefore believes that his success with a bill is often commensurate with his success in publicizing it." [31]

From the reporter's point of view, an undue emphasis on legislative leaders may result in a myopia that ignores, or at least diminishes, the importance of the views of so-called ordinary legislators. Legislators, particularly those with several years' experience, recognize the effect of favorable press coverage, perhaps more so than freshman legislators. In a study of Texas legislative coverage, for example, journalism researcher John Merwin found that, "Subjects serving in the Texas Legislature more than two years rated newspapers significantly more potent than their colleagues serving two years or less. Perhaps after one session in the Legislature the new legislator becomes more acutely aware of the potency of newspapers because of personal experience with adverse editorial comment and news stories." [32] The result may be coverage that focuses on "leaders" at the expense of other legislators, that leaves the neophytes with relatively low profiles, even to their own constituents.

Earlier in this chapter, Washington correspondent Littlewood was quoted as noting that the real pros in the legislative process were the managerial people. Certainly, the legislative aide, or research staff person, is a valuable source for the reporter. Such persons can often steer the reporter to the relevant background material on important legislative issues, and can just as often supply the names of other "experts" both in and out of government. A well-staffed city manager's office, with experts on population trends, housing, transportation needs, and other crucial issues, can be invaluable to the reporter looking for hard information that is likely to be less biased than the public statements of interested officials. The same is true of the legislative research staff.

Lobbyists are among the most durable of legislative figures, and often exert immense influence on the legislative process. They are usually experts in their fields, and although they are almost certainly biased toward a particular position, their range of knowledge may include opposing viewpoints. There are many kinds of lobbyists, ranging from a corporation attorney for a major industry, such as mining or railroads, to "citizen" lobbyists for the League of Women Voters. In many states, and in the Congress, lobbyists greatly outnumber lawmakers. The relationship between them is frequently clouded, and every capital city, during a legislative session, is awash with rumors of sumptuous dinners paid for by "big lobbies" for legislators and, sometimes, the press. More sober examination, however, suggests that the lobby provides an important service to lawmakers by presenting the opposing positions of special interest groups. Yet the key question is still how much influence the lobbies exert; and recently, states have begun to enact strict lobbyist-disclosure laws and rules.

In an article examining a professional lobbyist, John N. Cole, editor of the *Maine Times,* wrote that Loyall Sewall, a lobbyist, "will write, or have a hand in writing, nearly half the bills in any given legislature." Sewall "has no real power base, no vote, and usually represents a minority view. But he often prevails, because he maintains his credibility, performs a unique and otherwise unobtainable legal service, and is on duty on the third floor every day of every session." [33] "There is one group of statehouse regulars," according to Whitehead and Ziff, "that serves as a stable source of information: the lobbyists. A 1969 study of lobbying in four states—Utah, Oregon, North Carolina, Massachusetts—reports that the typical lobbyist has been on the job for an average of ten years." [34]

Other Sources for Coverage

The resources available to the reporter covering an aspect of the legislative process are growing. Organizations, associations, libraries, and research staffs all can help the reporter in his search for the background materials necessary to provide the daily events of legislation with context.

Law libraries in many state capitols contain compilations of state laws, and often, the laws of nearby states. Many also have records of state legislation, including committee minutes and background documents on important issues. Many state historical societies collect important state documents and historical sources.

Increasingly, legislatures are providing themselves with research staffs to develop "fact statements" on various issues. Also, many large cities have research personnel, sometimes under the wing of the city manager or city coordinator, who help plan the city's direction in such fields as transit and housing. These research groups draw on the resources within various state and municipal departments. The New York Department of Transportation, for example, maintains a planning and research division that supplies data on traffic flow, movement patterns, and forecasts for urban travel.

A number of organizations can help the reporter learn what is being done in the same field in other parts of the country. Such organizations include the National League of Cities, the Council of State Governments, the Citizen Conference on State Legislatures, the Eagleton Institute of Politics at Rutgers University, the National Conference of State Legislative Leaders, the Ford Foundation, and Common Cause. Other such groups may be valuable at the local level such as citizens' leagues and the League of Women Voters.

Conclusions and Summary

Legislative coverage is among the most demanding assignments for public affairs reporters, and the obstacles to sound, informative coverage are many. The reporter needs to watch, particularly, the *process* by which proposals become law, or are defeated, for in doing so, he will gain an understanding of the pressures and influences that affect specific proposals.

Understanding the process, however, will serve little purpose unless the reporter succeeds in interesting his reader in that process by showing him how its results have an effect on his daily life. After all, that's the assumption with which legislative coverage began.

NOTES

1. Delmar D. Dunn, *Public Officials and the Press* (Reading, Mass.: Addison-Wesley, 1969). See particularly Chapter 9, "The Impact of the Press on the Policy-making Process," pp. 165–71.
2. Ibid., pp. 169–70.
3. Ibid., pp. 167–68.
4. For overviews of state government, see John Burns, *The Sometimes Governments* (New York: Bantam, 1971); and John C. Wahlke et al., *The Legislative System* (New York: Wiley, 1962).
5. Thomas B. Littlewood, "What's Wrong with Statehouse Coverage," *Columbia Journalism Review* 10 (March-April, 1972), 42. See also Paul Simon, "Improving Statehouse Coverage," *Columbia Journalism Review* 12 (Sept.-Oct., 1973), 51–53.
6. Michael Green, Obstacles to Reform: Nobody Covers the House." *Washington Monthly* 2 (June, 1970), 68; reprinted in *Congress and the News Media,* ed. Robert O. Blanchard (New York: Hastings House, 1974), p. 328.
7. Quoted by Ralph Whitehead, Jr., and Howard M. Ziff in "Statehouse Coverage: Lobbyists Outlast Journalists," *Columbia Journalism Review* 12 (Jan.-Feb., 1974), 12.
8. Ibid.
9. Carol S. Hilton, "Reporting the Legislature: A Study of Newsmen and Their Sources" (Unpublished M. A. thesis, University of Washington, 1966).

10. Charles W. Wiggins and J. Paul Yarbrough, "Reporters and the Legislative System: A Study of Perceptions and Performance" (Paper delivered at the Midwest Political Science Association, Chicago, Ill., May 3–5, 1973.) See also Walter Gieber and Walter Johnson, "The City Hall Beat: A Study of the Roles of Sources and Reporters," *Journalism Quarterly* 38 (Summer, 1961), 289–97; Arthur Garcia, "A Study of the Opinions and Attitudes of California's Capital Correspondents," *Journalism Quarterly* 44 (Summer, 1967), 330–33; and John Merwin, "How Texas Legislators View News Coverage of Their Work," *Journalism Quarterly* 48 (Summer, 1971), 269–74.

11. Todd Phipers, "Rep. Traylor's Job Bill Survives—For Two Days," *Denver Post* (Feb. 23, 1975), p. 2.

12. Ibid.

13. "Walker Weighing 15 Justice Reforms," *Chicago Tribune* (Feb. 12, 1975), p. 1.

14. Bruce Keppell, "The Capitol Correspondents," *feed/back*, the Journalism Report and Review for Northern California 1 (Oct., 1974), 11–12.

15. David Nimmer, "St. Paul Decision Makers," *Minneapolis Star* (June 20, 1969), p. 1.

16. Emily Gantz McKay, in William L. Rivers, ed., *The Adversaries: Politics and the Press* (Boston: Beacon Press, 1970), p. 120.

17. Whitehead and Ziff, "Statehouse Coverage," p. 10.

18. Ibid., pp. 11–12.

19. Thomas B. Littlewood, "The Trials of Statehouse Journalism," *Saturday Review* 49 (Dec. 10, 1966), 82.

20. Paul Hoffman, "The Neglected Statehouse," *Columbia Journalism Review* 6 (Summer, 1967), 22–23.

21. Phyllis Austin, "What Interest Does Your Legislator Represent?" *Maine Times* (Dec. 7, 1973), p. 1.

22. Ben H. Bagdikian, "Congress and the Media: Partners in Propaganda," *Columbia Journalism Review* 12 (Jan.-Feb., 1974), 10. See also Bernard C. Cohen, *The Press and Foreign Policy* (Princeton: Princeton University Press, 1963); Dan D. Nimmo, *Newsgathering in Washington* (New York: Atherton Press, 1964); James Reston, *The Artillery of the Press* (New York: Harper & Row, 1967); and Leo Rosten, *The Washington Correspondents* (New York: Harcourt, Brace, 1937).

23. Bagdikian, "Congress and the Media," p. 5.

24. Lewis W. Wolfson, "The Local Congressman's Lament: Doesn't Anybody Know My Name?," *Washingtonian* 9 (Feb., 1974), 130.

25. Tom Berg and Charles Weaver, "Capitol Coverage: How Does It Look from the Statehouse?" *Twin Cities Journalism Review* 2 (July-Aug., 1974), 14.

26. Rivers, *"The Adversaries,"* p. 253.

27. Douglass Cater, "The Congressional Hearing As a Publicity Vehicle," *The Fourth Branch of Government* (Boston: Houghton Mifflin, 1959).

28. Robert M. Smith, "Why So Little Investigative Reporting?" *(MORE)* 3 (Nov., 1973), 7.

29. Berg and Weaver, "Capitol Coverage," p. 15.

30. Dunn, *Public Officials and the Press,* p. 116.

31. Ibid., p. 119.

32. John Merwin, "How Texas Legislators View News Coverage of Their Work," *Journalism Quarterly* 48 (Summer, 1971), 274.

33. John N. Cole, "The Lobbyist," *Maine Times* (Feb. 23, 1973), 2.

34. Whitehead and Ziff, "Statehouse Coverage," p. 12.

SUGGESTED READINGS

BLANCHARD, ROBERT O., ed. *Congress and the News Media.* New York: Hastings House, 1974. Contains many provocative articles on Congressional coverage.

KRISTOL, IRVING, "The Underdeveloped Profession," *The Public Interest* 6 (Winter, 1967), 36.

SIGAL, LEON V., *Reporters and Officials: The Organization and Politics of Newsmaking.* Lexington, Mass.: D. C. Heath and Company, 1973. Studies news decisions at the *New York Times* and the *Washington Post*.

chapter eleven

Specialized Coverage

The growth of specialized reporting is one of the most stimulating aspects of modern American journalism. . . . The old notion that any good reporter can cover any story, and do it well, is dying. Slowly, perhaps even reluctantly, American journalism is turning to the specialist.

JOHN HOHENBERG
The Professional Journalist

Sometimes it is hard to say where specialization in public affairs reporting begins. After all, the journalists who cover courts, government agencies, legislative bodies, and politics must have a specialized knowledge that enables them to interpret for their readers the events and processes that take place in these sectors of society. As processes in these areas have become more and more complex, however, the need for expertise in coverage has increased to a degree that the best of the journalists assigned to them have indeed become specialists. Watch a panel of Washington journalists—Peter Lisagor, White House correspondent for the *Chicago Daily News;* Charles Corddry, who covers the Defense Department for the *Baltimore Sunpapers*; Eileen Shanahan, economics writer for the *New York Times,* and Neil McNeil, congressional correspondent for *Time* magazine—quiz each other on television about the week's developments in their domains of competence, and the importance of specialization in reporting on government becomes readily apparent.

But there is another aspect of specialization in public affairs reporting. It, too, has developed to answer the challenge of complexity. But more than that, its development has usually been in response to demands by readers for information about aspects of their culture that may affect them even more directly than the activity of government. Why can't Johnny read? these readers want to know. How advanced is the science of cancer detection? Is the energy crisis really a crisis? How can I judge the shelf life of the canned goods at the supermarket? How is the current round of labor negotiations in the steel industry going to affect my job? These and hundreds of similar questions trouble the reader of today's newspaper, and for most of them there is no simple answer of the kind that might have been furnished in an earlier time by the generalist in journalism.

It is to answer such questions that a number of reporting specializations have evolved, some of which are treated briefly in this chapter. An extended analysis would require separate courses and separate textbooks. The following discussions are intended only to suggest the challenge these fields represent.

Reporting Urban Problems

America's cities have been marked by rapid and radical change in the years since World War II. They have experienced:

Explosive growth of suburbs, leading to the balkanization of government and services.

Massive migration of rural and southern blacks to the cities of the North, fueling the flight of middle-class whites to the suburbs.

Deterioration of the inner cores of central cities, followed by an exodus of industry and the resulting fiscal crises for municipal governments.

The civil-rights movement, ghetto riots, black consciousness, and the rising expectations of ethnic and racial minorities.

Environmental pollution, and a belated awareness of its danger.

From this fusion of accelerated growth, social conflict, and environmental decay, "urban journalism" was spawned. For a time, it was the pepperoni pizza of the news business—hot, popular, and a mélange of ingredients. It focused on the new and the important. It embraced subjects as diverse as architecture and race relations, ecology and zoning, transportation and mental illness. It promised approaches to news-gathering and news-writing that would accommodate both complex subject matter and an audience suffering from information overload.

Some observers contend that to a large degree urban journalism has lived up to these expectations. It has gained an identity: a small but growing literature, and an index category in *Journalism Quarterly*. It has gained visibility and respectability: the Urban Journalism Center was established at Northwestern University in 1967, and urban course work has been introduced at major schools of journalism across the nation. It has gained adherents: an Urban Writers Society was founded in 1968, and news executives speak of urban journalism as an integral part of the news structure. It has also recorded some successes in changing journalistic practice, notably by an assault on the media's Berlin Wall of divisiveness: the self-limiting beat system.

What it hasn't yet achieved is a definition. Most reporting specialties are defined by subject matter. Writing styles are defined by method of presentation. Urban journalism, a hybrid of both content and method, has evaded easy identification. Its subject matter runs through many of the existing journalistic specialties; its style varies with content. It is a presence more than a specific field, testifying to a conceptual change in news definition and presentation. As a result, urban journalism is a specialty in fact rather than in name at most large city newspapers.

Paul Goldberger is the "architecture and urban specialist" for the *New York Times*. At the Chicago *Daily News*, Dennis Byrne reports on "urban affairs." George McCue has been art and urban design critic for the *Saint Louis Post-Dispatch* since 1956. In Seattle, Hilda Bryant is the "social issues reporter" for the *Post-Intelligencer*. At the *Atlanta Constitution*, Chuck Bell covers ecology and the environment, perhaps the most common of the current urban reporting subfields. The varying titles signify but do not exhaust the breadth of subject matter coming under the urban journalism umbrella. Whatever the title—and many news organizations use no special designation for urban reporters—the function is similar: to identify and examine urban problems.

From this description, urban reporting may seem no different from any other species. And indeed, some journalists limit the definition to specific topical areas, to governmental functions such as transportation, sewage disposal, crime, education, water supply, public health, land use and zoning, housing and urban renewal, recreational facilities. But urban reporting also extends to concerns not solely within the scope of government, like pollution, race relations, and architecture. Reporters have in the past, and will continue in the future, to report on these subjects as they surface in the form of public events.

There is another way to look at urban reporting, however, that goes beyond the simple coverage of selected subjects. A common thread links all the urban problem topics listed above. Each involves several—and often competing—interest groups. Each involves decision processes that cut across conventional beat lines. Each affects layers of civic and social strata other than the parties directly involved in a single news event. In this perspective, urban reporting serves to integrate the multidimensional reality of complex social systems. These are systems in which events rarely occur in isolation, in which the shock waves of decisions travel past intended limits of their points of origin.

The urban reporter's function, then, is to sort out what communication researcher Jack Lyle describes as the "complex systems of interrelated parts" that constitute urban problems and solutions. For the reporter, urban problems do not start and stop on the steps of city hall or the county courthouse. Though necessarily local in nature, an urban subject may involve several levels of government, and any number of formal and informal civic organizations. A decision to develop a mass transit system, for example, may include participation by federal and state agencies, local government, and citizens' organizations of several kinds. In addition, the effects of the transit decision may be felt by other groups and individuals not direct parties to the process—retail businessmen, employers, bankers, commuters, taxi drivers, residents along the transit route—including some not even aware of the implications it has for them. The decision also may have profound meaning for other communities and their constituent groups, both short term and long term. The reporter's horizon must include these in order to present the dynamics of the news situation.

The process of urban reporting, under this definition, begins with the systematic identification of (a) the interest groups that *should* be represented in stories as information sources, and (b) the various audiences for the specific story subject, so that information serving their needs may be included. Making these procedures explicit helps the urban reporter to avoid missing significant story elements. For instance, when the police chief and the city council meet to discuss rising juvenile crime, the urban approach suggests that judges, probation officials, criminologists, community help organizations and similar groups may be relevant to the story. So may, for that matter, seemingly unrelated agencies such as schools and building inspection departments.

As with other reporting specialties, urban journalism implies specialized knowledge. Because the field includes so many subjects, formal training may range from public administration, land-use planning, and economics for some reporters, to architecture, sociology, and criminal justice studies for others. This training enables the urban specialist to see more clearly than the generalist the dimensions of public issues. Journalism Professor Gene Burd describes the result this way:

> Because of the complexity of cities, the urban specialist is better trained than the general assignment reporter to see the relation of cause and effect. He is better able to detect defective building code enforcement than report on slum fires; better able to analyze poor street planning than report on auto accident fatalities; and better able to detect high tension areas than report on mass murders.[1]

Urban problems don't often respect journalism's news beat boundaries. The action taken on a shopping center proposal in one suburb is likely to have profound implications for nearby suburbs and the central city itself. A housing program in the inner city may have some of its story roots in the state capital's political beat. The beat structure works against such cross-sectional reporting, however. Burd suggests an "urban renewal" program in newspaper city rooms to adapt to these conditions. Such a program could involve organizing reporting teams around urban subjects and urban functions—land development, social problems, public services. Reporters on the teams could continue to operate on narrower beat levels, with an urban "generalist" overseeing each team to assure integration. Such teamwork might result in reporting on water supply and control rather than an occasional flash flood; on highway planning and politics rather than the freeway jam; on slum conditions and causes rather than the tenement fire.[2]

For a time in the late 1960s, the urban crisis and urban reporting in the eyes of many journalists seemed synonymous with racial conflict. Following the ghetto riots in Newark, Detroit, the Watts district of Los Angeles, and other cities, news executives began a searching, painful, and public examination of their role in both the riots and the conditions that led up to them. Conferences were held; studies were conducted; reports were written. Much of the focus was on the behavior of the media during the disturbances, and the self-searching produced endless sets of guidelines on how to cover riots. The *Chicago Sun-Times*, for example, adopted "Eight Rules for Handling News of Racial Tension," ranging from "We do not report trivial incidents" to "We try to tell the story without slant or bias." [3]

The impetus for this approach came from a suspicion—sometimes an accusation—that news media practices may have been responsible for the escalation of minor disturbances into full-scale riots. The National Advisory Commission on Civil Disorders (the Kerner commission) was asked to investigate this question of press influence on ghetto riots. It reported these conclusions:

> First, that despite incidents of sensationalism, inaccuracies, and distortions, newspapers, radio and television, on the whole, made a real effort to give a balanced, factual account of the 1967 disorders.
> Second, despite this effort, the portrayal of the violence that occurred last summer failed to reflect accurately its scale and character. The overall effect was, we believe, an exaggeration of both mood and event.
> Third, and ultimately most important, we believe that the media have thus far failed to report adequately on the causes and conse-

quences of civil disorders and the underlying problems of race relations.[4]

The report went on to fault the media for reflecting "the biases, the paternalism, the indifference of white America" to black and other minority groups.[5] It also urged bringing more members of minority groups into journalism as practitioners, to remedy its conviction that "the press has too long basked in a white world, looking out of it, if at all, with white men's eyes and a white perspective." [6]

Many newspapers and broadcast operations attempted to correct for this myopia in the late 1960s. Their stories described the horrors of ghetto life. They attempted to explore the multiple causes of minority unemployment and underemployment, of educational inequality, of social discrimination. Blacks began to appear regularly on television. News executives searched for minority journalists, and, finding few with desired training or experience, launched training and scholarship programs. Aspects of minority life long ignored, such as social and organizational news, found a place in the paper. Language that expressed bias or perpetuated stereotypes began to recede from the mass media.

Some of the effects of that sudden minority consciousness are still evident in newsrooms today. Many of them vanished, however, as the memory of Watts and Newark waned and the media reverted to traditional news values. Events make news, and riots are easier to report about than the subtleties of job discrimination or lack of transportation. As one critic observed in 1974:

> Today, although blacks can be seen on television, and although some white media seriously attempt to cover the urban ghetto experience, most metropolitan and suburban newspapers and broadcast stations think of blacks only in terms of crime stories and bussing stories. Mainstream American media write white. News is covered by whites for whites. Feature sections rarely recognize the existence of blacks. Columns on beauty hints are of value only to white women. It is a small wonder that blacks often ignore white newspapers and feel the need for a black press.[7]

The few urban reporters specializing in race relations and related subjects must first overcome the inertia and disinterest that seems to reside in their industry. Adequately interpreting and representing minority interests requires skill, knowledge, and sensitivity. Whether the effort is worthwhile may be judged from this observation by a Cornell sociologist: "Negro and white Americans of comparable education and economic position share a large number of very important values, beliefs, hopes, fears, and ordinary human experiences. Communications that convey a sense of this commonality may be expected to enhance favorable prospects for orderly social change in race relations." [8]

If this assessment is correct, then human relations reporters have a rare journalistic opportunity to directly improve the quality of life in their communities. To realize this opportunity, obstacles that don't confront other urban affairs writers must be overcome. Foremost among these is the need to develop trusting and trustworthy news sources. The white reporter working in the Chicano, Indian, Puerto Rican, or black communities may face language barriers, indifference, and cynicism, along with more common news-gathering hazards. He must get to know and talk with the welfare recipient as well as the welfare director, the postman as well as the NAACP president, the pool-hall operator as well as the mortuary owner. The visible leaders of minority groups sometimes aren't the real opinion leaders of the community, and the reporter who develops a spectrum of sources is well served.

Race relations presents a broad landscape to the reporter. It includes routine organizations coverage, from fraternal, church, and social groups to activist associations. It includes coverage of the civil-rights and equal-opportunity programs of government and industry. It includes keeping current with the literature of human relations, and the movements active in the field. It includes the searching out of individuals worthy of news attention because of personality, activities, or achievement. The human relations reporter should also monitor indicators of the status and relative condition of minorities, particularly in regard to employment, education, and income. It was the absence of this early-warning approach to news that led to white America's shock and incomprehension at the riots of the sixties.

A final caution: sensitivities are great and source relationships fragile in urban minority communities. Not covering an event is likely to be interpreted as evidence of racism, not as a news value judgment based on available space and manpower. Some community groups expect overt participation by reporters in their activities as a sign of support and sympathy. A story critical of a group or individual may destroy irreplaceable sources. Human relations reporters must develop suitable mechanisms to cope with these and other ethical dilemmas.

Covering the Environment

In the hamlet of Topsham, Maine, two journalists launch a weekly newspaper, the *Maine Times,* and regularly publish hard-hitting articles about the impact of proposed oil refineries on the Maine coast. A few miles away in Portland, *Maine Sunday Telegram* reporter Bob Cummings examines just how much electric power will be produced by a hydro-electric project that would flood one of northern Maine's wild rivers. Halfway across the country, *Chicago Today* reporter R. Milton Carleton writes about phosphate pollution in Lake Michigan. On the West Coast, *San Francisco Chronicle* reporter David Perlman examines the energy needs of California, a state with a shrinking supply of power.[9] These articles, and many more like them in publications large and small, reflect the extensive coverage being devoted to environmental issues. Discussion of the environment has become "in," and the topic is not likely to diminish in importance in a time when terms like "energy crisis," "land use planning," "smog" and "zero population growth" have become commonplace.

Yet covering the environment has not been, in some critics' view, as professional as it might be. Colorado environmentalist H. Peter Metzger argues that some journalists "simply refused to consider the possibility that the U.S. Army or the AEC [Atomic Energy Commission] could, for any reason, create a situation of hazard to the public." He also maintains that all too many writers on the environment have a "general incompetence" in technical matters.[10] Moreover, the "event" approach of traditional news reporting is not well suited to covering environmental issues. Says *Los Angeles Times* environmental reporter Larry Pryor:

> Environmental writing is ideally suited to interpretive reporting. Here the writer turns theorist as well as reporter. He investigates and draws together seemingly unrelated facts into an understandable pattern. This takes time—literally months for one story—as well as good sources and the ability to communicate with them on technical topics.[11]

Journalism researchers Leonard Sellars and David W. Jones, Jr., take a similar view:

> Environmental change is often incremental, an equilibrium which shifts slowly and cumulatively over a period of years, seldom becoming an "event" that would normally be considered reportable. Event reporting is a linear, compartmentalized procedure that obscures the fact that environmental change is a process. It perforce focuses our attention on man's projects rather than nature's processes.[12]

Some of the danger zones for the environmental reporter ought to be evident from these comments. Environmental stories are complex and reporters should not rely on single sources. The translation of technical jargon is difficult. And the environmental reporter may find himself with a blind reliance on "experts" who present "doomsday" findings in "pseudo-events" such as news conferences.

Environmental coverage is, of course, complicated. Public policy decisions on the environment are based not only on scientific evidence but also on a sorting out of contrasting value systems. A major oil company may want one thing, the Sierra Club quite another. Both may marshal impressive scientific evidence to support their views. Both may also take moralistic positions: free enterprise versus conservation of natural resources. Complex messages coming from diverse voices confront the reporter at every turn. At a public hearing, for example, spokesmen for ecology groups may claim that certain action will lead to a contaminated water supply. They may back their argument with a battery of high-powered scientific talent. Industrial spokesmen, on the other hand, may be equally persuasive. They may have even higher-powered scientific support because their witnesses are likely to be paid consultants, whereas the ecology groups quite often have relied on volunteer talent. For the reporter this conflicting evidence means developing considerable sophistication in the particular field. He may want to seek out independent authorities with no ax to grind, read the leading journals, and consult with persons who can help him put the debate at the hearing in the proper context. The reporter must avoid becoming the moralist who always identifies with one side. And at times, there are dozens of sides, all in disagreement. Writer Dennis J. Chase concludes:

> By and large, journalists have been content to report the crisis by attributing it—to a study, a report, or the judgment of a prominent scientist or government spokesman—with no serious attempt to verify the conclusions or locate flaws in the findings. Most of these findings are of the "doomsday" variety and have scared the daylights out of readers and viewers. . . . This is most demonstrable in the cases of air pollution, water pollution and the population "explosion"—the Three Horsemen of the Apocalypse—all crises at once, and all containing the same flaws of the self-contradictory, the non-evidentiary, the non-verifiable, and the undefined. Eco-journalism (my term) is the journalistic practice of reporting ecological crises by ignoring, treating as unimportant, or mishandling the evidence on which the crises are based.[13]

These commentators suggest a changing role for the public affairs reporter who covers environmental topics. Rather than concentrating on the day-to-day events, the reporter should turn his attention to broader issues, and attempt to place events in context. What should be the objectives of the environmental reporter?

Expand Understanding of the Environment. By writing about the environment, the reporter can help promote a broader understanding of ecological sciences and their importance. While some might disagree that the reporter should advocate particular stands on environmental issues, it is hard to argue with the overall need of society to use natural resources in an intelligent fashion. The reporter, by providing careful analyses of proposals, can help decision-makers and the public make such choices.

Show the Interrelationships of Technical and Social Knowledge. Environmental writer David Hendin says that to most persons, "environment is synonymous with pollution of the air and water. But not to the Negro in Harlem. . . . To this person environment is rats, leaks in the roof and peeling lead-base paints that kill his children when they eat it. To this person environment is bad plumbing, no job and no coat to wear when he goes out in the snow." [14]

Some environmental reporting is beginning to reflect these larger concerns. In his article on a proposed hydroelectric dam, Cummings writes:

> Last winter's energy scare made an almost magic word of Dickey-Lincoln [the name of the project].
> The project, which would flood the wild Saint John River to generate electricity, is being touted as the answer to Maine and New England's long quest for a cheap and plentiful source of power.
> The truth is somewhat less dramatic. Dickey-Lincoln would produce useful volumes of power. But construction of the dams won't solve either the energy crisis in general or New England's need in particular.[15]

Cummings carefully examines reports by the Army Corps of Engineers on the project's potential and concludes that the project would "increase the electricity available to New England homes, businesses and industries by the grand total of seven-tenths of one percent." Against this gain, he weighs the loss of the river as a recreation area for canoeists and fishermen, and the loss of forest products that would be flooded. In an interview, Cummings describes his approach to environmental reporting. The "beat" typically takes him out of the office several days a week, and his major sources include local environmentalists, and state agencies, such as the Natural Resources Council, and the Land Use Regulation Commission. "I try to avoid the day-to-day coverage. A good, thorough story is worth more, and is more valuable to the reader than covering each development as it happens. The reader doesn't care week to week, so I try to do stories that tell where the overall issue is going." [16]

This same approach—looking for "where the overall issue is going"—was used by *Chronicle* reporter Perlman in his article on uses of power in California:

> Deep in the heart of the Pacific Gas and Electric Co.—hushed and tightly guarded—stand the airconditioned, pastel-tinted consoles of the giant system's Energy Control Center.
>
> Skilled men tend the center, but in the automated symbolism of the world's most energy-intensive society, the men seem little more than acolytes.
>
> They serve the machines, and to a degree control them; but the system itself holds the ultimate power, for upon it depend the economic life and social tranquility of nearly 9 million people in Northern California. . . .
>
> How much of all this energy is really needed? How much will be needed in the decades to come? How can what's needed be provided without ecological disruption? These questions are crucial to the public, to utilities companies, to government agencies and to politicians.[17]

While a number of magazines and newspapers have examined the impact of the Alaska pipeline on the natural tundra environment, free-lance writer Patricia Monaghan took a different approach in a three-part series in 1974 in the *Saint Paul* (Minn.) *Pioneer Press*. She examined the effect of the pipeline on Alaskan cities and social structure:

> But if Anchorage residents seem preoccupied with the massive construction project begun this spring, it is with good reason: Their city is the destination of tens of thousands of work-seekers who swarmed north this past summer in pursuit of what one welfare administrator bitterly calls "gold in the streets". . . .
>
> The number of migrants alone would cause problems, even if all were healthy, employed and law-abiding. Statistics suggest that as many as one-fifth of Anchorage's residents are newcomers who arrived after congressional approval of the pipeline project in April. Housing is scarce, schools bulging, and inflation soaring. Social services are strained to the limit.[18]

Such articles begin to put environmental issues in perspective, by recognizing that "impact" is not limited in effects to natural environments. So, clearly, the reporter assigned to cover environmental issues must bring broad understanding to the job. Hendin writes:

The environment is a unique subject. And the environmental reporter is a unique person. He isn't a layman and he isn't a scientist or environmentalist. He has to lie somewhere in between.

The problem here is that even the so-called environmentalists don't exactly know what an environmentalist is. He must be part biologist, part chemist, part architect, part physicist, part sociologist, part lawyer, part engineer, and more.

And the environmental writer must be all of those things, to a lesser extent, of course, and he must be able to write and be hardnosed too.[19]

Economic News:
Reporting on Business and Labor

Anyone who thinks that the bromide, "dismal science of economics," must infect economic news just hasn't read the *Wall Street Journal* or watched Louis Rukeyser's *Wall Street Week* on television. Day after day, the *Journal,* by dint of specific detail and superb writing, engages the interest of the country's second largest newspaper audience with its interpretation of finance and commerce, industry and labor. And week after week, Rukeyser's urbanity and wit brighten his insights into investment activity and the effect on it of government and politics.

These, unfortunately, are the exceptions. Media critic Chris Welles, writing in the *Columbia Journalism Review,* concludes that financial journalism is a great bore. As partial evidence, he relates:

> I recently visited with some journalism students at the University of Missouri and, in answer to my questions about why no more than one or two were even thinking of going into business writing, I was told that the subject just "didn't turn us on." All those numbers. Complicated financial statements. Factories full of grey machinery. Their feelings are understandable. When financial pages are filled with stories that XYZ Corp.'s earnings are up 23.2 per cent for the third quarter, that John Smith replaced John Jones as president, that a new assembly line was opened, that a new brand of shampoo was introduced, it is difficult to sense that anything really interesting or important is going on. Decades of pallid and boring business journalism have had an inevitable result.[20]

Yet a great deal that is both interesting and important *is* going on, although it would appear that more critics than business writers are talking about it. Given the lack of agreement among economic theorists as to what policies are good or bad medicine for the economy, the business writer can hardly be expected to solve economic ills. He should, however, be able to explain the theories of those who think they can. On a less authoritarian level, his aim should be to interpret accurately, as well as merely report, economic activity in his community; relate it to national and international trends; and identify the interaction between the economic and political-governmental spheres.

For this assignment, he needs a background of as much course work in economics and accounting as he can combine with his journalistic training. A native skepticism will prove equally valuable in reading corporate executives' faces, and their annual reports. And perhaps most of all, he needs the dogged persistence of the digger, for business rarely tells all to the press. Welles writes:

> Except for its glittery and self-serving advertising and public relations facade, American business remains shrouded from view. In secrecy as tight as that of the CIA, anonymous executives create the goods and services we buy, and determine, to the best of their ability, the prices we will pay for them. Some analysts would argue that they determine to a substantial degree the entire economic structure of society, the quality of our environment, the values that guide our lives.
>
> The corporate institution, wrote Ralph Nader in an introduction to *America, Inc.,* is "the most enduring, coordinated, and generic manager of power" in the country. One could make a fairly convincing case that the heads of any of the nation's 100 largest corporations have more influence over society than any but a very few Congressmen. Yet instead of an appreciation of this power, an effort to discover how and why it is exercised, and its impact on us, the nation's print and electronic media with rare exceptions offer us mere surfaces and facades, an unstructured flow of executive promotion announcements, earnings reports, speeches, and press conferences. On an average day, compare the overwhelming preponderance of stories on the financial pages of the New York *Times* that merely regurgitate handouts and spot news events against the investigative effort and thoughtful analysis in other parts of the paper. Yet the *Times'* financial section, as depressingly lackluster as it is, still is probably better than that of any other general circulation paper in the country. Beyond the *Times* is a bleak wasteland.[21]

Interpreting Economic Activity   The raw material from which the business writer works is mostly business statistics: company reports, bank statements, and reports of government agencies. It is what he does with them that spells the difference between service and disservice to his readers.

Of regular interest to business-page readers are annual reports of net profits, business volume, and size of dividends for the current year compared with those of previous years. For relating this information, the writer needs an understanding of the accounting systems employed. Edward Loeb, writing in *Columbia Journalism Review,* has criticized business writers generally for superficial reading of basic materials. One corporation's annual report, described uncritically on more than one business page, "showed earnings about the same as the previous year, but if the same accounting had been used both years, the company would have been in the red." [22]

Another critic, writing in *The Unsatisfied Man,* the Colorado journalism review, cites among many instances the following:

> One handout story, which appeared in all three [Denver] papers, brought the glad tidings that the directors of a shipping firm had not only declared a ten per cent stock dividend, but had approved a 15 cents per share cash dividend as well. The cash dividend was in fact bad news, as any business editor could have discovered from his own files, since it was a reduction from the earlier 20 cents a share. And the stock dividend alone was meaningless, since the market price was adjusted downward to reflect the increased volume of shares. The stock dividend merely diluted the impact of the cash dividend reduction. So the net effect of all this corporate largesse was that shareholders took a 17.5 per cent cut in cash dividends. But that never got into print. [23]

Another type of annual report of interest to the reader is the financial statements of local banks. Properly interpreted, they provide such indicators of the community's business activity as total deposits of all the community's banks as compared with those of previous years; total resources of these banks, ratio of loans to deposits, total investments in government bonds, and total checks drawn on local banks—all of these compared with previous years.

Relating to the Larger Picture. Many are the reports of government agencies that provide a context in which to consider local business activity. The Federal Reserve Board periodically reports on department-store sales in each of the system's districts, as well as on business loans at member banks. The Agriculture Department issues monthly crop reports. From the Commerce Department come monthly reports of the nation's imports and exports. From the Labor Department, reports on employment and unemployment, wholesale prices, and other cost-of-living indexes.

Another type of government source that may help the writer to view local business activity in a larger context is the regulatory agency, both federal and state. To what extent do the regulations of the Interstate Commerce Commission increase operating costs—and thus costs to the consumer—of local trucking firms? By what process does a state agency decide whether or not to grant a rate increase to a local utility?

Identifying Interaction. The points at which business intersects government—and they are many—may be useful to the business writer because government sources regularly talk more readily to the press than do corporate executives. As Welles has noted, major corporate exposés of recent times have come about through government-business involvement, with incriminating evidence leaked to the press by government employees.

The business writer, in any case, should be able to identify the movers and shakers of his community and how they wield power, because they are most often prominent business leaders. Some historians have observed that the caliber of elected officials in America declined in the post-Civil War period because business opportunities engaged the most venturesome talents, and these had no trouble imposing their will on elected officials. Today it is not uncommon for business leaders to find time to hold elective or appointive office, along with a number of corporate directorships, as Phyllis Austin showed in her study of Maine's power elite for the *Maine Times.*[24]

News of Labor   Whatever happened to labor news? The number of labor editors on daily papers declined from 150-odd in 1950 to about a dozen twenty years later, according to the *Editor & Publisher Yearbook*. So it is not a thriving specialization. Part of the answer lies in the criticism of labor coverage then and now: the only news of labor that gets attention is the event of conflict, the strike.[25] This lack of labor coverage is regrettable because many process or problem stories go untold in the press: industrial safety, pension plans, changes in the nature of the work force, job alienation versus the work ethic. How workers, blue collar and white, male and female, feel about their jobs can make engrossing reading, as Studs Terkel has proved in his volume of interviews, *Working*. But the reader must turn to books to get it.

Consumer Reporting

Closely related to economic news is consumer reporting, a relatively new branch of journalism, but one that has been widely praised and discussed. And little wonder. From New York to Louisville, Minneapolis to Los Angeles, newspapers and television stations are presenting interpretative reports about the quality of products and services in the American marketplace. And these reports have brought beneficial results. As the dean of consumer writers, Sidney Margolis, points out:

> Without the new interest of the press and often radio and sometimes TV, we probably would not have achieved the useful advances of the past 12 years such as truth-in-lending and other credit reforms on federal and state levels; the new product safety law; advances in regulations governing auto and tire safety; some reforms in food and cosmetic packaging; unit pricing and open dating of foods; the 1962 drug amendments requiring that drugs be proven efficacious as well as safe; the exposure and increasing regulation of multiple distributor investment schemes, and many other money-wasting deceptions whether actually illegal or barely inside the law. . . . What the new consumer journalism now needs urgently to develop is greater expertise. A new reporter assigned to cover consumer affairs sometimes does not know where to turn.[26]

Not all observers agree that consumer reporting is a form of journalism whose time has come. Francis Pollock, editor of *Media & Consumer,* has concluded that "consumer news may have 'arrived' in some media organizations. But its acceptance is far from universal." There is intense pressure from advertisers to blunt the impact of consumer reporting, and rather than praise consumer reporting, the dominant tendency of business has been to condemn the press for allegedly unbalanced and distorted reporting.[27] Researcher David C. Loveland, in a Freedom of Information Center report in 1971, surveyed 100 newspapers and 75 television stations about their consumer coverage, and found that the majority in both categories treated consumer news in the same manner as other news stories. "Everyone has his own ideas about what consumer news is, or what it should be," he says, "and how it should be approached. There is also the dilemma of professional objectivity versus advocacy that confronts the consumer reporter. He finds that if he is to serve the public, he must become an activist; if he is to satisfy his editor, and perhaps the advertising manager, he must attempt objectivity by telling both sides of the story." [28]

These considerations may be particularly important when a consumer story deals with the practices of a newpaper's advertiser. Publishers, perhaps particularly those on smaller papers where advertising revenue may come from only a few major accounts, remain sensitive to consumer stories that may ruffle advertisers. The safest path for the reporter here is still careful documentation for every statement and a story that is fair and balanced. Many consumer reports include sidebars in which the allegedly offending businesses are given a chance to respond to the charges.

The methods of the consumer reporter vary from topic to topic, and the reporter about to attempt a consumer affairs story might well consult with other papers to see how similar reporting has been conducted in other places. Here are some examples:

Supermarket Filth. Philadelphia Bulletin reporter Dorothy Brown in 1973 examined inspection reports by the Pennsylvania Agriculture Department and accompanied an inspector on his rounds. The store meat departments had various unsanitary conditions, such as "mold in the meat grinder." The report included surveys of bacteria counts, which revealed excessively high levels of bacteria in twelve of twelve samples of raw hamburger.[29]

Gasoline Additives. The *Detroit Free Press,* in 1973, surveyed prices, octane ratings and qualitative differences among gasolines sold in its area. Reporter Trudy Leiberman found that "for the most part, differences among brands measured in tenths of an octane, too small to be noticed by most automobile engines." [30]

Summer Camps. Houston Post reporter Martha Leibrum investigated safety standards at summer camps for children, and in a 1973 series, concluded that with some exceptions, "children are at the mercy of the good intentions of camp directors." [31]

Home Fire Alarms. The *Louisville Courier-Journal,* in a 1972 article, found that after a fatal fire, salesmen of home fire alarms visited homes near the fire and sold alarms for prices of more than $200. The article questioned the sales tactics, but was careful to say that fire alarm protection was important.[32]

Drug Prices. The *San Francisco Bay Guardian,* in 1973, surveyed drug prices in the San Francisco area and found wide price ranges. The paper concluded that the posting of prices, plus the sale of drugs by generic name, would substantially help the consumer.[33]

While some consumer stories expose abuses, others help the reader by making price comparisons and examining differences between similar products and services. Many newspapers regularly survey food stores for comparative pricing. Consumer stories can range from examining the differences between different types of life insurance to a guide on how to pick a nursing home for an elderly person.

Consumer affairs reporting often involves a closer working relationship between a reporter and a government agency than either may be used to. In her report on supermarket health standards, *Philadelphia Bulletin* reporter Brown worked closely with state officials. Similar relationships may develop with such agencies as the federal Food and Drug Administration, state attorneys' general offices, and the consumer protection agencies found in an increasing number of states and larger cities.

The reporter needs to be careful here, as sometimes a government agency will be a rubber stamp for a particular industry it is supposed to regulate. Nonetheless, the reporter should not overlook government sources and experts.

How does the consumer affairs reporter work? What methods does he use? What are the snares? *Minneapolis Star* managing editor David Nimmer, who worked on the paper's consumer-reporting team for more than a year, offers these guidelines:

> You can always do comparison shopping, such as with liquor or food, or any topic where you might find comparable items at different outlets.
>
> If you work for a newspaper which is not able to hire a private laboratory, you may be able to get a state agency to do the testing, such as the department of weights and measures, to see if companies are giving a full gallon of milk or ice cream. Or you may be able to use the facilities at your state university, such as asking the business administration department to explain the ins and outs of a homeowners insurance policy.
>
> I'd say you should plan to spend two weeks at a minimum to find out just what it is you're looking for in a particular product or service. Talk to government experts; talk to the people in the business. For example, if you're looking at television repair, you have to know what is reasonable for a television repairman to charge for a particular repair.
>
> Most importantly, don't overwrite your facts. If you find, for instance, bacteria counts of 10 million in hamburger, you have to point out that 10 million is generally considered an acceptable level. And if you find one sample with 100 million bacteria count, you should point out that no one will die from eating the meat, because most of the bacteria will be destroyed in cooking. At the same time, point out that a lot of people have meat that is cleaner than that, and that the meat is not as clean as it ought to be.[34]

Sources for the Consumer Reporter

There is a growing body of literature on consumer reporting, and a huge body of literature on various consumer investigations. Two important monthly publications are *Consumer Reports* and *Media & Consumer*. *Consumer Reports* is considered one of the leading consumer magazines; its investigations range from automobile performance to sales practices. *Media & Consumer* surveys the reporting on consumer issues being done at newspapers, magazines, and broadcast stations, and often reprints articles.

The *Freedom of Information Center* has issued a report (*No. 285;* June, 1972) on sources for the consumer affairs journalist. Many individual newspapers have done extensive consumer reporting, and an inquiry to them will often produce reprints or clips of specific articles.

There are many directories that are useful, including *Food Industry Sourcebook for Communication* (Washington: National Canners Association, 1972); *Consumers Directory 1971–1972* (The Hague: International Organization of Consumer Unions, 1971); *Directory of Government Agencies Safeguarding Consumer and Environment* (Alexandria, Va.: Serina Press, 1971); *United States Government Organization Manual* (Washington: Superintendent of Documents, 1972); *Guide to Federal Consumer Services* (Washington: Superintendent of Documents, 1971); *Standard Directory of Advertisers* (Skokie, Ill.: National Register Publishing Company, 1972); and *State Programs for Consumer Protection* (Raleigh, N.C.: National Association of Attorneys General, 1972).

Many periodicals for the consumer are also useful for the consumer reporter, including *Of Consuming Interest, Consumer Newsweek, Consumer Legislative Monthly Report,* and dozens of trade publications, such as *Advertising Age, Merchandising Week,* and *Supermarketing.*

Don't overlook such sources as the *Congressional Record,* which has reprints of many newspaper articles on consumer affairs inserted by congressmen, and the *Federal Register,* which has federal agency documents. Bibliographies for the consumer and consumer reporter include the short, but comprehensive one in *Media & Consumer* 1 (June, 1973); *Consumer Education Bibliography* (Washington: Superintendent of Documents, 1971); and *Consumer Law Bibliography* (Chestnut Hill, Mass.: National Consumer Law Center, Boston College Law School, 1971).

Science and Medical Reporting

Science and medical reporting in the American press has a long and colorful history. And, along with business news, it is probably the most firmly established area of specialty reporting.

Early science reporting tended toward sensationalism, exaggeration, and even hoaxes. The *New York Sun* in an 1835 series, for example, perpetrated the "moon hoax," reporting that a leading scientist had sighted "batlike men four feet tall bearing copper-colored fur, with yellow faces." [35] But by 1870, Horace Greeley was writing a regular science column (on scientific agriculture) for the *New York Tribune.* Other landmarks in science reporting were the introduction of Einstein's theory of relativity to newspaper readers by Carr Van Anda of the *New York Times* in 1919; the appointment of David Dietz as the first newspaper science editor by the Scripps-Howard newspapers in 1921; and the first Pulitzer Prize to a science writer (Alva Johnson of the *New York Times*) in 1923 for reporting scientists' acceptance of Darwin's evolution theory.

Carolyn D. Hay, in a 1970 master's thesis entitled, "A History of Science Writing in the United States," distinguishes three phases of science writing:

> The "gee whiz" phase, exemplifying an old "yellow journalism" dictum that a good story should make the reader say "Gee Whiz."
>
> The present era of increasingly professional analytic reporting of science, which has been a full-time journalistic occupation since the 1920s.
>
> A new phase in which science writers study the possible effects on society of science and technology.[36]

Science writing's place in American journalism has been solidified by university training programs in science reporting, the acceptance of trained science writers by the media, an active professional organization (National Association of Science Writers), and a continuing body of research about science reporting, readership, and the diffusion of scientific ideas.

As Hay suggests, science and medical writers have gone through different stages of development. As the space program evolved in the 1950s and 1960s, and as government came to play an increasingly important role in all phases of science, science writers often acted as mere translators for science and technology. With the coming of the ecology movement and similar social movements in the late 1960s, science writers became more critical. Jeff Carruthers, a science writer for Canada's Free Press newspapers, says the result was conflict between an old school of science reporting that relied almost exclusively on scientists as sources of news and a new school that went to other sources, which were occasionally embarrassing to the scientist.

Although science and medical reporting (medical is often, though not always, subsumed under science) seem light years ahead of other specialties that are just getting started, they may not indeed be far ahead at all. Perlman, for one, says science "is not covered properly. The writing is subject to whims, fashions, and fads in the scientific field." [37] In 1971 when David Perlman was president of the National Association of Science Writers, a survey conducted by that organization showed that "far fewer than 100 dailies have fulltime science writers. Most papers are just faking it." [38] To Boyce Rensberger of the *New York Times*, a major problem with science writing is that some "science writers are trying to write about things they don't understand. When you think about it, it's ludicrous. I have seen science writers struggling to write something they don't understand themselves even asking the source to read it to make sure they understood it and wrote it properly. They are assuming that if the source okays it, it is ready for the paper."[39]

In spite of its problems, science writing is an active and diverse field. And most writers migrate toward those subjects that especially interest them. Because science, technology, and other subjects the science reporter covers are so vast there is considerable latitude in selection of story topics. Writers like Mildred Spencer of the *Buffalo Evening News* focused her energies on biological science, medicine, and health whereas Alton Blakeslee of the Associated Press is more of a generalist who tries to cover all areas of science. Daniel Greenberg, formerly of *Science* magazine and now the director of his own science news service, specialized in the "politics of science." [40] Most science writers would agree that their assignments allow for considerable personal freedom as they advise the city desk about the science stories most appropriate for the day's coverage. Sometimes, of course, circumstances and events guide the science writer in story selection. For example, the 1974 operations of Mrs. Betty Ford and Mrs. Happy Rockefeller for breast cancer led to a series of stories on that subject. But, in the main, science writers might cover the physical and biological sciences, space exploration, medicine and public health, environmental sciences, social and behavioral sciences, and technology.

The public needs rapidly transmitted, accurate information about science and technology for several reasons. It is up to the science writer, therefore, to provide:

> Pragmatic advice about everyday life. Everything from weather information to items about personal health.
>
> Guidance on public issues. Before the critical, evaluative process ever begins, the knowledgeable citizen needs to know and understand a wide range of subjects from nuclear power plants to the funding of the National Science Foundation.
>
> Help in evaluating the relationship between science, technology, and society. When do advances in one area hamper developments in another? What is the nature of progress?

Similarly, in the subfields that make up science there are different categories of news. For example, medical news stories are usually of three kinds: (1) the condition of specific patients, (2) advancements in medicine and science, and (3) activities of hospitals and medically related organizations." [41] Because most scientific activity is in the public sector (even many private institutions rely on federal grants and contracts), it requires public understanding. Only through effective science writing can this come about. Here are three leads that demonstrate the functions mentioned above:

Pragmatic Advice about Everyday Life. Lou Joseph asked, "Is a thumb for sucking?" in an article in *Today's Health:*

The parents of Linus probably aren't worried about his thumb sucking. At his age, it's cute. And Linus will never grow up.

But as a real thumb-sucking child grows older, his parents begin to nibble on pencils and gnaw their fingernails when he doesn't quit. This vexing habit—thumb sucking, that is—not only worries parents but also generates considerable discussion and sometimes outright controversy among child health experts.[42]

Guidance on Public Issues. In a story that told the public that knowledge about air pollution and its effects was insufficient to justify pollution scares, David Spurgeon of the Toronto *Globe and Mail* began with one scientist's view:

Dr. H. N. MacFarland of York University gets annoyed whenever he hears some prophet of doom predict that air pollution will kill us all in 20 years.

An expert in inhalation toxicology, he says there simply is not enough known to make such statements. He even gets mildly irritated about the use of an air-pollution index, because he says there is no way of telling what the effects on health will be when the index is over a certain level: the basic scientific knowledge is just not available.[43]

Evaluating the Relationship between Science, Technology, and Society. In a television news story, George Dusheck of KQED-TV, San Francisco, began:

The Atomic Industrial Forum wound up its annual meeting at the St. Francis Hotel here today with a long and occasionally sharp debate on what the Forum calls "The Nuclear Controversy."

In one sense, the nuclear controversy is simply whether the United States shall depend more and more heavily on nuclear plants to supply its growing need for electrical power.

But in another sense, the nuclear controversy is about whether very large social decisions shall be made on technical or upon political grounds.[44]

The science writer's task is formidable. He must understand the scientific method, and the particular nuances of scientists and their language. Often these demands mean dealing with mathematics and statistics, translating jargon, and coping with complex content. Similarly, sources for science news are quite varied. They range from laboratories, scientific installations, and research institutions to journals and government reports. Scientific and professional meetings and conventions, such as the annual meetings of the American Association for the Advancement of Science, are also important sources of information. Not to be overlooked are personal interviews with local authorities on scientific subjects, whether or not they are scientists. As in other specialty reporting, science journalists must avoid simplistic translation and find varied bases for evaluation of the material they gather. Although science writers are moving closer to the methods of investigative reporting, they must take special care to avoid moral judgments and to evaluate scientific issues on a scientific basis.

Seasoned by coverage of demonstrations at scientific meetings, especially in the late 1960s and early 1970s, science reporters are moving toward a new style of tough-minded reporting. As John Lear of the *Saturday Review* has written, "If technology is to be brought under control, science reporters must move beyond mere description to evaluation that raises the hard questions." [45]

Covering Mental Health and Social Welfare

Like reporting of science and medicine, press coverage of mental health and social welfare has a colorful history. But unlike them, this has not been a highly successful field for specialty reporting. Only a few mental health-social welfare reporters are working for newspapers and broadcast stations, though hundreds are writing for specialized publications. In spite of a long history of press involvement with mental health-social welfare issues, editors have shown some reluctance to invest their personnel resources in this type of coverage.

Yet the problems and issues of mental health and social health have provided the press with considerable newsworthy material for many years. It may not have been the first time such a ploy was used, but Nellie Bly's "stunt" of the 1880s in which she feigned insanity in order to gain admission to a New York City asylum led to the writing of a classic exposé. Exposés of conditions in mental health and social welfare institutions became standard fare for the press. They were usually highly sensational, with little sensitivity for the people involved, and sought scapegoats for conditions they disclosed. This situation began to change in the years after World War II. As Arthur J. Snider, science and medical reporter for the *Chicago Daily News,* suggests:

Beginning in about 1945, there emerged a new type of story—an "exposé" with a constructive twist. Reporters entered mental hospitals and conducted investigations with the collaboration of superintendents and psychiatrists who were concerned over the lack of public interest in mental hospitals and the inability to obtain necessary funds from government agencies for operation, for rebuilding facilities that had deteriorated during the depression and for hiring staff. Today, most stories about state institutions are of this constructive type—calling attention to evils for the purpose of remedial action.[46]

In recent years the definition of mental health and social welfare has expanded greatly to encompass what are often referred to as "human services." In part this expansion is a consequence of the shift from isolated country asylums, homes for the elderly and juveniles, to community-based services. Furthermore, the term "mental health" has come to embrace, among other social maladjustments, alcoholism, drug abuse, and the problems of aging, adolescence, and minorities.

Coverage of mental health has often been rife with conflict between reporters and mental health professionals. As Paul I. Kliger, a Chicago community organizer, put it:

> The basic problem is communication. We have the uninformed journalist who knows nothing about mental health and the uninformed mental health professional who knows nothing about the media. The journalist comes to the mental health center looking for a good story. He brings with him all the usual popular beliefs and prejudices. He may come looking for an exposé or a more positive story to tell the public how well a center is doing.[47]

As early as 1956, the American Psychiatric Association, expressing concern over the lack of cooperation between mental health workers and the media, convened a conference to discuss mutual problems. Both sides agreed that it was in the public interest to cover mental health, and they attempted to work out an effective means of doing so. They agreed, as the conference report indicated, that "in supplying information and in presenting it to the public, members of both professions should avoid exaggeration, distortion, and sensationalism; seek to remove the stigmatization associated with mental illness; and bear in mind that some information about mental illness arouses anxiety." [48]

Snider lists three barriers that confront the writer trying to cover the mental health field: difficulty in conceptualizing the content of psychiatry, difficulty in communicating the language of psychiatry, and the negative attitude of psychiatrists toward the press. While Snider concentrates on only *one* of the several professions (such as psychologists, social workers, and rehabilitation counselors) dealing with mental health and social welfare, his critique could apply to all.

Schools of journalism have also been concerned with the coverage of mental health. In 1964 Robert W. Root organized a graduate program for journalists in mental health information at Syracuse University. The Root program and others at Kansas State University and the University of Texas were sponsored by the National Institute of Mental Health. Such organizations as the National Association for Mental Health, a citizens group; the American Psychological Association, a professional group; and the National Institute of Mental Health, a government agency, have expressed the view that adequate coverage of mental health—and the human condition—is crucial if the press is to tell the "people story" in human terms.

Mental health journalists face not only the barriers listed by Snider, but also considerable confusion because of the many schools of thought and interpretations in the mental health field. Often news sources will disagree about issues and it is necessary for the journalist to put these conflicts in context, indicating where they fit into the body of opinion about mental health. This confusion can be particularly disturbing in criminal trials where issues of tests for insanity are discussed. Virginia Grabowski has demonstrated the problems that different professional viewpoints can cause the journalist in her report on the conflicting psychiatric and psychological testimony in the trial of Sirhan Sirhan, the convicted assassin of Robert Kennedy. Day after day reporters covering that trial had to deal with sharply contrasting and contradictory testimony.[49]

Functions for Mental Health-Social Welfare Reporters   Because these fields embrace both publicly and privately supported institutions, services, and programs, the reporter has an especially difficult task in helping the public to understand the nature, purpose, and availability of particular services. He must put the service into clear view in the news story indicating how it is funded and to whom it is responsible. Functions for the mental health-social welfare reporter include:

> Helping the public know and understand human services and how they can be utilized.
>
> Examining the performance of officials who are responsible for those services through stories that monitor conditions, philosophies, and approaches.
>
> Utilizing the content of the mental health field to cover larger social problems.

The first two functions are self-explanatory; the third may not be. Those who work in the mental health and social welfare field are specialists who possess considerable knowledge about the human condition. They ought to be used by the reporter as sources of news in stories about housing, urban crowding, abortion, and other significant social issues. A psychiatrist, sociologist, or other professional concerned with human problems, for example, may be a good source on certain types of crimes, or on stories about shoplifting. The range of possible stories is great and the mental health-social welfare professional can be helpful.

Frank Angelo, a *Detroit Free Press* editor and former president of Sigma Delta Chi, has said that, "the 'people story,' who they are and how they live, is the most important story of the decade—this one or any other." The reporter concerned with mental health issues can do much to capture the essence of this story. For example, this story from the *National Observer* demonstrates the kind of vital, human information that can be delivered to the public:

> The door to a rickety, condemned shanty creaks open, exposing the distrusting gaze of an obese, 48-year-old Negro woman. Resigned to the regular intrusion of do-gooders, she admits the latest man-and-woman team with a shrug. An unconventional family waits inside: the woman's 72-year old, blind husband; her two illegitimate daughters, one 35 and pregnant and the other 12; and the pregnant daughter's three children. Leaking pipework has forced all seven of them into three murky rooms. The children run naked through the living room, where the stench from human excrement lying about is gagging. Cockroaches frolic openly.
>
> The woman interloper is a social worker, accustomed to such surroundings. But her partner, a psychiatrist, is radically far afield from the comfort of a tasteful office and cozy clientele. He is Dr. Fernando de Elejalde, director of an east Topeka community project, designed, as never before, to bring the services of a psychiatrist to the masses.[50]

While many mental health and social welfare services are covered in the context of government agencies (see Chapter 8), the reporter delving into this subject must make an effort to educate himself to the nature of the field: the government organizations responsible for services; the professional groups who carry it out, and the citizen groups that monitor it and lobby for it. Further, there is a considerable body of knowledge in each of the fields concerned with human problems. Public information offices at the various professional organizations, such as the American Psychiatric Association, American Psychological Association, and National Association of Social Workers, publish glossaries, journals, and other helpful information. Similarly, important scholarly and professional publications, and national meetings and conventions can serve as important sources. The National Institute for Mental Health, for example, has a free service for reporters at its Clearinghouse for Mental Health Information. A reporter asking a question about certain types of services or social problems can obtain computerized abstracts of articles on the subject.

Mental health and social welfare is a specialty field that requires considerable knowledge on the part of the reporter. Unfortunately, there are few mental health social welfare beats, and thus the serious reporter must learn about this subject on his own so that he can apply the knowledge to general assignment work or a specialty like science writing or urban affairs.

Reporting on Education

The origin of special coverage of education is generally credited to *Time* magazine in 1923, so its history is shorter than those of business and science coverage, but older than those of urban, environmental, consumer, and mental health reporting. It shares with all of them the necessity for specialized knowledge and insight, as well as for the gifts of the translator, if the reader is to be well served.

Sometimes he isn't, as an entry in one competition for education reporters disclosed. This particular entry was impressive if only for its bulk: page after page displayed clippings of stories reporting enrollments, sports events, homecomings, school-board meetings, budgets, new construction, PTA fund raisers, graduation exercises—an exhaustively detailed log of a year's events in the school system of a city of 50,000.

It might as well have been the chronicle of School Year 1953–1954 or 1963–1964 instead of 1973–1974. Nothing, apparently, had changed. No educational innovations? No drug problems? No increase in pregnancies?

Along toward the end of the year's reportage, the contest entry includes the report of a school-board meeting at which an assistant superintendent submitted his resignation in a letter charging his superior with incompetence. All of a sudden and without warning, a long-standing and bitter controversy in the school administration was out in the open. It must have come as quite a surprise to parents and other taxpayers lulled by the innocuous reporting of routine events that constituted a year's newspaper "coverage" of education in that community.

Too much is happening in education today for any newspaper to be satisfied with public-relations handouts and conventional reporting of surface events. Such accounts are inadequate aids to the reader in understanding the educational process, and the educational process is what it's all about.

No institution in our society is so commonly shared as the school. We've all been there. So why does coverage of education need a specialist?

There are at least two good reasons. The kind of confidence that opens administration and classroom doors can only be built on a continuing relationship established by a reporter of proven responsibility. And genuine understanding of educational problems, trends, and developments requires a concentration that is physically impossible for the generalist. Without that openness and without that understanding, the education writer is going to be incapable of carrying out his assignment. For just as Snider listed barriers that confront the writer covering the mental health field, there are problems, according to educator George Gerbner, that also confront the education writer. He lists them this way: "(1) newsmen's feeling of secretiveness, lack of confidence on the part of schoolmen; (2) problems of occupational jargon, obscure or abstract language; and (3) different conceptions of 'news value'." [51]

The education assignment can be seen in terms of three objectives:

1. To tell readers about the student in the classroom from kindergarten to college seminar.
2. To inform readers and interpret for them new developments in education generally.
3. To report and interpret the substance and progress of proposed legislation and of court actions concerning schools on both the state and federal levels.

Focus on Students   It would seem to be elementary that the focus of an education writer should be on the student, but evidence to support that assumption is mixed, if not downright soft. Journalism educator Charles T. Duncan, reporting on survey responses from 52 major dailies in 1966, noted that 30 of the education writers visited schools regularly, 19, occasionally.[52] Gerbner, surveying 119 dailies in the early 1960s, concluded that "the 'hard news, local angle' policy sets the style of [education] reporting on most papers." [53] In translation, "hard news, local angle" means board of education and committee meetings. It does not mean classroom visits, talks with teachers, interviews with students. Interviewing students, establishing rapport at various ages and levels of sophistication, requires a quite different talent from that needed to monitor school board meetings, especially if the reporter is trying to find out why some students hate school and why some students see it as a jail.

Nor is "hard news, local angle" much help to the parent who wonders what mysteries transpire behind those walls for the six hours Johnny is there. Many parents are curious, yet school officials are less than enthusiastic about parental visits except for those specified consultations, and then, too often, the parents' curiosity is frustrated by pedagogese. Wilma Morrison, longtime education editor for the *Portland Oregonian,* once cautioned her fellow education reporters:

> Don't tell Mrs. Jones about the "whole child." It doesn't mean anything to her when she sees it in print even though she has a houseful of aggressively whole children. It will mean something to her if she is told that the good school is responsible for helping her Johnny get over stuttering, learn to swat a baseball, tell the truth on the playground as well as off.
>
> Don't try to sell her "enriched learning experiences" for the enriched tax dollar you want from her. It is Sanskrit to her and she is right. It doesn't mean anything except that the writer is lazy, or dull, or both. Tell her what the kids are doing and why.[54]

The opportunity for telling what the kids are doing and why has been considerably lessened since student unrest and consequent disturbances, particularly in inner-city schools, became commonplace. The press is not welcome at such times. It might find the school personnel less defensive if its presence were less episodic.

Education Is Change   Any school system worth its budget is looking for better ways to promote the learning process, to take advantage of research in psychology and sociology, yet mistrust of educational "fads" is strong among many parents—outraged among some if the innovation is called sex education. The mistrust may very well be justified, but it should be based on complete information, not rumor and misunderstanding. Pedagogues are notoriously bad communicators when it comes to getting across a message to their constituency. The education writer can help, with thoroughgoing reports of such educational alternatives as free schools, open schools, magnet schools, continuous progress schools, and such adjuncts of conventional schools as basic skills centers, learning centers, and work opportunity centers. Nor does the reporter have to wait for the new idea, the new theory to be manifested in the local school system. The journals of education will supply the information.

One difficulty, of course, is the matter of evaluation. How promising is the theory, how effective the new method? The education writer must rely on authority, and he is naïve indeed if he relies on the first one at hand.

Laws, Opinions, and Students   No school system is autonomous. All states provide financial aid to education, and along with it, varying degrees of supervision and regulation. In recent years, the federal government has assumed more and more of a funding role. The qualified education writer is familiar with the personnel and the policies of the state education agencies, and is alert to the significance of proposed legislation, both state and federal, concerning schools. Of the dozens of bills that a state department of education may seek to introduce in the legislature in any one session, the education writer will recognize those that will affect the students in the local system and take pains to explain to readers *how* they will affect them.

Nor will the reporter be a stranger to courts and the opinions thereof. No single institution has affected the public schools in this century more than the U.S. Supreme Court in *Brown* v. *Board of Education*. As such issues as school desegregation continue to be contested in the courts, the education writer will study each decision for possible relevance to his own community.

And so the province of one type of public affairs specialist—the education writer—is not isolated from the domains of those other specialists, the legislative reporter and the writer on judicial process. Nor is the interrelationship unique. The actions of administrators, the laws of legislators, the decisions of judges affect urban and environmental problems, business and labor, consumers, scientific and medical developments, mental health and welfare services. The implied question of this chapter's opening—where does specialization in public affairs reporting begin?— might well be rephrased to ask: where does such specialization end? The answer would seem to be: wherever the industrious and perceptive reporter finds it necessary to pursue a process affecting his specialization.

NOTES

1. Gene Burd, "Urban Renewal in the City Room," *Quill* 56 (May, 1968), 12.
2. Ibid., p. 13.
3. See also Richard Leonard, "Role of the Press in the Urban Crisis," *Quill* (May, 1968), 8–11; Charles U. Daly, ed., *The Media and the Cities* (Chicago: University of Chicago Center for Policy Studies, University of Chicago Press, 1968); and, "We Have Learned Something about Reporting Riots," *Editor & Publisher* (Sept. 2, 1967), p. 11.
4. *Report of the National Advisory Commission on Civil Disorders* (New York: Bantam Books, 1968), p. 363.
5. Ibid., p. 366.
6. Ibid., p. 389.
7. David S. Sachsman, "Mass Media and the Urban Environment," *Mass Comm Review* 1 (July, 1974), 11.
8. Robin M. Williams, Jr., "Implications for the Mass Media of Research on Intergroup Relations and Race," in *Behavioral Sciences and the Mass Media*, ed. Frederick T. C. Yu (New York: Russell Sage Foundation, 1968), p. 74.

9. The *Maine Times* has been praised for its consistent and aggressive coverage of the environment. As an example, see Peggy Fisher, "These People Say the Environmentalists Have Sold Out Southern Maine," *Maine Times* (Nov. 29, 1974), p. 1. Cummings's article on the proposed Dickey-Lincoln dam project, "Dickey: Boon or Boondoggle?" appeared in the *Maine Sunday Telegram* on April 7, 1974. Carleton's article, "Phosphate Pollution—Tempest in a Teapot?" was in *Chicago Today,* April 7, 1972. Perlman's article, "Electric Power Dilemma," appeared in the *San Francisco Chronicle* on April 10, 1972.

10. H. Peter Metzger, "Wanted: Rocky Mountain Post," *The Unsatisfied Man: A Review of Colorado Journalism* 1 (Nov., 1970), 3–4.

11. Larry Pryor, "The Ecology Thicket," in *Interpreting Environmental Issues,* ed. Clay Schoenfeld (Madison, Wis.: Dembar Educational Research Services, 1972), p. 35.

12. Leonard Sellers and David W. Jones, Jr., "Environment and the Mass Media," *Journal of Environmental Education* 5 (Fall, 1973), 52.

13. Dennis J. Chase, "Eco-journalism and the Failure of Crisis Reporting," *Quill* 60 (Oct., 1972), 20–21.

14. David Hendin, "Environmental Reporting," *Quill* 58 (Aug., 1970), 16.

15. Cummings, "Dickey: Boon or Boondoggle?" p. 1.

16. Interview by co-author Stephen Hartgen with Cummings, June 27, 1974.

17. Perlman, "Electric Power Dilemma," p. 1.

18. Patricia Monaghan, "Boom Brings Social Problems to Anchorage," *St. Paul Pioneer Press* (Dec. 3, 1974), p. 1.

19. Hendin, "Environmental Reporting," p. 16.

20. Chris Welles, "The Bleak Wasteland of Financial Journalism," *Columbia Journalism Review* (July-Aug., 1973), 40–49.

21. Ibid., p. 41.

22. Edward Loeb, "Flaws in Financial Reporting," *Columbia Journalism Review* 5 (Spring, 1966), 37–40.

23. Gerald R. Armstrong, "The Business Jungle—Who's Covering?" *The Unsatisfied Man: A Review of Colorado Journalism* 2 (Jan., 1972), 5.

24. Phyllis Austin, "There Are Five Men Who Form the Core of Maine's Power Elite," *Maine Times* (Feb. 15, 1974), pp. 2–5.

25. Sam Zagoria, "Equal Breaks for Labor News," *Columbia Journalism Review* 6 (Fall, 1967), 43–45. See also Lawrence A. Pryor, "The Labor Beat: Do's and Don'ts," *Quill* 59 (April, 1971), 16–17.

26. Sidney Margolis, "Enter the Specialist Consumer Reporter," *Media & Consumer* 1 (July, 1973), 11.

27. Francis Pollock, "Consumer Reporting: Underdeveloped Region," *Columbia Journalism Review* 10 (May-June, 1971), 38.

28. David C. Loveland, "A Survey of Consumer Reporting," *Freedom of Information Center Report No. 264* (July, 1971), 1–2.

29. Quoted in *Media & Consumer* 1 (July, 1973), p. 8.

30. Quoted in *Media & Consumer* 1 (Aug., 1973), p. 2.

31. Quoted in *Media & Consumer* 1 (May, 1973), pp. 6–7.

32. Quoted in *Media & Consumer* 1 (March, 1973), p. 6.

33. Jeanette Foster, "High Drug Prices," San Francisco *Bay Guardian* (March 28, 1973), pp. 1, 3–4.

34. Interview with David Nimmer, April 14, 1974. See also David Nimmer, "How One Newspaper Tells the Consumer Story," *Editor & Publisher* 106 (March 17, 1973), 32, 34.

35. "Science Reporting Has Grown Out of Its 'Gee Whiz' Phase," *Editor & Publisher* 103 (Sept. 12, 1970), 20. Also see Carolyn D. Hay, "A History of Science Writing in the United States" (M. A. thesis, Northwestern University, 1970).

36. Ibid.

37. Everette E. Dennis, "A Report on the Science Writing Seminar," mimeographed (Eugene: University of Oregon, 1971), p. 3.

38. Ibid., p. 3.

39. Ibid., p. 3.

40. See Daniel S. Greenberg, "The Politics of Science," *Bulletin of the American Society of Newspaper Editors* (Dec., 1967), pp. 1–4.

41. Howard Emerson, "Access to Medical News," *Freedom of Information Center Publication No. 163* (June, 1966), p. 1.

42. Lou Joseph, "Is a Thumb for Sucking." *Today's Health* 47 (Dec., 1969), 32.

43. David Spurgeon, "Knowledge Lacking for Pollution Scare, York Expert Insists," *Toronto Globe and Mail* (May 14, 1970), p. 1.

44. George Dusheck, "TV Script—KQED-TV—San Francisco," reprinted in *National Association of Science Writers Clipsheet* 10 (April, 1970).

45. John Lear, "The Trouble with Science Writing," *Columbia Journalism Review* 9 (Summer, 1970), 30–34.

46. Arthur J. Snider, "Interpreting Mental Health: Concerns of the Science Writer" (Paper presented at Mental Health-Mass Media Conference, Kansas State University, Manhattan, Kansas, May 15, 1969), p. 1.

47. Paul I. Kliger, "Understanding the Human Condition: Mental Health and the Mass Media" (Paper presented at the annual meeting of the American Orthopsychiatric Association, San Francisco, March 26, 1970), p. 3. See also Everette E. Dennis, "Improving Relations between Mental Health and the Mass Media," *Hospital & Community Psychiatry* 22 (June, 1970), 39–41.

48. American Psychiatric Association, *Psychiatry, the Press and the Public: Problems in Communication* (Washington: American Psychiatric Association, 1956), pp. 47–48.

49. Virginia Grabowski, "Battle of the Psychiatrists: Newspaper Media Coverage of Psychiatric Testimony in the Trial of Sirhan B. Sirhan" (M.A. thesis, Kansas State University, 1972).

50. Theodore W. Landphair, "Psychiatry Gets into the 'Action,'" *National Observer* (April 7, 1969), p. 20.

51. George Gerbner, "Newsmen and Schoolmen: The State and Problems of Education Reporting," *Journalism Quarterly* 44 (Summer, 1967), 218.

52. Charles T. Duncan, "The 'Education Beat' on 52 Major Newspapers," *Journalism Quarterly* 43 (Winter, 1966), 338.

53. Gerbner, "Newsmen and Schoolmen," p. 224.

54. Wilma Morrison, "Reporting the Schools," *Nieman Reports* 7 (April, 1953), 14.

SUGGESTED READINGS

Urban Problems

FEAGIN, JOE R., *The Urban Scene: Myths and Realities*. New York: Random House, 1973. A collection of essays that provide a useful overview of the scope and substance of urban problems.

LYLE, JACK, *The News in Megalopolis*. San Francisco: Chandler Publishing, 1967. Observations of urban problems and media practices in the Los Angeles region.

MIDURA, EDMUND, ed., *Why Aren't We Getting Through?* Washington: Acropolis Books, 1971. Reports of a conference addressed to the media's role in causing, preventing, and reporting urban unrest.

Environment

ROSS, STEVEN S., "Source Guide, Understanding Energy," *Columbia Journalism Review* 14 (May/June, 1975), 34–36. A useful list of publications on various aspects of the energy problem.

RUBIN, DAVID, and DAVID SACHS, *Mass Media and the Environment*. Stanford, Calif.: Department of Genetics-Stanford University School of Medicine, 1971. A three-volume report, of which Volume 2, *The Environmental Explosion: The Press Discovers the Environment,* is especially critical of media treatment of environmental news in the San Francisco Bay area.

SCHOENFELD, CLAY, ed., *Interpreting Environmental Issues*. Madison, Wis.: Dembar Educational Research Services, 1972.

Economic News

COMAN, EDWIN T., JR., *Sources of Business Information*. Englewood Cliffs, N.J.: Prentice-Hall, Inc., 1949.

HELFERT, ERICH A., *Techniques of Financial Analysis*. Homewood, Ill.: Richard D. Irwin, Inc., 1963.

MANLEY, MARIAN C., *Business Information: How to Find and Use It*. New York: Harper & Bros., 1955.

Science

BURKETT, WARREN, *Writing Science News for the Mass Media* (2nd ed.). Houston: Gulf Publishing, 1973. Excellent chapters on coverage of scientific conventions.

CHEVALIER, LOIS R., "Do Science Writers Raise False Hopes?" *Medical Economics* (April 13, 1959), 69–71, 288–95.

FUNKHOUSER, G. RAY, and NATHAN MACCOBY, "Tailoring Science Writing to the General Audience," *Journalism Quarterly* 50 (Summer, 1973), 220–26.

GILLMAN, WILLIAM, *The Language of Science*. New York: Harcourt, Brace & World, 1961. Suggests some approaches for coping with complexity, jargon, and other scientific language problems.

HAY, CAROLYN G., "A History of Science Writing in the United States" (M.A. thesis, Northwestern University, 1970).

KRIEGHBAUM, HILLIER, *Science and the Mass Media*. New York: New York University Press, 1967. General discussion of science reporting; particularly effective summation of the many readership and diffusion studies with which Professor Krieghbaum has been associated over the years.

PATTERSON, JOYE, LAUREL BOOTH, and RUSSELL SMITH, "Who Reads about Science?" *Journalism Quarterly* 46 (Autumn, 1969), 599–602.

TICHENOR, PHILLIP J., "Communication and Knowledge of Science in the Adult Population of the U.S." (Ph.D. diss., Stanford University, 1965).

WADE, SERENA, and WILBUR SCHRAMM, "The Mass Media as Sources of Public Affairs, Science and Health Knowledge," *Public Opinion Quarterly* 33 (Summer, 1969), 197–209.

Mental Health and Social Welfare

DENNIS, EVERETTE E., RAMONA RUSH, DAVID JORDAN, and JEANNE STUART, *Reporting the Human Condition*. Manhattan, Kans.: Kansas State University 1972.

YU, FREDERICK T. C., ed., *Behavioral Sciences and the Mass Media*. New York: Russell Sage Foundation, 1968. Media and social science practitioners express their views on cooperation that could lead to better coverage.

Education

BAGIN, DAN, FRANK GRAZIA, CHARLES H. HARRISON, *School Communications: Ideas That Work*. Chicago: McGraw-Hill Publications Company, 1972. Although directed primarily to school public relations practitioners, it is a useful resource as well for education reporters.

CARTER, RICHARD F., and JOHN SUTTHOFF, *Communities and Their Schools*. Stanford, Calif.: Institute for Communication Research-Stanford University School of Education, 1960. A report of a national survey that stresses the importance of communications in gaining public understanding and hence support of public education.

SILBERMAN, CHARLES, *Crisis in the Classroom: The Remaking of American Education*. New York: Random House, 1970. The widely-praised—and criticized —examination of the failure of American public education. See also A. HARRY PASSOW, ed., *Reactions to Silberman's Crisis in the Classroom*. Worthington, Ohio: Charles A. Jones Publishing Company, 1971.

WYNNE, EDWARD, *The Politics of School Accountability: Public Information About Public Schools*. Berkeley, Calif.: McCutchan Publishing Corp., 1972. A case for fact-finding instead of publicity-seeking, including a useful chapter for education reporters.

chapter twelve

Strategies for Tomorrow

Technology, while adding daily to our physical ease, throws daily another loop of fine wire around our souls.

ADLAI STEVENSON

Nothing is more hazardous than prediction. Author Peter Drucker once warned, "the unsuspected and apparently insignificant [will] derail the massive and seemingly invincible trends of today." [1] The seemingly invincible trends in public affairs reporting today are the building blocks of this book. A focus on audience needs, interpretation of complex subjects, and the adoption of powerful new research methods were suggested as the guiding principles of contemporary reporting. The expectation, of course, is that they will also serve well in the future. But that is a matter for prediction, based on today's interpretations of yesterday's experiences and the one great unknown: tomorrow's changes.

The principal change agents in journalism appear to be economics, audience desires, and technology. We already know a good deal about all three:

Rising production costs and diminishing supplies of newsprint may force profound changes on daily newspapers in the near future. Some will be forced out of business. Those that survive will be smaller, "about the size of a paper towel," according to Gene Roberts, executive editor of the *Philadelphia Inquirer*.[2] To combat rising costs and delivery problems, publishers will have to "lower their sights . . . and cut back on circulation," predicted *Chicago Sun-Times* managing editor Ralph Otwell in 1974.[3] Otwell, president of the Society of Professional Journalists at the time, also forecast a change in reporting emphasis to "concentrate on fewer, more specialized areas" for a "more sophisticated audience."

Audiences have already given a message to the news industry: Television is the preferred news medium for a majority of adults. In an age of communication overload—what Harvard political scientist Karl Deutsch has described as "the disease of the cities"—it isn't surprising that many would eschew the word jam of newspapers. The print medium, however, hasn't been abandoned by the public. There is greater demand than ever for special interest publications, where readers can turn directly to material that interests them.

Technology has already produced the seeds of a total communications revolution. Equipment for producing facsimile newspapers in the home has been field tested on a large scale. One-way cable television, bringing the possibility of vastly increased news delivery service, is spreading across the nation. Two-way interactive cable systems, by which the subscriber can request news and other information delivered to his home, is a threshold away from coming into the wage-earner's price range. This "wired city" stage, when it arrives, will enable distribution of information in bulk form from computers in central facilities to offices and homes. Electrostatic printing systems capable of producing 12,000 to 18,000 lines per minute were on the market in 1974. In 1973, the *New York Times Index* became available on computer to any subscriber able to pay the fee.

Given these observations about the cutting points in mass communication today, where does that leave the public affairs reporter? Will his methods of operation be changed substantially by economic, audience, and technology factors? Will there be more of him or less of him in the future? There is a truism in the trade that machines may replace printers, publishers, and editors, but there will always be a need for the live reporter. But truisms, as the Wright brothers proved, have a way of changing with conditions. The future role and scope of public affairs reporting must remain speculative. Consider, for example, this scenario:

The year is 1990, and a team of three reporters has just returned from covering a conference on prison reform. They confer for a few moments with an editor, and then sit down at electronic keyboards. One writes a general story about the conference and its results, running 1,200 words. He follows this with a much briefer story on the same material, of 200 words. The second reporter produces a lengthy story on the technical aspects of prison reform, geared to the information needs of penologists, lawyers, and other specialists. The third reporter pecks out an interpretative piece on the economic implications of the conference proposals for local, state, and federal treasuries. All of their words, as their fingers touch the keys, are transmitted almost instantly to a computer that corrects for spelling, style, and certain factual errors. Computer A then passes the stories along to computer B, the central storage point for national news stories. Computer B makes an index summary of the stories available to regional news computer facilities around the nation. Within a matter of minutes after the stories are written, they are available to home users. All that is required is a glance at the "menu" of available stories listed on the home screen, punching out a series of digits on a telephone-like keyboard, and the story selected appears on the screen. If the news consumer wants to retain the story for future reference, he can store it in his own minicomputer for later reference, or have it produced on an inexpensive home printer wired to the television set.

Speculative? Yes, but it fits the vision of what some scholars in the field predict is possible and likely as equipment costs are lowered. Information technologist Peter C. Goldmark sees news dissemination of this kind as only one aspect of the wired city of tomorrow. The object, he writes, is "to improve the city's capacity to move information rather than people and materials." [4] Goldmark points out that the interactive cable system described differs substantially from existing television and radio service, which is a one-way informational system. With two-way cable, the subscriber controls the screen's output and can get a printed copy from it. In Goldmark's view, cable used this way may greatly expand the public's desire for information. The differentiated public, no longer limited to the mass media, will be able to secure the information to satisfy special interests that today can't be marketed because of production and delivery expense. And that, of course, means more reporting and more reporters.

A similar assessment is made by press critic Ben Bagdikian, who in 1970 directed a major study into the impact of technology on media.[5] Examining cable system effects, Bagdikian wrote:

> Beyond the standard 'news package' there will be more diversity. More independent channels of communication to each information corporation and into each home will end the homogenizing of news that now occurs because it must be prepared for such a wide spectrum of consumers.[6]

Electronic communication of high sophistication doesn't mean the end of print communication, Bagdikian observes. It's the ratio of electronic to print that will change:

> If present patterns continue, the wider choice of electronically displayed news will whet the appetite for printed information, and in some cases will intensify the desire for related information reproduced in permanent form. . . . Thus, the rise of new electronic media will undoubtedly reduce the ratio of printed to nonprinted

information, presenting more images without documents. But the assertion that the 'tyranny of print' is ended and that sentences and paragraphs will be displaced almost entirely by nonverbal forms has no basis in present trends or in appreciation of how men think and learn.[7]

Perhaps not even the Shadow knows what portent technology holds for public affairs reporting for the long-term future. Unless we become a nation of pacified robots like the characters in Ray Bradbury's ominous science fiction portrait, *Fahrenheit 451,* however, the need for competent, professional reporting is likely to remain high. In these pages, a rationale and a set of unifying principles for the fruitful pursuit of public affairs reporting have been offered. Implicit in this presentation has been the belief that job skills alone are not enough for today's reporters. They must also thoroughly understand their readers and viewers, and direct news efforts to serving their needs. Reporters must also have a thorough grasp of the workings of the society in which they live, and a deep knowledge of the fields in which they write. The accomplished reporter must also learn to use nontraditional tools, such as social science research methods, both for gathering information and for evaluating that pro vided by others. And finally, reporters must develop professional standards (if not status) in order to function on a high ethical level. They must be able to resist the blandishments of the news source seeking special favor, and of the publisher attempting to protect an advertiser.

This book is a beginning, not an end. It suggests strategies and approaches for the public affairs reporter. If adapted to the individual reporter's style and personality, they can help him attain the goals for effective coverage suggested in the foregoing paragraphs. But, of course, this is not enough. No book, no course of instruction can adequately prepare the public affairs reporter for the future. What the individual needs to do is develop his own strategy, his own methods and procedures for keeping pace with the future. These are noble words transmitting noble ideas, but too often they ring hollow. Their emptiness stems from the fact that exhortation does not always lead to action. Well-trained journalists leave universities each year with ideals and good intent. Part of that intent tells them that they must stay current and at times leap ahead to be fully effective as public affairs reporters. But only a few succeed.

One of the greatest dangers is a primitive know-nothingism that pervades many newsrooms. This is an attitude that categorically and all too cheerfully rejects the work of communications researchers who are doing much to advance the art of human communication. (Admittedly, part of the problem can be traced to the researchers themselves, who often do a poor job of disseminating their findings where they can be used.) Similarly, the lessons of communication history are quickly forgotten. In this atmosphere, many reporters are not performing much differently than reporters did in 1920.

At the same time, there are thoughtful, attentive reporters who are doing much to advance the state of the art. Philip Meyer, whom we have mentioned repeatedly in this book, is one. He has become the middleman translating the methods of research into language that makes sense to the practicing journalist. Other reporters such as Edwin Newman of NBC News have become knowledgeable students of the American language. Still others become skillful commentator-scholars, both within and outside their news organizations. For example, Anthony Lewis of the *New York Times* or Fred Graham of CBS News. Reporters like these contribute to the intellectual life of the nation and to public understanding of the society and its problems.

Thus, there are good and bad examples. Reporters can avoid the know-nothing trap by developing an information retrieval system that keeps them in touch with current developments in journalism and mass communication as well as in selected subject areas that they are covering. This is done by systematic reading, visits to libraries and universities. Some do it by offering to teach an occasional course at a nearby college or school. For every reporter a different style, geared to his own personality is probably most appropriate. Such a strategy should not only include reading and synthesizing what is being written, but making active suggestions about what ought to be done. If, for example, communication research is to be truly relevant to the practitioner, then the practitioner must have an input, must make suggestions about his own needs.

Earlier in this book we suggested that the modern public affairs reporter needs to acquire skills in writing and reporting as well as sustained substantive understanding of the things he will be covering. Writing skill should not imply a static formula that once acquired is never lost. The art of writing changes frequently. The journalistic form is changing and, with it, so are definitions of news. Similarly, skills for reporters, whether those from the social sciences or methods of interviewing, are also advancing. In the area of substantive knowledge, the information-retrieval methods mentioned earlier should address this problem.

The world of public affairs reporting is exciting and vital both to its practitioners and to the people who consume their work in newspapers and in newscasts. It has been our goal in this book to reflect on this vibrant field and to suggest ways for its improvement. The public affairs reporter is on the firing line, making sense out of society and translating this message back to citizens who can and must use it. In realizing this great purpose, the public affairs reporter helps to advance the social order in these changing times.

NOTES

1. Peter F. Drucker, *The Age of Discontinuity* (New York: Harper & Row, 1969), p. ix.
2. Quoted in "Rising Paper Costs Reshaping Newspapers," *New York Times* (Nov. 21, 1974), p. 79.
3. Ralph Otwell, "President's Address" (Speech delivered at the annual convention of the Society for Professional Journalists, Phoenix, Nov. 13, 1974).
4. Peter C. Goldmark, "Communication and the Community," *Scientific American* 227 (Sept., 1972), 145.
5. Ben Bagdikian, *The Information Machines: Their Impact on Men and the Media* (New York: Harper & Row, 1971).
6. Ibid., p. 292.
7. Ibid., p. 200.

SUGGESTED READINGS

GERBNER, GEORGE, LARRY P. GROSS, WILLIAM H. MELODY, eds., *Communication Technology and Social Policy*. New York: Wiley, 1973. See especially part 2, "Institutional Powers and Controls: The Direction of Change"; part 4, "The New Field of Urban Communication"; and part 6, "Tracking the Future."

appendix a

The Newsman's Guide

to Legalese*

a

abstract of record: A complete history in short, abbreviated form of the case as found in the record.

abstract of title: A chronological history, in abbreviated form, of the ownership of a parcel of land.

accumulative sentence: A sentence, additional to others, imposed at the same time for several distinct offenses; one sentence to begin at the expiration of another.

action in personam (in per-sō-nam): An action against the person, founded on a personal liability.

action in rem (in rem): An action for the recovery of a specific object, usually an item of personal property such as an automobile.

adjudication: Giving or pronouncing a judgment or decree; also the judgment given.

adversary system: The system of trial practice in the United States and some other countries in which each of the opposing, or adversary, parties has full opportunity to present and establish opposing contentions before the court.

allegation: The assertion, declaration, or statement of a party to an action, made in a pleading, setting out what he expects to prove.

amicus curiae (a-mī′kus kū′ri-ē): A friend of the court; one who interposes, with the permission of the court, and volunteers information upon some matter of law.

ancillary bill or suit: One growing out of and auxiliary to another action or suit, such as a proceeding for the enforcement of a judgment, or to set aside fraudulent transfers of property.

answer: A pleading by which defendant endeavors to resist the plaintiff's allegation of facts.

* Published by permission of the Pennsylvania Bar Association, 401 North Front Street, Harrisburg, Penna.

appearance: The formal proceeding by which defendant submits himself to the jurisdiction of the court.

appellant: The party appealing a decision or judgment—which he considers unfavorable—to a higher court.

appellate court: A court having jurisdiction of appeal and review; not a "trial court."

appellee: The party against whom an appeal is taken.

arraignment: In criminal practice, to bring a prisoner to the bar of the court to answer to a criminal charge.

arrest of judgment: The act of postponing the effect of a judgment already entered.

at issue: Whenever the parties to a suit come to a point in the pleadings which is affirmed on one side and denied on the other, they are said to be "at issue" and ready for trial.

attachment: A remedy by which plaintiff is enabled to acquire a lien upon property or effects of defendant for satisfaction of judgment which plaintiff may obtain in the future.

attorney of record: Attorney whose name appears in the permanent records or files of a case.

b

bail: To set at liberty a person arrested or imprisoned, on security being taken, for his appearance on a specified day and place.

bail bond: An obligation signed by the accused, with sureties, to secure his presence in court.

bailiff: A court attendant whose duties are to keep order in the courtroom and to have custody of the jury.

banc (bangk): Bench; the place where a court permanently or regularly sits. A "sitting in banc" is a meeting of all of the judges of a court, as distinguished from the sitting of a single judge.

bench warrant: Process issued by the court itself, or "from the bench," for the attachment or arrest of a person.

best evidence: Primary evidence, as distinguished from secondary; the best and highest evidence of which the nature of the case is susceptible.

binding instruction: One in which the jury is told that if it finds certain conditions to be true it must find for plaintiff, or defendant, as the case might be.

bind over: To hold on bail for trial.

brief: A written or printed document prepared by counsel to file in court, usually setting forth both facts and law in support of his case.

burden of proof: In the law of evidence, the necessity or duty of affirmatively proving a fact or facts in dispute.

burglary: The breaking into and entering of a building with an intent to commit a serious crime.

c

calling the docket: The public calling of the docket or list of causes at commencement of term of court, for setting a time for trial or entering orders.

caption: The caption of a pleading, or other papers connected with a case in court, is the heading or introductory clause which shows the names of the parties, name of the court, number of the case, etc.

cause: A suit, litigation, or action, civil or criminal.

certiorari (s'er'shi-ō-rā'ri): An original writ commanding judges or officers of inferior courts to certify or to return records of proceedings in a cause for judicial review.

challenge to the array: Questioning the qualifications of an entire jury panel, usually on the grounds of partiality or some fault in the process of summoning the panel.

chambers: Private office or room of a judge.

change of venue: The removal of a suit begun in one county or district to another, for trial, or from one court to another in the same county or district.

circumstantial evidence: All evidence of an indirect nature; the process of decision by which court or jury may reason from circumstances known or proved to establish by inference the principal fact.

code: A collection, compendium, or revision of laws systematically arranged into chapters, table of contents, and index and promulgated by legislative authority.

codicil (kod'i-sil): A supplement or an addition to a will.

commit: To send a person to prison, to an asylum, workhouse, or reformatory by lawful authority.

common law: Law which derives its authority solely from usages and customs of immemorial antiquity, or from the judgments and decrees of courts. Also called "case law."

commutation: The change of a punishment from a greater degree to a lesser degree, as from death to life imprisonment.

comparative negligence: The doctrine by which acts of opposing parties are compared in the degrees of "slight," "ordinary" and "gross" negligence, frequently on a percentage basis.

competency: In the law of evidence, the presence of those characteristics which render a witness legally fit and qualified to give testimony.

complainant: Synonymous with "plaintiff."

complaint: The first or initiatory pleading on the part of the complainant, or plaintiff, in a civil action.

concurrent sentence: Sentences for more than one crime in which the time of each is to be served concurrently, rather than successively.

condemnation: The legal process by which real estate of a private owner is taken for public use without his consent, but upon the award and payment of just compensation.

contempt of court: Any act calculated to embarrass, hinder, or obstruct a court in the administration of justice, or calculated to lessen its authority or dignity. Contempts are of two kinds: direct and indirect. Direct contempts are those committed in the immediate presence of the court; indirect is the term chiefly used with reference to the failure or refusal to obey a lawful order.

contract: An oral or written agreement between two or more parties which is enforceable by law.

corpus delicti: (kor'pus dē-lik'tī): The body (material substance) upon which a crime has been committed, e.g., the corpse of a murdered man, the charred remains of a burned house.

corroborating evidence: Evidence supplementary to that already given and tending to strengthen or confirm it.

court reporter: A person who transcribes by shorthand or stenographically takes down testimony during court proceedings.

costs: An allowance for expenses in prosecuting or defending a suit. Ordinarily this does not include attorney's fees.

counterclaim: A claim presented by a defendant in opposition to the claim of a plaintiff.

courts of record: Those whose proceedings are permanently recorded, and which have the power to fine or imprison for contempt. Courts not of record are those of lesser authority whose proceedings are not permanently recorded.

criminal insanity: Lack of mental capacity to do or abstain from doing a particular act; inability to distinguish right from wrong.

cross-examination: The questioning of a witness in a trial, or in the taking of a deposition, by the party opposed to the one who produced the witness.

cumulative sentence: Separate sentences (each additional to the others) imposed against a person convicted upon an indictment containing several counts, each charging a different offense. (Same as accumulative sentence.)

d

damages: Pecuniary compensation which may be recovered in the courts by any person who has suffered loss, detriment, or injury to his person, property, or rights, through the unlawful act or negligence of another.

de novo (de nō'vō): Anew, afresh. A "trial de novo" is the retrial of a case.

declaratory judgment: One which declares the rights of the parties or expresses the opinion of the court on a question of law, without ordering anything to be done.

decree: A decision or order of the court. A final decree is one which fully and finally disposes of the litigation; an interlocutory decree is a provisional or preliminary decree which is not final.

default: A "default" in an action at law occurs when a defendant omits to plead within the time allowed or fails to appear at the trial.

demur (dē-mer'): To file a pleading (called "a demurrer"), admitting the truth of the facts in the complaint, or answer, but contending they are legally insufficient.

deposition: The testimony of a witness not taken in open court, but in pursuance of authority given by statute or rule of court to take testimony elsewhere.

direct evidence: Proof of facts by witnesses who saw acts done or heard words spoken as distinguished from circumstantial evidence, which is called indirect.

direct examination: The first interrogation of a witness by the party on whose behalf he is called.

directed verdict: An instruction by the judge to the jury to return a specific verdict.

discovery: A proceeding whereby one party to an action may be informed as to facts known by other parties or witnesses.

dismissal without prejudice: Permits the complainant to sue again on the same cause of action, while dismissal "with prejudice" bars the right to bring or maintain an action on the same claim or cause.

dissent: A term commonly used to denote the disagreement of one or more judges of a court with the decision of the majority.

domicile: That place where a person has his true and permanent home. A person may have several residences, but only one domicile.

double jeopardy: Common-law and constitutional prohibition against more than one prosecution for the same crime, transaction, or omission.

due process: Law in its regular course of administration through the courts of justice. The guarantee of due process requires that every man have the protection of a fair trial.

e

embezzlement: The fraudulent appropriation by a person to his own use or benefit of property or money entrusted to him by another.

eminent domain: The power to take private property for public use by condemnation.

enjoin: To require a person, by writ of injunction from a court of equity, to perform or to abstain or desist from some act.

entrapment: The act of officers or agents of a government in inducing a person to commit a crime not contemplated by him, for the purpose of instituting a criminal prosecution against him.

equitable action: An action which may be brought for the purpose of restraining the threatened infliction of wrongs or injuries, and the prevention of threatened illegal action. (Remedies not available at common law.)

equity, courts of: Courts which administer a legal remedy according to the system of equity, as distinguished from courts of common law.

escheat (es-chēt): In American law, the right of the state to an estate to which no one is able to make a valid claim.

escrow (es-krō'): A writing, or deed, delivered by the grantor into the hands of a third person, to be held by the latter until the happening of a contingency or performance of a condition.

estoppel (es-top'el): A person's own act, or acceptance of facts, which preclude his later making claims to the contrary.

et al.: An abbreviation of et alii, meaning "and others."

et seq.: An abbreviation for et sequentes, or et sequentia, "and the following."

ex contractu (ex kon-trak'tu): In both civil and common law, rights and causes of action are divided into two classes: those arising ex contractu (from a contract) and ex delicto (from a wrong or tort).

ex delicto (ex de-lik'tō): Rights and causes of action arising from a wrong or "tort."

ex parte (ex par'te): By or for one party; done for, in behalf of, or on the application of one party only.

ex post facto (eks pōst fak'to): After the fact; an act or fact occurring after some previous act or fact, and relating thereto.

exception: A formal objection to an action of the court, during the trial of a cause, in refusing a request or overruling an objection; implying that the party excepting does not acquiesce in the decision of the court, but will seek to procure its reversal.

executor: A person named by the decedent in his will to carry out the provisions of that will.

exhibit: A paper, document, or other article produced and exhibited to a court during a trial or hearing.

expert evidence: Testimony given in relation to some scientific, technical, or professional matter by experts, i.e., persons qualified to speak authoritatively by reason of their special training, skill, or familiarity with the subject.

extenuating circumstances: Circumstances which render a crime less aggravated, heinous, or reprehensible than it would otherwise be.

extradition: The surrender by one state to another of an individual accused or convicted of an offense outside its own territory, and within the territorial jurisdiction of the other.

f

fair comment: A term used in the law of libel, applying to statements made by a writer in an honest belief of their truth, relating to an official act, even though the statements are not true in fact.

fair preponderance: Evidence sufficient to create in the minds of the triers of fact the conviction that the party upon whom the burden is placed has established its case.

false arrest: Any unlawful physical restraint of another's liberty, whether in prison or elsewhere.

false pretenses: Designed misrepresentation of existing fact or condition whereby a person obtains another's money or goods.

felony: A crime of a graver nature than a misdemeanor. Generally, an offense punishable by death or imprisonment in a penitentiary.

fiduciary (fi-dū′shē-ā-rē): A term derived from the Roman law, meaning a person holding the character of a trustee, in respect to the trust and confidence involved in it and the scrupulous good faith and candor which it requires.

forcible entry and detainer: [The taking of land and possessions and] summary proceeding for restoring possession of land to one who has been wrongfully deprived of possession.

forgery: The false making or material altering, with intent to defraud, of any writing which, if genuine, might be the foundation of a legal liability.

fraud: An intentional perversion of truth; deceitful practice or device resorted to with intent to deprive another of property or other right, or in some manner to do him injury.

g

garnishment: A proceeding whereby property, money, or credits of a debtor in possession of another (the garnishee) are applied to the debts of the debtor.

garnishee (noun): The person upon whom a garnishment is served; usually a debtor of the defendant in the action; (verb): to institute garnishment proceedings.

general assignment: The voluntary transfer, by a debtor, of all his property to a trustee for the benefit of all of his creditors.

general demurrer: A demurrer which raises the question whether the pleading against which it is directed lacks the definite allegations essential to a cause of action or defense.

gratuitous guest: In automobile law, a person riding at the invitation of the owner of a vehicle, or his authorized agent, without payment of a consideration or a fare.

guardian ad litem (ad lī'tem): A person appointed by a court to look after the interests of an infant whose property is involved in litigation.

h

habeas corpus (hā'be-as kor'pus): "You have the body." The name given a variety of writs whose object is to bring a person before a court or judge. In most common usage, it is directed to the official or person detaining another, commanding him to produce the body of the prisoner or person detained so the court may determine if such person has been denied his liberty without due process of law.

harmless error: In appellate practice, an error committed by a lower court during a trial, but not prejudicial to the rights of the party and for which the court will not reverse the judgment.

hearsay: Evidence not proceeding from the personal knowledge of the witness.

holographic will: A testamentary instrument entirely written, dated, and signed by the testator in his own handwriting.

hostile witness: A witness who is subject to cross-examination by the party who called him to testify, because of his evident antagonism toward that party as exhibited in his direct examination.

hypothetical question: A combination of facts and circumstances, assumed or proved, stated in such a form as to constitute a coherent state of facts upon which the opinion of an expert can be asked by way of evidence in a trial.

i

impeachment of witness: An attack on the credibility of a witness by the testimony of other witnesses.

implied contract: A contract in which the promise made by the obligor is not expressed, but inferred by his conduct or implied in law.

imputed negligence: Negligence which is not directly attributable to the person himself, but which is the negligence of a person who is in privity with him, and with whose fault he is chargeable.

inadmissible: That which, under the established rules of evidence, cannot be admitted or received.

in banc: On the bench; all judges of the court sitting together to hear a cause.

in camera (in kam'e-ra): In chambers; in private.

incompetent evidence: Evidence which is not admissible under the established rules of evidence.

indeterminate sentence: An indefinite sentence of "not less than" and "not more than" so many years, the exact term to be served being afterwards determined by parole authorities within the minimum and maximum limits set by the court or by statute.

indictment: An accusation in writing found and presented by a grand jury, charging that a person therein named has done some act, or been guilty of some omission, which, by law, is a crime.

inferior court: Any court subordinate to the chief appellate tribunal in a particular judicial system.

injunction: A mandatory or prohibitive writ issued by a court.

instruction: A direction given by the judge to the jury concerning the law of the case.

inter alia (in ter a'li-ä): Among other things or matters.

inter alios (in'ter'a-li-ōs): Among other persons, between others.

interlocutory: Provisional; temporary; not final. Refers to orders and decrees of a court.

interrogatories: Written questions propounded by one party and served on adversary, who must provide written answers thereto under oath.

intervention: A proceeding in a suit or action by which a third person is permitted by the court to make himself a party.

j

jurisprudence: The philosophy of law, or the science which treats of the principles of positive law and legal relations.

jury: A certain number of people, selected according to law, and sworn to inquire of certain matters of fact, and declare the truth upon evidence laid before them.

  grand jury: A jury whose duty is to receive complaints and accusations in criminal cases, hear the evidence and find bills of indictment in cases where they are satisfied a trial ought to be had.

  petit jury: The ordinary jury of twelve (or fewer) persons for the trial of a civil or criminal case. So called to distinguish it from the grand jury.

jury commissioner: An officer charged with the duty of selecting the names to be put into a jury wheel, or of drawing the panel of jurors for a particular term of court.

l

leading question: One which instructs a witness how to answer or puts into his mouth words to be echoed back; one which suggests to the witness the answer desired. Prohibited on direct examination.

letters rogatory (rog'a-tō-ri): A request by one court of another court in an independent jurisdiction that a witness be examined upon interrogatories sent with the request.

levy: A seizure; the obtaining of money by legal process through seizure and sale of property. The raising of the money for which an execution has been issued.

libel: A method of defamation expressed by print, writing, pictures, or signs. In its most general sense any publication that is injurious to the reputation of another.

limitation: A certain time allowed by statute in which litigation must be brought.

lis pendens (līs pen'denz): A pending suit.

locus delicti (lo kus de-lik'ti): The place of the offense.

m

malfeasance: Evil doing; ill conduct; the commission of some act which is positively prohibited by law.

malicious prosecution: An action instituted with intention of injuring defendant and without probable cause, and which terminates in favor of the person prosecuted.

mandamus (man-dā'mus): The name of a writ which issues from a court of superior jurisdiction, directed to an inferior court, commanding the performance of a particular act.

mandate: A judicial command or precept proceeding from a court or judicial officer, directing the proper officer to enforce a judgment, sentence, or decree.

manslaughter: The unlawful killing of another without malice; may be either voluntary, upon a sudden impulse, or involuntary, in the commission of some unlawful act.

master: An officer of the court, usually an attorney, appointed for the purpose of taking testimony and making a report to the court. Used most frequently in divorce cases.

material evidence: Such as is relevant and goes to the substantial issues in dispute.

mesne (mēn): Intermediate; intervening.

misdemeanor: Offenses less than felonies; generally those punishable by fine or imprisonment other than in penitentiaries.

misfeasance: A misdeed or treaspass. The improper performance of some act which a person may lawfully do.

mistrial: An erroneous or invalid trial; a trial which cannot stand in law because of lack of jurisdiction, wrong drawing of jurors, or disregard of some other fundamental requisite.

mitigating circumstance: One which does not constitute a justification or excuse of an offense, but which may be considered as reducing the degree of moral culpability.

moot: Unsettled; undecided. A moot point is one not settled by judicial decisions.

moral turpitude: Conduct contrary to honesty, modesty, or good morals.

multiplicity of actions: Numerous and unnecessary attempts to litigate the same right.

municipal courts: In the judicial organization of some states, courts whose territorial authority is confined to the city or community.

murder: The unlawful killing of a human being by another with malice aforethought, either expressed or implied.

n

ne exeat (nē ek′sē-at): A writ which forbids the person to whom it is addressed to leave the country, the state, or the jurisdiction of the court.

negligence: The omission to do something which a reasonable man, guided by ordinary considerations, would do; or the doing of something which a reasonable and prudent man would not do.

next friend: One acting for the benefit of an infant or other person without being regularly appointed as guardian.

nisi prius (nī′sī prī′us): Courts for the initial trials of issues of fact, as distinguished from appellate courts.

no bill: This phrase, endorsed by a grand jury on an indictment, is equivalent to "not found" or "not a true bill." It means that, in the opinion of the jury, evidence was insufficient to warrant the return of a formal charge.

nolle prosequi (nol′e pros′ e-kwī): A formal entry upon the record by the plaintiff in a civil suit, or the prosecuting officer in a criminal case, by which he declares that he "will not further prosecute" the case.

nolo contendere (nō'lō kon-ten'de-rē): A pleading, usually used by defendants in criminal cases, which literally means I will not contest it.

nominal party: One who is joined as a party or defendant merely because the technical rules of pleading require his presence in the record.

non compos mentis (non kom'pos men'tis): Not sound of mind; insane.

non obstante veredicto (non ob-stan'te ve-re-dik'to): Notwithstanding the verdict. A judgment entered by order of court for one party, although there has been a jury verdict against him.

notice to produce: In practice, a notice in writing requiring the opposite party to produce a certain described paper or document at the trial.

O

objection: The act of taking exception to some statement or procedure in trial. Used to call the court's attention to improper evidence or procedure.

of counsel: A phrase commonly applied to counsel employed to assist in the preparation or management of the case, or its presentation on appeal, but who is not the principal attorney of record.

opinion evidence: Evidence of what the witness thinks, believes, or infers in regard to a fact in dispute, as distinguished from his personal knowledge of the facts; not admissible except (under certain limitations) in the case of experts.

ordinary: A judicial officer, in several of the states, clothed by statute with powers in regard to wills, probate, administration, and guardianship.

out of court: One who has no legal status in court is said to be "out of court," i.e., he is not before the court. For example, when a plaintiff, by some act of omission or commission, shows that he is unable to maintain his action he is frequently said to have put himself "out of court."

P

panel: A list of jurors to serve in a particular court, or for the trial of a particular action; denotes either the whole body of persons summoned as jurors for a particular term of court or those selected by the clerk by lot.

parties: The persons who are actively concerned in the prosecution or defense of a legal proceeding.

peremptory challenge: The challenge which the prosecution or defense may use to reject a certain number of prospective jurors without assigning any cause.

plaintiff: A person who brings an action; the party who complains or sues in a personal action and is so named, on the record.

plaintiff in error: The party who obtains a writ of error to have a judgment or other proceeding at law reviewed by an appellate court.

pleading: The process by which the parties in a suit or action alternately present written statements of their contentions, each responsive to that which precedes and each serving to narrow the field of controversy, until there evolves a single point, affirmed on one side and denied on the other, called the "issue" upon which they then go to trial.

polling the jury: A practice whereby the jurors are asked individually whether they assented, and still assent, to the verdict.

power of attorney: An instrument authorizing another to act as one's agent or attorney.

praecipe (prē′si-pe): An original writ commanding the defendant to do the thing required; also, an order addressed to the clerk of a court, requesting him to issue a particular writ.

prejudicial error: Synonymous with "reversible error"; an error which warrants the appellate court in reversing the judgment before it.

preliminary hearing: Synonymous with "preliminary examination"; the hearing given a person charged with crime by a magistrate or judge to determine whether he should be held for trial.

preponderance of evidence: Greater weight of evidence, or evidence which is more credible and convincing to the mind, not necessarily the greater number of witnesses.

presentment: An informal statement in writing by a grand jury to the court that a public offense has been committed, from their own knowledge or observation, without any bill of indictment laid before them.

presumption of fact: An inference as to the truth or falsity of any proposition or fact, drawn by a process of reasoning in the absence of actual certainty of its truth or falsity, or until such certainty can be ascertained.

presumption of law: A rule of law that courts and judges shall draw a particular inference from a particular evidence.

probate: The act or process of proving a will.

probation: In modern criminal administration, allowing a person convicted of some minor offense (particularly juvenile offenders) to go at large, under a suspension of sentence, during good behavior, and generally under the supervision or guardianship of a probation officer.

prosecutor: One who instigates the prosecution upon which an accused is arrested or who prefers an accusation against the party whom he suspects to be guilty; also one who takes charge of a case and performs the function of trial lawyer for the people.

prosecutrix: A female prosecutor.

q

quaere (kēw'rē): A query; question; doubt.

quash: To overthrow; vacate; to annul or void a summons or indictment.

quasi judicial (kwā'sī): Authority or discretion vested in an officer wherein his acts partake of a judicial character.

quid pro quo: "What for what," a fair return or consideration.

quo warranto (kwō wo-ran'tō): A writ issuable by the state, through which it demands an individual to show by what right he exercises an authority which can only be exercised through grant or franchise emanating from the state.

r

reasonable doubt: An accused person is entitled to acquittal if, in the minds of the jury, his guilt has not been proved beyond a "reasonable doubt"; that state of the minds of jurors in which they cannot say they feel an abiding conviction as to the truth of the charge.

rebuttal: The introduction of rebutting evidence; the showing that statements of witnesses as to what occurred is not true; the stage of a trial at which such evidence may be introduced.

redirect examination: Follows cross-examination, and is had by the party who first examined the witness.

referee: A person to whom a cause pending in a court is referred by the court to take testimony, hear the parties and report thereon to the court. He is an officer exercising judicial powers and is an arm of the court for a specific purpose.

removal, order of: An order by a court directing the transfer of a cause to another court.

reply: When a case is tried or argued in court, the argument of the plaintiff in answer to that of the defendant. A pleading in response to an answer.

rest: A party is said to "rest" or "rest his case" when he has presented all the evidence he intends to offer.

retainer: Act of the client in employing his attorney or counsel, and also denotes the fee which the client pays when he retains the attorney to act for him.

robbery: The taking or stealing of property from another with force or the threat of force.

rule nisi, or rule to show cause (nī'sī): A court order obtained on motion by either party to show cause why the particular relief sought should not be granted.

rule of court: An order made by a court having competent jurisdiction. Rules of court are either general or special; the former are the regulations by which the practice of the court is governed; the latter are special orders made in particular cases.

S

search and seizure, unreasonable: In general, an examination without authority of law of one's premises or person with a view to discovering stolen contraband or illicit property or some evidence of guilt to be used in prosecuting a crime.

search warrant: An order in writing, issued by a justice or magistrate in the name of the state, directing an officer to search a specified house or other premises for stolen property. Usually required as a condition precedent to a legal search and seizure.

self-defense: The protection of one's person or property against some injury attempted by another. The law of "self defense" justifies an act done in the reasonable belief of immediate danger. When acting in justifiable self-defense, a person may not be punished criminally nor held responsible for civil damages.

separate maintenance: Allowance granted to a wife for support of herself and children while she is living apart from her husband but not divorced from him.

separation of witnesses: An order of the court requiring all witnesses to remain outside the courtroom until each is called to testify, except the plaintiff or defendant.

sheriff: An officer of a county, chosen by popular election, whose principal duties are aid of criminal and civil courts; chief preserver of the peace. He serves processes, summons juries, executes judgments and holds judicial sales.

sine qua non (sī'ne kwā non): An indispensable requisite.

slander: Base and defamatory spoken words tending to prejudice another in his reputation, business, or means of livelihood. "Libel" and "slander" both are methods of defamation, the former being expressed by print, writings, pictures, or signs; the latter orally.

specific performance: A mandatory order in equity. Where damages would be inadequate compensation for the breach of a contract, the contractor will be compelled to perform specifically what he has agreed to do.

stare decisis: (sta're de-si'sis): The doctrine that, when a court has once laid down a principle of law as applicable to a certain set of facts, it will adhere to that principle and apply it to future cases where the facts are substantially the same.

state's evidence: Testimony, given by an accomplice or participant in a crime, tending to convict others.

statute: The written law in contradistinction to the unwritten law.

stay: A stopping or arresting of a judicial proceeding by order of the court.

stipulation: An agreement by attorneys on opposite sides of a case as to any matter pertaining to the proceedings or trial. It is not binding unless assented to by the parties, and most stipulations must be in writing.

subpoena (su-pē'na): A process to cause a witness to appear and give testimony before a court or magistrate.

subpoena duces tecum (su-pē na dū sēz tē kum): A process by which the court commands a witness to produce certain documents or records in a trial.

substantive law: The law dealing with rights, duties, and liabilities, as distinguished from adjective law, which is the law regulating procedure.

summons: A writ directing the sheriff or other officer to notify the named person that an action has been commenced against him in court and that he is required to appear, on the day named, and answer the complaint in such action.

supersedeas (sū-per-sē-dē-as): A writ containing a command to stay proceedings at law, such as the enforcement of a judgment pending an appeal.

t

talesman (tālz'man): A person summoned to act as a juror from among the bystanders in a court.

testimony: Evidence given by a competent witness, under oath; as distinguished from evidence derived from writings and other sources.

tort: An injury or wrong committed, either with or without force, to the person or property of another.

transcript: The official record of proceedings in a trial or hearing.

transitory: Actions are "transitory" when they might have taken place anywhere, and are "local" when they could occur only in some particular place.

traverse: In pleading, traverse signifies a denial. When a defendant denies any material allegation of fact in the plaintiff's declaration, he is said to traverse it.

trial de novo (dē nō′vō): A new trial or retrial had in an appellate court in which the whole case is gone into as if no trial had been had in a lower court.

true bill: In criminal practice, the endorsement made in a grand jury upon a bill of indictment when they find it sufficient evidence to warrant a criminal charge.

u

undue influence: Whatever destroys free will and causes a person to do something he would not do if left to himself.

unlawful detainer: A detention of real estate without the consent of the owner or other person entitled to its possession.

usury: The taking of more for the use of money than the law allows.

v

venire (vē-ni rē): Technically, a writ summoning persons to court to act as jurors; popularly used as meaning the body of names thus summoned.

venire facias de novo (fā′she-as dē nō′vō): A fresh or new venire, which the court grants when there has been some impropriety or irregularity in returning the jury, or where the verdict is so imperfect or ambiguous that no judgment can be given upon it.

veniremen (vē′nī′rē-men): Members of a panel of jurors.

venue (ven′ū): The particular county, city, or geographical area in which a court with jurisdiction may hear and determine a case.

verdict: In practice, the formal and unanimous decision or finding made by a jury, reported to the court, and accepted by it.

voir dire (vwor dēr): To speak the truth. The phrase denotes the preliminary examination which the court may make of one presented as a witness or juror as to his qualifications.

w

waiver of immunity: A means authorized by statutes by which a witness, in advance of giving testimony or producing evidence, may renounce the fundamental right guaranteed by the constitution that no person shall be compelled to be a witness against himself.

warrant of arrest: A writ issued by a magistrate, justice or other competent authority, to a sheriff or other officer, requiring him to arrest the person therein named and bring him before the magistrate or court to answer to a specified charge.

weight of evidence: The balance or preponderance of evidence; the inclination of the greater amount of credible evidence, offered in a trial, to support one side of the issue rather than the other.

willful: A "willful" act is one done intentionally, without justifiable cause, as distinguished from an act done carelessly or inadvertently.

with prejudice: The term, as applied to a judgment of dismissal, is as conclusive of rights of parties as if action had been prosecuted to final adjudication adverse to the plaintiff.

witness: One who testifies to what he has seen, heard, or otherwise observed.

writ: An order issuing from a court requiring the performance of a specified act, or giving authority and commission to have it done.

writ of error coram nobis (ko'ram no'bis): A common law writ, the purpose of which is to correct a judgment in the same court in which it was rendered, on the ground of error of fact.

appendix b

Federal and State Court Structure

Though this textbook is not designed to provide the student with a comprehensive overview of court structure and jurisdiction, a brief sketch of the court structure in the United States may be helpful. Courts vary widely from state to state, and the reporter covering the legal process should be familiar with the nuances of the structure in his area.

Federal Court Structure

The Constitution of the United States (Article III, Section 1) vests the judicial power of the nation "in one supreme Court, and in such inferior Courts as the Congress may from time to time ordain and establish." The Supreme Court, with nine justices, has included within its powers that of judicial review in cases involving constitutionality, that is, whether federal or state laws, and lower court rulings, conform with the United States Constitution.

There are two other courts in the federal court system that the reporter may cover. These are the federal district court, and the circuit court of appeals. The circuit court is an intermediate level court between the district court and the Supreme Court. There are eleven circuits in the United States, each with its own judges. Each circuit includes at least three states, except the District of Columbia circuit. In addition to reviewing, on appeal, cases from the district courts, circuit courts review the administrative actions of some federal administrative agencies for errors of law. Many cases that are appealed to the circuit courts receive their final review there. Under certain circumstances, a case may bypass the circuit court, and go directly for review from the district court to the Supreme Court. This was the situation in the Watergate tapes case, in which the Supreme Court was asked to rule on executive privilege questions directly from the district court level.

The federal district court is the federal court most likely to be covered by the public affairs reporter. There are ninety-four district courts in the fifty states and territories. Each state has at least one federal district court, and some states have two or three. New York State has four. These courts have original jurisdiction in cases involving federal statutes, federal constitutionality, and some reviews of state court rulings, such as the deprivation of constitutional rights.

Federal courts also have jurisdiction in cases where the United States is a party to the action, and in cases involving disputes between states, between a state and citizens of another state, and between citizens of different states. Federal courts also have jurisdiction in cases involving ambassadors, and in cases involving foreign states.

Federal districts normally have a prosecutor, called a U.S. attorney, who represents the federal government in criminal cases and in cases where the United States is a party to the action. U.S. attorneys and their assistants may be helped by staff from the U.S. Department of Justice.

There are other courts in the federal system with which the reporter may have contact on an infrequent basis. One is the U.S. Court of Claims, which handles cases in which a monetary claim is made against

United States Court System

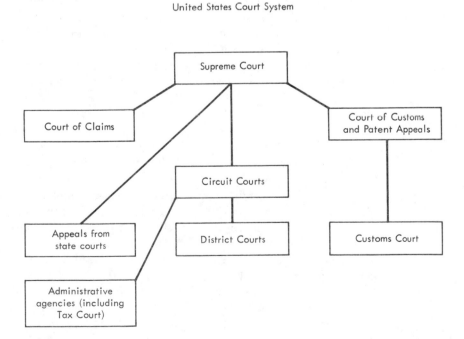

the United States. Another is the U.S. Court of Customs and Patent Appeals, which hears appeals from the Customs Court, the Patent Office, and the Tariff Commission. There are also U.S. Tax Courts, which hear cases, often on appeal, involving Internal Revenue Service rulings. While these specialized courts do not often make the news, the public affairs and the investigative reporter should know of their existence. A company that has had a recent case in a tax court, for example, at either the state or federal level, may have filed documents revealing its holdings and corporate structure, information which is difficult to obtain unless it is filed as part of a "public record."

Federal courts have their own rules of procedure, and the reporter assigned to cover them should begin with acquainting himself with the court's operations and functions.[1]

State Court Structure

As with the United States Constitution, state constitutions vest their judicial power in a supreme court, and in other inferior courts that are created by state legislatures. There is considerable variety in the structure of courts at the state level, and there is considerable variety in what these courts are called.

Typically, a state will have a supreme court, or an intermediate supreme court of appeals, whose major function is to hear cases on appeal from lower courts in the state system. At the state level, judges usually are appointed to the bench by the governor, and then stand for election to regular terms. Judges on federal courts, by the way, are appointed by the President and confirmed by the Senate. They do not stand for election.

Beneath the supreme court at the state level, the court system varies considerably with the size of the state and its major metropolitan areas. State district courts, sometimes called circuit courts, superior courts, or county courts, are usually organized by county in large metropolitan areas, and by districts that may include several counties in rural areas. Normally, such courts have original jurisdiction to hear felony cases, civil suits where the damages are over a certain amount, divorces, juvenile cases, equity cases, and matters dealing with real estate and probate. Sometimes, the court will have specific judges assigned to specific divisions, such as juvenile and divorce (sometimes called family court). The district or county courts are probably the main source of important trial news for the reporter. It is here that major crimes are tried, and where major civil suits are argued.

State Court System

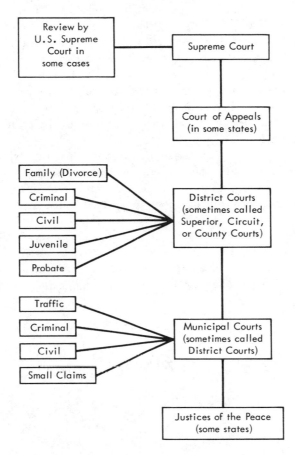

Beneath the district or county courts in the state court structure there is also considerable variety. The reporter may find municipal courts, which handle misdemeanors and act as courts of first appearance for felony cases, which are then referred to district courts, for arraignment and trial. Traffic offenses normally are handled at the municipal court level. So are small claims, which are sometimes handled by a separate division called small claims or conciliation courts. Minor civil suits are often handled at this level as well.

Beneath the municipal courts, some states have a justice of the peace system, which usually consists of individuals (not necessarily learned in the law) who can hear certain minor offenses, such as certain traffic violations.

Prosecution of cases at the state level is normally divided among three types of prosecutors. Typically, most felonies will be prosecuted by a county attorney, sometimes called a "state's attorney" or "district attorney." These officials are generally elected. The district attorney sometimes handles investigations through grand juries, and has considerable discretion about if and when a person should be charged with a crime.

The district attorney may have assistants, who are generally hired by the attorney. They may have civil service status, and thus, may be less "political" than the district attorney, who must keep his eye on the upcoming election.

States generally also have an attorney general, who is also an elected official. The attorney general's office represents the state in civil suits, and may handle some criminal cases. Some attorney general's offices have consumer protection divisions, organized crime investigation units, and other quasi-legal, quasi-law enforcement functions.

Misdemeanors and municipal ordinance violations are sometimes prosecuted by the district attorney's office, particularly in sparsely populated areas. In urban areas, there may be a city attorney who handles such prosecutions. A city attorney is normally an appointee of the village or city council.

NOTES

1. House Committee on the Judiciary, *The United States Courts* (Washington: U.S. Government Printing Office, 1973).

appendix c

Criminal Justice
and Criminal Trial Process

Criminal cases are handled in different ways in different states, but most criminal court matters follow a typical pattern.

The Criminal Process
from Arrest to Sentencing

A criminal case in court begins with either an arrest or a "tag" charge, such as for a traffic violation. Most states have different categories of crimes, and they are handled in different ways and in different courts. These crimes are characterized as felonies, gross misdemeanors, misdemeanors, and ordinance violations.

Felonies are serious crimes for which a term in a penitentiary may be imposed. Such crimes include treason, murder, rape, and robbery.[1]

Gross misdemeanors are less serious crimes, which usually carry a jail term (not in a penitentiary) of between 90 days and one year. Gross misdemeanors often include certain thefts, depending on the dollar value of the loss, and inciting a riot.

Misdemeanors are statutory offenses for which a fine (often up to $300) or jail term (usually less than 90 days in other than a penitentiary) may be imposed. Traffic violations are usually misdemeanors, as are such offenses as simple assault, when a life is not threatened. Aggravated assaults, in which the victim is in "great bodily harm," are usually considered felonies.

Ordinance violations are infringements of a municipal law rather than of a state law. These violations normally carry a penalty of up to 90 days in jail or a fine, or both.

Normally, felonies and gross misdemeanors must be tried in the court of original jurisdiction, usually the district (or county or superior) court. Misdemeanors and ordinance violations may be handled in the court of limited jurisdiction—the municipal court or by a justice of the peace; a conviction there may be appealed to the district court.

The municipal court also handles the initial court appearance of

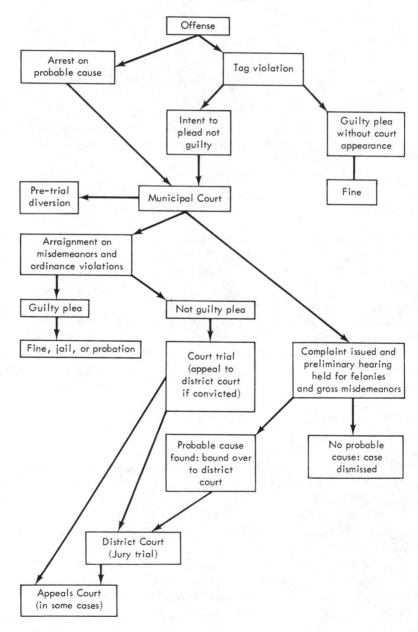

The Criminal Justice System
Municipal Court System

defendants arrested for committing a felony or gross misdemeanor. A preliminary hearing is held, and if probable cause is established, the case is then referred to—bound over to—the district court for arraignment and trial.

In felony cases where police believe they have enough evidence, they will draw up a legal document, called a complaint, which is presented to a judge. A warrant for arrest on probable cause is then issued, based on the complaint.

The reporter who finds defendants appearing in court on such complaints needs to exercise considerable caution. A complaint is not a verdict, not even an indictment. It does not establish guilt. It merely asserts that there is probable cause to believe that a crime has been committed, and probable cause to believe that the defendant committed it. A complaint does not convict the defendant of anything.

Because the charge is a felony, the defendant would appear first in municipal court for a preliminary hearing, at which the state would attempt to show through witnesses that there is, indeed, probable cause to believe that (1) a crime or crimes were committed, and (2) that the defendant named in the complaint committed it. In the preliminary hearing, the defense may attempt to rebut the state's case by attacking the credibility of the witnesses. If probable cause is established, the judge will bind the defendant over to the district (higher) court for arraignment and trial. At the district court, the complaint will be superseded by a court document called an information. An information, issued by the court, is similar to a complaint in that it informs the defendant of the charges against him.

In cases involving homicides, most prosecutors use the indictment process. The indictment, issued by a grand jury, constitutes the finding of probable cause, and brings the defendant directly to the trial court of original jurisdiction without going through the preliminary hearing. Indictments may also be sought by prosecutors for lesser felonies.

Once in district court, the typical felony case becomes more complex. There is normally an arraignment before the judge, at which a formal plea of guilty or not guilty is entered, and this may be followed by motions, the setting of a trial date, and pretrial evidentiary hearings. Most criminal cases never go to trial. The typical defendant pleads guilty to the charge for an agreed-upon limited sentence, or to a reduced charge. This process, called plea bargaining, involves negotiations between the defense attorney and the prosecutor with the approval of the judge.

Often, the case will be disposed of following an evidentiary hearing prior to trial. In these hearings, the judge hears testimony on evidence to be introduced at trial, and rules whether the evidence is admissible or not. He may also rule on the admissibility of a "confession" by the de-

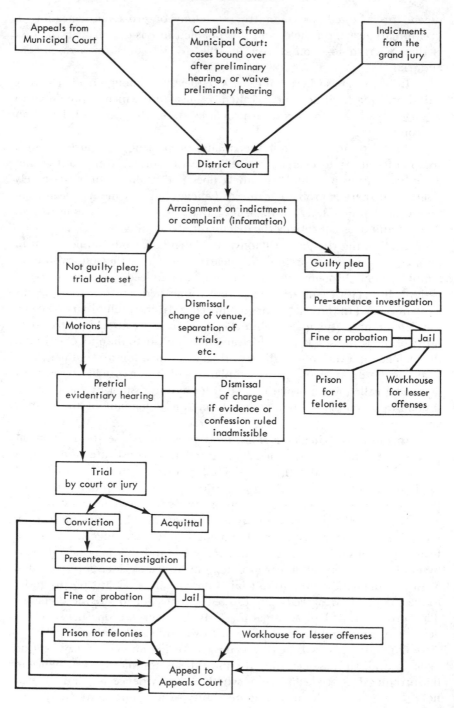

The Criminal Justice System:
District Court Process

Appeals from Municipal Court

Complaints from Municipal Court: cases bound over after preliminary hearing, or waive preliminary hearing

Indictments from the grand jury

District Court

Arraignment on indictment or complaint (information)

Not guilty plea; trial date set

Guilty plea

Pre-sentence investigation

Motions

Dismissal, change of venue, separation of trials, etc.

Fine or probation

Jail

Prison for felonies

Workhouse for lesser offenses

Pretrial evidentiary hearing

Dismissal of charge if evidence or confession ruled inadmissible

Trial by court or jury

Conviction

Acquittal

Presentence investigation

Fine or probation

Jail

Prison for felonies

Workhouse for lesser offenses

Appeal to Appeals Court

fendant, and whether the confession was given in a constitutional manner.

Covering a pretrial evidentiary hearing presents special problems for the court reporter. If certain evidence is ruled admissible, the reporter might well report that fact, as well as the nature of the evidence. But if the evidence is ruled inadmissible, the reporter who specifically identified the evidence might be prejudicing potential jurors.

There are numerous kinds of motions that may be filed in a criminal trial—either before arraignment, before the trial, or during the trial. A change of venue motion, for example, asks that the trial be moved to another county or district because circumstances, often pretrial publicity, are believed to make it impossible to impanel a fair and impartial jury. If there are codefendants in a case, they may all move that their trials be conducted separately. A motion to dismiss the charge or the indictment may be based on grounds that it was improperly drafted. Such motions normally precede arraignment. Some may be filed after, but heard before the trial. Defense attorneys are particularly prone to present the court with a variety of motions.

Cases that go to trial are handled according to rules of procedure that are described generally in the next section of this appendix. Following a trial with a guilty verdict, a judge may sentence a defendant directly from the bench, or may withhold sentencing until a presentence investigation is completed, normally by a division of the court or welfare department. A presentence investigation is normally confidential, and it often includes the defendant's previous criminal record, if any, background information on his employment, family, home, and personality. Investigators often recommend a particular kind of sentence, and judges frequently take such recommendations into account, though they are not bound by them.[2]

The Criminal Jury Trial:
Structure and Process

A criminal trial begins with the selection of a jury from a panel of potential jurors, called veniremen. Potential jurors are chosen from the district in which the trial court has jurisdiction, and potential jurors normally undergo careful questioning by the judge and defense and prosecution. This process is called voir dire, and it may take considerable time. A potential juror may be challenged or "struck" for "cause," meaning there is some reason that he or she is unacceptable. A juror may also be struck by either the prosecution or defense in a "peremptory challenge," in which no reason need be given.

Criminal Trial Process

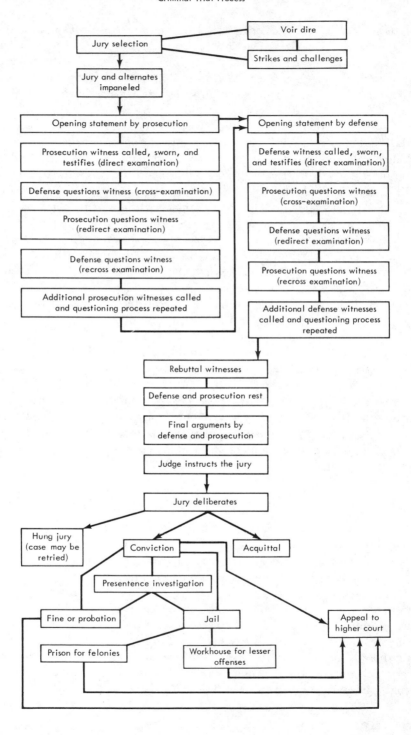

Some attorneys consider jury selection the most important part of any criminal trial. They argue that potential jurors come to a trial with lifetimes of experiences which incline them in one way or another, and that no amount of testimony, however persuasive, is likely to change basic beliefs. It is therefore crucial, they argue, that the right jury be impaneled. Others disagree with this approach, and argue that juries are fully capable of laying aside prejudices to consider cases on the merits.

Once a jury is impaneled, it is normally instructed not to read news accounts of the trial, or to watch broadcast accounts. The jury may be sequestered if the judge believes it may become tainted by outside influences.

Following the selection of a jury, the prosecution in the typical criminal trial will make an opening statement, explaining to the jury what it intends to prove. The prosecution's statement, like that of the defense's, is not testimony. The opening statements are usually very important because they give the court reporter a capsule of both sides of the case.

Depending on the rules of criminal procedure, and perhaps on the tactics of the attorneys, the defense may withhold its opening statement until after completion of the prosecution's case.

The next step in a trial is the calling of witnesses. Witnesses for the prosecution, called "state's witnesses," are called first, and each is questioned first by the prosecuting attorney under what is called "direct examination." After questioning is completed, the defense may question the witness in a process called "cross-examination." The prosecutor may then question the witness again on items brought up in the cross-examination; this questioning is termed "redirect examination." It may be followed with a recross examination.

The same process is followed with each witness, and is conducted in the same way when the defense begins to call witnesses. A defense witness will be questioned first—direct examination—by the defense counsel; he may then be questioned—cross-examination—by the prosecutor.

One witness may contradict another, and the purpose of calling a particular witness may not be clearly stated, but only inferred. The reporter must take special care to balance his reports: a too-heavy emphasis on either the prosecution or defense performance is likely to bring protests. At the same time, the reporter must watch out for the grandstand play by an attorney, the remark intended as much for the press as for the jury.

Unlike the Perry Mason television "trials," very few criminal cases have dramatic moments when "the truth" is suddenly revealed. Witnesses provide pieces of a puzzle, and the experienced attorney presents witnesses to the jury in a careful, methodical fashion, building the case brick by brick.

After the prosecution and defense have called their witnesses, each may call "rebuttal" witnesses to attack specific points made by the other side. Both sides then rest their cases, and prepare for final arguments. Final arguments may provide the reporter with an outline of what each side believes it has shown, but the reporter should realize that final arguments, like opening statements, are not testimony.

The judge will then instruct, or "charge," the jury, telling them what aspects of the law they are to consider and the meaning of certain legal terms, such as "proof beyond a reasonable doubt." The judge's instructions to the jury are often crucial in the outcome of the case, and both defense and prosecution normally submit various rules of law that they would like the judge to give the jury. The option to include them in his charge or not, of course, is the judge's.

After the jury has been instructed, it will deliberate until it reaches a verdict or an impasse. A unanimous vote is usually required for conviction, although several states allow less-than-unanimous votes in some cases. If a jury cannot agree on a verdict, it may be declared a "hung" jury by the judge, and a new trial ordered. If the defendant is convicted, sentencing may be immediate, or follow a presentence investigation by probation officers.

NOTES

1. Legal terms often have very precise definitions. See Henry C. Black, *Black's Law Dictionary* (St. Paul: West Publishing, 1968).
2. There are several summaries of the criminal trial process. One of the best is by Jerold H. Israel and Wayne R. LaFave, *Criminal Procedure in a Nutshell* (St. Paul: West Publishing, 1971). See also the other titles in the "nutshell" series, including Ernest Gelhorn, *Administrative Law;* Paul F. Rothstein, *Evidence*; and Delmar Karlen, *Procedure before Trial.*

appendix d

How to Use

the New 1974 FOI Act

Federal Agency Fees & Procedures
For Info Requests Made Under 1974 FOI Act

Passage of the 1974 amendments to the federal Freedom of Information Act in November of last year placed a duty on each federal agency to promulgate detailed regulations by February 19 implementing the substance of the amendments and outlining information request procedures, appeal procedures, and search and duplicating costs (see *PCN VI*, pp. 15-17 for a digest of the substantive amendments to the Freedom of Information Act)

Federal agency implementation of the FOI amendments has varied, both in procedures to search for the requested information and in the fees to be charged for search and duplication.

Search Procedures   Some agencies have specifically designated Freedom of Information search squads to locate the information sought and make decisions regarding its release. These squads are generally affiliated with the agency press information office or the general counsel's office and comprise both clerical and professional personnel.

FBI. The FBI "Freedom of Information Unit" within the Justice Department appears to be the largest search unit established with a staff of 25 full-time employees—20 clerks who do the raw processing and five attorneys who make decisions regarding classification or release of the information. When an information request comes in, clerical personnel locate the file and forward it to the professional staff. That staff checks with the agents originally in charge of the case to discover whether the file contains material the Bureau would like to withhold. Once alerted to

Reprinted by permission of *The Reporters Committee for Freedom of the Press*, the Freedom of Information Clearinghouse, the Department of the Army (Office of Public Affairs), and members of the Staff of the Senate Judiciary Committee.

this "sensitive material," the professional staff determines whether the material qualifies under one of the exemptions to the Freedom of Information Act.

CIA. The CIA "Information Review Staff" is a coordinating group of eight persons including five professional and three clerical members affiliated with the general counsel's office. The review staff locates the requested information and coordinates examination of the file by the various departments within the agency which may have an interest in it. Information sought to be withheld is referred to the general counsel's office for a final determination regarding its release or withholding.

Department of Defense. The Department of Defense "Office of Information" has not set aside a separate staff to review incoming information requests on a file-by-file basis. All files handled by DOD are "classified" according to various established secrecy classifications by the persons who originally process the file. Under this system, the outside of the file jacket would notify an information seeker that the file was either classified or unclassified and until what point in time. The clerk processing an incoming information request would then merely check the file jacket to determine whether the file was classified or available for release.

Search & Reproduction Fees   The 1974 amendments to the Freedom of Information Act also require agencies to promulgate uniform fee schedules. These fees include the cost of search and duplication of the information requested. In a December 11 memorandum to the heads of all federal departments and agencies, then Attorney General William Saxbe outlined general guidelines to be followed in implementing fee schedule regulations and suggested procedural formats that agencies could adopt depending upon their needs.

Among his suggestions were that agencies consider whether they would furnish estimates of fees, require payment in advance and notify information requesters of expected costly charges. Saxbe suggested that agency regulations might specify a ceiling fee above which the requester would have to give express consent to the agency to proceed after agreeing to bear the expected high costs. Saxbe said that such a provision would also toll the 10 day time response period until the requester agreed to assume the anticipated costs.

In addition, Saxbe said that agencies may no longer charge for time spent determining whether "an exemption can and should be asserted" or for time spent deleting exempt matter or for time spent "monitoring a requester's inspection of agency records." Search fees may be charged even when "no records are found or no records not exempt from disclosure are found," the memo said.

Because of the large number of federal agencies promulgating search fee regulations and the differences in fees, space limitations prevent a listing of all fee schedules here. However, a representative sampling is noted below and all others may be obtained from the agency involved or from *The Reporters Committee* upon request.

Office Of Management And Budget

Search:
-$5 per hour for clerical employee search
-$8 per hour for professional employee search
-no charge for searches less than an hour
-direct costs to be assessed for computer time (around $55 an hour)
-transfer charges to be assessed if records elsewhere than D.C.
-costs assessed even if record not located after "reasonable effort"
-costs to be assessed if record found but exempted
-requester will be notified of anticipated fee exceeding $25
-advance deposits required for searches exceeding $25
-payment by personal check acceptable
-fee may be waived when info deemed to be in public interest

Duplication:
-first three page reproduction free, $.25 per page after that

Central Intelligence Agency

Search:
-$4 per hour clerical search
-$8 per hour profession search
-$55 per hour computer search

Duplication:
-$.10 per page reproduction
-direct cost for non paper reproduction

Department of Defense

Search:
-$6.50 per hour clerical search
-$13.00 per hour professional search (includes computer programmer)
-fee assessed even if no records found
-charge assessable even if no records not exempt found

Duplication:
-$2 minimum for up to six reproductions, $.05 per page after 6 pages
-waiver of fees for non-profit activity or state or local government

Atomic Energy Commission

Search:
-less than one hour search is free
-$5.70 per hour for clerical employee search
-$16.00 per hour professional search
-computer time to be billed as direct cost (undetermined yet)
-security deposit required
-public interest waiver provision

Informal Information Inquiries

Who May Ask for Information: The Act says that any "person" may make a request under the Freedom of Information Act. The press has no more and no fewer rights under the Act although you may find the agency Press Information Office helpful. You do not have to offer any reason or explanation for your request, although it is advisable to inform the agency that you are a news reporter.

The First Step: You must be able to "reasonably describe" the information you want. You don't have to know a specific document or docket number, but your request must be specific enough to permit a government employee reasonably familiar with the agency to identify the information you are seeking.

Contacting the Agency: Call the agency involved identifying yourself as a news reporter and request the information. If you are turned down on the telephone, try the agency press officer who frequently tends to be more understanding of the press' problems than are other agency employees. Make a point of telling any officials you talk to that you intend (if you do intend) to make a formal request and if denied to take an appeal and if denied to file a law suit.

The Punitive Provision: The new Act contains a punitive provision which declares that an "arbitrary" or "capricious" denial of information sought under the Freedom of Information Act can subject the government employee to administrative penalties including the loss of salary by the Civil Service Commission.

Therefore, it would be wise for a reporter to find out by telephone what particular official has made the decision to refuse to release the information and to inform both the press office and that official that you consider the information clearly releasable under the FOI Act and that you consider his denial to be clearly "arbitrary" under the Act (use your descretion in mentioning to him the Civil Service penalty provision).

The mention of the penalty provision in your negotiations with the agency is expected to frequently have the effect of causing lower level government employees either to release the information or to pass the decision on to the next higher level—but not to turn you down because the lower level government official does not want to assume the financial penalty of a salary suspension.

Search Fee Inquiries: You should obtain some idea of the volume of the information you want (either from talking with the agency official or from outside sources) and should be able over the telephone to decide about how long it should take the agency to "search" for the information. Therefore, inquire about the search fees which the agency may impose on you. If you think these fees are too high (perhaps a tactic to discourage you), complain to the press office or to the general counsel's office (*The Reporters Committee* has available search fee information established by all federal agencies.)

Fee Waiver Arguments: If you think the fees are too high—or if the fee is fair but the volume makes it too expensive—you may request a "waiver" of the fees. The agency is required to waive the fee, in whole or in part, when it decides that the "information can be considered as primarily benefiting the public interest." In addition, some agencies have promulgated regulations allowing fee waivers when the agency determines that release of the information would "be in the interest of the agency."

Inspection vs. Document Reproduction: If you believe that the document production costs (see above) or the time to reproduce the documents would unduly delay your story, you may save both money and time by agreeing to visit the agency and inspect the documents in person. Most government agencies will make a typewriter available to take notes on and once you are there, they will probably let you do modest copying without charge. Once again, the Press Information Office may be your best friend.

Document Reproduction Fees: (See list of reproduction fees) Bear in mind that the standard commercial copying cost is no more than 10 cents a page and that any government charge in excess of 25 cents a page (to cover cost of copying machine operator) would appear to be an effort to discourage you.

The Formal Request: If all else fails, you should write a letter to the agency you think has the information and send a copy to the FOI office (see address pages) if there is one—if not to the press office. It may help to send a copy and a short covering letter to the Division head and the general counsel.

For fastest results, you should consult agency regulations to determine which department within the agency actually has the information you seek and send your request directly to the department FOI office (if there is one) listed in the regulations. Many of the agency addresses listed on pages 312–14 have FOI offices attached to their sub-departments or outlying regional offices.

Information sought, for example, from a regional office of the National Labor Relations Board should be sent to the regional office of the Board. Information sought from the National Institute of Health (NIH), a department within the Department of Health, Education and Welfare (HEW), should be sent directly to NIH. When in doubt about which department actually has the information, send your request to the main agency listed in the address pages. The main agency will forward the request to the appropriate department.

Form Request Letter

Agency name   Return Address
Address   Date

Dear

    I hereby request personal access to (a copy of—describe the document, report, or information sought as specifically as you can)—under 5 U.S.C. 552 et seq., The Freedom of Information Act.

    If you agree to this request in whole or in part, please inform me of the search fees and the reproduction fees in advance of fulfilling the request (or please supply me with the information if the search and copy fees do not exceed a total of $).

    If any part of this request is denied, please inform me of your appeal procedures. I will consider my request denied if I have no communication from you within 10 working days of receipt of this letter.

    Please be put on notice that I consider this information clearly releasable under the Freedom of Information Act and that I consider your refusal to release the information to be arbitrary and capricious as defined in the Act.

    Thanking you for your kind attention, I remain,

                                        (signature)

Form Appeal Letter

Head of Government department,   Return address
commission or agency   Date

My dear Mr. Secretary:

    On (date), I sent a letter requesting access to (use the same description of the information sought as in your request letter) under 5 U.S.C. 552, The Freedom of Information Act.

    On (date), I received a letter from (name, title, address) denying my request.

    I hereby appeal that denial and if I do not hear from you within 20 working days, I will consider my appeal denied.

    I consider the information requested clearly releasable under the Freedom of Information Act and I hereby inform you that I would consider your denial to be clearly arbitrary and capricious as defined by the Act.

    Enclosed please find a copy of my original request and the response, and I remain,

                                        Sincerely,

                                        (signature)

Court Action: If your request is denied by the Secretary, or head of the agency, Commission, or Department or if he does not answer within 20 working days, you may file a Freedom of Information Act law suit in the United States District Court most convenient to you. (The FOI Act provides that your law suit must be given "expedited" treatment which means your case, if it has been properly filed, will be given precedence over other litigation.) Sample complaints and case studies by exemption number are available upon request from *The Reporters Committee.*

Court Action Costs: Filing a complaint under the Freedom of Information Act should be relatively inexpensive. After you file your complaint, the burden is on the government to come forward and justify the withholding of the information. Courts are becoming more demanding on the government for precise and detailed reasons as to why the government refuses to release the information. It is at this point—when the government replies—that you and your attorney should obtain a fairly accurate idea of how much it would cost to continue the law suit.

The Act provides for the payment of your attorney fees and costs if a judge decides that the government has "arbitrarily" withheld the information.

Disclosure Exemptions to the Act

The exemptions and the type of information *not available* under each are as follows:

1. (a) Specifically authorized under criteria established by an Executive Order to be kept secret in the interest of national defense or foreign policy and (b) are in fact properly classified pursuant to such Executive Order.

The documents exempt under this section are those, like the Pentagon Papers, that are officially stamped Top Secret, Secret, or Confidential, terms which are defined in a Presidential Executive Order. The 1974 amendments, however, make it clear that courts have a duty to determine whether the claim of national security is justified. Courts will not necessarily take an official's word on the propriety of the classification, but may look at the information itself to see if it is properly classified according to the terms of the Executive Order. This should be especially helpful in securing access to historical records, and documents which were obviously classified merely to prevent domestic political repercussions. Also, the fact that a few pages of a report are properly classified does not mean that the remaining non-sensitive portions can be cloaked in secrecy. Remember, too, that just because information is in the possession of the

Departments of Defense or State does not necessarily mean that it is classified. For instance, material such as results of drug-testing done on GI's returning from overseas is not generally classified, and so is not exempt under this provision.

2. Related solely to the internal personnel rules and practices of an agency.

This exemption covers such things as employee parking and cafeteria regulations, as well as certain manuals that relate only to the internal management and organization of particular agencies. But staff manuals instructing inspectors or agents how to perform their jobs are *not* exempt.

3. Specifically exempted from disclosure by statute.

This covers documents and information specifically exempted from disclosure by other laws. Examples are income tax returns, patent applications, and completed census bureau forms. In those cases information which relates to individual submitters is exempt.

4. Trade secrets and commercial or financial information obtained from a person and privileged or confidential.

The agencies under this section may withhold information only if it is either a trade secret or commercial or financial information. In addition, the government must prove that the information is confidential and that its disclosure would be likely to either impair the agency's ability to obtain necessary information in the future or to cause substantial competitive injury to the submitter. This exemption applies only to information submitted *to* the government; government-prepared documents based on government information are never exempt under this section.

5. Inter-agency or intra-agency memoranda or letters which would not be available by law to a party other than an agency in litigation with the agency.

This is the exemption most widely used by the government. In general, two somewhat overlapping dividing lines may be drawn between what must be disclosed and what may be withheld under this exemption. First, factual portions of documents generally should be disclosed, but advice and recommendations on legal and policy matters may be withheld. Second, preliminary drafts, and unfinished reports may be withheld, but once finished, such memoranda and reports should generally be disclosed. To illustrate, a memo from a staff person to a supervisor recommending that a particular policy be established would be exempt except for factual portions. But factual reports or analyses of facts are not exempt.

6. Personnel and medical files and similar files, the disclosure of which would constitute a clearly unwarranted invasion of privacy.

This exemption is self-explanatory, although it may be difficult to apply in some instances. The difficulty of application results from the fact that this is the only exemption which allows a balancing of interests between disclosure and non-disclosure—the one case, in other words, in which the reason for your request may be material. If your request involves this exemption, a brief explanation of why you want the information should be made so that it can be determined whether the invasion of privacy resulting from disclosure would be "unwarranted."

7. Investigatory records compiled for law enforcement purposes, but only to the extent that the production of such records would (a) interfere with enforcement proceedings, (b) deprive a person of a right to a fair trial or an impartial adjudication, (c) constitute an invasion of personal privacy, (d) disclose the identity of a confidential source, and, in the case of a record compiled by a criminal law enforcement authority in the course of a criminal investigation, or by an agency conducting a lawful national security intelligence investigation, confidential information furnished only by the confidential source, (e) disclose investigative techniques and procedures, or (f) endanger the life or physical safety of law enforcement personnel.

This is another over-used exemption. Congress amended it in 1974 in order to avoid broad agency claims of exemption for almost anything which could be called an "investigatory file." Under the new amendments, the government must prove that the documents were compiled for civil or criminal law enforcement purposes, and that disclosure would actually result in one of the six enumerated harms. Thus, documents such as annual surveys or inspections may be investigatory, but they are not compiled for law enforcement purposes, and, therefore, are not exempt under this section.

8 and 9. These are special-interest exemptions relating to banking and oil well information which are not relevant to most applications of the Act.

Federal Agency Addresses and
Telephone Numbers
Washington, D.C. Area Code 202

Department of Agriculture
Office of the Secretary
Director of Public Affairs
Washington, D.C. 20250
447-3845

Department of the Air Force
Headquarters U.S.A.F. (DADF)
Washington, D.C. 20339
695-4992

Department of the Army
William J. Donohoe
Special Consultant
Office for the Freedom of
  Information, OCP-OSA
The Pentagon
Washington, D.C., 20330
697-4122

Department of Commerce
Freedom of Information
Central Reference and
  Records Inspection Facility
Room 7043
Washington, D.C. 20230
967-7470

Department of Health, Education & Welfare
Director of Public Affairs
330 Independence Ave., S.W.
Washington, D.C. 20201
245-7470

Department of Housing and Urban Development
Office of Public Affairs
Attn: FOI
Washington, D.C. 20410
755-6980

Department of the Interior
Harmon Kallman
Office of Communications
18th & C. Streets, N.W.
Washington, D.C. 20240
343-3171

Department of Justice
Robert Saloschin
Public Information
Freedom of Information Committee
Constitution Avenue (between 9th
  & 10th)
Washington, D.C. 20530
739-2674

Department of Labor
Sofia Peters
Department of Labor
Washington, D.C. 20210
523-8065

Department of Navy
Chief of Information
Department of Navy
Washington, D.C. 20350
697-7371

Department of State
FOI Staff—Barbara Ennis, Head
Room 5835
Department of State
Washington, D.C. 20520
632-9322

Department of Transportation
H. David Crowther
Freedom of Information Officer
Department of Transportation
Washington, D.C. 20590
426-4570

Department of Treasury

1. Freedom of Information Request
   Office of the Secretary
   1500 Pennsylvania Ave., N.W.
   Washington, D.C. 20220
   964-2041

2. Internal Revenue Service
   (send to regional office)

3. Customs Service
   (send to regional office)

Energy Research and Development Administration
   (formerly AEC)

Walter Kee
Mail Facility
300 7th Street, S.W.
Washington, D.C. 20545
245 3330

Central Intelligence Agency

Mr. Angus Thuermer
Ass't to the Director
Washington, D.C. 20505
351-7676

Civil Aeronautics Board

Office of the Secretary (B-10)
1825 Connecticut Ave., N.W.
Washington, D.C. 20428
382-4356

Small Business Administration

Paul Lodato
Director of Public Information
Small Business Administration
Washington, D.C. 20416
382-1891

U.S. Postal Service

Bernard Roswig
Public and Media Relations
U.S. Postal Service
Washington, D.C. 20260
245-4144

Veterans Administration

Central Office
Vermont Ave., N.W.
Washington, D.C. 20420
389-3007

U.S. Civil Service Commission

Assistant Executive Director
Freedom of Information
1900 E. Street, N.W.
Washington, D.C. 20415
632-4458

Environmental Protection Agency

Freedom of Information Officer
   (A-101)
401 M Street, S.W.
Washington, D.C. 20460
755-0377

Equal Employment Opportunity Commission

Office of the General Counsel
Attn: Legal Counsel Division
2401 E Street, N.W.
Washington, D.C. 20506
343-8425

Federal Bureau of Investigation

Clarence M. Kelley
Director, Federal Bureau of
   Investigation
Attn: Freedom of Information
   Act Unit
10th and Pennsylvania Aves., N.W.
Washington, D.C. 20535
324-2935

Federal Communications Commission

Barbara O'Malley
Office of the General Counsel
1919 M Street, N.W.
Washington, D.C. 20554
632-6444

Federal Maritime Commission

Francis C. Hurney
The Secretary, FMC
1100 L Street, N.W.
Washington, D.C. 20573
523-5725

Federal Power Commission

William L. Webb
Office of Public Information
825 N. Capitol Street, N.E.
Washington, D.C. 20426
386-6102

Federal Trade Commission

Freedom of Information Act
Office of the Secretary
Federal Trade Commission
  Building
6th St. and Pennsylvania Ave.,
  N.W.
Washington, D.C., 20580
962-3321

General Services Administration

Richard Q. Vawter
Director, Office of Public Affairs
ALVP
Room 6117
18th and F Streets, N.W.
Washington, D.C. 20405
343-4511

Interstate Commerce Commission

Warner L. Baylor
Public Information Office
12th St. & Constitution Ave., N.W.
Washington, D.C. 20423
343-4141

**National Aeronautics and
Space Administration**

Freedom of Information (JH)
National Aeronautics and
Space Administration
Washington, D.C. 20546
755-2320

National Labor Relations Board

1. Standau E. Weinbreht
   Freedom of Information Officer
   1717 Pennsylvania Avenue, N.W.
   Washington, D.C. 20570
   254-9350

2. For information relating to
   a specific National Labor
   Relations Board case: contact
   regional director where
   case is being litigated.

National Science Foundation

Freedom of Information Officer
National Science Foundation
Washington, D.C. 20550
632-4397

Office of Management and Budget

Velma Baldwin
Ass't. Director for Administration
Office of Management and Budget
Washington, D.C. 20503
395-5600

**Securities and Exchange
Commission**

Richard Nathan
Security Exchange Commission
Washington, D.C. 20549
755-1224

ABOUT THE AUTHORS

GEORGE S. HAGE is professor of Journalism and Mass Communication and chairman of the News-Editorial sequence at the University of Minnesota School of Journalism and Mass Communication. He has taught Public Affairs Reporting for twenty-five years and has been an active participant in public affairs as a member of the Minneapolis Planning Commission for eight years. He is the author of *Newspapers on the Minnesota Frontier* (St. Paul: Minnesota Historical Society, 1967), and holds a Ph.D. from the University of Minnesota in American Studies.

EVERETTE E. DENNIS, assistant professor of Journalism and Mass Communication at Minnesota, has had professional experience as a public information officer for state agencies in New York and Illinois and has also worked for newspapers. Dr. Dennis has taught at Kansas State University and the University of Oregon and has a Ph.D. in mass communication from Minnesota. A frequent contributor to legal and journalistic periodicals, he is co-author of *Other Voices: The New Journalism in America* (Canfield/Harper, 1974) and editor of *The Magic Writing Machine* (Oregon, 1971). He is a consultant on communication to various government agencies.

ARNOLD H. ISMACH is an assistant professor at the University of Minnesota School of Journalism and Mass Communication and is in charge of the school's urban journalism program. He spent fifteen years as a reporter and editor on daily newspapers in Washington and California, and was city editor of the San Bernardino (California) *Sun and Evening Telegram*. He has been a consultant to the Public Relations Center, Los Angeles, on political campaign communication, and is a candidate for a Ph.D. in communication theory and methodology from the University of Washington.

STEPHEN HARTGEN teaches Public Affairs Reporting, investigative reporting, and other courses at the School of Journalism, Ohio State University. For six years he was a reporter for the Minneapolis *Star* and covered such public affairs beats as courts, municipal politics, and corrections. He holds an M.A. in American history from Brandeis University, and is a Ph.D. candidate in American Studies at the University of Minnesota, where he taught for three years as guest lecturer in the School of Journalism and Mass Communication. He is a former president of the *Twin Cities Journalism Review* and has written articles for *Journalism Educator*, the *Quill, Audubon,* the *Twin Cities Express,* and *Minnesota Preview*. He is the author of *A Guide to Public Records in Minnesota* (Minneapolis Star and Tribune Company, 1975).

Index